ECONOMICS FOR GCSE

ALAIN ANDERTON

COLLINS EDUCATIONAL

The publishers would like to thank the following for permission to reproduce photographs:

Unit 1 — British Coal/Earthscan/Massin Furs/National Trust/John Mannion; Unit 3 — John Mannion/Health Education Council/Manpower Services Commission; page 17 — John Mannion; Unit 7 — Barnaby's Picture Library (× 3)/Sally and Richard Greenhill; Unit 8 — Imperial War Museum/Sally and Richard Greenhill; Unit 9 — Fine Fare Ltd/John Mannion (× 2); Unit 14 — Ellis Copp Estate Agents/John Mannion (× 4); Unit 15 — British Rail/John Mannion (× 3); Unit 16 — John Mannion (× 2)/Barnaby's Picture Library/Henry Grant; Unit 18 — Sally and Richard Greenhill/Wiggins Teape (× 2)/Imperial Tobacco/John Mannion; Unit 19 — Sally and Richard Greenhill; Unit 20 — British Steel Corporation/Vidal Sassoon/T A Wilkie/Sally and Richard Greenhill; Unit 22 — Glasgow District Council/Barnaby's Picture Library/St Bartholomew's Hospital/Wimpey Homes; Unit 25 — Barnaby's Picture Library; Unit 28 — Mobil; Unit 32 — William Collins & Sons; Unit 34 — European Ferries Group PLC; Unit 35 — Janine Wiedel; Unit 37 — The Pharmaceutical Society of Great Britain; Unit 38 — Oliver Hatch, London Borough of Hackney; Unit 43 — Fagor Domestic Appliances, Reeve Wodehouse Easton Ltd; page 110 — Campaign for Real Ale; Unit 46 — Oliver Hatch, London Borough of Hackney/Washington Development Corporation (× 2)/John Mannion; Unit 48 — Sally and Richard Greenhill/BBC Hulton Picture Library; page 135 — Abbey National Building Society/Popperfoto; Unit 52 — Royal Mint; Unit 53 — Johnson Matthey; Unit 55 — Sally and Richard Greenhill/John Mannion (× 2)/Ministry of Defence/South West Thames Regional Health Authority/Barnaby's Picture Library (× 2); Unit 57 — Anne Bolt/John Mannion; Unit 59 — Keystone Press Agency; Unit 60 — Honeywell Computers; page 152 — Sally and Richard Greenhill; Unit 61 — Sally and Richard Greenhill; Unit 62 — Mark Abrahams, Network; Unit 65 — Central Electricity Generating Board; Unit 66 — Ford Motor Company Ltd; Unit 67 — Mansell Collection; Unit 68 — Barnaby's Picture Library/John Mannion; Unit 70 — The Stock Exchange; page 176 — Sally and Richard Greenhill; Unit 74 — BBC Hulton Picture Library; page 186 — Popperfoto; Unit 79 — British Tourist Board; page 208 — John Mannion; Unit 81 — Topham Picture Library; Unit 83 — Oxfam/Earthscan (× 4); Unit 86 — Xinhua News Agency; Unit 97 — Sally and Richard Greenhill.

For permission to reproduce copyright material the Publishers would like to thank the following:

Barclays Bank Group; City of Birmingham Development Unit, Rawlinson Cattel Picken Ltd; Department of Energy; Department of Environment; European Ferries Group PLC; Lambeth County Council; Lloyds Bank PLC; National Westminster Bank PLC; Midshires Building Society; Times Newspapers Ltd.

Artwork by John Booth, Capricorn Graphics: Units 1–17, 48–74; Richard Geigar: Units 18–47, 75–87.

Cartoons by Bill Stott and Peter Shrank.
Designed by The Pinpoint Design Company.

First published 1986 by Collins Educational, 8 Grafton Street, London W1X 3LA.

Reprinted 1986 twice, 1987

ISBN 00 327386 5

Typeset by CG Graphic Services, Aylesbury, Bucks
Printed by Scotprint Ltd, Scotland

Contents

Preface

The change from CSE and 'O' level examinations to GCSE marks an evolution in teaching and examining in Economics at 16+. The old CSEs and GCEs had the teaching of knowledge as the basis of their curriculum, and were heavily dependent upon factual recall. With the GCSE, 'recall of knowledge' is just one of the main objectives. Because of this, knowledge-based textbooks, which have served CSE and GCE well in the past, are unlikely to be as successful for GCSE.

This book aims to serve the needs of young economists in the late 1980s and 1990s. Throughout, there is an underlying emphasis on data collection, data interpretation, trends and sequences, application of basic economic concepts, decision-making and policy-making. The overall aim of the book is to help pupils develop economic understanding – to get them to think and act like economists. To help achieve this aim an active approach to learning has been adopted. Each of the 87 units begins with a piece of stimulus, with accompanying 'study points'. This may be used in a variety of ways: as the basis for full class discussion, small group work or individual work. The purpose of the stimulus is to focus attention immediately on the particular topic and to get the pupils to develop and use the skills needed at GCSE. It is envisaged that each unit will form the basis of one to two hours' study in the classroom.

The basic text is designed to act as a resource for pupils in using their economics. The workings of the British economy are described, and terms, concepts and theories explained. Data are used to emphasise the link between economic theory and the real world.

Questions, called 'checkpoints', accompany each unit. These questions are designed as a basic check of understanding. Each unit also includes a 'coursework suggestion'. For GCSE, candidates have to research and write one or more projects. The suggestions in the book are not intended as project synopses – indeed it would be totally against the spirit of GCSE if such synopses were commercially available. They are, however, there as a starting-point from which pupils can develop their own unique projects. It is hoped that no final project will resemble exactly any of the suggestions given. 'Key terms' are provided as a further resource for pupils. They should prove particularly useful in examination preparation. 'Key terms' for each unit are identified in small capitals and defined in the boxed area on each right-hand page. Italics are used for emphasis throughout and other economic terms may therefore appear in italic.

Interspersed throughout the units are pages of data-response and essay questions. All GCSE examinations require candidates to answer data-response questions. This again reflects the move towards testing a candidate's ability to *understand* and *use* economics as opposed to being able simply to recall knowledge.

The book is ordered in logical sequence. However, there are many paths which teachers and pupils can take through GCSE, and the splitting up of the material into 87 units has been done in part so that teachers can use the book in as flexible a manner as possible.

I would particularly like to thank Sheila Collins who typed the manuscript, Ronald Bramham, Julian Stanley and Linda Thomas who made invaluable comments on the manuscript and all the editorial staff at Collins who have worked so hard getting this book into print in such a short period.

A. G. Anderton

Scarce Resources and Infinite Wants

SCARCE RESOURCES

INFINITE WANTS

S T U D Y   P O I N T S

1 Look at photograph 1. Make a list of the most important items that you think the woman would want to have.

2 What do you think are the ten most important wants of a 20-year-old woman in Britain?

3 What do you think are the ten most important wants of a 10-year-old child in Britain?

4 What wants are illustrated in photographs 3, 4 and 5?

5 Coal is a 'resource' and can be used to produce goods and services which satisfy people's wants. Look at photograph 2. Why is there only a fixed or 'finite' amount of coal available in the world today?

6 Look at photograph 6. Roads are an economic resource, and there are only a finite number of these resources in any area. Why might the situation shown in the photograph be caused?

7 Describe how the photographs show your wants now and in the future. It is an economic fact that nearly all resources in the world are scarce. Explain why many of your wants will never be satisfied.

8 Explain whether you think the wants of a poor person, such as the woman shown in photograph 1, differ from those of somebody better off like yourself.

Scarce Resources

- '40 000 children die every day in the developing world.' (*Source:* Unicef)
- 'Diarrhoea kills 4 million children a year.' (*Source:* Unicef)
- '2.8% of households in the UK still did not have an inside toilet in 1981.' (*Source: Regional Trends*)
- 'In 1984 average weekly pocket money in the UK dropped to £1.09 from a record £1.22 in 1983.' (*Source: Daily Express*, 16 March 1985)
- 'Sir Keith Joseph, the Education Secretary, said that there was no more money available for teachers' pay.' (*Source: The Guardian*, May 1985)

All of these situations have one thing in common. They all illustrate the problem of *scarce resources* or ECONOMIC SCARCITY. There is only a finite (or limited) number of resources such as workers, machines, factories, acres of land and reserves of oil on the planet earth. Because these resources are finite, it is not possible to produce an infinite number of goods and services. About 40 000 children die every day in the poorer countries of the world because of lack of food, decent housing, clean water and medicine. Four million children die each year of diarrhoea, caused mainly by lack of clean water to drink and wash. Closer to home, 1 household in every 36 does not have an inside toilet, because it cannot afford one. Children are limited in what they can buy, because their parents do not give them an unlimited supply of pocket money. Teachers want more pay, but the government says that the resources are not there to pay them the increase.

Infinite Wants

Scarce resources wouldn't be a problem if individuals didn't want more than they have at present. 40 000 child deaths a day wouldn't matter, if children, parents and others didn't object to the situation. It wouldn't matter if children didn't care that they were receiving less pocket money in 1984 than in 1983.

But human beings do care. They want more resources to be available to them. They want better food, better housing, better transport, better health care, better education . . . the list is infinite. Economists say that WANTS are INFINITE. Whether it is a person struggling to feed herself in the developing world, or a multi-billionaire seeking to increase her fortune in the USA, there is always something more an individual wants.

The Economic Problem

The world's resources are scarce. But human wants are infinite. So there is a problem and it is this problem that is called the BASIC ECONOMIC PROBLEM. The economic problem would not exist:

- if resources were infinite, *or*
- if human wants were limited, *or*
- if all resources were totally *free*, like the air we breathe, *or*
- if we were all Buddhist monks seeking poverty.

If the economic problem were to cease to exist, so too would the study or science called Economics.

World resources are limited. Human wants aren't.

C H E C K P O I N T S

1 What is meant by 'scarce resources' in Economics?

2 Write down ten resources that are scarce in the world.

3 What free resources are there in the world?

4 In three minutes, write down as many items as you can think of that you would like to own or consume. Are there still any items that you would like to have, but didn't have time to write down? Why is it unlikely that you could ever write down everything you want?

5 (a) Give five examples of human wants.
   (b) What is meant by the word 'infinite'?
   (c) Why are human wants infinite?

C O U R S E W O R K   S U G G E S T I O N

Take any scarce resource in the world – for example, oil, coal, land, labour. Try to measure how much of this resource is available and show that it is scarce. Then look at the wants of individuals for this resource. What is it used for? How is it used? Would people use more of the resource, if it were totally free? Explain why all this illustrates the basic economic problem. Do you think the scarce resources available in the world today could be better used?

K E Y   T E R M S

ECONOMIC SCARCITY – a situation where there is only a limited or finite number of resources available.

INFINITE WANTS – human beings' unlimited desire to own or consume resources.

THE BASIC ECONOMIC PROBLEM – the problem arising because resources are scarce, but human wants are infinite.

FREE RESOURCE – a resource that is not limited in supply for human beings.

Choice, Opportunity Cost and Allocation

STUDY POINTS

1 Imagine you had a place on Training for Skills (YTS). You live at home with your parents and it costs you £2.50 a week in bus fares to travel to and from your place of work. Draw up a budget as follows, showing how you would spend your money.

2 If the YTS grant were increased by £5 a week, how would you choose to spend your extra income and why?

3 The OPPORTUNITY COST of something is the benefit lost from the next most desirable course of action. For instance, if Mars bars and Wispas were your two favourite chocolate bars, each costing 20p, and you only had enough money to buy one bar, then the opportunity cost of a Mars Bar would be the benefit you give up by not being able to eat a Wispa.

What would be the opportunity cost for you on the YTS of £1 spent on clothes?

4 What would be the opportunity cost for you of joining YTS?

5 YTS is paid for by the government mainly from taxpayers' money. Raising the YTS grant to young people by £2 a week would cost taxpayers up to £25 million a year.
(a) Who would be better off as a result of a rise in the grant?
(b) Who would be worse off as a result of a rise in the grant? What might they have to give up in order to pay for the rise?
(c) Should the government raise the grant by £2 a week per trainee? Explain your answer carefully.

Allocation of Resources

Here are three sets of statistics relating to the basic economic problem.

- 'The UK is planning to spend £1250 million on 100 Tornado fighter aircraft.' (*Source: The Guardian*, 19 January 1985)

- '£95 million has been given by the British government for famine relief in Africa, but the money has all come from reducing foreign aid to other parts of the world.' (*Source: Daily Express*, 23 May 1985)

- '£23 million was spent in 1984 in the UK on toy advertising. The total UK toy market in 1984 was worth £800 million.' (*Source: Financial Times*, 7 February 1985).

In Unit 1, it was argued that human wants are infinite. Governments would like to spend more on defence. Starving people in Africa want more food. Parents would like to spend more on toys for their children and advertisers are happy to spend money encouraging them to do just that.

But resources are scarce. There aren't enough raw materials, or workers, or time to produce everything that people want. So *choices* have to be made. Individuals, firms, nations, the whole world all have to choose between the various alternative uses of scarce resources. The government has to choose whether to buy 100 Tornado fighter aircraft or give 12 times as much to famine relief in Africa. Parents have to choose between spending money on toys for their children or buying goods and services for themselves. Toy firms have to choose between advertising and more machinery for their factory. Economists say that resources have to be *allocated* between all the different uses that those resources could have been put to.

Opportunity Cost

Whenever resources are allocated and choices made, something has to be given up as a result. If the government chooses to buy 100 Tornado aircraft, it means that it cannot give £1250 million to help the starving round the world. If you choose to spend £2 on magazines, it means that you cannot buy £2 worth of sweets. Economists call what has to be given up the OPPORTUNITY COST of a particular choice. The opportunity cost of a choice is the benefit which is given by the next most desirable alternative that is forgone (given up) as a result of making that choice.

The opportunity cost of a choice is what economists call a REAL COST – 'real' as opposed to 'money'. The money cost of an LP record might be £4.99. The real cost is what could have been bought instead – for example, 10 magazines or a T-shirt. The opportunity cost of a choice should always be expressed as a real cost, not a money cost.

Any individual, organisation or nation has to make three fundamental types of choices about how to allocate the scarce resources available to it. It has to decide:

- *what* to produce – food or industrial machinery, books or newspapers, and so on;
- *how* to produce – how many workers will be used, with what machinery, etc.;
- *for whom* it will produce – will some people get a bigger share of resources than others? Will some people get so few resources that they cannot survive, while others

live in luxury? Will resources be evenly distributed?

ECONOMICS, then, is the study or science of human behaviour in relation to how scarce resources are allocated and how choices are made between alternative uses.

1 **Indicate how you allocated your scarce resources last week by drawing up a budget. Divide a sheet of paper in two. On the left-hand side, put a title 'Income' and on the right-hand side 'Expenditure'. Then write down all the money you received last week (your 'income') and all the money you spent (your 'expenditure'). Provide as much detail about different types of income and expenditure as possible. If you borrowed money or spent part of your savings, record this under the income column. If you saved money or repaid any loans, record it under the expenditure column. Add up income and borrowing and record the total as 'total incomings'. Add up expenditure and savings and record the total as 'outgoings'. 'Incomings' should equal 'outgoings'.**
   (a) **What is meant by 'opportunity cost'?**
   (b) **What was the opportunity cost to you of 50p of your expenditure?**
   (c) **Why did you face the problem of the allocation of scarce resources last week?**

'If you let **ME** spend our last £5 on this book, I'll hum the tape for you.'

2 **Give three examples of the real cost of a Mars Bar.**
3 **If you were given £10 000 to give to one charity of your choice, which charity would you choose to give it to? Why?**
4 **Why do resources have to be allocated in an economy?**
5 **'Famine in the world today is a problem caused not by finite (i.e. limited) world resources, but by the poor allocation of those resources.' What do you think this means?**

Consider how a person's time is allocated. Conduct a survey of ten people of your own age. Ask them to keep a calendar record of how they spend their time over two days, preferably a Sunday and a Monday (a day of rest and a day of work). The record should be a detailed one, giving meal times, sleep times, work times (with a breakdown of what work was done when) and recreation times. Compare how different people used their scarce time. What does it reveal about the choices they faced and the opportunity cost of their decisions? Consider whether or not their time was spent in the best way.

ALLOCATION OF RESOURCES – how scarce resources are distributed between competing uses.

ECONOMIC CHOICE – deciding between different uses of scarce resources.

OPPORTUNITY COST – the benefit obtained from the next most desirable alternative forgone because of a particular choice.

REAL COST – the cost of an item in terms, not of money, but of the resource, good or service that has had to be given up to obtain that item.

ECONOMICS – the science of human behaviour in relation to the allocation of scarce resources between alternative uses.

Economic Decision-Making

WITH MY AMAZING **X-RAY VISION** I CAN SEE THE **HARM** CIGARETTES DO INSIDE PEOPLE'S BODIES. THAT'S WHY I DON'T **SMOKE!**

STUDY POINTS

1 What are the benefits of smoking: (a) to the smoker and (b) to non-smokers?

2 What are the costs of smoking: (a) to the smoker and (b) to non-smokers?

3 When a smoker smokes a cigarette, do you think that he or she considers the short-term costs and benefits and/or the long-term, lifelong costs and benefits of smoking?

4 Why do you think people start smoking?

5 Why is it more difficult to give up smoking than, say, going to the cinema or eating chocolate?

6 Would it be better for individuals and society if the government were to make cigarette smoking illegal in the UK?

'Young people' said Mrs Thatcher recently, 'ought not to be idle. It is very bad for them. It starts them off on the wrong foot.' (*Source: Daily Mirror*, 15 February 1985)

The Prime Minister was talking about the problem of youth unemployment. In 1984, 1 in every 4 people under the age of 20 who had left school or college was unemployed. Over half a million of those in 'employment' were on Training for Skills placements. This scheme was costing the government approximately £1000 million a year to run. The problem and costs of unemployment will be considered in Units 57 and 58. Here, we wish to consider how individuals, organisations and society come to make decisions about, say, unemployment or any other economic issue facing them.

Rationality

Economists start by assuming that economic decision-makers act in a **RATIONAL** manner. What this means is that decision-makers act according to reason, rather than in any odd way. For instance, if a person wanted to increase his or her income, it is assumed that he or she would try to work longer hours, rather than shorter hours. Equally, if there were two identical packets of soap powder on the supermarket shelf, one priced at £2.00, the other on 'special offer' at £1.80, it is assumed that shoppers would buy the cheaper packet.

Maximisation

A second economic assumption is that economic decision-makers attempt to **MAXIMISE**. This means that they try to get the best out of any economic situation. If a person can choose to work for 38 hours a week instead of 40 hours, everything else being the same including the wage, then he or she will choose to maximise leisure time by working 38 hours. Equally, a business will prefer to earn as much profit as possible, rather than a lower profit, if all other considerations are equal. A government would prefer to spend £15 billion on the National Health Service rather than £14 billion, if there were no opportunity cost involved in this.

Costs and Benefits

In order to decide what is 'best' in any economic situation, a decision-maker has to assess the costs and benefits of any particular course of action. For instance, in the case of the £1000 million spent each year on the Training for Skills, the government could decide to scrap the scheme. What would be the costs and benefits of this decision?

- The benefits would include saving £1000 million, which could be spent on something else or used to reduce taxes or borrowing.

- The costs would include extra welfare benefits for the young people now on the dole, a less well trained workforce in the future, and lost production in the economy because half a million young people were not at work. There would be further costs in terms of anger and frustration on the part of unemployed teenagers.

Some costs and benefits are paid and received by individual economic decision-makers. The individual teenager would benefit from training and from a grant from the government, which would probably be better than unemployment benefit. The company taking on the young person would benefit from free labour, but might have to pay some money towards training. These are examples of PRIVATE COSTS and PRIVATE BENEFITS. It is these private costs and benefits which form the basis for private decision-making.

But there may well be other costs

What are the costs and benefits of the YTS to an individual unemployed teenager? What are its costs and benefits to society as a whole?

and benefits of a decision. SOCIAL COSTS and SOCIAL BENEFITS are the costs and benefits to society as a whole of an individual decision. It is these social costs and benefits which should form the basis for decision-making in society as a whole. Social costs and benefits are discussed in more detail in Unit 47.

CHECKPOINTS

1 What is meant by 'rational economic behaviour'? Give two examples of such behaviour.

2 If you were given £5, how would you spend this money? Explain why this would be the 'best' way of spending the money for you.

3 Describe how you spend a typical Monday when you are at school, from getting up in the morning to going to bed at night. Why does this represent the 'best' use of your time so far as you are concerned? What could you do with your time which would be less worth while?

4 Explain the difference between a private cost and a social cost.

5 What are the private costs and benefits to you of spending an evening travelling around your area on a motorbike which you own? What would be the social costs of this?

6 What are the private costs and benefits to you of being at school this year? What are the social costs and benefits of your schooling? (Consider here the costs and benefits to others of your schooling.)

COURSEWORK SUGGESTION

Examine the private costs and benefits of running a motorbike. Describe both monetary and non-monetary benefits. What are the social costs and benefits of motorbikes in the UK? Would it be better for (a) motorcyclists and (b) society as a whole if the minimum age for driving a motorcycle were raised to 18?

KEY TERMS

RATIONALITY – making decisions in a reasoned way.

MAXIMISATION – securing the optimal or best situation.

PRIVATE COSTS AND BENEFITS – costs and benefits paid and received by individual economic decision-makers.

SOCIAL COSTS AND BENEFITS – the costs and benefits which accrue to society from a given course of action.

Spending Wisely

Figure 4.1 Time Diary for a typical week

	Mon	Tues	Wed	Thurs	Fri	Sat	Sun
Sleeping							
Eating							
Paid work							
Household duties							
School							
Homework							
Leisure activities:							
Television							
Reading							
Other main activity							
All other activities							

S T U D Y P O I N T S

1 Copy out Figure 4.1 and fill in the time spent on each activity for a typical school week.

2 Assume that you are given one hour's extra homework a night and two hours' extra at the weekend.
   (a) What would you give up doing to make room for this?
   (b) What would be the benefits of this change?

(c) What would be the costs of the change?
(d) Would the benefits outweigh the costs of the change?
Explain your answers.

3 The television breaks down and your parents can't afford to replace it for another two months.
   (a) How would you use the extra time available?

(b) Why do you prefer to watch television rather than allocate your time in this other way?

4 (a) What is the opportunity cost for you of time spent doing household duties?
   (b) Do the benefits gained from your doing household duties outweigh the costs (i) for you; (ii) for your parents?

'In 1968, Proctor and Gamble launched Ariel, the popular washing powder, onto the UK market. In the same year, Schweppes put out a drink called Cresta and Cadbury launched a product called Appletree. The year also saw Rank Hovis McDougall introduce Scotts' hot cereals in strawberry and raspberry flavours. Today, only Ariel remains a market leader.' (*Source: Financial Times*, 7 March 1985)

Firms launch many new products each year. Most of them are failures, because customers don't want to buy them. Like Cresta and Appletree, they soon disappear from the supermarket shelves. Only a few products, like Ariel, survive to sell year after year. Why is this? Why is it that consumers buy some products and not others? Why is it that consumers allocate their scarce resources in one way rather than in another way?

Costs and Benefits

In the previous unit, we saw that consumers for the most part are rational. So they would consider the *costs* and *benefits* of a particular purchase. Take the purchase of a Mars Bar.

- The cost of a Mars Bar to the consumer is the *opportunity cost* – the benefit gained from the most desirable item the consumer has to give up because of the purchase of the Mars Bar. This may be another type of chocolate bar or an ice cream or a magazine. There may be other real costs. The sugar and fat content of a Mars Bar may damage the health of the consumer. There may be purchase costs as well. Buying a Mars Bar might involve a five-minute walk to a shop, whereas the next best alternative, like a magazine, might be available there and then.

- The benefits of a Mars Bar would include relief of hunger and the giving of energy (because of the sugar content). A consumer might also like the taste and sensation of eating a Mars Bar. A Mars Bar might also be available there and then, whereas the next most desirable alternative might involve a walk or time cost. In economics, the benefits resulting from the consumption of an item are often called the SATISFACTION or UTILITY to be gained from consumption.

If the benefits of a Mars Bar outweigh the costs, then the consumer will buy a Mars Bar. If, however, the consumer could get better value for money by buying a Twix or a can of lemonade, then he or she will buy the other product.

The Margin

When a consumer makes a decision about how to spend money, he or she will make that decision at the MARGIN. To understand what this means, imagine a housewife going round a supermarket deciding what to buy. She has £30 to spend. She doesn't fill up 10 baskets and then decide which basketful of goods to buy. In other words, she doesn't compare how she is going to spend *all* her £30. What she does is to think about each individual purchase separately. Would it be better to buy this brand of baked beans rather than another? Would it be better to buy pork this week or beef? Is it worth not buying any biscuits so that she can afford to buy some batteries for the radio? The housewife is here deciding how to spend each *extra* pound of her money. She is making a decision at the margin of what she has to spend.

You do the same when deciding how to spend your time. When you decide whether or not to go out to the cinema, for instance, you don't decide how to spend *all* your time for the next week, or month or year in order to make that decision. What you do is to weigh up the advantages and disadvantages of spending this *extra* part of your time. You are making a decision about how to spend your marginal time.

1 Try to name one product that was put onto the market by a company and that is now no longer sold. Why do you think this happened?

2 Assume that you decide to buy a packet of crisps. What would be the costs and benefits of this action to you personally?

3 Giving examples, explain what is meant by 'utility' in economics.

4 What is meant by 'the margin'?

5 Why might a shopper decide to buy:
(a) size 1 eggs rather than size 6 eggs?
(b) a chicken rather than a leg of lamb?
(c) a Sony television rather than a Philips television?

COURSEWORK SUGGESTION

Ask each member of your household to keep an account of what they spend over a period of time (say, a week). Analyse how spending has been allocated between different categories of consumption goods (see Unit 6 for details of how consumption is broken down nationally). Consider why different members of the household allocated resources in the way that they did. Did each member make the best use of scarce resources? What do you mean by 'best' use?

KEY TERMS

SATISFACTION or UTILITY – the benefit to be gained from the consumption of a good or service.

THE MARGIN – the last (or next) part of a whole. Taking a decision at the margin, therefore, involves decision-making about the last (or next) part of a larger whole.

Measuring Resources

STUDY POINTS

1 Conduct a survey amongst five of your friends. Ask them how much pocket money they received on average per week one year ago, and how much they receive today. Some may reply that their pocket money includes an allowance for clothes. *Either* ask five people whose pocket money includes a clothes' allowance *or* ask five people whose pocket money does not cover clothes, but do not mix the two. Copy Figure 5.1 into your books and record your results on it.

2 Display your results on a bar graph, rank ordering your respondents in terms of pocket money received today. Figure 5.2 is an example.

3 Now convert your figures into INDEX NUMBER form. This means that you will call one of your figures '100'. This is the 'base' figure. Then you will compare all the other figures with this base figure and convert them into index numbers in proportion to the base. For instance, converting the figures on the graph (Figure 5.2) into index number form and using David's pocket money today (i.e. £2.00) as a base would give the results shown in Figure 5.3.

Choose as your base figure (i.e. the figure you are going to call 100), the middle figure of today's pocket-money figures you have collected from your friends. Convert both pocket money today and one year ago to an index with this base.

4 Display your results on a bar chart. What do you notice about this bar chart compared with the first bar chart you drew?

5 Did £1 buy more, less or the same quantity of goods one year ago as it does today? If your pocket money had been £1 a year ago, how much would you need today to buy the same amount of goods and services? (To answer this, ask your teacher for the inflation rate over the past twelve months.)

6 Work out how much each of the people in your survey would have needed to increase their pocket money by to be able to buy at least as many goods and services as they did one year ago. Which people are better off and which worse off compared to a year ago?

7 Calculate the percentage increase in pocket money over the past twelve months:
(a) in money terms;
(b) in real terms.

Money as a Measure

Figure 5.4

	1973	1983
Production of wheat (UK) (million tonnes)	5.0	10.9
Admissions to cinemas (GB) (million)	134	63

(*Source*: CSO, *Annual Abstract of Statistics 1984*)

Consider the figures in Figure 5.4. If an economist is to comment on the availability of resources and their allocation in an economy, then it is important for there to be some common measure of resources. The statistics show that wheat production went up, but admissions to cinemas went down over the period 1973–83. What the statistics don't tell us is whether the growth in wheat production was more or less important than the decline in cinema admissions. One step towards measuring this would be to put the statistics into monetary terms. Money acts as a measuring rod in economics. Figure 5.5 shows the same statistics expressed in monetary values.

Figure 5.5 £ million

	1973	1983
Production of wheat (UK)	230	1368
Cinema admissions (GB)	58	120

(*Source*: CSO, *Annual Abstract of Statistics 1984*)

The figures look completely different. Both the value of total wheat production and the value of cinema admissions have increased. Does this show that output has definitely increased in the economy?

Inflation and Real Values

The answer is probably no. Much of the increase in values will have been caused by inflation – a general increase in prices without any corresponding increase in output. If we are to

Figure 5.1

Name	Pocket money per week (£)	
	A year ago	Today

Figure 5.2

£ per week

Figure 5.3

	One year ago		Today		
	£	Index number	£	Index number	
Jennie	2.25	→ 112.5	4.50	→ 225.0	
Liz	2.50	→ 125.0	4.00	→ 200.0	
David	1.50	→ 75.0	2.00	→ 100.0	Base
Steve	1.60	→ 80.0	1.75	→ 87.5	
Wayne	1.50	→ 75.0	1.50	→ 75.0	

compare like with like, the inflation element of a change in monetary values has to be taken out. Economists call this changing from MONEY VALUES or CURRENT PRICES to REAL VALUES or CONSTANT PRICES.

On average, prices in the UK rose by approximately 3½ times between 1973 and 1983. So £1 of wheat in 1973 would have cost about £3.50 in 1983 for the same quantity. That means that £230 million worth of wheat produced in 1973 would have cost £819 million in 1983 at 1983 prices (i.e. £230 million multiplied by approximately 3½). The 1983 value of £58 million spent on cinema admissions in 1973 was £207 million (i.e. £58 million multiplied by approximately 3½). In making these calculations, we are assuming that wheat and cinema tickets rose in price by the same as the average for all goods and services in the UK.

Now we can compare the value of output *after* inflation has been removed from the figures. They are shown in Figure 5.6.

Figure 5.6

		£ million at 1983 prices
	1973	1983
Production of wheat (UK)	819	1368
Cinema admissions (GB)	207	120

This now gives the REAL change in the value of money output; or, as economists sometimes put it, this shows the change at CONSTANT (1983) PRICES. It shows that the real value of wheat production increased, but the real value of cinema admissions declined.

Index Numbers

Another way in which these statistics could be presented is in the form of INDEX NUMBERS. An index number is a way of showing proportional changes in a set of statistics. One particular figure is chosen as the BASE figure and given the value of 100. Changes in the figures are shown as changes on this base of 100. For instance, assume there were 30 pupils in the class at the start of the year and 27 at the end of the year. Taking the 30 pupils as the base figure of 100, the index of pupils would change from 100 to 90. The proportions (30 to 27 and 100 to 90) have remained identical.

Going back to the original figures for the production of wheat and cinema admissions, and calling 1973 the base year, the statistics would look like those in Figure 5.7.

Figure 5.7

	1973 = 100	
	1973	1983
Production of wheat (UK)	100	218
Admissions to cinemas (GB)	100	47

It is important to realise that, in calling figures for wheat production and for cinema admissions 100 in 1973, we are not saying that they are equal. The 100 figure only means that that is the starting point for comparing other figures in the same series in other years.

Index numbers are particularly useful when it comes to comparing averages of several figures. This aspect will be discussed in more detail in Unit 61.

CHECKPOINTS

1 A farmer produces 20 tonnes of apples, which he sells at £400 a tonne. What is the monetary value of the 20 tonnes of apples?

2 A shop sells 1000 pairs of jeans at £30 each. What is the monetary value of 1000 pairs?

3 What is the pecentage increase in price in the following examples?

	Old price	New price
(a)	£100	£110
(b)	£100	£150
(c)	£200	£250
(d)	£500	£1000

4 A family spends £400 a month. How much would it need to spend to maintain the real value of its spending (i.e. buy the same amount of goods and services as before), if prices increased by: (a) 10%; (b) 20%; (c) 50%; (d) 100%?

5 A chocolate bar cost 30p in 1985. How much would it have cost in 1975, if the prices of chocolate bars had increased by: (a) 100%; (b) 50%; (c) 20% over the period 1975–85?

6 A child receives yearly increases in pocket money. Convert these figures into an index, using 1985 as a base year:

	1984	1985	1986	1987	1988
Pocket money (in pence)	20	50	60	100	150

COURSEWORK SUGGESTION

Take a particular set of economic statistics – for example, the gross national product (GNP), the retail price index (RPI) or the current account on the balance of payments. Explain how the statistics are calculated and what they calculate. Explain how money values are used to measure physical quantities. Show how the statistics can be converted to real values and to an index. Discuss the economic significance of the statistics: in particular, how they might illustrate the basic economic problem.

Data Response Questions
Units 1–5

Unit 1 Scarce Resources and Infinite Wants

Lack of money means library pleas rejected

Councillors have been forced to turn down pleas for new libraries in Lichfield and Tamworth because of lack of money. They had been asked to consider building libraries at Boley Park and Stoneydelph.

Members of the libraries, arts and archives committee were told that Lichfield only had one library and the growing number of residents at Boley Park had to travel up to three miles to use it.

But county librarian Mr Louis Livesey said that it was impossible to provide a new building within the budget.

"It will cost at least £100,000 just for the initial costs and then there are the running costs on top of that," he said.

And he added that if the committee provided a mobile library on the site it would not be able to cope with demands for similar libraries in other areas of the county.

Source: Express and Star, 1 June 1985

1 What 'wants' have been expressed by the citizens of Lichfield and Tamworth? *(2 marks)*

2 What is meant by 'scarce resources' in economics? *(2 marks)*

3 Explain how councillors in Lichfield are faced with the problem of scarce resources. *(3 marks)*

4 Explain how the article illustrates the basic economic problem. *(3 marks)*

Unit 2 Choice, Opportunity Cost and Allocation

Whitehall 'is stingy with the starving'

THE BRITISH people have shown magnificent generosity to African famine victims while the Government has been downright stingy, according to an all-party committee of MPs.

The public has given £67 million to famine charities, including sales of the Band Aid record Do They Know It's Christmas.

But the Government has not put up a single penny extra. All the £95 million earmarked for victims of the disaster has been diverted from the existing foreign aid budget.

In a hard-hitting report, the Foreign Affairs Select Committee says transferring the cash could severely damage other projects, many of them aimed at preventing a recurrence of such tragedies.

The report concludes: "Unfortunately the generosity of the British people has not been matched by the British Government."

Source: Daily Express, 23 May 1985

1 (a) How much have individuals given to help African famine victims, according to the article?
  (b) What has been the opportunity cost of that to the individuals concerned? *(3 marks)*

2 (a) How much has the British Government given for famine relief?
  (b) What has been the opportunity cost of that? *(3 marks)*

3 (a) What would be the costs and benefits for the UK if individuals and the UK Government were to allocate more resources to famine relief?
  (b) What would be the costs and benefits of such a move for famine countries? *(4 marks)*

Essay Questions
Units 1–5

1 Mr Spencer has £200 saved in his building society account. He wants to buy a washing machine (cost £199.99) and a colour television set (cost £189.99).
  (a) What can Mr Spencer afford to buy with his savings? *(4 marks)*
  (b) Give *two* reasons why he might want to buy the washing machine. *(4 marks)*
  (c) What is meant by 'opportunity cost' and what is the opportunity cost to Mr Spencer of buying a washing machine? *(6 marks)*
  (d) Why does Mr Spencer face the basic economic problem? *(6 marks)*

Unit 3 Economic Decision Making

Sunday Shopping

The law against Sunday trading will be scrapped by Christmas or early next year.

The Cabinet is now ready to repulse all attacks from the churches and the trade unions.

Shopworkers' leaders are already lobbying back-bench MPs, urging them to defeat the proposals.

ESSENTIAL

Mrs Thatcher, the daughter of a corner shop grocer, is personally in favour of the right to "open all hours."

She regards freedom to shop on Sundays as an essential part of modern Britain.

It will be Parliament's twentieth attempt to introduce Sunday trading.

Studies have shown it could produce a shopping boom, and not simply spread the same spending over seven days instead of six.

But the shopworkers' union USDAW claims Sunday trading will push up prices. Counter assistants get double-time for working on the Sabbath.

Source: *Daily Express*, 10 May 1985

1 What is meant by 'Sunday trading'? (1 mark)
2 What are the likely (a) benefits and (b) costs to the consumer of allowing Sunday trading? (6 marks)
3 What are (a) the costs and (b) the benefits to workers of Sunday trading? (6 marks)
4 Is society likely to be better off or worse off following the abolition of the Sunday Trading laws? Give reasons to support your answer. (4 marks)

2 Jane Harris, an apprentice engineer, has decided to buy a motorbike at a cost of £750.
(a) What is the private cost to Jane of buying and operating the motorbike? (6 marks)
(b) What might be the private benefits to Jane of owning the motorbike? (6 marks)
(c) What might be the social costs of Jane using a motorbike? (8 marks)

Unit 4 Spending Wisely

Record survey

A survey published this week shows that most people have already decided which LP record they want to buy before they go into a shop. Only 32% of people questioned in the survey said that they chose LPs mainly by browsing through stock in shops and even fewer (21%) chose singles in this way. Price seemed to have little influence upon choice of records. 77% of people said that they were rarely put off buying a record because of its price. If a record was expensive, people said that they would still buy even though it meant that they had to buy less of something else. 35% of people said that they bought records because "they were in the charts", 32% because friends had bought the record, 44% because they had heard the record on radio or television and only 5% because the record had been cheap. But price was important in deciding where records were bought. 55% of people said that they bought records from shops where they thought price would be lowest.

1 According to the survey, what made people decide to buy a particular record? (3 marks)
2 According to the survey, in what way was the price of a record important in deciding to buy a record? (1 mark)
3 What is the opportunity cost of buying an expensive record? (2 marks)
4 What benefits or utility might a consumer gain from buying a record? (4 marks)

Unit 5 Measuring Resources

Index of consumers' expenditure on food and services (1980 = 100)

	At current prices		At constant (1980) prices	
	Food	Services[1]	Food	Services[1]
1975	52	44	96	88
1980	100	100	100	100
1984	123	149	98	108

[1] excluding rent and rates.
(*Source*: CSO, *Economic Trends Annual Supplement 1985* and CSO, *Monthly Digest of Statistics, August 1985*)

1 What is meant by an 'index'? (2 marks)
2 By what percentage did expenditure on food increase between 1980 and 1984 (a) in money terms and (b) in real terms? (2 marks)
3 a) How has expenditure on food changed between 1975 and 1984 compared to expenditure on services?
b) Suggest why the change has been different in each case. (6 marks)

Patterns of Spending

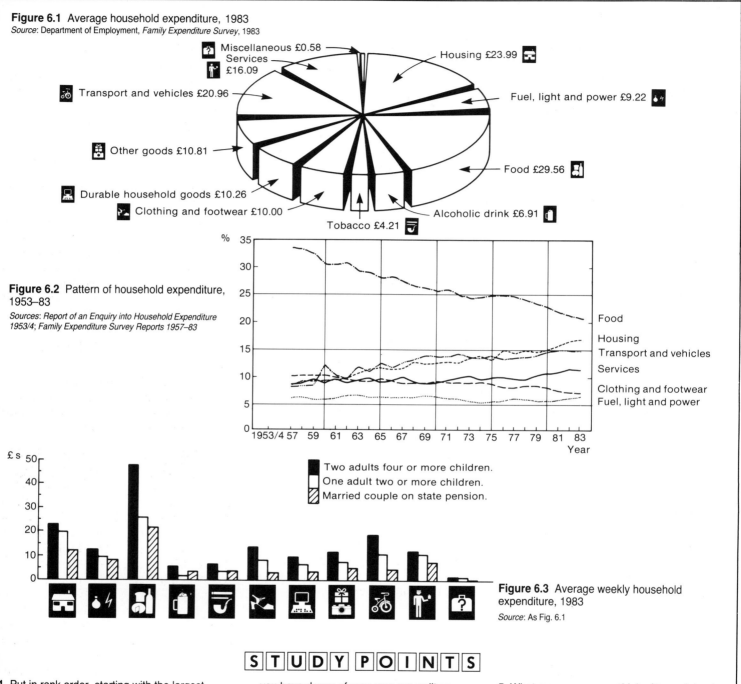

Figure 6.1 Average household expenditure, 1983
Source: Department of Employment, *Family Expenditure Survey*, 1983

Miscellaneous £0.58
Services £16.09
Transport and vehicles £20.96
Other goods £10.81
Durable household goods £10.26
Clothing and footwear £10.00
Tobacco £4.21
Alcoholic drink £6.91
Food £29.56
Fuel, light and power £9.22
Housing £23.99

Figure 6.2 Pattern of household expenditure, 1953–83

Sources: *Report of an Enquiry into Household Expenditure 1953/4; Family Expenditure Survey Reports 1957–83*

Food
Housing
Transport and vehicles
Services
Clothing and footwear
Fuel, light and power

Two adults four or more children.
One adult two or more children.
Married couple on state pension.

Figure 6.3 Average weekly household expenditure, 1983

Source: As Fig. 6.1

STUDY POINTS

1 Put in rank order, starting with the largest expenditure first, the components of average weekly household expenditure (1983) shown in Figure 6.1.

2 Write down how much your household spends on average in a typical week on each of the categories in Figure 6.1. Draw a pie chart showing your household expenditure.

3 Using Figures 6.1 and 6.3, and the pie chart you have drawn of your own expenditure, explain why different households spend different proportions of their income on housing, food, alcoholic drink, etc. For instance, why do pensioner households spend so little on housing? Why do single-parent families spend so little on alcoholic drink?

4 Using Figure 6.2, describe how household expenditure has changed over time.

5 What reasons can you think of to explain why patterns of expenditure have changed over time. In your answer, remember that real household income doubled (i.e. households could buy twice as many goods and services) over the period 1953–83. Has there been any difference in spending on necessities and goods and services that could be called 'luxuries'?

The Typical Household

Households face the same basic economic problems common to all economic decision-makers. They have a limited income and therefore can buy only a limited number of goods and services. This unit considers what consumers do buy in the UK and how this has changed over time. Figure 6.1 shows how the average household in the UK spends its money. The figures are taken from the *Family Expenditure Survey*. Each year, the government picks 11 000 households and ask those households to record their expenditure in detail for a two-week period. An average is then worked out for all the households and also for special households, like pensioner or one-parent households. The SURVEY is not totally accurate because:

- the information given by households to the government is not always completely accurate;

- as in any survey, only a *sample* of the population is taken. Around 19 000 people live in the households surveyed, out of a total UK population of nearly 57 million. Every effort is made to try and make sure that the households surveyed provide a representative cross-section of the population, but it is not possible to be totally accurate.

Expenditure

Figure 6.1 gives the breakdown of CONSUMER EXPENDITURE in a typical household. Most of the categories of spending are self-explanatory: namely, housing, food, alcoholic drink,

tobacco, and clothing and footwear. Of the others:

- 'fuel, light and power' refers to gas, electricity, coal and oil paid for by the consumer;

- 'DURABLE HOUSEHOLD GOODS' refers to household goods which last over a long period of time, such as furniture, televisions, hi-fi equipment and refrigerators;

- 'other goods' includes sports goods, jewellery, books, newspapers, toys, medicines and cosmetics;

- 'transport and vehicles' refers to cars, petrol, bus fares, train fares, etc.;

- 'services' include hair cuts, holidays, restaurant meals and cinema visits;

- 'miscellaneous' is a category which covers any items of expenditure not covered in the other specific categories, and includes pocket money to children.

Trends Over Time

Figure 6.2 shows how the composition of consumer expenditure has changed over time. Households have been spending a larger proportion of their income on housing and a lower proportion on food, clothing and footwear. The fact that households are spending relatively less on food and clothes may be due to the fact that these are NECESSITIES rather than LUXURIES. As households receive higher and higher incomes, they choose to spend extra income on luxuries such as bigger and better housing or on videos or holidays, rather than on food and clothing.

Different Households

Figure 6.3 shows the differences in spending between three different types of household. The first is a large family household with two adults and at least four children. The second is a one-parent family household with two or more children. The third type is the retired couple whose main income is the state old age pension. The stimulus will help you to draw out the difference in spending between these three types of household.

C H E C K P O I N T S

1 Explain the purpose and methods of the *Family Expenditure Survey*.

2 Using the categories found in Figure 6.1, say which category each of the following expenditures would fall into: a pair of jeans, a motorcycle, a gas bill, an electric cooker, a weekend break to Paris, a packet of cigarettes, a bottle of lemonade, a magazine, a bed, a can of beer.

3 Give ten examples of 'durable goods'.

4 Explain the difference between a 'necessity' and a 'luxury'. Would you classify (a) housing and (b) food as necessities or luxuries?

C O U R S E W O R K S U G G E S T I O N

Compare your own household with the typical household in the UK. Find out the characteristics of the typical household from the latest edition of the *Family Expenditure Survey* (published by HMSO). Then collect the corresponding data from your own household. This will necessitate the members of your household keeping a diary of their expenditure over a short period of time. Collate the data you collect from your household so that it is in the same form as that to be found in the *Family Expenditure Survey*. Then compare the allocation of resources between the 'typical' UK household and your own household. Explain why the two differ or are similar. Evaluate whether or not each household is making the 'best' use of its *scarce resources*.

K E Y T E R M S

SURVEY – the collection of data from a representative sample.

CONSUMER EXPENDITURE – spending by consumers on goods and services.

DURABLE GOODS – goods, such as furniture and hi-fi equipment, which are consumed over a long period of time.

NECESSITIES – goods or services whose consumption is seen as essential in order to maintain a minimum standard of living in a society.

LUXURIES – goods and services whose consumption is seen as contributing to a higher standard of living than the minimum.

Interdependence

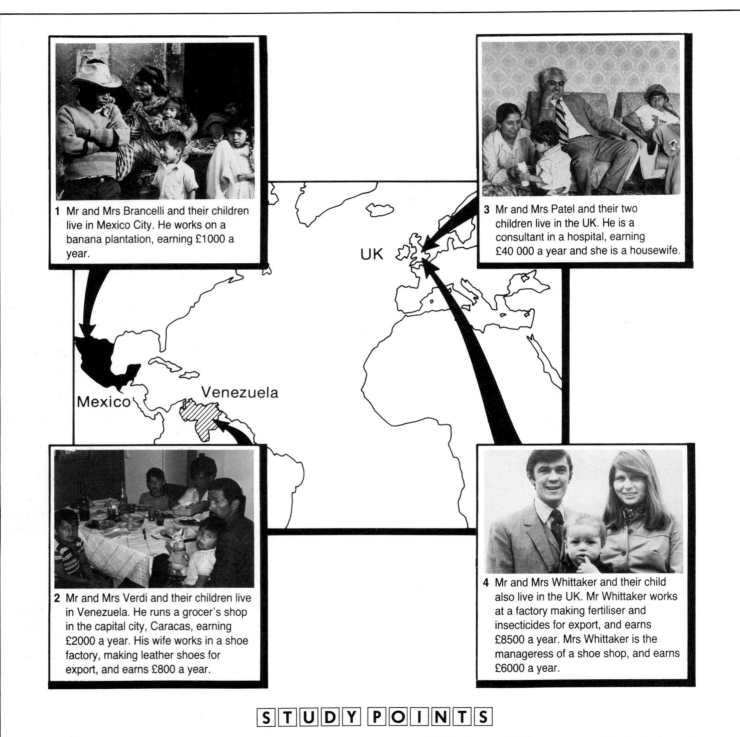

1 Mr and Mrs Brancelli and their children live in Mexico City. He works on a banana plantation, earning £1000 a year.

2 Mr and Mrs Verdi and their children live in Venezuela. He runs a grocer's shop in the capital city, Caracas, earning £2000 a year. His wife works in a shoe factory, making leather shoes for export, and earns £800 a year.

3 Mr and Mrs Patel and their two children live in the UK. He is a consultant in a hospital, earning £40 000 a year and she is a housewife.

4 Mr and Mrs Whittaker and their child also live in the UK. Mr Whittaker works at a factory making fertiliser and insecticides for export, and earns £8500 a year. Mrs Whittaker is the manageress of a shoe shop, and earns £6000 a year.

UK

Mexico

Venezuela

STUDY POINTS

1 Mr Whittaker is made redundant. What might have caused this? What might be the effects of this on the other three families?

2 An earthquake hits Mexico. As a result there is heavy damage to agriculture. What might the effects of this be on the non-Mexican families?

3 (a) What would be the costs to the Whittaker family of making themselves independent of the other families?

(b) Would there be any possible benefits?

4 If there were a world catastrophe, such as a nuclear war, which of these families is least dependent on others to maintain its standard of living and why?

The Division of Labour

The average household in the UK, according to the government's *Family Expenditure Survey*, contains approximately 2.7 people. When people live together, they co-operate in many different ways. One important way in which they co-operate is to share work between themselves. This sharing of work is known as the DIVISION OF LABOUR.

Thirty years ago, division of labour in a household with a husband, wife and two children was usually quite clear. The husband went out to work to earn money for the household. He would also do any 'heavy' jobs round the house, like woodwork, decorating or other DIY activities. He would also be responsible for looking after and driving the family car. The wife would be responsible for cleaning the house, cooking, shopping and bringing up the children. The children would 'work' at school, and when they were older might do some simple tasks like setting the table or cleaning the dishes. Today, with many wives going out to work and with more husbands sharing the household tasks, there isn't such a clear-cut division of labour. But, it is still true that, in most households, some *specialisation* occurs.

Reasons for the Division of Labour

There are a number of reasons why the members of a household specialise in doing certain tasks. The major reason is that by specialisation the household can produce more goods and services with the same number of limited resources. This is because:

- each 'worker' in the household can concentrate on doing what he or she is best at doing; for instance,

because men have traditionally been paid more than women, it has made more sense for men to earn money, while women concentrate on other tasks (note, though, that there is nothing 'right' about this);

- the 'worker' can build up an expertise in a particular task which would not be possible if work were shared.

The members of the household can also choose to specialise in what they most enjoy doing.

The Household and the Wider Economy

Members of a household specialise within their household. But the household itself is INTERDEPENDENT with the rest of the economy. The household does not attempt to be totally self-sufficient. It does not grow all its own food, make all its own clothes, build its own furniture or house, for instance. What it does is to buy in many of these goods and services. In *exchange*, the typical household will provide workers to make highly specialised goods and services for other households. The household can then obtain all manner of goods and services – everything from oranges to televisions and foreign holidays – which it would not be able to obtain if it produced in total isolation.

The whole of the modern economy is built upon the division of labour. Each household depends upon millions of other workers all round the world to provide goods and services. That is why households are 'interdependent' and not 'independent' in a modern society. That is also why, if there were a

complete breakdown of society (such as might follow a nuclear war), very few people in the UK would be able to survive. Workers have become so specialised that they do not have the skills to be a builder, own food-grower-cum-fuel-gatherer-cum-doctor, etc. What is more, without other workers such as oil drillers and mechanics, very few machines would work and without machines people can produce very little.

This division of labour in industry will be discussed further in Unit 19.

1 **What is meant by the division of labour?**

2 **Describe the division of labour in your own household.**

3 **Would you be better off if you tried to be totally self-sufficient (i.e. if you lived on your own and you produced everything you needed yourself)? Explain your answer.**

4 **What would a household have to produce in order to be totally self-sufficient? Is it possible, do you think, for a household to be totally self-sufficient in the UK today? Explain your answer.**

5 **Describe how your household is interdependent with (i.e. depends upon) other households: (a) in your local area; (b) in the UK; and (c) in the world economy.**

KEY TERMS

DIVISION OF LABOUR – a system whereby workers concentrate on performing a few tasks and then exchange their surplus for other goods and services. The division of labour is an example of *specialisation*.

INTERDEPENDENCE – a situation where one economic unit is economically reliant upon other economic units, for instance for food or raw materials or services.

Exchange

German prisoner-of-war camps consisted normally of 1200 to 2500 people. They were housed in large bungalow huts, 200 prisoners to each hut. Supplies came from two sources. Rations were provided by the Germans. More importantly, Red Cross food parcels were given out containing items such as tinned milk, jam, butter, biscuits, chocolate, sugar and cigarettes.

A complicated system of trade and exchange operated. The cigarette was the standard of value. At the start, people wandered through the bungalows calling their offers – 'cheese for seven' (cigarettes). The hours after a Red Cross parcel issue were chaos. The inconveniences of this system soon led to its replacement. Exchange and Mart notice boards were put up in every bungalow. Under the headings 'name', 'room number', 'wanted' and 'offered', sales and wants were advertised. When a deal went through, it was crossed off the board. Prices became generally known throughout the camp. Although cigarettes were the normal currency, barter deals continued.

Cigarettes performed more or less well the functions of metallic currency or money: as a medium of exchange; as a measure of value; and as a store of value. Cigarettes also shared many of the characteristics of metallic money. They were homogeneous, reasonably durable, and of convenient size for the smallest or, in packets, for the largest transactions.

Prices changed frequently. Part of the problem was that cigarettes were also used for smoking. While the Red Cross issue of 50 or 25 cigarettes per man per week came in regularly, the cigarette currency worked well. But when Red Cross parcels weren't distributed for some reason, prices fell. Then less trade took place and bartering increased. On the other hand, several hundred thousand cigarettes might arrive in the space of a fortnight. Prices would rocket and then begin to fall, slowly at first, but more rapidly as stocks of cigarettes in the camp ran out – until the next big delivery.

(*Source*: Adapted from R. A. Radford, 'The Economic Organisation of POW Camps', *Economica*, vol. XII, November 1945)

STUDY POINTS

1 What was a German prisoner-of-war camp?

2 Why did prisoners exchange items from their rations and Red Cross parcels?

3 Why was there no money in the form of notes and coins used in the camps?

4 What is 'barter'? Why was it used in the camps?

5 Why did trading in cigarettes prove more popular than bartering?

6 Why did cigarettes come to be used as money?

7 What problems were there, do you think, in using cigarettes as currency?

Production in the world economy is based upon the division of labour. Workers specialise in producing particular goods and services. What they then do is EXCHANGE these for other goods and services. This unit considers exchange and its importance in the economy.

Barter

Before money came into existence, all exchange was conducted through BARTER. A farmer might want a cow and be ready to pay 20 hens for it. He then had to find a farmer with a cow who might want 20 hens. If he was lucky enough to find one, the two farmers could then barter the cow for the 20 hens. But what if the farmer with the cow didn't want 20 hens, but wanted a horse instead? This was the major problem of barter – it was difficult for one person to find somebody else who was willing to barter exactly what he or she wanted. The result was that trade and exchange didn't form an important part of the economy.

Money

The appearance of money changed this. MONEY is anything that is acceptable to a wide number of people and organisations as payment for goods and services. Money allows a person to sell something – for example, his or her time as a worker – and then to buy something at a later date. Anything which is money has three main jobs or *functions*.

- It is a *medium of exchange* – that means that when buyers and sellers get together to exchange, money is an acceptable means of payment.

- It is a *store of value* – that means that when a seller sells something for money, it will keep its value until it can be spent at a later date.

- It is a *measure of value* – money is used to put a value on goods and services. If a book is priced at £2 and a pair of shoes at £20, then we know that 10 books have the same value as one pair of shoes.

In theory, anything can act as money. In the past, everything from cowrie shells, to pigs, to cigarettes have been used. It helps, however, if what acts as money has certain *characteristics* or features. These include:

- *limited supply* – this means that there must be only a limited amount of money available. If it were not limited, it would not have any value. So gold is a good money in this sense, whereas sand would be very poor.

- *divisibility* – it is easier if the money can be broken down into small units. Pigs were not very useful as money, because it is not possible to chop off a small part of the pig to make a payment and keep the pig intact.

- *portability* – it should be easy to carry around.

- *durability* – it should last. Cigarettes, for example, are not a very good form of money, because they deteriorate quickly when passed from person to person.

- *homogeneity* – money of the same value should be the same in size, shape, etc.

Without money, the whole system of the division of labour, specialisation and exchange would collapse. Money is therefore a very important resource in the economy. What constitutes money in a modern economy is considered in Unit 53.

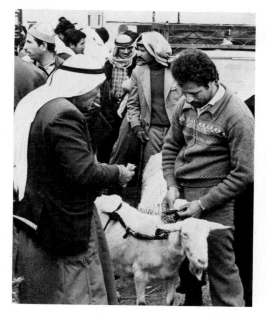

Money must be a medium of exchange, a store and a measure of value.

1. What is meant by 'barter'? Describe any experiences of barter that you have had. What difficulties did you encounter?

2. Explain why exchange is essential if there is to be a division of labour in the economy.

3. What is the difference between the functions of money and the characteristics of money?

4. Explain why a £1 coin today (a) fulfils the three functions of money and (b) possesses the characteristics of good money.

COURSEWORK SUGGESTION

Examine the use of gold, notes and bank current-account assets as money. Explain why gold was once used as money and why it lost its function to notes and bank current-account assets in the modern industrial world. Analyse the advantages and disadvantages of the use of these three types of money. Evaluate the extent to which notes will cease to be used as money over the next 100 years, as electronic banking becomes a reality.

KEY TERMS

EXCHANGE – the exchange of goods and services for goods (bartering) or for money.

BARTER – the direct exchange of goods and services for other goods and services without using money.

MONEY – anything that is generally acceptable as a means of payment.

The Market

S T U D Y P O I N T S

1 What is happening in each of the three photographs?

2 What do you understand by the term 'a market'? Why are all three situations shown in the photographs examples of markets?

3 What influences car owners in their decision (a) to buy petrol rather than other products and (b) to buy petrol at one petrol station rather than another?

4 (a) What will happen to the price of apples, if there is a shortage of apples on the market? Why?
  (b) How might apple producers respond next season to this?

5 What will happen to the production of a particular toy if it proves so popular that supplies are continually running out in the shops? Why?

6 How might a shop react if it had ordered 30 dresses at £19.99 in September, but found that it had only sold 20 of them by 24 December?

7 Who decides what is bought and sold in a market? Is it consumers? Is it producers? Is it the government? Give examples of particular markets in your answer.

- A new hospital is built in Liverpool
- Cadbury's increases its production of chocolate bars
- Consumers buy less butter

Who decides that all this will happen? Who decides what is to be produced and consumed? (Or, as economists might say, who decides how scarce resources are to be allocated?) Economists argue that there are two main ways in which decisions about the allocation of resources are made.

- The *market mechanism* links individual consumers and producers. We will start to consider the workings of the market mechanism in this unit.
- The *state* allocates resources too. This will be considered in Units 54–56.

The Market

A **MARKET** is a place where goods are bought and sold. In a local street market, shoppers who want to buy goods can meet stall holders who want to sell goods. The market is the place where buyers and sellers meet and goods and services are exchanged. Most markets, though, are not situated in one place like a street market. Consider this extract:

> 'Cold weather across most of Europe yesterday gave the oil market its first boost since October, raising prices of oil to between $26.25 and $26.50 a barrel.' (Adapted from the *Financial Times*, 8 January 1985)

The oil market is not a visible market like a street market. You cannot pinpoint the oil market to a particular town or city. The oil market here is a worldwide market. Buyers and sellers in the market are linked by telephone and telex. Millions of pounds or dollars will exchange hands in a typical transaction. Markets, in fact, come in all shapes and sizes, from a local market for, say, petrol or potatoes to an international market in, say, oil or diamonds.

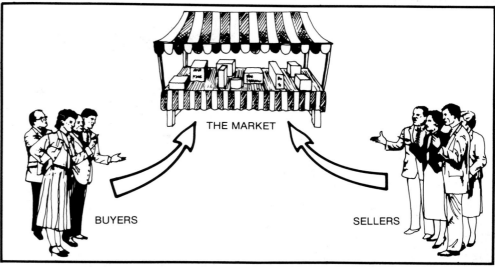

For any market to exist, there must be buyers and sellers.

Price

Read again the extract about oil. Notice the fact that the price of oil is said to have gone up. Buying and selling can only take place when a **PRICE** is agreed upon, for a given *quantity* to be sold. In the case of oil, the price is between $26.25 and $26.50 for one barrel of oil. In the market for cassettes, blank cassette tapes might be £9.99 for five tapes. In the textile market, jeans might be £19.99 per pair.

Price is determined (i.e. fixed) by buyers and sellers reacting to each other. In the case of the oil price rise, cold weather meant that consumers and businesses wanted to buy more oil to heat their houses, factories and offices. So sellers of oil could put up the price of oil to take advantage of this situation. When shops cannot sell the goods they have on their shelves, what do they do? They reduce the price: for instance, in a sale. The lower prices attract more customers to buy the products. The goods are sold at a lower price.

Conclusion

A market exists whenever buyers wishing to exchange money for a good or service come into contact with sellers wishing to exchange a good or service for money. The price of the good or service and the quantity bought and sold are decided by the actions of the buyers and sellers.

CHECKPOINTS

1 What is meant by a 'market' in economics?
2 Give five examples of markets.
3 Why is it not possible for a market to exist where there are only sellers?
4 How are prices fixed in a market?
5 Explain the purpose of a 'sale' in a shop.

COURSEWORK SUGGESTION

Investigate a particular market. It could be a local market or a national or international market. Find out who are the buyers and sellers in the market. Analyse why the market exists and why prices and output are at their present level. Consider the economic consequences if the market were to collapse (i.e. sellers would no longer be willing to sell goods to buyers).

KEY TERMS

MARKET – where buyers meet sellers to exchange money for goods and services.

PRICE – the value put on a commodity at the point of exchange.

Data Response Questions
Units 6–9

Unit 6 Patterns of Spending

Variation of expenditure with household income: transport and vehicles

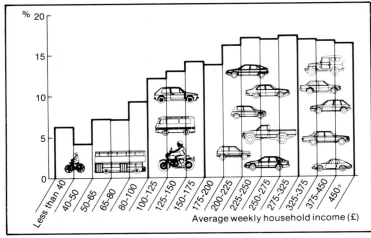

Source: Department of Employment, *Family Expenditure Survey*, 1983

1 What percentage of total expenditure did the average household earning less than £40 a week spend on transport and vehicles? *(1 mark)*

2 Approximately how much (in £s) did a typical household earning £90 a week spend on transport and vehicles? *(2 marks)*

3 (a) How does average expenditure on transport and vehicles change as the weekly income of households increases? *(3 marks)*

   (b) Suggest reasons why this might be the case. *(4 marks)*

Unit 7 Interdependence

Fall in sales hits cigarette jobs

A drop in cigarette sales is expected to cost nearly 300 jobs.

The cutbacks are planned for the three Rothmans factories in Co Durham, following a slump in demand from smokers.

Leaders of the four unions at the cigarette manufacturing plants at Darlington and Spennymoor, which each employ about 900 people, and the treatment plants at Peterlee where 80 people work, were meeting management today.

A big drop in demand in the UK and the Middle East is blamed for the drop.

Source: Express and Star, 19 September, 1985

1 Explain what is meant in the passage by 'a slump in demand' for cigarettes. *(2 marks)*

2 Explain how cigarette workers and cigarette smokers are interdependent. *(4 marks)*

3 Who else, apart from workers at Rothmans, might be affected by the 'slump in demand' and how will they be affected? *(4 marks)*

Essay Questions
Units 6–9

1 (a) Explain how you spend your money. *(4 marks)*

   (b) Give *four* ways in which the way in which you spend your money might be different from the way in which a pensioner spends his or her money. *(6 marks)*

   (c) Explain, giving *two* examples, what is meant by a 'consumer durable'. *(5 marks)*

   (d) Why has spending on necessities, such as food, been declining as a proportion of total expenditure in the UK over the past 20 years? *(5 marks)*

2 The Price household live in their own house in Wapping, London. The father is a print worker, the mother works in a local supermarket and their two children are still at school.

   (a) Explain *four* different ways in which this family is dependent upon others in the UK economy. *(8 marks)*

   (b) Give *two* ways in which the Price household are interdependent with households in other foreign economies. *(4 marks)*

   (c) Why are markets important for the Price household in the way in which they earn money and spend money? *(8 marks)*

Unit 8 Exchange

Funny money

Money comes in something less than billions, as an irritated Milan reader has pointed out to *The Economist*.

Italy has been suffering from chronic shortages of small change for years, but now, he says, the situation is becoming ridiculous. Sweets, and then postage stamps, have for years done duty for small coins. The state autostrada tollgates freely give change in meticulously packed postage stamps which, however, they do not always accept back again in payment from the motorist. Italians can only eat so many gumdrops, and the mail works too dismally for it to be worth posting a letter any more. So Milan has come up with a new substitute: the convertible bus ticket.

At 100 lire apiece, unused tickets have gained wide acceptance at grocers' and small businesses. And, our correspondent adds, at banks. The other day, he walked into a bank, asked for change for a 1,000 lire note and was offered a book of ten bus tickets. One rumour has it that a Milan bank distributes 1m lire worth of tickets daily to its branches to use in lieu of small change. But in Rome and Florence, where bus fares are a paltry 90 lire, the relentless pursuit of small change will persist until more change is minted (the government says not until late 1976) or inflation elevates their bus tickets into a convertible paper currency too. Good news for counterfeiters, bad news for confectioners.

Source: The Economist, 15 November 1975

1 What is being used as money in Italy, according to the article? *(1 mark)*

2 Why has this situation come about? *(1 mark)*

3 To what extent are the new monies a good medium of exchange? *(3 marks)*

4 What might happen if the Italian Government banned the use of the new monies but didn't mint more small coins to replace them? *(5 marks)*

Unit 9 The Market

From 186.9p to 201p in the forecourt fiasco

THE £2 gallon holds no fears for the inhabitants of the Scottish island of Islay — they broke through the barrier two years ago and now pay £2·01.

At the other end of the country — and the other end of the scale — is Page's Filling Station in Southampton.

Its customers are top of the smiles-per-gallon league with prices of just 186·9 pence per gallon.

And in Bristol, the two garages run by Cut Price Petrol were selling at 187·5p yesterday, although this rose by 2p during the day.

This compares with the average of 194·6 pence per gallon elsewhere in the country.

Source: Daily Express, 8 March 1985

1 How does the price of petrol vary between different areas of the country? *(1 mark)*

2 Suggest reasons why the price of petrol varies between different parts of the country. *(5 marks)*

3 Explain why Islay and Southampton form:
(a) part of the same market for petrol and
(b) different markets for petrol. *(4 marks)*

Demand (1)

'Sony, the Japanese consumer electronics company, launched the first of the new generation of 8 mm video camera and recorders to become available in Britain yesterday. It will cost £1100. Sony expects that the UK market for portable video systems will be about 75 000 units, and combined camera-recorders, like Video 8, 48 000.' (*Source: Financial Times*, 22 March 1985)

Why might 48 000 combined camera-recorders a year be sold in Britain? Why not 30 000 or 100 000 or 1 million? What determines the quantity that consumers are willing or able to buy of combined camera-recorders or, indeed, of any product? Or, as economists put it, what constitutes the **EFFECTIVE DEMAND** for a product? To make a start on answering these questions, consider this news item:

'Austin Rover, BL's volume cars division, achieved sales of 37 000 cars in January and 36 300 cars in February, but only with the help of incentive schemes. BL cannot afford to carry on selling cars at a discount if it is to return to profitability.' (Adapted from *Financial Times*, 19 March 1985)

This extract points out that Austin Rover sold approximately 37 000 cars a month in early 1985, but only achieved this with the help of price cuts. If the company had tried to sell cars at its ordinary 'list' price, it would not have been able to sell as many. This is because at higher prices some car buyers would have bought other makes of cars (Fords, Vauxhalls, etc.), and others would have decided not to buy a car at all. Economists find that this relationship between price and quantity demanded holds true for nearly all products. The higher the price, the less will be purchased or demanded. The lower the price, the more will be demanded. Or, as economists say, a rise in price will lead to a **CONTRACTION** of demand, whereas a fall in price leads to an **EXTENSION** of demand.

Figure 10.1

Figure 10.2

STUDY POINTS

1 Conduct a survey of eight of your classmates. Ask them how many they buy a week of (a) standard-size packets of crisps and (b) bars of chocolate such as Mars Bars. Then ask them how many packets or bars they would buy if prices went up by 2p and 4p and if they came down by 2p and 4p. Make a table like Figure 10.1 and record your answers in it.

2 Plot a graph for each of the eight classmates you have interviewed for their consumption of crisps. For each graph, on the horizontal *x*-axis put 'Quantity' (i.e. numbers demanded per week) and on the vertical *y*-axis put 'Price'. Give a title to each graph as follows: *Individual demand curve for* * and put in the name of your classmate instead of the *.

3 Copy out Figure 10.2 and fill it in. To do this you will need to calculate how many packets of crisps would be demanded at each price for all eight of your respondents.

4 Using the figures in question 3, plot two 'market demand curves', one for crisps and one for chocolate bars. Label the axes as in question 2. Plot total quantity demanded for crisps against price on one graph and total quantity demanded for chocolate bars against price on the other graph.

5 Explain why you think customers buy more of a product when its price falls.

A Graphical Analysis

The relationship between the quantity of a product demanded and factors such as price and income can be shown on a graph. Read again the extract from the *Financial Times* about Austin Rover. Then study Figure 10.3.

Figure 10.3

Price per car (£)	Number of cars sold per month
6000	10 000
5000	30 000
4000	50 000
3000	70 000

This table is a crude estimate of the number of cars that Austin Rover would sell at a given average price per car sold. It assumes that all other factors remain constant when prices change. If this is now plotted on a graph, then the result is as shown in Figure 10.4. The line drawn on the graph is known as the DEMAND CURVE (even though in this case the line is not a curve, but a straight line). The demand curve shows how much

Figure 10.4

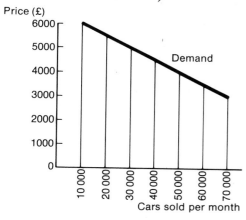

would be bought at any given price over a period of time. So, if British Leyland sold 37 000 cars in a month, it can be seen from the graph that the average price per car sold was £4650. If British Leyland dropped its average price to £4000 per car, then there would be an *extension* of demand to 50 000 cars per month. This is shown by a *movement along* the curve. If price rose to £5000 per car, then there would be a *contraction* of demand to 30 000 sales per month, again leading to a movement along the curve from the previous level of demand.

C H E C K P O I N T S

1 Explain, giving an example, what is meant by 'effective demand'.

2 Give five examples of goods or services you have demanded recently. What price did you pay? How much of the product did you buy?

3 A teenager is thinking of buying a double LP album at £11.99, but decides in the end not to buy it because it is too expensive. Why is this NOT an example of effective demand?

4 Draw a demand curve from the following data:

Price (£)	Quantity demanded
10	100
8	250
6	400
4	550

Indicate on the curve a contraction of demand from a quantity demanded of 250 units.

Figure 10.5

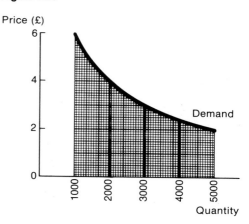

5 From Figure 10.5, how much would be demanded at prices of £4 and £6? What would be the extension in demand, if the price fell from £4 to £2?

C O U R S E W O R K S U G G E S T I O N

This project involves the collection of data over a six-month period. Find out what fruit and vegetables are purchased in your household and where they are commonly purchased. Then, every week, preferably on the same day of the week, note on a record sheet the survey prices in the shops of these fruit and vegetables. On the record sheet, also note down the weekly quantity of each fruit and vegetable purchased by your household. On the basis of the six months' evidence, describe your findings. Draw a demand curve (quantity demanded per week against price) for each fruit and vegetable surveyed. Explain the problems you encountered in gathering your evidence and in analysing it. Try to decide the extent to which the demand curve for fruit and vegetables is downward sloping.

K E Y T E R M S

EFFECTIVE DEMAND or DEMAND — the quantity that a buyer is willing and able to purchase over a period of time.

EXTENSION OF DEMAND — the increase in quantity demanded, due to a fall in price.

CONTRACTION OF DEMAND — the fall in quantity demanded, due to a rise in price.

DEMAND CURVE — the line that shows the relationship between price and quantity demanded over a period of time.

Demand (2)

Figure 11.1 Cinema admissions, UK

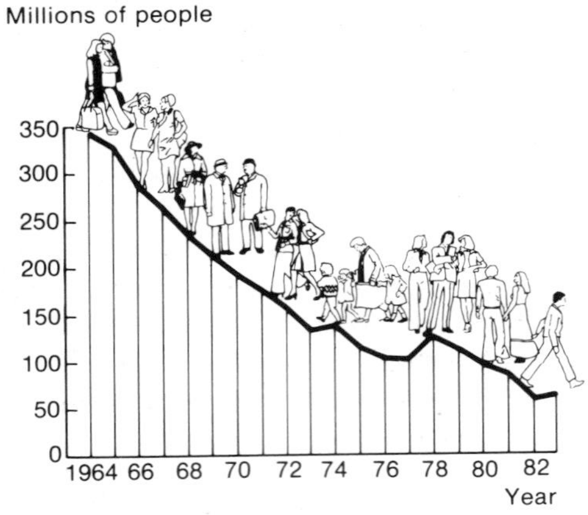

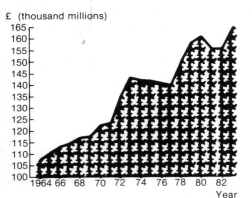

Millions of people

Source: CSO, Annual Abstract of Statistics, 1974 and 1985

Figure 11.2 Average price of admission (at constant 1980 prices)

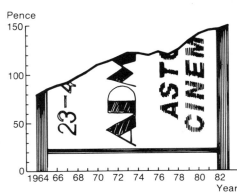

Pence

Source: as 11.1 and CSO, Economics Trends Annual Supplement, 1985

Figure 11.3 Real personal disposable income, UK

£ (thousand millions)

Source: CSO, Economic Trends Annual Supplement, 1985

Figure 11.4 Percentage of people aged 15 and over living in a household with television

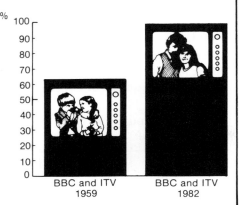

%

BBC and ITV 1959 — BBC and ITV 1982

Source: CSO, Social Trends, 1984

It was shown in the previous unit that the quantity of a product demanded varied according to the price charged for the product. But price is only one factor that determines demand. Consider Figure 11.5.

In 1974, the average disposable income per person in the UK (at 1980 prices) was £2538. 15 million car licences were purchased or demanded (i.e. there were 15 million cars on the road in 1974). By 1983, the average disposable income had risen to £2866 and the number of cars on the road had risen to 17·6 million. Economists have found that this relationship of rising income and rising demand is typical for most goods. A good where an increase in income leads to an increase in demand is called a **NORMAL GOOD**. But for some goods, the opposite occurs – as income rises, demand falls. These goods are known as **INFERIOR GOODS**. Possible examples of inferior goods are bread (where people switch to more expensive foods such as meat, as their incomes rise) and bus services (where people switch to cars as their incomes rise).

Other factors, apart from price and income, affect the level of demand for a product. These include:

- *The price of other products.* If, for instance, the price of beef goes up, then consumers are likely to demand more pork.
- *Advertising.* Heavy advertising should increase the demand for a product.
- *Population.* An increase in the population should raise demand for products.
- *Fashion.* Tastes change over time, and as tastes change, so does demand for particular products.

A Graphical Presentation

This can all be shown on a price/quantity graph. Consider Figure 11.6. A downward-sloping demand

STUDY POINTS

1 How many times have you been to the cinema over the past year?

2 What influences your decision as to whether or not you decide to go to the cinema? (You might mention the price of tickets, availability of good films, transport, alternative forms of leisure activity, your income, etc.)

3 Look at the data provided in Figure 11.1. Describe what has happened to cinema admissions over time.

4 What might have caused this change in demand for cinema admissions to take place? Consider the evidence shown in Figures 11.2–

11.4: changes in price; changes in real income; changes in alternative forms of entertainment.

5 How has this change in demand for cinema admissions altered the demand for other goods and services in the economy? For instance, what has been the effect on the demand for buildings to be used as cinemas, the demand for workers in the cinema industry, the demand for workers in other leisure industries?

6 How might the cinema industry set about reversing the trend in cinema admissions?

Figure 11.5

Year	Income (real personal disposable income per person, UK, £ at 1980 prices)	Quantity demanded (Number, in millions, of vehicle licences purchased, private cars and light goods vehicles, UK)
1974	2538	15·0
1978	2663	15·5
1983	2866	17·6

(*Sources*: CSO, *Annual Abstract of Statistics*; CSO, *Economic Trends Annual Supplement*)

curve, D, is drawn for cars. What it shows is that as the average price of cars increases, the quantity of cars demanded falls. Assume that 1 million cars a year are bought at £5000 each. If the incomes of consumers were to increase, what would happen? At the same price of £5000, consumers would buy more cars. Indeed, at any price more cars would be bought with higher income levels. So the increase in income pushes the demand curve out to the right. In Figure 11.6, it pushes the curve out from D to D′. At a price of £5000, consumers now want to buy 2 million cars, instead of 1 million – so the increase in income must have been fairly large. But this INCREASE IN DEMAND could have been caused by other factors. The price of petrol might have gone down, making motoring cheaper, so that consumers wanted to buy more cars. Or the government might have shut down the whole of British Rail, forcing people to buy more cars to travel.

A FALL IN DEMAND, as shown in Figure 11.7, means that at any given price, less is demanded. So this is shown by a leftward shift in the demand curves from D to D′. A fall in demand could be caused by a fall in consumers' incomes or a fall in the price of competing goods.

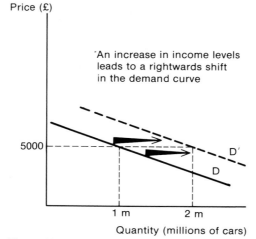

Price (£)

'An increase in income levels leads to a rightwards shift in the demand curve'

5000

1 m   2 m

Quantity (millions of cars)

Figure 11.6

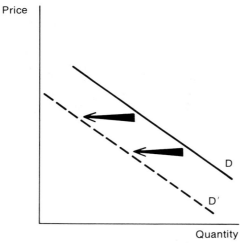

Price

D

D′

Quantity

Figure 11.7

CHECKPOINTS

1 Explain carefully how and why the demand for tennis rackets will change:
   (a) if the incomes of all consumers rise by 20%;
   (b) if the price of admittance to tennis courts doubles;
   (c) if exciting matches at Wimbledon are shown on television;
   (d) if there is very poor weather during the summer.

2 Explain carefully how and why the demand for LP records will change:
   (a) if the price of decks halves;
   (b) if the income of teenagers falls;
   (c) if the price of pre-recorded cassettes halves.

3 Using a price/quantity graph, show how the demand curve might shift in each of the four cases described in question 1.

4 Explain, with examples, the difference between a normal good and an inferior good.

5 Draw a demand curve from the following data:

Price (£)	Quantity demanded
20	1
15	3
10	5
5	7

Now assume that incomes increase and, as a result, quantity demanded increases by one unit at each price. Draw the new demand curve.

COURSEWORK SUGGESTION

Construct a sample of ten young people of your own age with varying incomes. Ask them to keep a diary of their income and expenditure over a period of one or two weeks. Analyse how they have spent their money, using the standard categories to be found in Unit 6. Classify their income. Explain any link you feel there might be between the income of an individual and his or her spending or saving. Consider the possible impact on demand if these ten people experience a doubling of their incomes.

KEY TERMS

NORMAL GOOD – a good or service for which demand increases when incomes increase.

INFERIOR GOOD – a good or service which experiences a fall in demand when incomes increase.

INCREASE and FALL IN DEMAND – a change in quantity demanded, which results from changes in factors such as income and tastes, but *not* price.

Supply

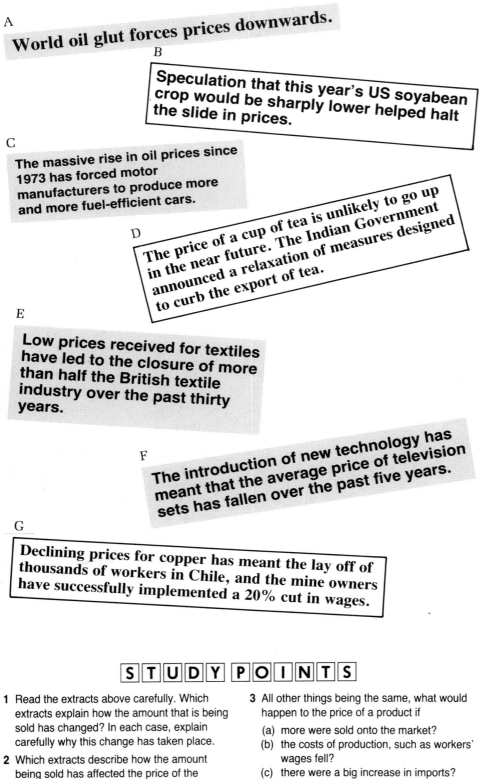

A World oil glut forces prices downwards.

B Speculation that this year's US soyabean crop would be sharply lower helped halt the slide in prices.

C The massive rise in oil prices since 1973 has forced motor manufacturers to produce more and more fuel-efficient cars.

D The price of a cup of tea is unlikely to go up in the near future. The Indian Government announced a relaxation of measures designed to curb the export of tea.

E Low prices received for textiles have led to the closure of more than half the British textile industry over the past thirty years.

F The introduction of new technology has meant that the average price of television sets has fallen over the past five years.

G Declining prices for copper has meant the lay off of thousands of workers in Chile, and the mine owners have successfully implemented a 20% cut in wages.

STUDY POINTS

1 Read the extracts above carefully. Which extracts explain how the amount that is being sold has changed? In each case, explain carefully why this change has taken place.

2 Which extracts describe how the amount being sold has affected the price of the product? In each case, explain carefully why this has been so.

3 All other things being the same, what would happen to the price of a product if
(a) more were sold onto the market?
(b) the costs of production, such as workers' wages fell?
(c) there were a big increase in imports?
(d) new technology were introduced into the production process?

In 1970, the price of oil stood at less than $5 a barrel. The amount of oil known to exist underground stood at 533 billion barrels. By 1980, the price of oil had reached $30 a barrel. Known oil reserves had risen to 608 billion barrels – and this was despite the fact that 20–25 billion barrels of oil were taken out of the ground and sold each year between 1970 and 1980. What had happened was that the large increase in price had encouraged oil companies to find new reserves of oil to sell to households, firms and governments. They went to places like the North Sea or Alaska, which were difficult to work in and until then had not been explored or exploited. On average, the oil men found more new oil than was actually sold in any year in the 1970s.

This illustrates a very important principle in economics. As the price of an item rises, more will be supplied to the market. So as the price of oil rose, more oil fields were offered for exploitation. If the price of potatoes rises over a long period, more farmers will grow potatoes and supply them to the market. This relationship is shown in Figure 12.1. At a price of 60p, 150 units per week will be supplied to the market by producers. At a price of £1, producers will want to supply more to the market. The supply curve shows

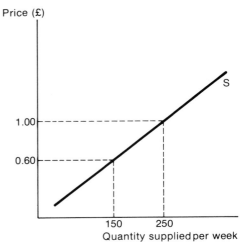

Figure 12.1

that they will want to supply 250 units per week. The definition of the word 'SUPPLY' here is the quantity of a commodity that is offered for sale at any given price over a period of time. As with demand, a change in price affecting quantity supplied is shown by a *movement along* the supply curve and is called an EXTENSION or CONTRACTION OF SUPPLY.

Other Factors Affecting Supply

Consider this:

> 'Renewed frosts in Brazil over the weekend pushed coffee prices up again.' (*Source: Financial Times*, 14 June 1985)

The weather is an important determinant of the supply of agricultural products like coffee or wheat or rice. Frost in Brazil means that, at any given price, less coffee will be supplied to the market because frost has damaged the crop. So the frost has led to a fall in the supply of coffee to the market.

Other factors affect the supply of coffee too. For instance, coffee supply could be increased, if new higher-yielding plants were developed. Each coffee bush would produce more beans and this would increase the supply of coffee to the market. On the other hand, an increase in wages paid to coffee workers would reduce supply. For any given quantity of coffee beans supplied, growers would now want a higher price to cover the cost of the higher wages. If coffee prices were to remain the same, some coffee growers would no longer be able to make a profit from growing coffee, because of the new higher wages. They would either grow less coffee or stop growing coffee altogether, thus reducing the supply of coffee to the market.

These changes in supply can be shown on a diagram. The frost in Brazil which led to a fall in supply would be shown by a *shift* to the left of the whole supply curve from S to S′, as shown in Figure 12.2. If the price, for instance, had been OA, growers would have supplied OC of coffee to the market. The frost has reduced the crop, so at the price of OA, growers are now only prepared to supply OB.

The introduction of higher-yielding coffee bushes, on the other hand, would push the supply curve to the right, as in Figure 12.3. At any given

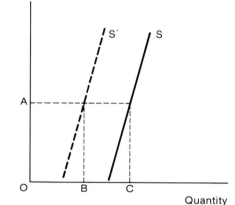

Price per tonne

Figure 12.2

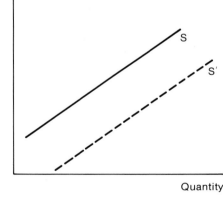

Price per tonne

Figure 12.3

price, more coffee will be supplied to the market.

CHECKPOINTS

1 Explain using examples, what is meant by 'supply'.

2 What effect would the following have on the supply of cars:
   (a) a fall in the price of cars;
   (b) a fall in wages of car workers;
   (c) the introduction of robots to replace humans so as to reduce costs?

3 What is the difference between an 'extension' of supply and an 'increase' in supply?

4 Draw a supply curve from the following data.

Price (pence)	Quantity supplied
10	4
20	16
30	28
40	40
50	52

What is the quantity supplied at prices of 35p and 45p?

5 Use supply curves to illustrate each of the three cases in question 2 above.

COURSEWORK SUGGESTION

In this project, you are considering the supply of labour by your peer group. Construct a simple questionnaire. From the questionnaire you need to find out who has got a paid job, what the job is and what wage rate is paid. From those who have not got a job, find out why not and what rate of pay would induce them to take on paid employment. Find out from all respondents what their other sources of income are. Ask about 25 of your classmates to complete the questionnaire. Describe your findings. Construct a supply curve for labour of your group. Analyse what would happen to supply, if wage rates were to increase. Consider the extent to which a cut in pocket money would increase the supply of labour.

KEY TERMS

SUPPLY – the quantity of a commodity that is offered for sale at a price over a period of time.

EXTENSION OF SUPPLY – the increase in quantity supplied, due to an increase in price.

CONTRACTION OF SUPPLY – the fall in quantity supplied, due to a decrease in price.

Price

Park Bridge Garage, Elliots Lane, Park Bridge, Wolverhampton, WV2 1NC

21 June 1986

The Marketing Manager, Caraco Petroleum
Caraco House, Springway
Birmingham

Dear Mr Bird

The recent 5p rise in the price of petrol forced upon us by Caraco has led to a decline in petrol and derv sales at our garage. Sales were 3000 gallons a day when petrol was priced at £2.10. At £2.15 sales have dropped to 2500 gallons a day. We feel that this latest price increase was totally unjustified given that no other major oil company has increased its prices and it has crippled our trade.

I gather that there is a possibility that you will be re-introducing your special subsidy scheme for selected garages and I suggest that we be one of those selected garages. If petrol was £2.05, I am sure that we could sell 3500 gallons a day.

I will give you a ring later this week to discuss matters further.

Yours sincerely

Bill Graham
Bill Graham

CARACO PETROLEU[M]
Caraco House Springway Birmingham

26 June 1986

Mr W Graham
Manager, Park Bridge Garage
Wolverhampton WV2 1NC

Dear Mr Graham

Thank you for your letter of 21 June. We at Caraco fully understand your plight. However, for the past four years our petrol sales have resulted in losses for the company. Selling more petrol than we currently sell at £2.15 would result in greater losses. If we were to sell 3000 gallons a day through a garage such as yours, we would need a minimum price of £2.20. To sell 3500 gallons a day would mean that we would have to buy petrol from other companies, pushing costs up even further and we would need a minimum price of £2.25. It would not be profitable for us to sell more than 2500 gallons a week at £2.15 per gallon, or 1500 gallons a week at a price of £2.05 per gallon.

We believe that the other oil companies will soon raise their prices. Until then, we can offer no prospect of increased sales.

Yours sincerely

W B Bird
W B Bird

STUDY POINTS

1 Bill Graham was worried because of falling *demand* for petrol at his garage. As an economist working for Caraco Petroleum, explain:
   (a) how sales have decreased. You may want to plot a demand curve to illustrate your answer.
   (b) why demand has fallen. Have motorists stopped buying petrol? Have they switched demand to other petrol stations?

2 How much is Caraco prepared to sell at different prices at Park Bridge Garage? You may want to draw a supply curve to illustrate your answer.

3 Why is Caraco prepared to sell different quantities of petrol at different prices?

4 (a) How much petrol are customers prepared to buy at a price of £2.05? How much petrol is Caraco prepared to sell at that price?
   (b) How much petrol are customers prepared to buy at £2.10? How much petrol is Caraco prepared to sell at that price?
   (c) How much petrol are customers prepared to buy at £2.15, and how much petrol is Caraco prepared to sell at that price?
   (d) How much petrol are customers prepared to buy at £2.20 and how much is Caraco prepared to sell at that price?
   (e) How much petrol are customers prepared to buy at £2.25 and how much is Caraco prepared to sell at that price?
   (f) What is the price at which the amount customers are prepared to buy is equal to the amount Caraco is prepared to sell? (i.e. at what price does demand equal supply? This price is known as the **EQUILIBRIUM PRICE**).

5 Draw a demand and supply curve for petrol at Park Bridge Garage and mark on it the equilibrium price and the equilibrium level of sales.

6 What would happen to the price of petrol if:
   (a) more people bought cars?
   (b) the cost of oil to the oil companies increased?
   (c) the government reduced the taxes on petrol?
   If possible, show the effects of these using a demand and supply diagram.

> 'Petrol poised to burn up the £2-a-gallon barrier. Petrol prices will shoot up to within ½p of £2-a-gallon at Esso pumps around the country. This latest rise is the third in under a month.'
> (*Source: Daily Express*, 8 March 1985)

What fixes the price that households pay for petrol, or indeed any commodity?

Demand and Supply

Price in a free market is fixed or 'determined' by the forces of demand and supply. Take the price of petrol. If oil companies want to sell more petrol (i.e. if they want to increase the supply of petrol), then they can only do this by persuading motorists to buy more petrol. The easiest way to do this is for the oil companies to drop the price of petrol. If, on the other hand, oil companies reduce the supply of petrol to the market, most motorists would be prepared to pay higher prices to obtain the petrol supplies available, i.e.

- a decrease in demand or an increase in supply will *reduce* prices;
- an increase in demand or a fall in supply will *raise* prices.

A Graphical Analysis

Price determination can be shown by using a demand and supply diagram. In Figure 13.1, a demand and supply curve is drawn for a commodity. At a price of £5 − 250 units will be

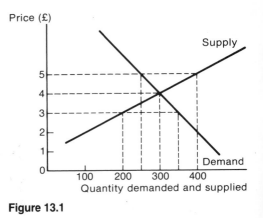

Figure 13.1

demanded, but 400 units will be supplied. The result will be that 150 units will be left unsold. The price of £5 is too high for everything produced to be sold. Economists say therefore that EXCESS SUPPLY (i.e. too much supply in relation to demand) exists. If the price is £3, then producers will only want to sell 200 units, but buyers will want to buy 350 units. Many buyers will be disappointed because there will not be enough goods to buy. EXCESS DEMAND (i.e. too much demand in relation to supply) will exist.

Only at a price of £4 will demand exactly equal price. This price is known as the EQUILIBRIUM PRICE or the MARKET CLEARING PRICE. It is the price where the forces of demand and supply are matched so that there is no tendency to change. When there is excess supply, suppliers will not continue for ever to produce more than they can sell. They will cut back production, and reduce prices, until supply again equals demand. If there is excess demand, firms will push up prices and expand output to take advantage of the situation where buyers want to buy more.

Changes in Prices

A change in price will come about when either demand or supply changes. For instance, the reason why petrol prices went up in March 1985 was because the price of oil to the oil companies increased. So the oil companies increased the price of petrol at the pumps. This would be shown by an upwards shift in the supply curve for petrol, shown in Figure 13.2. Before the price rise, the market or equilibrium price was £1.90 – that was the price where demand

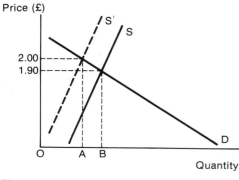

Figure 13.2

equalled supply. After the price rise, the oil companies wanted a higher price to supply the same amount of petrol. So the supply curve shifted upwards from S to S'. A new equilibrium price of £2 was achieved, but the oil companies had to accept that they would not sell as much petrol as before. At £1.90, motorists were prepared to buy OB of petrol. At £2.00 they would only buy OA.

Figure 13.3 shows an increase in demand from D to D'. This pushes up the equilibrium price from OA to OB, and increases the equilibrium quantity bought and sold from OE to OF.

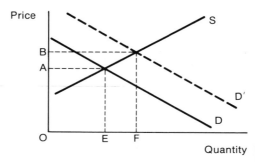

Figure 13.3

CHECKPOINTS

1 What determines the price of a product?
2 Explain how and why the price of beef will change in a free market:
   (a) if the demand for beef increases;
   (b) if the supply of beef decreases;
   (c) if farmers keep more sheep instead of cows;
   (d) if a disease reduces the number of calves born;
   (e) if there is a successful advertising campaign for beef;
   (f) if a report is published linking beef with ill health.
3 In each of the cases (a) to (f) in question 2, draw a demand and supply diagram showing the effect of the change on price and quantity demanded and supplied.

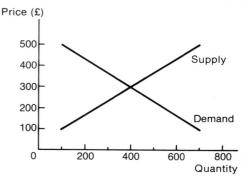

Figure 13.4

4 Look at Figure 13.4.
   (a) What is the equilibrium price?
   (b) What is the equilibrium quantity demanded?
   (c) How much is demanded at a price of £100? How much is supplied? What is the excess demand at this price?
   (d) What is the excess supply at a price of £500?

COURSEWORK SUGGESTION

This project requires research into the change in price of one good or service over a period of time and an analysis of the causes of this change. Take a particular period of time and find out how the price of a commodity or group of commodities has changed over that period. Possibly the best source of data is the Retail Price Index, a detailed breakdown of which can be found in the *Department of Employment Gazette* and *British Labour Statistics: Year Book* (both published by HMSO). Then suggest reasons as to why prices have changed for this commodity, and try to find statistical evidence to support your hypothesis. Evaluate possible future trends in prices. Use demand and supply diagrams wherever possible to support your analysis.

KEY TERMS

EQUILIBRIUM PRICE or MARKET CLEARING PRICE – the price at which demand equals supply.
EXCESS DEMAND – a situation where demand is greater than supply, leading to shortages of commodities.
EXCESS SUPPLY – a situation when supply is greater than demand, leading to a glut of commodities on the market.

Data Response Questions
Units 10–13

Unit 10 Demand (1)

Source: Wolverhampton Adnews, 5th September 1985.

1 What is meant by:
(a) a 'stock clearance'? and
(b) a 'discount'? *(4 marks)*

2 (a) What will be the likely result of the discount being offered by the Car Centre?
(b) Use a diagram to illustrate your answer. *(6 marks)*

Unit 11 Demand (2)

Fare freeze boosts bus rides

A massive increase in the number of rides being taken on West Midlands buses has been hailed as the prize for freezing fares for a record three years.

Latest figures show that journeys on buses spiralled by 19 million — nearly four per cent — in 1984-85 to 490 million.

At the same time 26 million rides were taken on cross-country rail routes, an increase of two million over the previous year.

Passenger Transport Executive director-general, Mr James Isaac, said: "This increase has taken place during a recession and answers the critics of bus services."

Source: Express and Star, 14 June 1985

1 What happened to the number of rides made on public transport in the West Midlands in 1984–85? *(2 marks)*

2 (a) Explain why this has happened.
(b) Draw a demand and supply diagram to illustrate your answer. *(5 marks)*

3 What would be the likely effect on rides taken of a 20% rise in fares? *(3 marks)*

Essay Questions
Units 10–13

1 The price of a Mars Bar goes down from 20p to 18p.
(a) What is likely to happen to the consumer demand for Mars Bars? *(2 marks)*
(b) Explain *one* other way in which the manufacturers of Mars Bars could change the demand for Mars Bars. *(4 marks)*
(c) What would you expect to happen to the demand for Mars Bars if the average pocket money of children increased and why? *(4 marks)*
(d) If the price of other competing chocolate bars went up by an average of 20%, how would you expect the manufacturers of Mars Bars to react and why? *(5 marks)*

(e) Draw two demand diagrams showing the difference in effect on demand of a fall in price of Mars Bars and a rise in consumer incomes. *(5 marks)*

2 The price of one LP record is £4.99 whilst the price of another is £2.99.
(a) Suggest *four* reasons why the price of these two records is different. *(8 marks)*
(b) Explain how and why the price of records might change if more were spent on advertising by record companies. *(4 marks)*
(c) Using a demand and supply diagram, explain how and why the quantity bought of records might change if the price of record players increased. *(8 marks)*

Unit 12 Supply

Poor crops put pepper in a pickle

A worsening shortage of pepper, has caused wholesale prices to rocket to record levels in recent months.

A disastrous crop last year in Brazil and low harvests in all the three other main producing countries have conspired to bring on the supply squeeze.

Prices of white pepper have doubled and those of black pepper have trebled over the past 18 months.

Estimates of supply and demand in the fragmented and relatively unsophisticated world pepper trade are notoriously unreliable. But pepper brokers and buyers believe that demand is certain to exceed supplies this year by a substantial margin — for the second consecutive season.

The pepper market is feeling the after-effects of years of relatively low prices, which have discouraged production in some countries and led to bad husbandry in others.

As to what happens after this year, opinions are divided. Optimists point to the possibility of relatively new suppliers such as China dramatically stepping up their production. They also forecast that the present price levels will eventually encourage traditional suppliers to boost output.

Pessimists underline the long lead-times involved in pepper production. It takes three years from planting for the first crop to appear, and the pepper vine does not attain its maximum yield until six years after that.

Source: Financial Times, 16 May 1985

1 Explain what is meant by 'supply of pepper'. *(2 marks)*

2 Why did the supply of pepper change in 1984–5? *(2 marks)*

3 Use a diagram to show this change in supply. *(2 marks)*

4 What is likely to happen to pepper supplies in the future and why? *(2 marks)*

5 Show these future changes on a diagram. *(2 marks)*

Unit 13A and 13B Price

Accidents push up cost of basic chemicals

Prices of ethylene and propylene, base materials for the chemicals industry are rising sharply as the result of an extraordinary series of accidents at chemicals plants in Europe.

On May 16, Esso's ethylene cracker at Stenungsund in Sweden was put out of action by the collapse of its cooling tower. Three days later, Italian producer Enchem's cracker at Prolo in Sicily was damaged by fire. Together with an explosion in January at the Rheinische Olefinwerke (ROW) cracker in West Germany, jointly owned by Shell and BASF, accidents have taken out 10 per cent of Europe's total ethylene capacity.

As a result, says Enichem, prices of both ethylene and propylene (also produced by all three crackers) have risen by more than 10 per cent in the past 30 days.

Source: Financial Times, 4 June 1985

1 What has been happening to the prices of ethylene and propylene? *(1 mark)*

2 Explain why the prices of these materials have changed. *(5 marks)*

3 Draw a demand and supply diagram to show how prices have changed. *(4 marks)*

Banks's put 4p on pint

Banks's-Hanson's announced today that the price of bitter is going up by 4p a pint and lager and mild by 3p from September 16.

Brewery chiefs today blamed the increases on inflation and rising costs over the past year.

The new increase means that bitter in Banks's and Hanson's pubs will cost 66p, with mild and lager at 61p and 75p.

Marketing director Mr Derek Andrew said: "Our prices have been increased in line with inflation and increased overheads during the year."

The news was greeted with dismay by licensees, who described it as "another nail in the coffin" of pubs.

"We are just lurching from one crisis to another. Our sales are down anyway, thanks to the weather, and now we have to put up with a price rise as well," said a Wolverhampton Banks's manager.

"Things are getting to the stage where the pubs will be empty.".

Source: Express and Star, 5 September, 1985

1 How much did a pint of bitter in Banks's pubs cost:
(a) before 16th September 1985?
(b) on 16th September 1985? *(1 mark)*

2 What effect is the rise in price likely to have on sales of beer? *(2 marks)*

3 Why did the brewery put up its prices? *(2 marks)*

4 Draw a demand and supply diagram to show why prices have risen. *(5 marks)*

The Cookseys

John Cooksey – aged 40, an English teacher in a comprehensive school;
Sally Cooksey – aged 38, housewife;
Miriam Cooksey – aged 15, still at school;
Mathew Cooksey – aged 13, at school;
Michael Cooksey – aged 11, at school

3 Mayfield Road
lounge, dining room, kitchen, bathroom, 3 bedrooms.

BUDGET
(Incomings and Outgoings per Month)

	£		£
Food and small domestic purchases	170	Take home salary	570
Mortgage	50	Child Benefit	90
Rates	40		
Clothes	30		
Holidays	30		
Car	120		
Pocket Money and Presents	40		
Bills (gas, electric, insurance etc.)	170		
Other	10		
TOTAL	660		660

Put yourself in the place of John and Sally Cooksey.

1 Analyse your expenditure by completing the bar graph in Figure 14.1, putting the costliest item first on the left and ending up with the least costly item on the right.

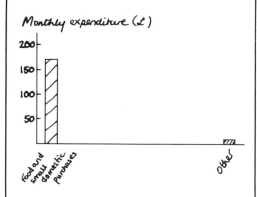

Figure 14.1

2 Building societies put up their interest rates and your monthly mortgage repayment goes up to £60. How will you reallocate your scarce resources as a result? i.e. what item or items of expenditure will you cut to pay for this? Explain the reason for your decision.

3 The cost of food and other small domestic purchases (washing powder, newspapers etc.) goes up by 10% but all other costs remain the same.
  (a) Explain how and why you will reallocate your resources.
  (b) Calculate the price elasticity of demand for food and other small domestic purchases revealed by your decision.
  (c) Calculate too the cross elasticity of demand for any categories of expenditure which have changed as a result of the increase in price.

4 More textile imports are allowed into the country and as a result the price of clothes falls by 20%.
  (a) Explain how and why you will reallocate your resources as a result.
  (b) Calculate your price elasticity of demand for clothes.
  (c) Calculate too the cross elasticity of demand for any other categories of expenditure which have changed as a result.

5 Teachers get a pay rise which adds 5% to take home pay.
  (a) Explain how and why you will reallocate your resources.
  (b) Calculate the income elasticity of demand for each of the categories of expenditure on the budget.

- **The price of a packet of crisps goes up by 10%.**
- **Pocket money falls by 5%.**
- **The price of chocolate bars goes up by 20%.**

What effect might any one of the above changes have on the quantity of crisps demanded? Economists measure the responsiveness of changes in quantity demanded to changes in factors such as price, income, price of other goods, etc. by something called ELASTICITY.

Price Elasticity of Demand

For instance, PRICE ELASTICITY OF DEMAND measures the responsiveness of changes in the quantity demanded of a product to changes in its price. The exact formula for price elasticity of demand is:

$$\frac{\text{Percentage change in quantity demanded}}{\text{Percentage change in price}}$$

If the quantity demanded of a good rose by 10% due to a fall in price of 5%, the price elasticity of demand for a product would be $^{10}\!/_5$ or 2. (To be totally accurate, the answer is -2, since the fall in price of 5% should have been shown by a '-5'. But since changes in price and quantity nearly always move in opposite directions, economists usually do not bother to put in the minus sign.)

Special names are given to various values of price elasticity of demand, as is illustrated below.

If the price elasticity of demand is 0 (i.e. the same amount is demanded, whatever the price), then demand is said to be *perfectly inelastic*. (See Figure 14.2.)

If the price elasticity of demand is between 0 and 1 (i.e. the percentage change in quantity demanded from A to B is smaller than the percentage change in price), then demand is said to be *inelastic*. (See Figure 14.3.)

If the price elasticity of demand is 1 (i.e. the percentage change in quantity demanded is exactly the same as the percentage change in price), then demand is said to be of *unitary elasticity*. (See Figure 14.4.)

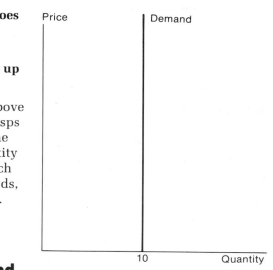

Figure 14.2

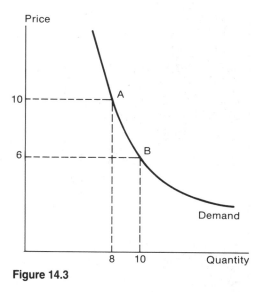

Figure 14.3

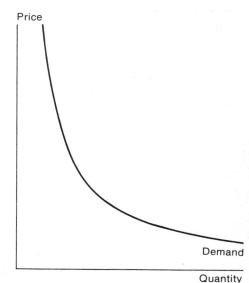

Figure 14.4

If the price elasticity of demand is between 1 and infinity (i.e. the percentage change in quantity demanded from A to B is larger than the percentage change in price), then demand is said to be *elastic*. (See Figure 14.5.)

If the price elasticity of demand is infinite (i.e. purchasers will buy all that is available at the existing price), then demand is said to be *perfectly elastic*. (See Figure 14.6.)

Figure 14.7

Change in quantity demanded:		Change in price (£):		Percentage change in quantity demanded	Percentage change in price	Elasticity
from	to	from	to			
1000	900	2	3	$\frac{100}{1000} \times 100$	$\frac{1}{2} \times 100$	$\frac{1}{5}$
500	200	10	11	$\frac{300}{500} \times 100$	$\frac{1}{10} \times 100$	6
100	20	5	6	$\frac{80}{100} \times 100$	$\frac{1}{5} \times 100$	4
50	40	5	7	$\frac{10}{50} \times 100$	$\frac{2}{5} \times 100$	$\frac{1}{2}$

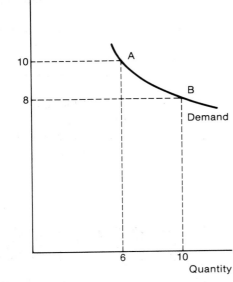

Figure 14.5

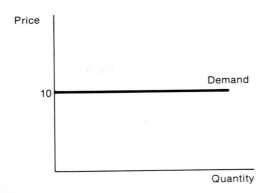

Figure 14.6

To illustrate the concept of price elasticity of demand, consider the market for petrol. Assume that the price of petrol at the pumps increases by 10%. Petrol consumers are unlikely to decrease their consumption of petrol by very much: lorries still need petrol for business, commuters still have to get to work, families will still want to shop at their nearest supermarket. So, in the short term at least, the quantity demanded of petrol is unlikely to fall greatly. If demand fell by, say, 2%, then petrol would have an elasticity of 2/10 or 0.2 (i.e. demand is inelastic). Over a long period, consumers are likely to react to the 10% increase in petrol prices by switching to more fuel-efficient motor vehicles. This will reduce the demand for petrol further. Over a ten-year period, demand might fall by, say, 15%. Then the long-term elasticity of demand for petrol would be 15/10 or 1.5. Further examples are given in Figure 14.7.

Income Elasticity of Demand

INCOME ELASTICITY OF DEMAND is the relationship between a change in quantity demanded and a change in income. The exact formula for income elasticity is:

$$\frac{\text{Percentage change in quantity demanded}}{\text{Percentage change in income}}$$

For a normal good, an increase in income will lead to an increase in quantity demanded. Income elasticity of demand is therefore positive. For an inferior good, an increase in income will lead to a fall in demand for the good, and so income elasticity is negative. (For a fuller discussion of normal and inferior goods, see Unit 11.)

Cross-elasticity of Demand

CROSS-ELASTICITY OF DEMAND measures the responsiveness of changes in quantity demanded of a product to change in the price of another product. The exact formula for cross-elasticity of demand for product X is:

$$\frac{\text{Percentage change in quantity demanded of product X}}{\text{Percentage change in price of another product}}$$

For instance, if the cross-elasticity of demand for crisps were 2 and the price of chocolate bars went up 10%, then there would be a 20% increase in demand for crisps.

Price Elasticity of Supply

The concept of elasticity is just as applicable to supply. PRICE ELASTICITY OF SUPPLY is the relationship between change in quantity supplied and a change in price. The exact formula for price elasticity of supply is:

$$\frac{\text{Percentage change in quantity supplied}}{\text{Percentage change in price}}$$

Its value is normally positive, because an increase in price is likely to increase the quantity supplied to the market and vice versa. A downward-sloping supply curve, where an increase in price led to a fall in quantity supplied, would obviously have a negative elasticity.

The concept of elasticity is considered further in the next unit.

CHECKPOINTS

1 Explain what is meant by price elasticity of demand. If demand for a good is 'price elastic', what does this mean?

2 How does the income elasticity of demand for a normal good differ from that of an inferior good? Why?

3 Calculate the price elasticity of demand from the following data:

Percentage change in quantity demanded	Percentage change in price	Elasticity
10	20	
5	1	
20	10	
50	30	

4 The following data show how quantity demanded for a good changes as income changes. Calculate the income elasticity of demand for a change in income:
(a) from £100 to £200;
(b) from £200 to £300;
(c) from £300 to £400;
(d) from £100 to £400.

Quantity demanded	Income (£)
10	100
20	200
60	300
180	400

5 For the data in Figure 14.8, calculate the price elasticity of supply for a change in price:
(a) from £10 to £20;
(b) from £20 to £30;
(c) from £30 to £40;
(d) from £40 to £20.

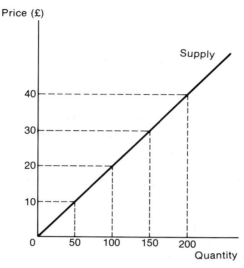

Figure 14.8

6 The cross elasticity of records for pre-recorded cassettes is + ½. Calculate:
(a) the percentage change in demand for records if the price of cassettes went up by 10%;
(b) the percentage change in the price of cassettes that occurred to cause a 10% rise in the demand for records;
(c) the percentage rise in the demand for records if the price of cassettes went up from £5 to £6.

7 What do you think the elasticity values might be in the following cases? Explain your reasoning carefully.
(a) Price elasticity of demand for records.
(b) Price elasticity of demand for tickets to a concert featuring a top British rock group.
(c) Income elasticity of demand for a Mars Bar.
(d) Income elasticity of demand for motorcycles.
(e) Income elasticity of demand for private health care.
(f) Cross elasticity of demand of Dunlop and Slazinger tennis rackets.
(g) Cross elasticity of demand of petrol and mini cars.
(h) Cross elasticity of demand of new houses and large cars.

COURSEWORK SUGGESTION

Keep a record of your spending over a six-month period. Over the same period, make a weekly survey of the prices of ten goods and services that you commonly purchase. Also, keep a summary of changes in your weekly income. Explain the concept of elasticity and estimate the price, income and cross-elasticities of demand for the products you have purchased over the six-month period. Explain the difficulties of measuring elasticity from your data. Consider the extent to which elasticity is a useful tool in economics, given the difficulties of measurement when using actual data.

KEY TERMS

ELASTICITY – the responsiveness of the quantity of a product to a change in the value of a factor determining its quantity. PRICE ELASTICITY OF DEMAND measures the responsiveness of quantity demanded to a change in price; INCOME ELASTICITY OF DEMAND measures the responsiveness of quantity demanded to a change in income; CROSS-ELASTICITY OF DEMAND measures the responsiveness of quantity demanded of one product to the change in price of another product; PRICE ELASTICITY OF SUPPLY measures the responsiveness of quantity supplied to a change in price.

Elasticity (2)

STUDY POINTS

The price of each of the products or services shown in the photographs goes up by 10 per cent.

1 What, in your opinion, is likely to happen to the quantity purchased of the product in percentage terms?

2 For each product, explain why demand is likely to change in the way you have described.

3 What, then, in your opinion, is the price elasticity of demand for each product?

Determinants of Price Elasticity of Demand

'Electricity prices set to rise by 5%.'

How will electricity consumers react to this in the short term? The answer is probably that there will be almost no change in the quantity of electricity demanded – in other words, the demand for electricity is inelastic in the short term. Why is this the case? There are three main reasons:

- Electricity has few good *substitutes*. A **SUBSTITUTE GOOD** is a good that can be used instead of another good; for example, gas is a substitute for electricity, but only under certain conditions. If a householder wishes to run a television or freezer, or have lighting, then electricity is almost the only option. Even those households with electric cookers and heating are unlikely to change hundreds or thousands of pounds of equipment, just because of a 5% rise in running costs. In the longer term, when households do have to replace worn out equipment, they may change to another form of fuel. So in the long run, the demand for electricity will be more elastic than in the short run.

'This wasn't what I expected when you said we'd have a candlelit dinner instead of paying that huge electricity bill.'

- Electricity is seen as a *necessity*. Consumers are likely to cut back on goods and services which they see as luxuries, rather than on cooking or lighting or heating.

- For many households that only use electricity for lighting and running a few appliances like a television, electricity is a very *small part* of their *total spending*. A 5% rise in prices will hardly make them turn off their televisions or not turn on their lights.

In general, demand for a good will tend to be inelastic when there are no good substitutes, where the proportion spent on the product out of total income is relatively small, and where the good is considered a necessity.

Elasticity and Expenditure or Revenue

It has been argued that electricity, at least in the short run, is price inelastic. For instance, with an elasticity of $(-)\frac{1}{2}$, a rise in electricity of 5% would result in a fall in demand for electricity of 2½%. What this means is that total spending on electricity will increase following the price rise, resulting in higher **REVENUE** for the electricity company. On a bill of £100, the price rise would be £5. But the 2½% fall in demand for electricity would mean that the final bill would only come to about £102.50. So if demand is inelastic, a rise in price will lead to a fall in quantity demanded, but overall there will be a rise in expenditure or revenue. On the other hand, a fall in price with inelastic demand will lead to a fall in revenue *and* expenditure.

The opposite is true if demand is elastic. Assume that foreign holidays have an elastic demand and that the value of that elasticity is $(-)2$. Then a fall in the price of foreign holidays of 10% will raise demand by 20%. That means that total spending by households and total revenue received by the foreign tourist trade will rise. On the other hand, if the price of foreign holidays goes up, the fall in demand for foreign holidays will result in a fall in total spending and revenue.

K E Y T E R M S

SUBSTITUTE GOOD – a good that can be used instead of another good for a particular purpose; for example, gas can be used for electricity for cooking.

(SALES) REVENUE – the sum of money received from the sale of a product. It can be calculated by multiplying the average price received by the total quantity sold.

Saving

John Harris: 19, getting married in three months' time, wants to buy a house.

Sylvia Thistle: 43, married with two teenage children, just inherited £10,000.

Wendy Carrol: 10, at school.

Liz Bertram: 63, retired, husband still alive, children all left home, has saved up £5,000.

MONEY MAKER

Instant Access. No Penalties
Monthly Income Option

£20,000+ invested
10·30% *NET
10·57% †
COMPOUNDED ANNUAL RATE

10·05% *NET
£5,000+ invested
10·30% †
COMPOUNDED ANNUAL RATE

£1,000+ invested
9·75% *NET
9·99% †
COMPOUNDED ANNUAL RATE

* Current net rate to investors paying basic rate Income Tax at 30%.
† Compounded annual rate is earned when half-yearly interest is added to the account.

Coventry
Building Society

The Piggy Bank Account

The PIGGY BANK savings account is specially designed for young children. It requires a minimum of £3 to open an account, of which £1 goes towards the cost of the Piggy Bank pack, and the rest is credited to the account. In addition NatWest will put in £2 FREE when you save the 15 tokens from Cadbury packs.

The Piggy Bank pack consists of Woody (the first in a set of 5 ceramic piggy banks), a wall chart, folder and colour pencil set. In addition, members regularly receive a magazine and, provided they have the appropriate balance in the account, receive the next piggy bank in the family free, every six months. Interest is paid each June and December.

NB. If the account is opened for a child under the age of seven the signature of a parent or guardian is required for all transactions.

£64,000* FOR YOUR FAMILY IF YOU DIE. £21,000* FOR YOU IF YOU DON'T.

Contrary to popular opinion you don't have to cash in on your life assurance.

For just £20 a month Abbey Life has a plan that will insure your life for over £64,000.* Until the age of 60, we can also maintain your policy if you're sick or disabled and we may be able to help if you're made redundant.

But that's not all. The plan will also provide a substantial lump sum on retirement.

Nationwide

for extra interest

Bonus-90 Accounts

Net	Compounded Annual Rate	Gross Equivalent CAR	Minimum Investment
10.00%	10.25%	14.64%	£200 or £2,000 if monthly income
Half Yearly Income Per £1,000	Monthly income Per £1,000 (minimum £2,000)	Withdrawal notice or penalty Up to £10,000 / Over £10,000	
£50.00	£8.33	90 days	NIL Provided £10,000 remains invested

'Get the Abbey habit', reads the advertising slogan for the Abbey National Building Society. Building societies are interested in your **SAVINGS**. Saving takes place when a household or a firm or a government decides not to spend the money available to it. If a household earned £200 after tax, etc. and spent £150, then it must have saved the extra £50.

Why Save?

Saving takes place for a number of reasons. Much saving is for purchases of goods and services in the future. A family might want a car or a new washing machine, so they save to pay for it. People also save for their retirement, when their income from their job will disappear. Saving now will provide an income for the worker when he or she retires. Saving also takes place because savers want to protect themselves against future problems. The car might break down.

S T U D Y   P O I N T S

1 Why do people save money?

2 Where can they put their savings?

3 What is the link between interest and savings?

4 What type of saving scheme might be suitable for each of the four people above and why?

5 Is it a good thing for teenagers to save and why? To answer this, weigh up the costs and benefits of saving.

6 Find out how many of your class are saving up for something in particular and how many save all the time anyway.

The roof might start to leak. The worker might be made redundant. So households save up to provide themselves with a financial cushion against such events. Third, savers might be attracted by the fact that savings will grow in value over time. For instance, **INTEREST** is usually paid on savings. Or the value of savings in, say, shares or a house might grow. By not spending now, more goods and services can be bought in the future.

Savings Institutions

Figure 16.1 shows how savers held their savings in 1983. Approximately 5.9% were held in *bank deposit accounts*. Banks borrow money, some of it from the ordinary person in the street. Bank deposit accounts are designed for the saver, and interest is given on money in the account.

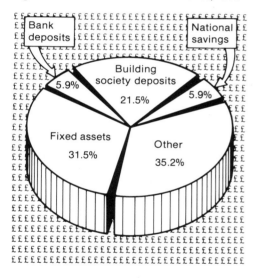

Figure 16.1 Personal sector use of funds, 1983

Deposit accounts are unlike a bank current account, which is designed for the person who wants to move money around.

Approximately 21.5% of savings were held in **BUILDING SOCIETY** *accounts*. Building societies borrow money from households and then lend that money out again in the form of **MORTGAGES** – loans to buy property. Building societies offer a variety of accounts for customers. Ordinary share accounts allow customers to pay in and withdraw money at will. For higher interest rates, though, savers must have accounts where they either promise to save regularly (like a Save-As-You-Earn account) or they keep a fixed amount of money in the account and have to give at least 7 days' notice of withdrawal.

The 5.9% in National Savings are held in various schemes, including National Savings Certificates, Premium Bonds, the National Savings Bank, Income Bonds and Save-As-You-Earn. National Savings are run by the government, mainly through the Post Office. The government needs to borrow money to pay for its spending.

'Fixed assets' are mainly houses. A house is not used up or consumed in the same way as, say, a car. Most houses, in fact, sell for more than they were bought for. So a house is a form of saving.

'Other' is the most important category at 35.2%. It includes ownership of stocks and shares. More importantly, it includes money held in *assurance* and **PENSION** funds. Assurance or life insurance companies offer savings schemes whereby a saver promises to pay money (known as **PREMIUMS**) at regular intervals to the company. Then, at the end of, say, 25 years, the assurance policy of the saver will come to an end (or *mature*), and the money will be paid back with interest and profits. These companies and other pension companies also offer **PENSION** schemes. Savers pay money to the company, usually on a regular basis, and the company promises to pay them a regular fixed pension when they retire. The assurance and pension fund companies use the money lent to them to save money themselves, much of it in the form of stocks and shares, although they also invest in property.

CHECKPOINTS

1 **What is the difference between consumption and saving?**

2 **Explain why (a) a 15-year-old, (b) a 25-year-old and (c) a 55-year-old person might save.**

3 **Have you got any savings at the moment? Where do you keep them? Why do you keep them there?**

4 **What is the opportunity cost of keeping savings in a building society account?**

5 **Convert Figure 16.1 to a bar chart. Why do you think that over half of all UK savings are held in the form of houses, assurance policies and pension funds?**

KEY TERMS

SAVING – income and wealth that is not spent on goods and services.

INTEREST – a sum of money paid as a reward for the loan of money. The INTEREST RATE is the proportion of interest paid in comparison with the size of the loan; it is expressed as a percentage.

BUILDING SOCIETY – a financial institution that specialises in borrowing money from personal savers and lending the money out again for the purpose of home loans.

MORTGAGE – a loan of money for the purchase of property.

PREMIUM – a sum of money paid regularly for insurance or assurance cover.

PENSION – a sum of money paid at regular intervals when a person has retired.

COURSEWORK SUGGESTION

Describe in detail four different savings schemes. Assess the relative merits of each savings scheme. Analyse why different savers (e.g. a pensioner, a woman at home looking after her family, a young married couple) might decide to choose one saving scheme rather than another. Assess the effects these choices will have on the way resources are used in the economy.

Income, Wealth and Inequality

STUDY POINTS

From Figure 17.1:

1 How much of the total wealth of the UK is owned by the most wealthy 1% of the adult population?

2 If a typical 100 people owned a total of £100, how much would
   (a) the average person own?
   (b) the most wealthy person own?
   (c) the most wealthy 25 people own?
   (d) the least wealthy 50 people own?
   (e) the average person amongst the least wealthy 50 people own (hint: divide your answer to (d) by 50).

From Figure 17.2:

3 How much did the top 1% of income earners earn in 1949 and 1981/2?

4 Which group(s) saw a rise in its share of total income over the period 1949 to 1981/82?

From Figure 17.3:

5 What happens to benefits received and taxes paid as income rises?

6 What is the largest source of income for the bottom fifth of the population?

7 What is the difference in income between the bottom fifth and top fifth of income earners
   (a) in £s and
   (b) in percentage terms?

From Figures 17.4 and 17.5:

8 What percentage of dwellings in England and Wales in 1981 was unfit for human habitation?

9 If there were 20 million dwellings in 1983 in Great Britain, how many did not have a fixed bath or shower?

From all the Figures:

10 Describe how differences in income and wealth have changed over recent years in the UK.

11 Explain why the most wealthy in the UK are also likely to be among the top income earners.

12 How could the distribution of income and wealth be made more equal? What would be the consequences of this?

Figure 17.1 Concentration of wealth among adult population

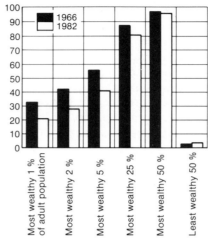

% of total UK wealth

(*Source:* Inland Revenue statistics, 1984)

Figure 17.2 Shares of pre-tax income: by selected quantile groups of income

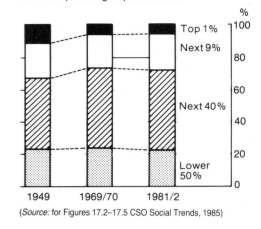

(*Source:* for Figures 17.2–17.5 CSO Social Trends, 1985)

Figure 17.3 Distribution of income before and after tax 1982 (£)

	Income before tax and benefits	Benefits	Tax[1]	Income after tax and benefits
Bottom fifth	150	2680	10	2820
Next fifth	2620	1960	430	4160
Middle fifth	6690	890	1430	6150
Next fifth	10040	680	2280	8440
Top fifth	17390	530	4100	13820

[1] Income tax and National Insurance Contributions.

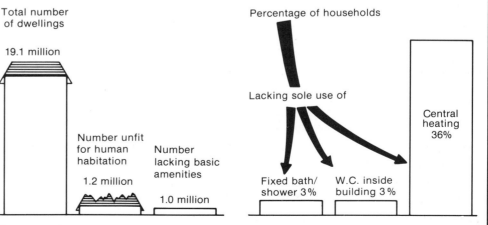

Figure 17.4 Dwellings in England and Wales, 1981 (in millions)

Figure 17.5 Housing standards in the UK, 1983

- 'Miss J. Lewis, of 16 Hicks Avenue, left £773 000 in her will.'

- 'Mr B. James is currently the top income earner in the company with a salary of £37 500 a year.'

Miss Lewis owned money, property and valuables that amounted to £773 000 at the time of her death. This was the value of her WEALTH. The value of a person's wealth (or indeed of the wealth of a company or a country) can be measured *at a point in time* such as 31 December 1985. We are not told how wealthy Mr James is, but he does earn an income of £37 500 over the period of a year. INCOME can only be measured *over a period of time*. Various types of wealth give rise to various types of income. In particular:

- HUMAN WEALTH or HUMAN CAPITAL yields EARNED INCOME. Human wealth is the economic value of a person. A person's human wealth can be increased by education, training and work experience. The greater a person's human wealth, the higher should be the income that that worker receives from an employer.

- NON-HUMAN WEALTH yields UNEARNED INCOME, such as interest, profit and dividends. Non-human wealth is the value of a person's possessions – money, houses, stocks and shares, building society deposits, etc. By lending or making available money or other assets to other people, an individual can receive an income that is not earned by going out to work.

Human wealth and non-human wealth are unevenly distributed in the UK. Figure 17.1 shows how unequally non-human wealth was distributed in the UK in 1982. A mere 1% of the population (that is, one person in every 100) owned one-fifth of the available non-human wealth in the UK. Half the population only owned 4% of the wealth. No figures exist for the value of human wealth in the UK, but it is likely to be as unevenly distributed as non-human wealth, given that in 1982 some workers earned less than £25 a week, whereas others earned over £2000 a week.

Figure 17.2 shows how income is distributed before tax and benefits. Half of all income earners received a mere 22% of the total income in the UK in 1981/2. Some people's income had to be increased through benefits such as the state pension and unemployment benefit. These benefits are paid for by taxing the better off. Figure 17.3 shows the distribution of income after taxes and benefits have been taken into consideration. The differences between income earners have been reduced, but there is still a big difference between high- and low-income earners.

Figures 17.4–17.5 give some simple facts about what it means to be poor in Britain in the 1980s – no inside toilet, no running hot water, etc.

Are Inequalities Inevitable?

Does an economy *have* to have inequalities in income and wealth? In practice, every economy produces inequalities, but the degree of inequality is the *choice* of society. For instance, in Britain we could solve the problem of poverty amongst pensioners by doubling the state pension. But that has to be paid for. Is it better to have the higher-paid workers paying more taxes to provide higher pensions? Or is the situation better as it is? This is a difficult choice to make, but it is one that every society has to face.

K|E|Y T|E|R|M|S

HUMAN WEALTH or HUMAN CAPITAL – the skills and abilities of an individual that enable that person to produce goods and services.

NON-HUMAN WEALTH – the material possessions of an individual, such as money, houses, cars, and stocks and shares.

EARNED INCOME – income derived from working.

UNEARNED INCOME – income derived from non-human wealth, such as interest, rent, profit and dividends.

Production

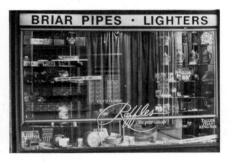

Types of Production

Yoghurts, tights, boxing gloves, jumbo jets, education and nuclear bombs are just a few of the goods and services produced in the world economy today. Because there is such a wide variety of goods produced, economists tend to split up or *classify* production in various ways. Here are some of them:

- primary, secondary and tertiary production – considered in Unit 49;
- public-sector production and private-sector production – considered in Unit 54;
- production for consumption and production for investment is a distinction made in Unit 64;
- CAPITAL-INTENSIVE PRODUCTION and LABOUR-INTENSIVE PRODUCTION. In some production industries, a great deal of capital (machines, building, etc.) is needed in relation to the number of workers employed. The chemical industry or the motor-vehicle production industry are examples. In other industries, very little capital is needed compared to the number of workers involved. Many industries, such as the tourist industry or the retailing industry, are labour-intensive.

The Chain of Production

Production in a modern economy is a complicated business. Figure 18.1 shows a simple production process. Existing products are combined with machinery, raw materials and labour. A product is then made. For instance, a car manufacturer would need workers, land and other raw materials and machinery to produce a finished car. The manufacturer would also use products purchased from other firms – components such as lights or brakes, or semi-manufactured products such as steel. A CHAIN OF PRODUCTION can be drawn which shows some or all of the links between the factors of production and the consumer. A simple chain is shown in Figure 18.2.

STUDY POINTS

1 Make a list of all the industries involved in the making and selling of cigarettes.

2 From your list construct a CHAIN OF PRODUCTION. This is a flow chart. At the top put those industries which come first in the production process. At the bottom, put those which are last (in this case, they will be the shops that sell cigarettes). An example of a chain of production for cars is given in Figure 18.2 which accompanies the text for this unit.

3 Why are cigarettes produced in the economy?

4 What would be the effect on other industries if the number of cigarettes smoked per year in Britain declined?

5 Is it desirable that there should be a decline in cigarette smoking in Britain? To answer this, explain;
   (a) the social costs (e.g. poor health) and
   (b) the social benefits (e.g. employment in the cigarette industry) of cigarette smoking.

The Purpose of Production

What is the purpose of production in society? The ultimate aim of all production should be to create goods and services to satisfy consumer wants. These wants may vary enormously from bread to health care to a cleaner environment. In an economy like that of the UK, households indicate their consumer preferences either through *markets*, by spending money on products for sale, or through the *ballot box* by voting in governments which will spend money on behalf of households. Producers of goods and services should therefore be the servants of consumers. When CONSUMER SOVEREIGNTY exists, consumers tell producers what to produce.

But it is not always the case that production takes place with this in mind.

- Governments and workers may try to produce goods and services which consumers do not demand. The main reasons for this are either to keep wages at too high a level or to keep workers in jobs (both of

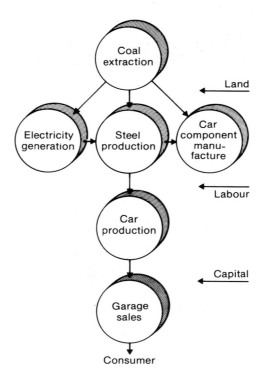

Figure 18.2 A chain of production for cars

these can be seen clearly at work in the Common Agricultural Policy of the EEC discussed in Unit 81.) When a factory is closed down, workers often argue against the closure on the grounds that a demand for their product still exists.

- Governments and firms may exploit the market for their own purposes. Firms can sell consumers products which consumers do not really want to buy. Firms can do this, for instance, through advertising, where they try to CREATE a demand for a product. In the EEC agriculture industry, farmers have successfully persuaded governments, and

ultimately taxpayers, to pay them to grow far more food than consumers want to buy. 'Mountains' of food are destroyed or fed to animals or sold at rock-bottom prices overseas.

Production just to keep people in jobs is unlikely to be an *efficient* use of scarce resources. Why produce too much butter or too much coal, when the factors of production employed in those industries could be used to produce goods and services that consumers do want?

CHECKPOINTS

1 **Construct a chain of production for (a) a bar of chocolate; (b) a school tie; (c) a bus ride; (d) a record and (e) any good or service of your choice.**

2 **What is the purpose of producing goods and services?**

3 **A farmer produces milk, which is turned into butter. The butter is then bought by the Common Market and eventually sold at a fraction of its cost to the USSR.**
   (a) Who benefits from this?
   (b) Who loses out?
   (c) Is this an efficient use of resources in the economy?

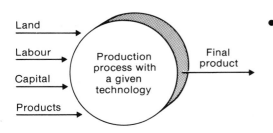

Figure 18.1 The production process

COURSEWORK SUGGESTION

Take a firm or government organisation that is closing down a production unit in your area. Describe what is being closed, how many workers will be made redundant and what products will cease to be produced. Analyse the effects of this on the local economy in terms of employment, incomes, and the environment, and on the national economy in terms of output, lost tax revenues, and greater government spending (for example, on unemployment benefits). Analyse also why the closure is taking place. Try to decide whether the closure is good or bad overall. Consider, in particular, whether or not the goods and services previously being produced were demanded by consumers.

KEY TERMS

CAPITAL-INTENSIVE – an industry or production process where a relatively high amount of capital is used in relation to labour.

LABOUR-INTENSIVE – an industry or production process where a relatively high amount of labour is used relative to capital in production.

CHAIN OF PRODUCTION – shows the various production stages through which a good or service passes before being sold to a consumer.

CONSUMER SOVEREIGNTY – a situation where consumers tell producers what to produce, rather than producers dictating to consumers what they can and cannot buy.

Data Response Questions
Units 14–18

Unit 14 Elasticity (1)

Variation of expenditure with household income

Average weekly household income (£)	Average weekly household expenditure on fuel, light and power (£)
45	5.40
90	8.10
135	9.72

(Adapted from *Department of Employment Family Expenditure Survey*, 1983)

1 How much did the average household earning £45 a week spend on fuel, light and power? *(1 mark)*

2 By how much (a) in money and (b) in percentage terms did expenditure on fuel, light and power increase when incomes increased from £45 to £90? *(2 marks)*

3 Calculate the income elasticity of demand for fuel, light and power for an increase in income:
   (a) from £45 to £90;
   (b) from £90 to £135. *(4 marks)*

4 Explain why the income elasticity of income changes as income increases. *(3 marks)*

Unit 15 Elasticity (2)

Brewery defies 'vicious circle' of price rises

A Shropshire brewery is making a stand against the beer barons who, it claims, push up the price of a pint every year to cover falling sales.

The brewery has written to all of its customers explaining why its prices have not gone up and asking for their support in trying to keep them pegged.

"This time I feel there is little justification for any price increase other than pumping up profits as a hedge against falling beer sales," said Mr Wood of Wood's Brewery.

"We hope to persuade our retailers to point out to their customers what good value for strength and quality our beers are while keeping the Wood Brewery beers at a steady price."

Source: *Express and Star*, 5 October 1985

1 What does Mr. Wood say has been happening to beer sales in recent years? *(1 mark)*

2 Why might a brewery increase its profits by pushing up prices? *(3 marks)*

3 (a) Explain what is meant by 'price elasticity of demand'.
   (b) If the price elasticity of demand for beer is less than one, explain why an increase in the price of beer will benefit a brewery's revenue. *(6 marks)*

Unit 16 Saving

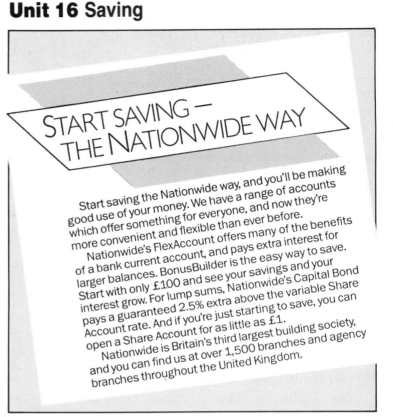

START SAVING – THE NATIONWIDE WAY

Start saving the Nationwide way, and you'll be making good use of your money. We have a range of accounts which offer something for everyone, and now they're more convenient and flexible than ever before. Nationwide's FlexAccount offers many of the benefits of a bank current account, and pays extra interest for larger balances. BonusBuilder is the easy way to save. Start with only £100 and see your savings and your interest grow. For lump sums, Nationwide's Capital Bond pays a guaranteed 2.5% extra above the variable Share Account rate. And if you're just starting to save, you can open a Share Account for as little as £1.
Nationwide is Britain's third largest building society, and you can find us at over 1,500 branches and agency branches throughout the United Kingdom.

Source: Nationwide Building Society.

1 Give four reasons why an individual might be attracted to save with the Nationwide Building Society. *(2 marks)*

2 Why does a building society like the Nationwide offer a variety of savings schemes to its customers? *(4 marks)*

3 How can a building society attract more customers to save with it? *(4 marks)*

Essay Questions
Units 14–18

1 British Rail decide to increase all their fares by 20%, whilst the price of petrol and bus fares stay the same.
   (a) What effect do you think this will have on the numbers of travellers at peak times during the day when most travellers are people who are going to and from work? *(5 marks)*
   (b) What effect do you think this will have on off peak travel when many passengers are shoppers or families going out for the day. *(5 marks)*
   (c) To what extent will this increase in fares increase the total revenue from sales of tickets for British Rail? *(10 marks)*

Unit 17 Income, Wealth and Inequality

HELP!

PRINCE Charles pleaded yesterday for the Government to step in and help Britain's breadline families.

He told 4,000 businessmen of the "inhuman" conditions, squalor and despair he had seen in inner city slums.

He also told of communities throughout Britain "shattered" by the loss of the industries on which they had depended.

"It is only when you visit these areas, as I do from time to time, that you begin to wonder how it is possible that people are able to live in such inhuman conditions," he said.

The problem was greatest in single-industry areas made redundant by changes in demand or technology.

"The hopelessness felt in such communities is compounded by the decay all around, the vandalism and the inability to control their lives in any way beyond the basic requirement of day to day survival in a hostile environment" he said.

Praise

Prince Charles praised community building schemes he had visited in Liverpool and Macclesfield but warned that the end of housing improvement grants could be disastrous for such schemes.

Source: Daily Mirror, 27 February 1985

1 What is a 'breadline family'? *(2 marks)*

2 What are the effects of poverty on the poor according to Prince Charles? *(2 marks)*

3 Why was 'the problem greatest in single-industry areas'? *(2 marks)*

4 (a) Suggest four ways in which the Government could help 'Britain's breadline families'.

(b) What would be the opportunity cost of these measures? *(9 marks)*

2 Linda Philpott is managing director of a company which she owns. She has savings of £200,000 and is the owner of a block of flats in Mayfair.

(a) Suggest *four* different types of income which she is likely to receive. *(8 marks)*

(b) Distinguish between 'earned income' and 'unearned income'. *(6 marks)*

(c) Which of the different types of income you mentioned in (a) was unearned income? *(2 marks)*

(d) Describe *two* savings schemes which she could have used for her £200,000. *(4 marks)*

Unit 18 Production

Tomorrow's big spenders

Feona McEwan on advertising aimed at children

Children have become a major market and one which the advertising industry has also learned to take seriously. In the UK there are advertisements for confectionery, soft drinks and even bank accounts aimed directly at children. Average pocket money for a child in the UK is £3.11 a week, 80 per cent of it spent on confectionery, the rest on toys. Adults are said to spend £70 on average per child a year; the total UK toy market is worth £800m.

Television, not surprisingly, takes the lion's share of UK spending on toy advertising, which last year amounted to about £23m (at rate card), according to Media Expenditure Analysis Limited. This shows a drop of some £6m over 1983 figures, largely thought to be due to the collapse of the video games market. This year in the UK Rainbow Toys, one of the brightest companies on the UK market, and Palitoy will spend £6.4m and £10m respectively, on advertising and promotion, and Mattel expects to spend £6m on TV advertising alone.

Advertisers can pay anything up to £50,000 for a 30-second network slot in peak time children's programming, which tends to be Saturday mornings, and evenings between 5 pm and 7 pm.

Yet for all its importance, television is by no means the sole influence on children's buying habits "though it receives disproportionate attention," according to Glen Smith. "What the child on the other side of the fence has is far more influential. There's also lots of competition for a child's attention in schools which is more real."

Source: Financial Times, 7 February 1985

1 How much was spent on advertising in the UK according to the article? *(2 marks)*

2 Why is children's advertising mainly placed by toy and confectionery companies? *(2 marks)*

3 What influences how a child consumer spends his or her money? *(3 marks)*

4 To what extent can toy and confectionery companies persuade children to buy goods they don't really want to buy? *(3 marks)*

The Division of Labour

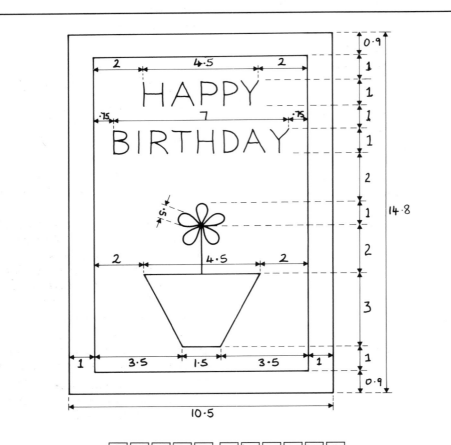

STUDY POINTS

- You are going to produce 8 birthday cards.
- Form a team of four workers.
- You will need 4 pencils, 4 rulers, 1 rubber, 8 sheets of A4 paper.
- Spend *five* minutes deciding how you as a team are going to produce the cards.
- All cards must be identical in scale to the card shown above. The figures shown represent measurements in centimetres.
- Do not show any measuring lines. All that should be visible on the card is (a) a border (b) 'Happy Birthday' and (c) a flowerpot with a 5 leaved flower.
- To construct the card, fold the sheet of A4 paper in two from top to bottom. Then fold again from side to side to produce a free standing card. The picture should be drawn on the front of the card.
- On the inside of the card on the right hand sheet, the words 'For my love' in capitals 1 cm high should be written. The message should be centred 5 cm from the top of the page. The team may decide whether or not to

use one or two lines. All cards, however, must be identical.

- The team has *fifteen* minutes to make up to eight cards.
- The aim of the exercise is to produce birthday cards as *efficiently* as possible.

Follow Up

- Describe how your team organised its production.
- In what ways was your organisation (a) efficient, (b) inefficient at producing cards? For instance, did the team produce 8 cards in the time given? Were the cards of good quality? Would it have been possible to produce more cards in less time if the organisation had been different?
- Imagine you worked for a small company which produced hand made cards like this. To what extent would this type of work be satisfying?
- What limited the extent to which work could be divided up between members of the team?

Specialisation and the division of labour have already been discussed in relation to householders in Unit 7. In this unit, we will consider its application in industry and commerce.

Adam Smith, who is often considered to have been the founder of modern-day economics, wrote in his most famous book, *An Inquiry into the Wealth of Nations* (1776), that the division of labour was an important source of efficiency in the economy. To explain the workings of the division of labour, he described a factory making pins:

'One man draws out the wire, another straightens it, a third cuts it, a fourth points it, a fifth grinds it at the top for receiving the head; to make the head requires two or three distinct operations to put it on is a peculiar business; to whiten the pins is another; it is even a trade by itself to put them into paper; and the important business of making a pin is, in this manner, divided into about eighteen distinct operations.'

If making a pin can be split into eighteen separate processes, each being done by a different worker, then it is obvious that making something as complicated as a car would involve thousands of different processes.

Efficiency

There are several reasons why the division of labour is such an efficient way of producing goods and services. Products can be produced at low cost. This is because specialist workers can be employed who are obviously far quicker and more skilful at their jobs than a worker who tries to do all the tasks by him or herself. A specialist worker is also less likely to lose time moving between jobs. A pin worker who makes and packs pins is going to have to move between a pin-making machine and a packing table. This movement wastes time compared to a situation where workers specialise in each task. Less time and effort are also needed to train workers. Specialist tools can be developed to help with the production of part of the finished product. These tools will also be in far greater use than in a situation where each worker had to have his or her own set of tools, which for most of the time would lie idle.

The division of labour is also efficient because it is only by sharing and co-operating that complex modern products can be created and produced. No individual, for instance, could alone have produced a pocket calculator, or a television set or a modern office block.

But there are also disadvantages in the division of labour.

- Workers may become bored and *alienated* by doing the same job day after day. This is not only unpleasant for the worker, but could lead to poorer work effort and standards.

- Although the division of labour allows more goods to be produced at a cheaper price, these goods tend to be similar mass-produced products. Traditional craft goods, which are individual and pleasing, may disappear.

- Specialisation means that the factors of production may be unemployed, if demand for them declines. If, for instance, a worker has been trained as a steel worker, he may find it difficult to find another job because he lacks the necessary skills

Limitations of the Division of Labour

Although specialisation has many advantages, there is a limit to just how far the division of labour can be taken.

- There are physical limitations as to how far work can be broken up. Adam Smith identified eighteen separate processes in pin-making. It would not have been possible to break it down into more processes.

- The division of labour is limited by exchange. If a farmer wants to specialise in producing wheat, but nobody wants to buy it, then it would not make sense for him to grow wheat. He would do better either growing food he wants to eat himself, or food that can be sold on the open market.

- The division of labour is limited by the extent of the market. It is not possible, for instance, to mass produce Porsche cars, because their high price means that few consumers want to buy them. So Porsche cannot afford to break down its production into as many processes as, say, British Leyland can with its Metro.

- It is not possible for large-scale specialisation to take place, if poor transport means that goods cannot be moved easily from factory to market.

- Consumers may not want to buy mass-produced goods, but may

prefer the individuality that comes from craft products.

- Some products, like hairdressing or tourism, cannot be mass produced in the same way that a car can be mass produced.

CHECKPOINTS

1 Describe how there is a division of labour in (a) a school; (b) a hamburger restaurant; (c) a newsagents.

2 Why do firms organise production on the principle of the division of labour?

3 Explain why a worker (a) on a till in a supermarket and (b) on an assembly line in a factory may become bored with his or her job. What effect may this have on the quality of his or her work?

4 Explain why it is easier for specialisation to occur in the production of television sets than in the production of a restaurant meal.

5 What is meant when it is said that 'the division of labour is limited by the extent of the market'?

COURSEWORK SUGGESTION

Find out the names of all the people who have a job in your school. Give a job description for each worker. Explain how this illustrates the principle of the division of labour at work. Analyse why work is divided up in this way. Consider whether more could be achieved by the school if its scarce resources were allocated in a different way, so that the division of labour were more effective.

The division of labour – tuna fish being cleaned and canned

Economic Resources

A hairdresser

A blast furnace in a steelworks

Workers in a factory

A farm and farming land

STUDY POINTS

1 Make a list of the factors of production shown in each of the photographs.

2 What factors of production are used to provide you with education?

3 Explain why these factors of production are scarce.

4 To what extent can factors of production be substituted for each other in each of the situations shown in the photographs, e.g. capital for labour in farming?

Types of Resources

Economic resources are scarce. What are these resources? Economists distinguish between three types of resources called the FACTORS OF PRODUCTION. These three factors of production are land, labour and capital.

Land

In 1976, the UK produced the first oil from the North Sea. About 12.2 million tonnes were extracted. By 1984, production had increased to 125.9 million tonnes. This crude oil is an example of what economists call LAND. 'Land' in the economic sense is the natural resources of this planet. It is not only land itself, but also what lies under the land (like coal and gold), what grows naturally on top of the land (like forests and wild animals), what is over the land (like the air), and what is around the land in the seas and oceans and under the seas and oceans (like fish and oil). Only one major resource is for the most part free – the air we breathe. The rest are scarce, because there are not enough natural resources in the world to satisfy the demands of consumers, producers, etc.

Labour

LABOUR is the human input into the production process. There are approximately 4 billion people on this planet. Many of these are too young, too old or too ill to work. In the UK, of about 56 million inhabitants only approximately 35 million are of working age (16–64 years for men and 16–59 for women), and of those only about 24 million have paid jobs. Two important points need to be remembered about labour as a resource:

- Just because a person has not got a paid job, it does not mean that he or she does not produce goods and services. A housewife, a keen gardener and a DIY enthusiast all produce goods and services, but they do not get paid for them.

- Not all labour is of the same quality. Some workers are more productive than others because of the education, training and experience they have received. This is called HUMAN CAPITAL. The greater the human capital of a worker, the more productive he or she will be.

Capital

CAPITAL is a man-made resource. It is the machines, roads, factories, schools and office blocks which human beings have produced in order to produce other goods and services. A modern industrialised economy possesses a large amount of capital, and it is continually increasing. Increases to the *capital stock* of a nation are called *investment*. This capital is sometimes called *physical capital* or *non-human capital* in order to distinguish it from human capital.

Entrepreneurship

Sometimes a fourth factor of production is distinguished. An ENTREPRENEUR is an individual:

- who risks his or her own resources (money in most cases) in a business venture; and

- who organises the business – that is, organises the other three factors of production.

An entrepreneur is a special type of worker. Many economists agree that entrepreneurs should be classed as part of the factor 'labour'.

Labour and capital will be considered in more detail in Units 21 and 22, respectively.

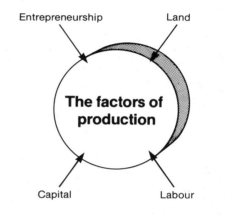

The factors of production

C H E C K P O I N T S

1 What is a 'factor of production'?

2 Which of the factors of production are the following; (a) a factory; (b) a teacher; (c) a road sweeper; (d) a forest; (e) a shoal of fish; (f) a gold mine; (g) a deposit of gold; (h) a business person who owns and runs his/her own business; (i) an MP?

3 Why does the factor 'labour' not include the whole population of the UK?

4 What is the difference between human capital and non-human capital?

5 What is the role of the entrepreneur in the economy?

C O U R S E W O R K S U G G E S T I O N

Identify the factors of production used in your education. Explain how these factors are combined to provide your education. To what extent could these factors be combined more efficiently to produce the same result at a lower cost or a better result for the same cost?

K E Y T E R M S

FACTORS OF PRODUCTION – resources of land, labour and capital used to produce goods and services.

LAND – natural resources available for production.

LABOUR – human effort available for production.

CAPITAL – man-made physical goods used to produce other goods and services.

HUMAN CAPITAL – the skills and abilities of workers resulting from investment in education and training.

ENTREPRENEUR – a worker who organises the factors of production and risks his or her capital.

Figure 21.1 Employment trends in the UK, 1970–84

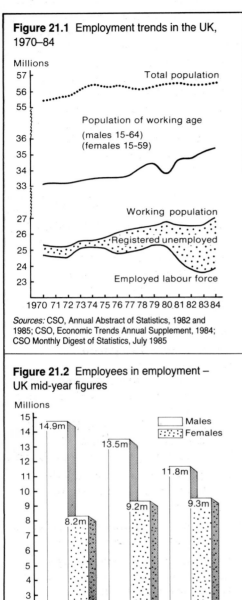

Millions

Sources: CSO, Annual Abstract of Statistics, 1982 and 1985; CSO, Economic Trends Annual Supplement, 1984; CSO Monthly Digest of Statistics, July 1985

Figure 21.2 Employees in employment – UK mid-year figures

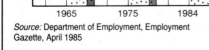

Millions

- Males
- Females

14.9m / 8.2m — 1965
13.5m / 9.2m — 1975
11.8m / 9.3m — 1984

Source: Department of Employment, Employment Gazette, April 1985

Figure 21.3 Percentage of school leavers getting two or more GCE 'A' level passes or three or more SCE 'H' grade passes

1973/4	13.0
1977/8	13.2
1982/3	14.5

Source: CSO, Annual Abstract of Statistics, 1985

From Figure 21.1:

1 State the population of working age in 1970 and 1984.

2 Describe what has happened to employment over the period 1970 to 1984.

From Figure 21.2:

3 Compare male employment with female employment over the period 1965 to 1984.

From Figure 21.3:

4 What has happened to the educational qualifications of the labour force in the UK over the period 1973/4 to 1982/3? How might this have helped make the labour force more productive?

From Figure 21.4:

5 Describe how the structure of employment has changed in the British economy over the period 1951 to 1985.

From Figure 21.5:

6 Construct a bar chart showing the distribution of employment and unemployment in the UK, putting numbers in millions on the vertical axis and regions along the horizontal axis.

From all the data:

7 Why has the quantity of labour available for production increased in the UK since 1970?

8 Explain what you think will happen to the quality of labour as a factor of production in the future.

9 Give four reasons why there has been a change in the pattern of employment in recent years.

10 In what ways have the changes in the labour force in recent years been (a) desirable and (b) undesirable?
Explain your answers carefully.

Figure 21.4 Shares of total civilian employment in the UK, 1951–85

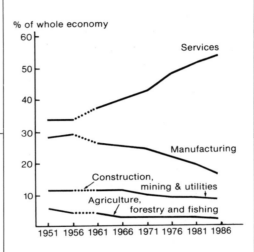

% of whole economy

Services
Manufacturing
Construction, mining & utilities
Agriculture, forestry and fishing

Sources: The Treasury, Economic Progress Report, February 1984; Department of Employment, Employment Gazette, April 1985

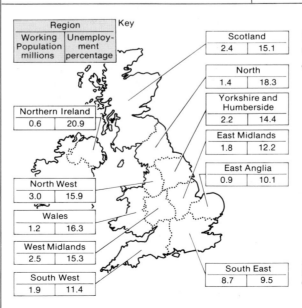

Region	
Working Population millions	Unemployment percentage

Key

Scotland	
2.4	15.1

North	
1.4	18.3

Yorkshire and Humberside	
2.2	14.4

East Midlands	
1.8	12.2

East Anglia	
0.9	10.1

Northern Ireland	
0.6	20.9

North West	
3.0	15.9

Wales	
1.2	16.3

West Midlands	
2.5	15.3

South West	
1.9	11.4

South East	
8.7	9.5

Figure 21.5 Working population and unemployment by region in the UK, June 1984

Sources: CSO, Regional Trends 20, 1985; Department of Employment, Employment Gazette, November 1985

The Quantity of Labour Available for Production

Labour is one of the factors of production. In this unit, we will consider how much of this scarce factor is available for production in the UK and its quality.

Not everybody in the UK is available for work. Figure 21.1 shows that the current population of the UK is over 56 million people. But many of these are either children aged 0–15 or persons of retirement age – 60 years and over for women, and 65 and over for men. The rest – known as the POPULATION OF WORKING AGE – is theoretically available for work.

In practice, many of these do not take on paid work. Young people stay on at school, college or university after the age of 16. Many women leave work to bring up children, as do some men. A smaller number of people are infirm or permanently handicapped, have sufficient income not to work or simply choose not to seek paid employment.

Currently this removes about 8.4 million people from the population of working age. The remaining 27 million people form the WORKING POPULATION – the number of people either in work or seeking work. As can be seen from Figure 21.1, the working population has been rising since 1970. This is because:

- more and more women want to work, as can be seen in Figure 21.2.
- more and more school leavers have entered the job market. This is because between 1951 and 1965 the UK experienced a 'baby boom'. Every year, more babies were born. The number of school leavers is now set to decline, however, because after 1965 the birth rate

declined. (This is the reason why schools today are being closed or merged.)

Not all the working population works. Over three million were unemployed in 1985. So the EMPLOYED LABOUR FORCE stood at just under 24 million people. The unemployed represent a huge waste of scarce resources. If each of the one in nine workers at present unemployed were to produce just £5000 a year in goods and services (and the average worker was paid nearly twice that much in 1985), extra production of £15 000 million could be obtained.

The Quality of the Labour Force

The numbers available for work are just one measure of the factor of production called labour. Of equal, if not greater importance is the quality of those workers. The workforce of a poor country like Bangladesh is larger than that of the UK, but it is less productive because the average UK worker has had more education, more training and more experience than the Bangladeshi worker. It is relatively easy to measure the size of the workforce, but it is not possible to give a precise measure of the quality (or *human capital* – a concept explained in Unit 20) of a labour force. One very simple measure of the improvement in the UK's labour force over time is given in Figure 21.3, which shows that the number of people leaving school with 2 or more 'A' levels has increased over time.

Choice

Where are the 24 million or so workers employed in the UK? Figure 21.4 shows what industries these workers are in. Notice the rise in service-sector employment and the fall in

manufacturing-sector employment over the last 30 years. The reasons for this trend are explored in more detail in Unit 49. Today, more than half of all workers are in service-sector industry.

Figure 21.5 shows the geographical distribution of the workforce. Notice that the workforce is concentrated particularly in the south of England. Notice also that unemployment is particularly high in all areas other than the south of England. If scarce resources are not to be wasted in the future, industry and jobs will have to be created in those areas, or migration encouraged.

CHECKPOINTS

1. State whether each of the following are part of (i) the population of working age; (ii) the working population and or (iii) the employed labour force:
   (a) each person who lives in your household;
   (b) a teacher;
   (c) a housewife aged 45;
   (d) a pensioner;
   (e) an unemployed steel worker;
   (f) a 15-year-old girl with a paper round;
   (g) an unemployed handicapped worker looking for a job.
   (Note: each *may* be part of all three).

2. Suggest two ways in which the working population could be increased.

3. Why does unemployment represent a waste of scarce resources?

4. Explain how your schooling will help to improve the quality of the labour force in the future.

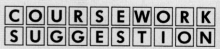

COURSEWORK SUGGESTION

Using *Regional Trends* (published by HMSO) and other sources, describe the changes in the labour force in your local area or region in recent years. Analyse why these changes have taken place, and what effect they have had on the prosperity of the region. Discuss further patterns of employment, and whether or not these are likely to bring greater prosperity to the region.

KEY TERMS

POPULATION OF WORKING AGE – all those people between the school-leaving age and the retirement age who are theoretically available for work.

WORKING POPULATION – all those people in paid employment and those who are unemployed.

EMPLOYED LABOUR FORCE – all people who are in paid employment.

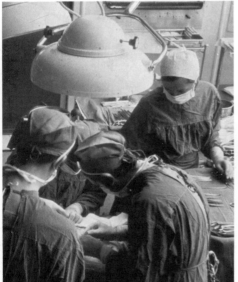
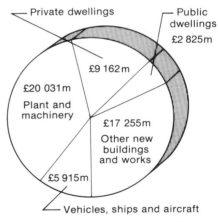

Private dwellings — Public dwellings £2 825m

£9 162m

£20 031m
Plant and machinery

£17 255m
Other new buildings and works

£5 915m

Vehicles, ships and aircraft

Figure 22.1 Gross domestic fixed capital formation, 1984 (£ millions)
Source: CSO, *Monthly Digest of Statistics*, April 1985

STUDY POINTS

The photographs show different types of *capital*. Capital is the machinery, factories, tools, offices, roads, etc, which are used to produce other goods and services. Figure 22.1 gives statistics relating to *investment* (called 'Gross Domestic Fixed Capital Formation') in the UK economy. Investment is the increase in capital over a period of time – in this case a year.

1 Make a list of all the different examples of capital that you can see in the photographs.

2 What goods and services can be produced by each of the pieces of capital shown in the photographs?

3 From the pie chart, what was the largest type of investment in the UK in 1984?

4 How much was invested in new housing in 1984?

5 What do you think is meant by 'other new buildings'?

6 Why do you think it is important for investment to increase each year?

7 Investment in public sector dwellings (mainly council houses) fell in the early 1980s. What effect do you think this had on (a) existing council house dwellers and (b) on people who wanted to move in to a council house?

8 What do you think is the opportunity cost of investment in an economy?

'Industrial investment in Britain should rise by nearly 8% in real terms next year, according to an official survey published yesterday.' (Source: *Financial Times*, 14 December 1984)

Industry needs to update and increase its CAPITAL STOCK. Capital is the machinery, factories, tools, offices, etc. that are used to produce other goods and services. A capital good such as a machine is different from a *consumption good*, because a consumption good is one which, like a chocolate bar, a skirt or an LP record, is bought for the satisfaction or enjoyment that it brings.

INVESTMENT is the addition to the stock of capital. So the extract above stated that the addition to capital would be 8% greater in 1985 than it was in 1984.

Types of Capital

There are different types of capital. It is very difficult, if not impossible, to measure the capital stock of an economy. It is obviously not possible to add up so many factories, so many machines, so many hospitals, etc. and produce a figure for square metres of capital or tonnes of capital. It is also difficult, if not impossible, to add up the monetary value of the capital stock. For instance, what value would you put on a school building: the cost of replacing it, or the price it would fetch if it was let or sold on the open market? It is, however, possible to calculate how much is spent on investment each year. Figures for UK investment are shown in Figure 22.1. This figure shows that in 1984:

- Approximately 22% of investment was devoted to dwellings (i.e. new housing). A house is a form of capital, because it is used to produce living accommodation over a long period of time.

- Approximately 31% went in other new buildings and works. This category includes investment in factory buildings, office blocks, new school buildings, hospitals, roads and airports.

- Approximately 11% was invested in vehicles, such as lorries and trucks, ships and aircraft, which were all used to produce other goods and services.

- The single largest category of investment (36% of the total) was plant and machinery – everything from a chemical works to a computer to a typewriter. 'Plant' is the term used to describe large fixed machinery, machinery so large that it is the size of a factory unit.

Some of this addition to the capital stock is SOCIAL CAPITAL. This is capital mainly owned by the state and used to produce goods and services that are not, on the whole, sold for money. Examples of social capital are roads, schools, hospitals, sewage works and libraries.

Part of the capital stock is INFRASTRUCTURE. This is the man-made environment – the canals, the railways, etc. (but not, for instance, machinery, vehicles, ships or aircraft).

The Importance of Capital

Capital is essential if a country is to produce the vast quantity of sophisticated goods and services available for consumption today. If an economy is to produce more, it needs to add to that capital – that is, it must invest. The poor investment record of the UK is something that will be returned to in Unit 66.

returned to in Unit 66.

CHECKPOINTS

1 Explain the difference between investment and the capital stock of an economy.

2 Distinguish between capital goods and consumption goods.

3 Consider this list of goods. The dates indicate when they were produced and sold:
 factory building (1985)
 school building (1956)
 dumper truck (1985)
 packet of corn flakes (1985)
 motorway (1985)
 jewellery (1985)
 office desk (1985)
 Which of these:
 (a) were part of the capital stock of the economy at 31 December 1985?
 (b) formed part of investment in 1986?
 (c) are consumption goods?
 (d) represent part of the infrastructure of the economy?
 (e) are examples of social capital?

COURSEWORK SUGGESTION

Describe the social capital in your local area. You will almost certainly find it helpful to draw a map to do this. What investment is currently taking place? What are the costs and benefits of (a) improving the existing stock of social capital (e.g. undertaking repairs) and (b) adding to the stock of social capital in an area? (For example, what would be the costs and benefits of building a new sports complex or school?)

KEY TERMS

CAPITAL STOCK – the total amount of capital.

INVESTMENT – the addition to the capital stock.

SOCIAL CAPITAL – mainly state-owned capital used to produce goods that are not usually sold via the market mechanism.

INFRASTRUCTURE – the man-made environment.

Data Response Questions
Units 19–22

Unit 19 The Division of Labour

Household division of labour in Great Britain: by marital status (Percentages)

	Married people[1]		
	Actual allocation of tasks		
	Mainly man	Mainly woman	Shared equally
Household tasks:			
Washing and ironing	1	89	10
Preparation of evening meal	5	77	17
Household cleaning	3	72	24
Household shopping	5	51	44
Evening dishes	17	40	40
Organisation of household money and bills	29	39	32
Repairs of household equipment	82	6	10

[1] 1,209 married respondents.
Source: CSO *Social Trends*

1 What is meant by the 'division of labour'? *(2 marks)*

2 (a) Describe how, according to the data the division of labour is organised in a typical household.
  (b) How does this compare with your own household? *(2 marks)*

3 Suggest economic reasons why this division of labour exists in households. *(4 marks)*

4 Would it be more efficient if members of households were to share all tasks equally? *(3 marks)*

Unit 20 Economic Resources

False Economy

THE Employment Minister, Tom King, must soon decide, whether to close down 29 of Britain's Skill-centres which teach a trade to thousands of youngsters and adults.

It is a ludicrous suggestion, made by a committee of the Manpower Services Commission by a majority of only one — and that one has since changed his mind.

The first Skillcentre was opened in 1919. There are now 87 of them. The training they give ranges from electronics to carpentry and from computers to plumbing.

Obsessed

At the end of it, a trainee can enter employment as a professional.

Several hundred experienced instructors will be sacked if the closures go ahead and their skills will be left to decay.

The proposal could only be entertained by a Government so obsessed with saving money as the present one.

The Skillcentre network is expected to lose about £10 million this year. It cannot meet its instruction from the MSC to break even by 1986-87. That is why 29 of them are threatened with being shut down.

Silly

But in the short run and the long run — through the unemployment of the instructors and the absence of skills for the young — closure will cost more than it will save.

The Government repeatedly boasts about the training it is giving to those seeking work.

If he is really serious about helping the unemployed, Mr King will throw out this silly idea.

Source: Daily Mirror, 13 February 1985

1 What suggestion has been put forward by the Manpower Services Commission according to the article? *(1 mark)*

2 Describe the factors of production used in training workers at Skillcentres. *(3 marks)*

3 How do Skillcentres help increase the value of the factors of production available to producers? *(4 marks)*

4 What would be (a) the costs and (b) the benefits to society of the Manpower Services Commission proposal? *(4 marks)*

5 Should Mr King approve the proposal? Explain your answer carefully. *(3 marks)*

Unit 21 Labour

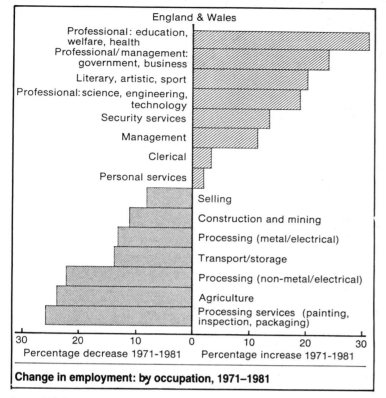

Change in employment: by occupation, 1971–1981

Source: CSO, *Social Trends*, 1985

1 Name *two* occupations which have increased in employment between 1971 and 1981. *(1 mark)*

2 What has been the percentage change in employment in agriculture between 1971 and 1981? *(1 mark)*

3 Which of the three sectors of industry has seen an increase in employment over the period? *(1 mark)*

4 What do the statistics suggest has happened to the demand for services in comparison with manufactured goods over the period? *(3 marks)*

5 How might the changes shown have led to unemployment being created? *(4 marks)*

Unit 22 Capital

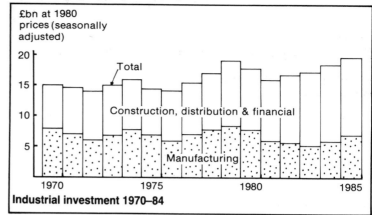

Industrial investment 1970–84

Source: Financial Times, 14 December, 1984

1 What was the value of total industrial investment in 1977? *(1 mark)*

2 Approximately what percentage of total industrial investment was undertaken by manufacturing in (a) 1975 and (b) 1985? *(2 marks)*

3 (a) What has happened to manufacturing investment compared to construction, distribution and financial investment between 1970 and 1985? *(4 marks)*

  (b) What will have been the likely effect of this on the capital employed in the two sectors over the period? *(4 marks)*

  (c) How will this have affected the ability of companies to produce goods and services? *(4 marks)*

Essay Questions
Units 19–22

1 (a) Describe the main stages in the production of a can of baked beans, starting with the raw materials used and finishing at the point of sale to the consumer. *(6 marks)*

  (b) Draw a chain of production diagram to illustrate your answer to (a). *(4 marks)*

  (c) Give *two* examples of the division of labour in the production of baked beans. *(4 marks)*

  (d) What limits the extent to which the division of labour can be applied in this production process? *(4 marks)*

2 (a) Describe the factors of production that would be needed to produce a take-away fish and chip supper. *(8 marks)*

  (b) What is 'social capital'? Give two examples. *(6 marks)*

  (c) Why would it be difficult for consumers to buy fish and chips in Birmingham if there were no social capital in the UK? *(6 marks)*

The Demand for Labour

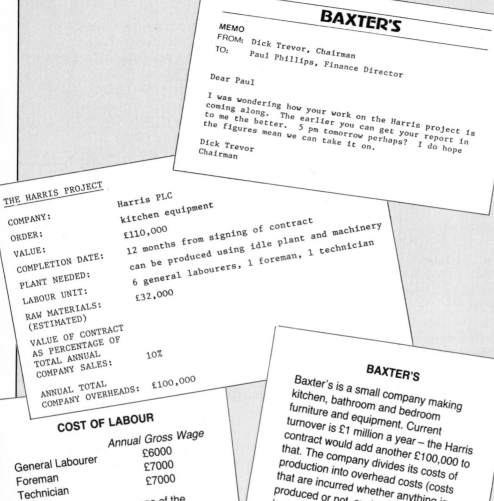

BAXTER'S

MEMO
FROM: Dick Trevor, Chairman
TO: Paul Phillips, Finance Director

Dear Paul

I was wondering how your work on the Harris project is coming along. The earlier you can get your report in to me the better. 5 pm tomorrow perhaps? I do hope the figures mean we can take it on.

Dick Trevor
Chairman

THE HARRIS PROJECT

COMPANY:	Harris PLC
ORDER:	kitchen equipment
VALUE:	£110,000
COMPLETION DATE:	12 months from signing of contract
PLANT NEEDED:	can be produced using idle plant and machinery
LABOUR UNIT:	6 general labourers, 1 foreman, 1 technician
RAW MATERIALS: (ESTIMATED)	£32,000
VALUE OF CONTRACT AS PERCENTAGE OF TOTAL ANNUAL COMPANY SALES:	10%
ANNUAL TOTAL COMPANY OVERHEADS:	£100,000

COST OF LABOUR

	Annual Gross Wage
General Labourer	£6000
Foreman	£7000
Technician	£7000

In addition to the gross wage of the worker, the company has to pay 10% of gross wages to the Government in Employers' National Insurance Contributions, and 5% of gross wages to the company pension scheme.

BAXTER'S

Baxter's is a small company making kitchen, bathroom and bedroom furniture and equipment. Current turnover is £1 million a year – the Harris contract would add another £100,000 to that. The company divides its costs of production into overhead costs (costs that are incurred whether anything is produced or not, such as interest on loans, rates, office staff) and variable costs (costs which are incurred due to the fact that a particular contract is undertaken).

STUDY POINTS

You are Paul Phillips, Finance Director of Baxter's.

1. Prepare a report arguing whether or not the company ought to take on the Harris contract. In your report you will need to calculate the costs to the company of the contract and compare it to the revenues obtained.

2. The company workforce is awarded a 10% wage rise. Would your decision still be the same and why?

3. If wages went up by 20%, what would you recommend the company to do and why?

4. What determines the number of workers employed by Baxters?

'General Motors is to take on another 217 employees at its Fisher Body plants in Belfast in the next two months. The US group employs 983 people at the factories in east and west Belfast which make seat belts and seat belt mechanisms. The new workers will produce a new lightweight seat belt for export to the USA.' (*Source: Financial Times*, 17 January 1985)

General Motors needs more workers for its Belfast factories – or, as economists would say, General Motors has *demanded* more labour. Workers are only demanded by employers because they want to use that labour to produce goods and services. Labour is therefore a **DERIVED DEMAND**. In the case of General Motors, labour has been demanded because American motorists have demanded Oldsmobile and Buick cars, which are produced by General Motors.

What causes the demand for labour to change? Several factors can be distinguished.

Wage Rates

One factor is the wage rate. The **WAGE RATE** is the price of labour – how much an employer has to pay a worker to hire him or her for a period of time. If the wage rate falls, it is unlikely that an employer would sack workers. Either the employer will keep the same number as before, or the fall might lead to more workers being taken on. So economists suggest that lower wage rates will lead to employers taking on more workers, whereas higher wage rates will lead to employers taking on fewer workers. This is shown in Figure 23.1 If the wage rate per worker is £200 a week, then the firm will demand or employ 600 workers. If the wage rate went down to £150 a week, then the firm would demand 800 workers. Economists give a number of reasons why the demand curve for labour is downward-sloping:

- One theory, the *marginal revenue productivity theory*, argues that if a firm keeps on employing workers

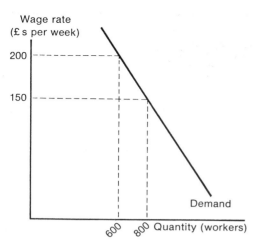

Wage rate (£s per week)

Figure 23.1

with a given quantity of machines, raw materials, etc., then the output per man will eventually start to go down. Each extra worker (or *marginal* worker) will produce less than the last man employed. A firm will only be prepared to pay a worker for the value of what he or she produces. If a worker can add £120 to the value of production, the firm will be prepared to pay that worker up to £120. As the value of the output of each extra worker employed goes down, so will the wage rate the firm is prepared to pay to the last worker it employed. Since workers tend to be paid the same if they are of the same grade, then the more workers a firm employs, the lower will need to be the wages paid to all workers.

- Another theory argues that if a firm is to sell more products, it will need to become more competitive and that means lowering its prices. In order to lower price, the firm will have to reduce costs and that could be done by reducing wage rates. If the firm does sell more products, it will need more workers to produce them. So a fall in wage rates leads to

extra demand for labour. One of the reasons why General Motors is producing seat belts in Northern Ireland for export to America is almost certainly because wage rates in Northern Ireland are lower than in America. So the Belfast plants are more competitive than their US rivals – that is, more labour is demanded in Belfast because of lower wage rates.

- Another argument is that people can be replaced by machines. The higher the wage rate, the more firms will install machines which can replace humans.

Other Factors

The demand for labour is not determined by price alone. The demand for labour is a derived demand. If, say, consumers' incomes went up in the USA, more labour in Belfast would be demanded, because Americans would buy more cars. So the level of total or AGGREGATE DEMAND for goods and services in the economy is an important determinant of the demand for labour. For an individual industry, the level of demand for its products is important too. Wage cuts in a firm are not going to help keep workers employed if demand for the good being produced is falling. Technology, too, is important. Advances in technology can make labour uneconomic at any wage rate. For instance, you cannot make television sets without machinery, even if you pay workers only £10 a week.

As we shall see in Units 59 and 60, what causes firms to demand workers is very important for the debate on the causes of unemployment. Can we solve unemployment by cutting wage rates, or is the solution to expand the demand for goods and services?

1 Explain what is likely to happen to the number of workers employed by a supermarket chain, if:
   (a) the supermarket opened ten new stores;
   (b) customers bought 10% more goods from the chain;
   (c) the wages of the staff increased by 10%;
   (d) the government put VAT on food;
   (e) the chain installed new computerised cash tills.

2 Explain why the demand for farm workers is a derived demand.

3 (a) On graph paper, draw a demand curve for labour using the following data. (The wage rate goes on the *y*-axis, and the quantity is put on the *x*-axis.)

Wage rate (£ per week)	Quantity demanded
200	10
180	12
160	14
140	16

   (b) How many workers will the firm employ, if the wage rate were £150 a week?
   (c) What is likely to happen to the demand curve, if there is a fall in total spending in the economy?

COURSEWORK SUGGESTION

Arrange to interview the personnel officer of a local firm (or whoever is in charge, or would be aware, of labour recruitment policies in the firm). Before the interview, draw up a questionnaire to help you find out the factors that would influence the hiring or sacking of workers in the firm. From your findings, estimate the price elasticity of demand for labour (i.e. assess the extent to which the level of employment in the firm is dependent upon the level of wage rates). Try to assess the effect of a significant increase in government spending on the level of employment in the firm.

KEY TERMS

DERIVED DEMAND – demand that arises because another good or service is demanded.

WAGE RATE – the rate of pay for a fixed amount of work.

AGGREGATE DEMAND – the demand for all goods and services produced in an economy.

The Supply of Labour

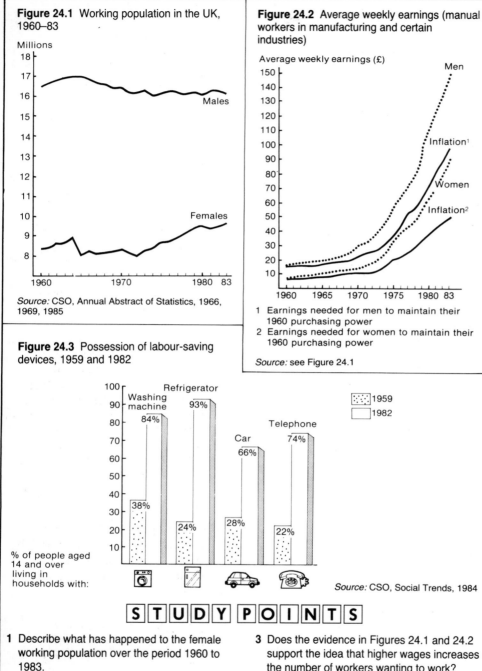

Figure 24.1 Working population in the UK, 1960–83

Millions

Source: CSO, Annual Abstract of Statistics, 1966, 1969, 1985

Figure 24.2 Average weekly earnings (manual workers in manufacturing and certain industries)

Average weekly earnings (£)

Men
Inflation¹
Women
Inflation²

1 Earnings needed for men to maintain their 1960 purchasing power
2 Earnings needed for women to maintain their 1960 purchasing power

Source: see Figure 24.1

Figure 24.3 Possession of labour-saving devices, 1959 and 1982

Refrigerator
Washing machine
84%
93%
Telephone
Car
66%
74%
38%
24%
28%
22%

1959
1982

% of people aged 14 and over living in households with:

Source: CSO, Social Trends, 1984

In 1970, the working population (the number of people who either had a job or who wanted a job, but were officially registered as unemployed) was about 25 million. In 1984, this had risen to 27 million. Why had the number of people who wanted to work risen over the period? Or, as economists would say, why had the SUPPLY OF LABOUR risen? A number of possible reasons can be put forward.

- The total number of people who could work increased over the period. In 1970, there were 33.1 million people of working age (i.e. men aged between 16 and 64 years, and women aged between 16 and 59). By 1984 this had risen to 35 million.

- Wages increased at a faster rate than inflation. The average worker could earn more in 1984 than he or she could in 1970. This is likely to have encouraged more people to look for work.

- Technology in the home changed. Automatic washing machines, dishwashers, freezers, microwave ovens and a host of other appliances meant that women could do their housework in less time. These machines also fell in price relative to earnings, so more people could afford them. Women could go out to work more easily.

- The social climate changed too, with more women looking for jobs, encouraged by the Women's Movement.

These are some of the factors which possibly increased the supply of labour to the whole economy in the 1970s and 1980s.

We can also consider what might affect the supply of labour to an industry like manufacturing industry, or to a particular occupation like teaching. Consider this extract, which had as it headline 'Low pay hits civil service recruitment':

S T U D Y P O I N T S

1 Describe what has happened to the female working population over the period 1960 to 1983.

2 Why have these changes taken place? In your answer, explain how the benefits of going out to work (such as pay, and availability of new consumer goods like automatic washing machines and videos) have changed since 1960. Explain too how the costs of going out to work (such as time spent on housework like washing and cooking, and looking after children) have altered.

3 Does the evidence in Figures 24.1 and 24.2 support the idea that higher wages increases the number of workers wanting to work? Explain your answer carefully.

4 The Equal Pay Act 1975 stated that women had to be paid the same wage as men doing the same job. What effect do you think this might have had on the number of women wanting a job?

5 What do you expect to happen to the number of women wanting to go out to work in the future? Explain your answer carefully.

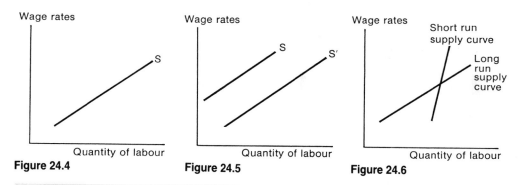

Figure 24.4

Figure 24.5

Figure 24.6

'The number of Civil Service vacancies increased by more than 29% last year – but job applications dropped by 2%. (*Source: Financial Times*, 25 April 1985)

Demand for new workers in the civil service increased, but fewer workers wanted those jobs (i.e. the supply of workers to the civil service went down). The article then went on to suggest why this might have been the case. It stated that civil service workers face 'poor' pay levels, lack of promotion prospects, low job interest, poor location and a decline in the standing of civil servants in the community. Workers are preferring to work in other jobs.

Pay, promotion prospects, job interest, etc. add up to what economists call the 'NET ADVANTAGES' OF AN OCCUPATION. If the net advantages increase, then more workers will want that job (i.e. supply will increase). If the net advantages decline, as seemed to be happening in the civil service, then fewer workers will offer themselves for hire in that particular job (i.e. supply will decrease).

A Diagrammatic Representation

The supply of labour can be shown on a diagram like any normal supply curve. It is likely that if wages increase, more workers will want to work in that job. So the supply curve shown in Figure 24.4 is upward sloping.

Figure 24.5 shows an increase in supply from S to S′. What this means is that at any given level of wage rates, more workers will want to work. This shift in supply is what was seen for the whole UK economy between 1970 and 1984. If Figure 24.5 showed an increase in supply for, say, electricians, then this might have come about because the net advantages of being an electrician have increased, or because there are now more people in the working population, or because the net advantages of other occupations such as plumbers have declined. A fall in supply would push the supply curve back, upwards and to the left on the diagram.

The Elasticity of Supply of Workers

Elasticity of supply (explained in Unit 14) is a measure of the responsiveness of changes in quantity supplied to changes in price – in this case, the wage rate. In the short term, the supply of labour to an industry is relatively inelastic. A rise in wage rates will not result in large numbers of workers wanting to become employed in that industry. This is because few workers are likely to have the necessary skills and because workers may see the rise in wages as temporary. Workers do not move jobs every time a small difference in wages between industries occurs. In the long term, however, if the increase in wages is permanent,

and if other wages have not increased by much, then supply is likely to be more elastic – that is, more workers will want to work in that industry compared to the short-run position. This is shown in Figure 24.6.

CHECKPOINTS

1 What is meant by the 'supply of labour'?

2 How and why will the supply of labour for the whole economy be affected:
   (a) if there are more school leavers this year compared to last year;
   (b) if fewer women want to go out to work;
   (c) if the retirement age for men is reduced to 60;
   (d) if wages increase at a faster rate in the UK than in Germany?

3 How and why will the supply of labour to the teaching profession be affected:
   (a) if the pay of teachers goes down compared to all other jobs;
   (b) if existing teachers are made redundant because of falling numbers of pupils in schools;
   (c) if the amount of money spent on school buildings, textbooks, materials, etc. goes down;
   (d) if the number of days' holiday in other jobs increases?

4 Draw supply diagrams to show the effects of each of the situations described in questions 2 and 3.

5 Explain how and why the elasticity of supply for teachers is likely to change in the short term and in the long term.

COURSEWORK SUGGESTION

Compare four different occupations with differing wages rates. Examine the net advantages of each occupation. Assess the supply of labour to each occupation in the short term and in the long term. Try to evaluate what is likely to happen to the supply of labour in each occupation over the next ten or twenty years.

KEY TERMS

SUPPLY OF LABOUR – the number of people who have a job or who want a job, but are officially registered as unemployed.

NET ADVANTAGES OF AN OCCUPATION – the difference between the private benefit and private cost to a worker of a particular occupation.

The Determination of Wages

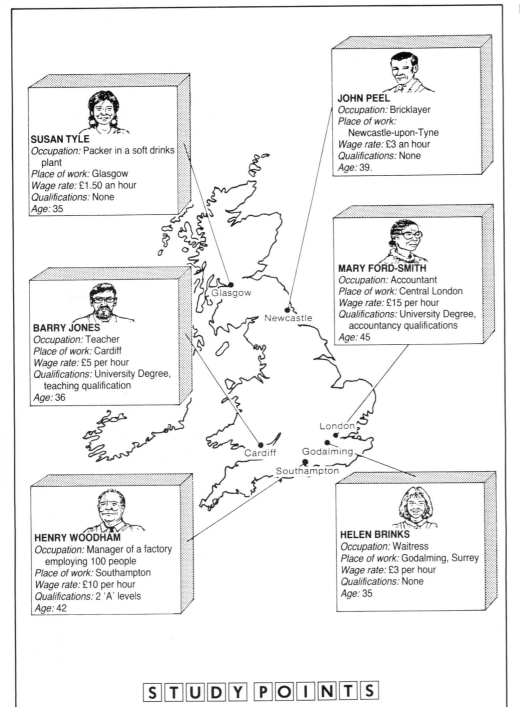

SUSAN TYLE
Occupation: Packer in a soft drinks plant
Place of work: Glasgow
Wage rate: £1.50 an hour
Qualifications: None
Age: 35

JOHN PEEL
Occupation: Bricklayer
Place of work: Newcastle-upon-Tyne
Wage rate: £3 an hour
Qualifications: None
Age: 39.

BARRY JONES
Occupation: Teacher
Place of work: Cardiff
Wage rate: £5 per hour
Qualifications: University Degree, teaching qualification
Age: 36

MARY FORD-SMITH
Occupation: Accountant
Place of work: Central London
Wage rate: £15 per hour
Qualifications: University Degree, accountancy qualifications
Age: 45

HENRY WOODHAM
Occupation: Manager of a factory employing 100 people
Place of work: Southampton
Wage rate: £10 per hour
Qualifications: 2 'A' levels
Age: 42

HELEN BRINKS
Occupation: Waitress
Place of work: Godalming, Surrey
Wage rate: £3 per hour
Qualifications: None
Age: 35

Glasgow
Newcastle
London
Cardiff
Godalming
Southampton

STUDY POINTS

1 Construct a bar graph showing the different wage rates of each worker.

2 Why are these six workers paid different wage rates?

3 Are these workers paid fairly? In your answer explain carefully what you understand by 'fairness' in wages.

4 How would a flat rate wage rise of £3 an hour for all workers affect the allocation of resources in the economy? Would a flat rate rise like this be fairer than a 50% rise for all workers in an economy and why?

'A nationwide campaign to establish a basic wage of £100 a week is being launched today by Britain's biggest union, the Transport Workers. The present average earnings for manual workers is about £150 a week. But skilled farm workers only get £82.80 a week; shop assistants, school cleaners, hotel and catering workers get about £70; and textile workers get less than £70.' (*Source: Daily Mirror*, 20 February 1985)

Workers are paid different wages. A textile worker in 1985 received less than £70 a week. In the same year, the average director's earnings were £676 a week, nearly ten times as much. Why is this so? How are wages determined?

Demand and Supply

Like any price, the price of workers – their wage – is fixed by the forces of demand and supply. If demand for a particular type of worker increases, or the supply falls, then wage rates will rise. If demand falls, or supply rises, then wage rates will fall.

This is shown in Figure 25.1. Assume there is a rise in demand for British textiles. Textile firms will want to take on extra workers – that is, the demand for textile workers will rise from D to D'. At the old equilibrium, where D and S intersected, 100 000 workers had jobs at £70 a week. The increase in demand pushes wage rates up to £80 a week and increases the numbers employed from 100 000 to 120 000.

Difference in Wages

Using the laws of demand and supply, we can now explain why a director is paid more than a textile worker, or a miner more than a cleaner. Wage rates will be higher on average:

- If the job requires special talents, qualifications and experience. Nearly all workers could become machine minders or refuse collectors, so the supply of these workers is very high. Very few workers have the right talents,

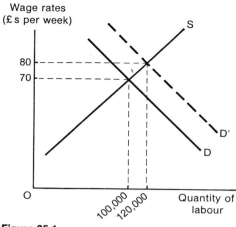

Figure 25.1

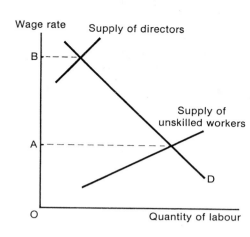

Figure 25.2

is virtually the only source of demand for many workers such as teachers or civil servants. Wages in these situations are fixed not by the laws of demand and supply, but by the relative bargaining strength of the employer and the employees.

qualifications and experience to become directors of companies, so the supply of these workers is very small. As can be seen from Figure 25.2, assuming that the demand for both workers is the same, then the shortage of supply of directors will result in high wages of OB, but unskilled workers will only receive OA.

- If the job is dangerous, unpleasant, or results in long hours of work. Few workers will want to work at the same wage as in safer or more pleasant jobs. So, again, the lower supply will push up wage rates.

Construction workers working on the Dungeness nuclear power plant. Dangerous work!

- If demand for the product that the worker makes is high, thus causing a high demand for workers in the industry. For instance, workers in the electronics industry today are paid more than shipyard workers. In part, this is because the demand for electronic goods is high, whereas the demand for ships is low.

- If the value or MARGINAL REVENUE PRODUCT of one worker is higher than another. The value of the extra output resulting from the employment of a director is greater than the value of the extra output resulting from the employment of an ordinary textile worker. Both this and the last point are shown in Figure 25.1, where the higher demand curve D' causes higher wages.

The above analysis assumes that markets are relatively free, such that there are a large number of buyers and sellers of labour in the market, none of whom are able to influence unduly the wage rate paid. But many labour markets are not free. Trade unions may exist, for instance, which can push wages above the free-market prices. (This is explained further in Unit 27.) Or employers may have immense power. The government, for instance,

C H E C K P O I N T S

1 What determines the wage rate paid to an individual worker?

2 Explain why:
   (a) a dustman is paid less than a teacher;
   (b) a shop assistant is paid less than a police constable;
   (c) an apprentice is paid less than a fully trained worker;
   (d) a secretary is paid less than a miner.

3 (a) Draw demand and supply curves for labour on a graph, using the following data.

Quantity demanded	Quantity supplied	Wage rate (£)
6000	3000	100
5500	4000	110
5000	5000	120
4500	6000	130

   (b) What is the equilibrium wage rate?
   (c) Draw a new supply curve, assuming that the supply of labour has increased by 1000 at every wage level.
   (d) What is the new equilibrium wage rate?

C O U R S E W O R K
S U G G E S T I O N

Find out about earnings and conditions of work in five different occupations. Establish the factors that determine the demand for labour and the supply of labour in each occupation. Explain why each worker is paid differently. Try to assess the extent to which the earnings of a worker correspond to the value of that worker to society.

K E Y P O I N T S

MARGINAL REVENUE PRODUCT – the addition to revenue gained by employing an extra factor of production such as a worker.

Trade Unions (1)

BREAKTHROUGH IN REDUCING HOURS

A BREAKTHROUGH in reducing hours has been achieved by the T&G at a firm in West Norwood. They now work a four-day week of 35 hours, and have also got a five per cent pay rise backdated to the beginning of July.

The new four-day week started last month at Winn & Coles, which makes cladding and other anti-corrosive products, mainly for oil pipelines.

Said T&G convenor David Napier: "The agreement has been so impressive that non-members are applying to join or rejoin, and we are hopeful of achieving 100 per cent membership again, although we have never been a formal closed shop."

Downgrading of posts led to boycott

TWO SENIOR Environmental Health Officers posts with Wokingham District Council are to be boycotted.

The request for the boycott arose as a result of the authority's decision to recruit two Senior Environmental Health Officers on grades below those established by the jointly agreed Job Evaluation Scheme used by the authority. Despite representations by NALGO that no recruitment takes place until agreement has been reached, the authority have advertised the above posts of Grades Scale 5 to SO 2.

Source: NALGO NEWS, 13 September 1985

Trade union education courses 1985/86

Tutor training — linked weekends

TWO national linked weekend tutor training courses are to be held this winter:

■ Moat Hotel, Oxford
8-10 November 1985 and 6-8 December 1985

■ Cairn Hotel, Harrogate
31 January-2 February and 21-23 February 1986

Source: Nalgo News, 13 September 1985

This Tutor Training course aims to help develop the teaching skills necessary for effective trade union education.

It is relevant to all the main types of trade union education activity at branch and district levels, e.g. membership education, briefings, and training and policy courses of various sorts.

You should apply for this course if you are (i) a branch education secretary or help the education secretary with branch level education activities, or (ii) nominated by a district with a view to helping on district courses.

STUDY POINTS

1 Read each of the extracts and summarise them in your own words.

2 Write a short report, using the information contained in the articles as examples, describing the work of trade unions.

3 Would you join a trade union at work? Explain your answer carefully by considering the costs and benefits of union membership.

4 Can trade unions fulfil a useful role in society and what should that role be?

- 'Teachers may disrupt exams.'
- 'Cleaners' battle likely to end.'
- 'Postal engineers act over trial manning.'

This sort of headline appears regularly in the news. Many people get the impression that these crises are everyday events for trade unions. In fact, they are most unusual, which is why they get into the news. If trade unions are not all about strikes, what are they about?

The Function of Trade Unions

Trade unions exist to protect the interests of their members. A TRADE UNION is concerned with:

- the level of wages and other forms of remuneration paid to its members;
- promotion prospects and opportunities;
- job security;
- hours of work and other conditions of work;
- health and safety at work;
- dismissal of members;
- benefits paid to workers who are ill, unemployed, retired or injured.

In order to improve the welfare of its members, a trade union needs to negotiate with and put pressure on employers, on other unions and other workers, and on government.

Before trade unions existed, a worker had to negotiate and bargain with an employer on his or her own. Employers were almost always in a more powerful position than workers. In the last resort, an employer could sack a worker and hire another one. The worker who was sacked would probably have found it difficult to get another job. By *combining* in unions, workers could begin to match the power that employers (and government) had over them. COLLECTIVE BARGAINING, where groups of workers appoint representatives to bargain with the representatives of employers, is an attempt to alter the balance of power in the worker–employer relationship.

Trade Union Organisation

Figure 26.1 shows the growth of trade union membership. Today, nearly half of all workers belong to trade unions. Many more workers belong to *professional associations*. These are organisations that perform many of the functions of a trade union, but are not registered as trade unions. They tend to cover better-paid, WHITE-COLLAR WORKERS.

Figure 26.1 Trade unions: membership[1] (*United Kingdom, millions and percentages*)

	Membership (millions)			As a percentage of all employees[2]		
	Men	Women	Total	Men	Women	Total
1951	7.7	1.8	9.5	56	25	45
1961	7.9	2.0	9.9	53	24	43
1971	8.4	2.8	11.1	59	32	49
1976	8.8	3.6	12.4	61	38	52
1977	9.1	3.8	12.8	63	39	53
1978	9.2	3.9	13.1	64	40	54
1979	9.4	3.9	13.3	66	39	55
1980	9.2	3.8	12.9	64	38	53
1981	8.4	3.8	12.1	59	38	50
1982	. .	. .	11.6	. .	. .	48

[1] Figures are for December each year.
[2] Employees in employment plus the registered unemployed.

Source: CSO, *Social Trends*, 1985

Figure 26.2 shows the typical organisation of a large trade union. Members of the trade union – often described as 'shop-floor' workers, because traditionally factory workers were said to work on the 'shop floor' – elect SHOP STEWARDS from their ranks in a place of work. Shop stewards are not paid for their trade union duties,

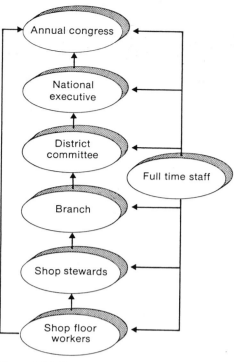

Figure 26.2 Trade union organisation

which they normally carry out in their own time. The shop steward will sort out the day-to-day problems of his or her members at work – everything from queries about last week's pay packet to changes in work duties to complaints about the state of the toilets.

Members in a local area are part of a branch, and all members are entitled to go along to branch meetings to discuss and vote on matters of union interest. The branch will discuss matters that affect the workers from different workplaces. For instance, the union might want its members' opinions on a matter like new health and safety legislation. Or the local branch may want to change union policy on pay bargaining.

Branches are combined on a regional basis (such as the Midlands or the South-East). A district committee is elected to look after the union affairs of the region. The National Executive of the union is elected to run the union nationally. It will be responsible for the finances of the whole union, important issues such as national strikes, considering new government legislation and other matters that affect all union members. The National Executive is responsible to the Annual General Meeting or the Annual Congress of the Union, where delegates from the shop floor meet and pass resolutions defining union policy. At a national level, the union also employs full-time staff, who work at every level of the trade union, assisting in its work.

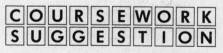

CHECKPOINTS

1 What is a 'trade union'?

2 Give the names of five different trade unions.

3 Describe three different functions of a trade union (i.e. describe three things a trade union does).

4 Explain why collective bargaining is likely to help a worker obtain higher wages than if he or she had to bargain individually with an employer.

5 Describe the organisation of a typical national trade union.

COURSEWORK SUGGESTION

Find out about a particular trade union (you could research the NUT or NAS/UWT), either on a national or a local level. Describe its activities. Analyse how it protects the interests of its members. Assess the extent to which it provides positive benefits for (a) its members and (b) the economy as a whole.

KEY TERMS

TRADE UNION – a group of workers who combine to protect their interests.

COLLECTIVE BARGAINING – where the representatives of workers negotiate with the representatives of their employers.

WHITE-COLLAR WORKER – a non-manual worker such as a teacher or a secretary, as opposed to a manual *blue-collar* worker, who works 'with his hands'.

SHOP STEWARD – an unpaid elected trade union representative of shop-floor workers, who protects their interests in their place of work.

Trade Unions (2)

Company Statistics[1]

| | Actual | | | | Projected |
	1986	1987	1988	1989	1990
Turnover (£ millions)	20	15	25	30	32
Profit (£ millions)	2	−3	1	2	1
Capital employed (£ millions)	40	44	41	45	47
Number of workers employed	1150	1200	980	1000	1000
Average earnings per worker (£)	9990	11080	11311	12000	—
Average pay rise (%)	10	12	2	6.1	—
Inflation rate (%)	5	5	5	6	7

[1]Provided by the company to the unions for the 1990 pay negotiations.

STUDY POINTS

1 Assume you were a full time official of one of the trade unions involved in the dispute which is taking place in 1990. Write a short report explaining the trade union arguments in favour of a pay rise.

2 Can the firm afford to give the workers a pay rise? What is the maximum it could afford to give?

3 What are the economic consequences of a pay rise: (a) for the workers; (b) for the company; (c) for the rest of the economy?

4 What would be the economic consequences of a strike (a) for the workers, (b) for the company, (c) for the rest of the economy?

5 Should the workers accept the 9% offered them by the company? Explain your answer.

Trade unions have always been controversial. But what effects do they have on the economy? Consider this news item:

'The threat of a rail strike loomed last night after union leaders were given a take-it-or-leave-it pay offer. British Rail's "final" offer is worth nearly five per cent on basic rates. The deal would boost railmen's weekly earnings from £89 to £93.50. The cost to BR's wage bill would be about £80 million a year.' (Source: *Daily Express*, 28 March 1985)

The rail unions have demanded a pay rise and British Rail has offered 5%. If the pay award were implemented, it would add £80 million to British Rail's wage bill and therefore to British Rail's costs.

Who would pay this? Different economists give different answers, but it is likely that the £80 million would be paid by one or more of the following:

- *consumers* – British Rail might put up its fares to passengers to cover the £80 million;

- *the owners* of British Rail (in this case the government) – the extra wages might be paid for by reducing profits paid to the owners of the company (or by making the owners pay bigger subsidies to run the business);

- *the workers* – British Rail might decide that it cannot afford to pay all its workers any more, so it might reduce its workforce;

- *nobody* – because British Rail would be forced to increase **LABOUR PRODUCTIVITY**. Productivity is defined as output per worker. An increase in wages would force British Rail to find ways of making workers produce an extra £80 million of output to cover the cost of the increased wage bill.

Trade unionists would argue that increased wages are likely to be paid for by increased productivity and reduced profits. They would argue that workers are always fighting to keep their share of the wealth that their company produces. Without trade unions, profits would be higher and the owners of the company would be richer at the expense of the workers. Others would argue that wage rises hit consumers by forcing firms to push up their prices. This could well lead to inflationary problems in the economy. They would also argue that wage rises cause unemployment. Trade unions, by pushing up wages, leave firms with no alternative but to sack workers. So, they argue, trade union power may be a major cause of unemployment.

A Diagrammatic Analysis

The effect of trade unions on wages and employment can be explained using demand and supply diagrams. In Figure 27.1, the demand for workers by company, such as British Rail, is given by the line D. The supply curve of workers to the company is given by the line S. The equilibrium level of wage rates is therefore OA and the company will employ OE workers. Now assume that trade unions force the company to pay higher wages, say OB. What this means is that, due to union pressure, the company can't hire any workers at a wage of less than OB. So the supply curve of labour becomes horizontal between B and F. To the right of F, the supply curve becomes upward sloping again – trade unions aren't going to prevent wages going even higher than

OB if market conditions force British Rail to pay these higher wages. In Figure 27.1 the new equilibrium wage is therefore OB. Note, however, that British Rail now only want to employ OC workers, whereas before, at the wage rate of OA, it wanted to employ OE workers. CE workers will therefore lose their jobs. Trade unions have raised wages but at the expense of jobs in the rail industry.

What if the company itself paid for the pay rise out of its profits? This situation is shown in Figure 27.2. Here the company is prepared to employ the same number of workers, whatever the wage rate. It might be prepared to do this, if, for instance, these workers formed only a very small part of the cost of production, but were essential none the less. If, for instance, wages counted for only 1% of the cost of the product, an employer would be unlikely to sack workers if they received a pay rise of 10% rather than 5%. Equally, a company might need an exact number of workers to staff a factory, if it is to produce at all. Here, the choice is between operating the factory or not, irrespective of the wage paid. In both these situations, the demand for labour is perfectly inelastic and is shown in the demand curve D. The company is prepared to employ OC workers, whatever the wage rate. Assume that the factory was profitable at a wage level of OB. Then if the company can pay lower wages at

OA, it will be even more profitable. Trade unions in this situation would be trying to push up wages at the expense of profits.

CHECKPOINTS

1 Explain the possible effects of a wage rise given to car workers:
  (a) on the car workers;
  (b) on the owners of the car company;
  (c) on the buyers of cars;
  (d) on workers in companies making components for cars.

2 Explain whether or not trade unions can cause (a) inflation and (b) unemployment.

3 (a) Plot a demand curve for farm workers on a graph, using the following data.

Wage rate (£)	Employment (hundreds)
200	100
150	300
100	500
50	700

  (b) If the wage rate was £60, how many workers would be employed?
  (c) The farm workers' trade union negotiates a pay rise to £75. How many workers would now be employed? How many workers would lose their job as a result of the wage increase?
  (d) At what level of wages would employment fall below 200 000?

COURSEWORK SUGGESTION

Research a recent pay dispute in a local business, where a trade union won a pay rise on behalf of its members. Describe the causes, the conduct and the outcome of the dispute. Analyse the effect of the strike on pay, jobs and prices. Try to assess the benefits and costs given by the trade union to its members and to other individuals and/or organisations in the economy.

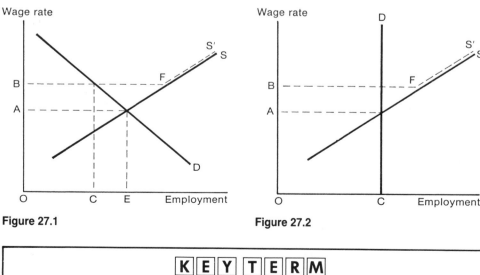

Wage rate

Figure 27.1

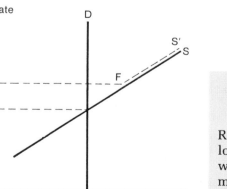

Wage rate

Figure 27.2

KEY TERM

LABOUR PRODUCTIVITY – output per worker.

Data Response Questions
Units 23–27

Unit 23 The Demand for Labour

Warning over pay rises

Employment Secretary Tom King issued a fresh warning today that British workers are pricing themselves and others out of jobs.

The warning came after new Government figures showed that wages are running well ahead of inflation.

Pay awards in April were 9.4 per cent higher than 12 months earlier. Although the underlying increase is put at 7.5 per cent, that is still considerably higher than the 6.9 per cent inflation figure for April.

But what is worrying Ministers most is that the big pay rises are not being matched by comparable increases in productivity.

"Efficiency and competitiveness are the key to jobs. Yet the increase in unit wage costs in Britain's manufacturing industries over the last year is now 6.4 per cent," said Mr King.

He went on: "This has risen steadily and now stands at twice the level of a year ago. And this moreover at a time when our overseas competitors' unit wage costs are either low or falling.

"It is the clearest possible warning of the risk we run of pricing British goods out of foreign markets," said the Employment Secretary.

Anxious

"Pay negotiators on both sides of industry must realise the long-term effects of excessive pay claims and settlements. What is needed is the realism that a lower rise in average real pay will mean more jobs and a more profitable and expanding industry in the long run."

Source: Express and Star, 19 June, 1985

1 Explain what is meant by:
   (a) 'inflation';
   (b) 'productivity';
   (c) 'overseas competitors'.   *(6 marks)*

2 Explain carefully the argument that pay rises lead to firms employing fewer workers.   *(4 marks)*

3 What are the costs to workers of low pay increases?   *(2 marks)*

4 Why might low pay increases lead to a fall in demand for British goods and British workers?   *(3 marks)*

Unit 24 The Supply of Labour

Trend to early retirement growing, survey shows

RETIREMENT before the state pension age is becoming the norm in many organisations, according to a study by Incomes Data Services, the research company. The numbers of people retiring early are at record levels after a dramatic rise in the past ten years.

Much of it has been "involuntary," caused by job cuts in the recession. But more employees are coming to expect early retirement and more employers want to establish permanent schemes allowing people to choose to go early.

For men aged 60 to 64, an Employment Department study combining several surveys showed an activity rate of just over 85 per cent in 1975. But the preliminary results from the 1983 Labour Force Survey show only 59.6 per cent of men in this age group as economically active.

Large employers such as British Rail and ICI said very few employees now stayed on at work until the statutory retirement age.

Source: Financial Times, 7 May 1985
Note: 'an activity rate of 85%' means that 85 out of every 100 people had a job.

1 What is happening to the age at which workers retire?
     (2 marks)

2 Suggest *three* possible reasons why this change in the age of retirement has occurred.   *(6 marks)*

3 (a) What is happening to the supply of labour in the economy as a result of these changes?
   (b) Draw a supply diagram to show these changes.
     (7 marks)

Essay Questions
Units 23–27

1 'Nurses are paid far less than pop stars and yet are far more important to people's welfare.'
   (a) Give *three* reasons why workers are paid differently.
     (6 marks)
   (b) Explain why a nurse is paid less than a pop star.
     (6 marks)
   (c) Describe, using a demand and supply diagram, how nurses' pay and the number of nurses employed would change if the Government decided to open 20 new hospitals in the UK.   *(8 marks)*

Unit 25 The Determination of Wages

Canteen lady stirs it up!

JULIE HAYWARD is a 'canteen assistant' with the Cammell Laird shipyard. She was paid much less than painters and other skilled workers.

She claimed that her work was of equal value to theirs and, by winning, her case has sounded a new signal for women workers and for those who employ them.

The European Court of Justice forced the UK Government to introduce new regulations which came into force on January 1st, 1984.

Under the Equal Pay Act, women were already entitled to be paid the same as men in the same firm, doing the same or similar work.

But now they could compare their pay with men doing different jobs but at a similar level of skill in the same firm.

Julie Hayward argued that the demands made on her in kitchen and canteen were no less than those made on painters and other skilled colleagues.

She said her qualifications as a cook/chef were equivalent to theirs. She had as much responsibility. And matching her work with theirs, an independent job evaluation expert held that the work was of equal value so that she should be paid no less than they were.

Source: Daily Mail, 23 January 1985

1 Explain the difference between the original provisions of the Equal Pay Act 1975 and the new regulations of January 1st 1984. *(2 marks)*

2 Describe Julie Hayward's case and explain why she won it. *(4 marks)*

3 Suggest *two* economic reasons why Julie Hayward may have been paid less than skilled workers at Cammell Laird before 1985. *(4 marks)*

4 Use a demand and supply diagram to show the possible effects of the decision on the employment of women. *(5 marks)*

2 Jimmy Plant starts work today as a trainee manager at a supermarket.
  (a) Suggest *four* reasons why he might want to join a trade union. *(8 marks)*
  (b) What is a 'shop steward' and how might he help Jimmy Plant and other workers at the supermarket? *(6 marks)*
  (c) Using a demand and supply diagram, explain the possible effects of a 10% pay increase for workers at the supermarket on the number of workers employed by the company. *(6 marks)*

Units 26 and 27 Trade Unions

Threatened steel plant seeks protection

UNIONS at British Steel's Tinsley Park works, near Sheffield, have asked the Government to consider a form of protection for their factory that would enable it to stay open saving 4,500 jobs.

Closure of the Sheffield works, which has been badly hit by rising imports of special steels, was announced in March. It employs 1,100 workers, but the unions claim that many more jobs in the area depend on it staying open.

Yesterday, the union handed British Steel management a 50-page analysis of the operation at Tinsley Park, arguing the case for a minimum British steel content in UK assembled vehicles and vehicle components.

The union document, drawn up by a multi-union committee at Tinsley Park, is being sent to political leaders, including the Prime Minister, and to the Commons Select Committee on Trade and Industry, which will discuss special steels next month.

Source: Financial Times, 5 June 1985

1 What is British Steel intending to do to its Tinsley park works? *(1 mark)*

2 How are trade unions protecting their members' interests at Tinsley Park? *(5 marks)*

3 What would be the cost of the union's plans
  (a) to consumers and
  (b) to industry? *(4 marks)*

Ford women's fiesta

A JUBILANT group of 270 women had a fiesta yesterday as they celebrated victory in their long-running battle with the Ford motor company.

The sewing machinists have fought for 16 years to have their jobs classified as skilled.

And now an independent arbitrator has ruled in their favour.

The decision means an extra £7 on top of their basic £133 a week. And it will be backdated to January 1.

Yesterday's verdict by the ACAS conciliation service comes as the climax to a campaign which began in 1969 and culminated in a six-week strike at the end of last year.

The walkout by the 270 machinists — all but seven of them female — at Dagenham and Halewood led to 10,000 other workers being laid off.

Source: Daily Express, 26 April, 1985

1 Why did the sewing machinists at Ford want a pay rise? *(1 mark)*

2 Explain how the sewing machinists achieved their pay rise. *(2 marks)*

3 Use a demand and supply diagram to show the change in pay for machinists at Ford. *(4 marks)*

4 (a) Why is it unlikely that the pay rise awarded will result in a loss of jobs?
  (b) What does this imply about the elasticity of demand for machinists at Fords? *(3 marks)*

Rent, Interest and Profit

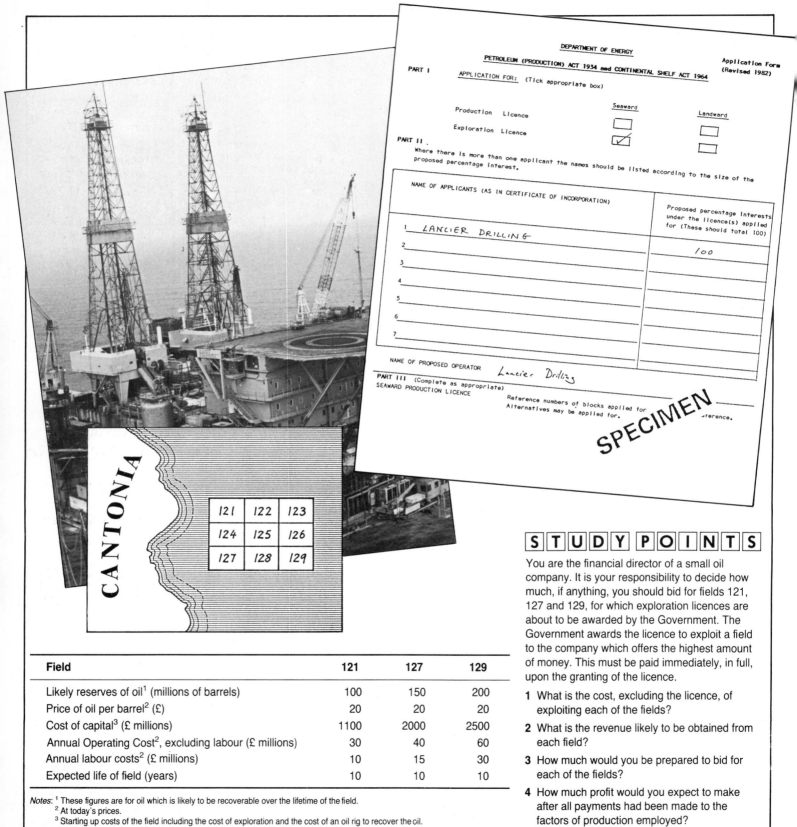

DEPARTMENT OF ENERGY

PETROLEUM (PRODUCTION) ACT 1934 and CONTINENTAL SHELF ACT 1964

Application Form
(Revised 1982)

PART I

APPLICATION FOR: (Tick appropriate box)

Production Licence   Seaward   Landward

Exploration Licence

PART II

Where there is more than one applicant the names should be listed according to the size of the proposed percentage interest.

NAME OF APPLICANTS (AS IN CERTIFICATE OF INCORPORATION)

Proposed percentage interests under the licence(s) applied for (These should total 100)

1   LANCIER DRILLING

2   100

3

4

5

6

7

NAME OF PROPOSED OPERATOR   Lancier Drilling

PART III (Complete as appropriate)
SEAWARD PRODUCTION LICENCE

Reference numbers of blocks applied for
Alternatives may be applied for.

SPECIMEN

CANTONIA

121	122	123
124	125	126
127	128	129

Field	121	127	129
Likely reserves of oil[1] (millions of barrels)	100	150	200
Price of oil per barrel[2] (£)	20	20	20
Cost of capital[3] (£ millions)	1100	2000	2500
Annual Operating Cost[2], excluding labour (£ millions)	30	40	60
Annual labour costs[2] (£ millions)	10	15	30
Expected life of field (years)	10	10	10

Notes: [1] These figures are for oil which is likely to be recoverable over the lifetime of the field.
[2] At today's prices.
[3] Starting up costs of the field including the cost of exploration and the cost of an oil rig to recover the oil.

STUDY POINTS

You are the financial director of a small oil company. It is your responsibility to decide how much, if anything, you should bid for fields 121, 127 and 129, for which exploration licences are about to be awarded by the Government. The Government awards the licence to exploit a field to the company which offers the highest amount of money. This must be paid immediately, in full, upon the granting of the licence.

1 What is the cost, excluding the licence, of exploiting each of the fields?

2 What is the revenue likely to be obtained from each field?

3 How much would you be prepared to bid for each of the fields?

4 How much profit would you expect to make after all payments had been made to the factors of production employed?

Costs

It was shown in Unit 25 how the forces of demand and supply determined how much it cost to hire a worker. In this unit, we will consider the cost or price of hiring the other factors of production. Just as the forces of demand and supply fix the wage paid to a worker, so too do the forces of demand and supply determine what the owners of land, capital and entrepreneurship receive when they hire out their factors of production.

Land

Total land is fixed in supply. There are only so many billion tonnes of coal on this planet, so many hectares of land, etc. But the supply of land for any particular use is not fixed. For instance, the supply of land for building can be increased by reducing the supply of agricultural land, or the land used for recreational activities. Figure 28.1 shows that an increase in the demand for building land from D to D′ will raise the price of building land from OA to OB and lead to an extension of supply from OE to OF. The price of hiring land is usually called *rent* (but, as will be shown in Unit 29, the term 'rent' has come to have a different meaning in economics to the everyday meaning of the word).

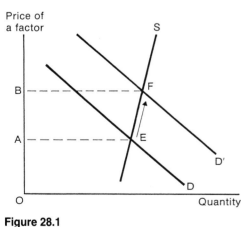

Figure 28.1

Capital

The price of capital, too, is fixed by the forces of demand and supply. In a free market, capital is demanded by business organisations in order to produce goods and services. Of course, a firm does not have to buy capital. It could, instead, save the money it

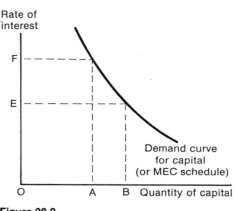

Figure 28.2

would have spent on capital goods by putting it in a bank or in stocks and shares (i.e. it could *save* the money instead of *investing it*). The price that a firm pays for its capital is the opportunity cost of the capital – what the firm has to give up in order to invest and hold capital. That price is the rate of interest it could have received if it had saved the money. So the reward to capital is generally considered to be interest.

Capital is supplied to the economy by individuals, business, government, etc. That supply of capital, too, has an opportunity cost. For instance, the household that buys new shares in a company could have used that money for spending or it could have saved the money. Again, the opportunity cost of having capital is the interest that is lost on that money, had it been saved. So the 'price' of capital is the rate of interest. The higher the rate of interest, the more households, firms and governments will choose to supply money to building societies and banks, rather than demand new capital.

This is shown in Figure 28.2. When interest rates are high at OF, the demand for capital, OA, is low. (The demand curve is given the special name of the 'marginal efficiency of capital (MEC) schedule'.) An increase in capital from OA to OB will reduce interest rates by EF.

Entrepreneurship

The reward for entrepreneurship is generally considered to be profit. The entrepreneur risks his or her money or capital in a business and organises the other factors of production. In practice, most output is produced either in the

public sector, where no single person owns and organises production, or in large PLCs (public limited companies) in the private sector, where the shareholders are different people from the directors and managers of the firm. Profit in the private sector, then, is paid to shareholders who have risked their money in buying the capital of the company – that is, profit is the return to capital and not entrepreneurship.

Profit is different from the other rewards to the factors of production. Wages, rent and interest are normally fixed in advance of production. Profit is the amount of money left over after all costs have been paid. For that reason, profit can be negative as well as positive, if cost exceeds revenue. Profit also tends to vary much more than the other payments to the factors of production over a period of time. The role of profits in the economy is discussed in Unit 35.

C H E C K P O I N T S

1 **Explain what determines the hire charge for an acre of farm land.**

2 **What is the opportunity cost of renting an office block?**

3 **Explain why the higher the rate of interest is, the lower the demand for capital will be.**

4 **Why does an entrepreneur earn profit?**

5 **Why can profits be negative, when wages cannot?**

C O U R S E W O R K S U G G E S T I O N

Investigate the prices of land in your locality. One major source of information would be local estate agents. The area under investigation should be large enough to include land used for housing, for industrial purposes, for recreation and for farming. Describe the pattern of land prices and rents. Using demand and supply analysis, explain why land values and rents differ. Consider what would happen to land values and rent, if there were a change in the permitted usage of the land.

Economic Rent, Costs and Profit

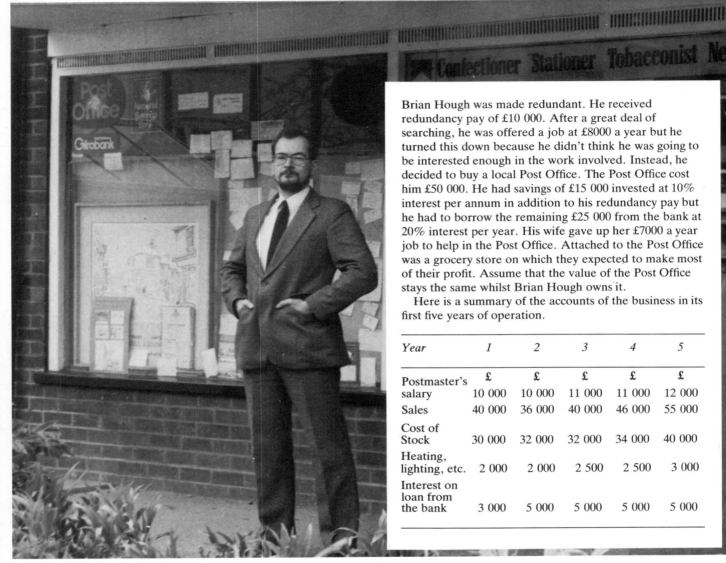

Brian Hough was made redundant. He received redundancy pay of £10 000. After a great deal of searching, he was offered a job at £8000 a year but he turned this down because he didn't think he was going to be interested enough in the work involved. Instead, he decided to buy a local Post Office. The Post Office cost him £50 000. He had savings of £15 000 invested at 10% interest per annum in addition to his redundancy pay but he had to borrow the remaining £25 000 from the bank at 20% interest per year. His wife gave up her £7000 a year job to help in the Post Office. Attached to the Post Office was a grocery store on which they expected to make most of their profit. Assume that the value of the Post Office stays the same whilst Brian Hough owns it.

Here is a summary of the accounts of the business in its first five years of operation.

Year	1	2	3	4	5
	£	£	£	£	£
Postmaster's salary	10 000	10 000	11 000	11 000	12 000
Sales	40 000	36 000	40 000	46 000	55 000
Cost of Stock	30 000	32 000	32 000	34 000	40 000
Heating, lighting, etc.	2 000	2 000	2 500	2 500	3 000
Interest on loan from the bank	3 000	5 000	5 000	5 000	5 000

STUDY POINTS

1 Make a list, in words, of all the costs that Brian Hough faces in running his business. Don't forget to include the costs he has has to pay directly, but also the hidden opportunity costs of his business such as the pay his wife could have been earning if she weren't employed at the Post Office.

2 Calculate the economic costs of the business in its first five years of operation. Don't forget that 'economic cost' must include the opportunity costs involved.

3 What revenues does the business receive?

4 Calculate the revenue earned by the business in each of its five years of operation.

5 Calculate the economic profit or loss (i.e. revenues minus costs) for each year.

6 How much money did Brian Hough and his wife make with their business in each year? Include not only the Postmaster's salary, but also any other earnings or profits they are taking out of the business.

7 If Brian Hough and his wife could have earned £15 000 by working for someone else

in year 5, how much more or less did they earn by working in their Post Office? (This is known as their ECONOMIC RENT).

8 What effect would a halving of the rate of interest have on (a) the costs of the business and (b) the profits of the business?

9 The Post Office decides to cut all postmasters' pay by 50%. Is the business now making a profit?

10 If the value of the Post Office increased by £5000 each year, what effect would this have on the profitability of the business?

Economic Rent and Transfer Earnings

The words 'rent', 'cost' and 'profit' have different meanings in ordinary language and in economics. Consider this sentence:

'The rent on the farmland was £5000 a year.'

Rent here is a term used to describe the payment for the hire of a piece of land. This is the ordinary everyday usage of the word. But in economics, the term has come to describe the earnings of any factor of production over and above its transfer earnings.

The TRANSFER EARNINGS of a factor are the earnings that a factor could receive in its next best occupation. For instance, assume that a piece of land could be used either as building land, at a rent of £15 000 a year, or as farming land, at a rent of £5000 a year. Then, the transfer earnings of the piece of building land are £5000 a year – what could be earned by renting out the land as farm land instead of building land.

ECONOMIC RENT is any earnings over and above the transfer earnings. So if the rent on the piece of land used for building were £15 000 a year, then the economic rent would be £10 000 – the £15 000 minus the transfer earnings of £5000.

The highest economic rent is earned by factors with very low transfer earnings in comparison to their actual payment. A pop star, for instance, might earn £250 000 a year. His next best job might be as a teacher, earning say £10 000. So with transfer earnings of £10 000, he is earning an economic rent of £240 000. Building land is a good example of high economic rent, because there tends to be a great difference between the rent paid on building land and land for alternative uses.

Economic Cost and Profit

Cost and profit, too, have special meanings in economics. COST includes not only what has to be paid directly, but also the hidden cost of factors that could be used in alternative ways. For instance, consider the businesswoman who works for her own business and who puts in £20 000 to start it off. Her costs will obviously include raw materials, hiring of other workers, etc. But in economics, costs will also include the costs of borrowing that £20 000. The money has an opportunity cost because it could have been lent, say, to a bank and earned interest. The businesswoman must also include a wage for herself, that being the wage that she could have earned in the next best alternative job. So if the businesswoman could have earned £15 000 a year in a job, the economic cost to her business is £15 000 a year.

ECONOMIC PROFIT is the difference between all revenues received and all costs incurred. For instance, if a company earned £30 000 in revenues and paid out £20 000 in costs, then the profit would be £10 000.

Economic profit may well differ from what is ordinarily called 'profit' in the business world by accountants. This is because an accountant considers mainly those revenues and costs that are actual flows of money into and out of the firm. But many costs and benefits are hidden. An economist takes into account all of these costs and revenues, both the accounting costs and revenues as well as these hidden costs and revenues.

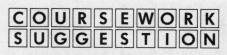

CHECKPOINTS

1 Explain what is meant by transfer earnings and economic rent.

2 Which of the following workers are likely to earn a high economic rent and why:
   (a) a pop star;
   (b) an international footballer;
   (c) a road sweeper;
   (d) a cashier in the supermarket?

3 Copy out and complete the table.

Current earnings (£)	Transfer earnings (£)	Economic rent (£)
10 000	5000	
20 000	8000	
40 000		2000
	6000	0

4 Explain the difference between the ordinary meaning of 'cost' and the economic meaning of 'cost'.

5 You decide to travel by bus into town to do some shopping. Which of the following are the economic costs of this to you and why:
   (a) the bus fare;
   (b) the petrol used by the bus;
   (c) the bus driver's time;
   (d) your time spent travelling and shopping;
   (e) wear and tear on your shoes;
   (f) the money you paid for the goods you bought?

COURSEWORK SUGGESTION

Investigate the market for either pop stars or football players. Find out and describe the earnings of a number of these workers. Explain why they are paid so much. Estimate their transfer earnings. (For instance, what does a football player earn after retirement and in what job? Give specific examples.) Estimate their current economic rent. Should this economic rent be taxed by the government? Put forward arguments for and against this idea.

KEY TERMS

ECONOMIC RENT – payment to a factor of production over and above its transfer earnings.

TRANSFER EARNINGS – the earnings of a factor in its next best use.

COST – the cost of an activity including not only monetary costs, but also the opportunity cost of factors owned by the producer.

ECONOMIC PROFIT – the difference between all revenues received and all costs incurred.

Factor Mobility

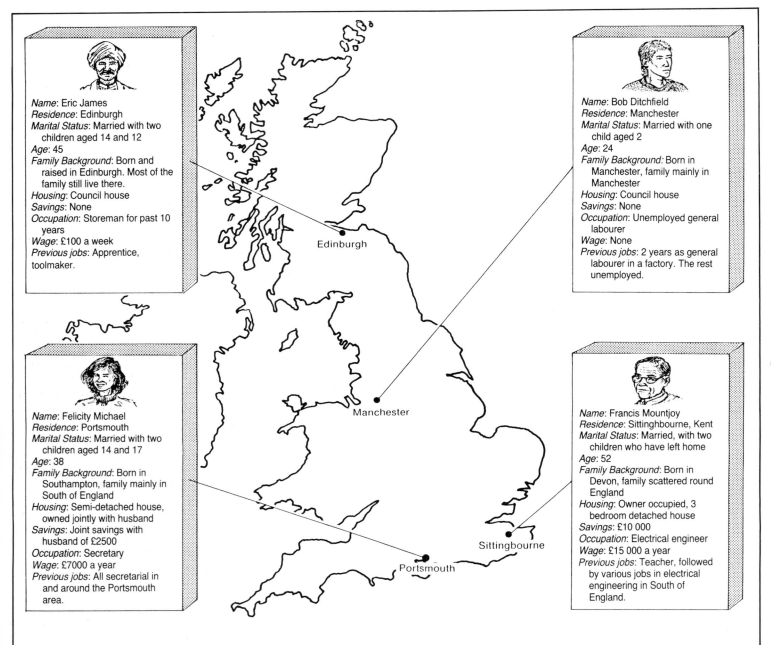

Name: Eric James
Residence: Edinburgh
Marital Status: Married with two children aged 14 and 12
Age: 45
Family Background: Born and raised in Edinburgh. Most of the family still live there.
Housing: Council house
Savings: None
Occupation: Storeman for past 10 years
Wage: £100 a week
Previous jobs: Apprentice, toolmaker.

Name: Bob Ditchfield
Residence: Manchester
Marital Status: Married with one child aged 2
Age: 24
Family Background: Born in Manchester, family mainly in Manchester
Housing: Council house
Savings: None
Occupation: Unemployed general labourer
Wage: None
Previous jobs: 2 years as general labourer in a factory. The rest unemployed.

Name: Felicity Michael
Residence: Portsmouth
Marital Status: Married with two children aged 14 and 17
Age: 38
Family Background: Born in Southampton, family mainly in South of England
Housing: Semi-detached house, owned jointly with husband
Savings: Joint savings with husband of £2500
Occupation: Secretary
Wage: £7000 a year
Previous jobs: All secretarial in and around the Portsmouth area.

Name: Francis Mountjoy
Residence: Sittinghbourne, Kent
Marital Status: Married, with two children who have left home
Age: 52
Family Background: Born in Devon, family scattered round England
Housing: Owner occupied, 3 bedroom detached house
Savings: £10 000
Occupation: Electrical engineer
Wage: £15 000 a year
Previous jobs: Teacher, followed by various jobs in electrical engineering in South of England.

STUDY POINTS

1 Eric James is made redundant. There is a vacancy for a storeman in Sittingbourne, Kent. Why is it most unlikely that Eric James would come to work in Sittingbourne?

2 What obstacles are there to Bob Ditchfield finding a job (a) other than a general labourer in Manchester or (b) as a general labourer elsewhere in the UK?

3 If a worker is likely to find it difficult to be offered, or to take a job, in another area of the UK, economists say that that worker is *geographically immobile*. Why is Felicity Michael likely to be geographically immobile? Why is Francis Mountjoy likely to be geographically immobile too?

4 If a worker is likely to find it difficult to change his or her occupation or job, then economists say that the worker is *occupationally immobile*. Why is Francis Mountjoy likely to be occupationally immobile? Why is Felicity

Michael likely to be occupationally immobile too?

5 To what extent do you think you are likely to be geographically *mobile* when you are in work? Would you, for instance, consider taking a job in the nearest large town or city to yours? Would you consider moving to a different region of the UK? Would you consider working abroad? Explain your answer carefully.

Specialisation and Exchange

The economy is built upon the principles of specialisation and exchange. Workers, firms, regions and countries specialise in the production of certain goods and services, and exchange them for others. For this type of economy to work efficiently, it is important that the factors of production (land, labour and capital) be *mobile*. If they are not mobile, then workers can become unemployed, firms can go bankrupt, and regions and countries can fail to share in growing world prosperity.

Mobility can be of two types:

- GEOGRAPHICAL MOBILITY describes the movement of a factor of production from one area to another area within a region or within a country or between countries.
- OCCUPATIONAL or VERTICAL MOBILITY describes the movement of a factor between one job and another.

The Mobility of Land

Land is geographically immobile. It is impossible to move land from, say, Glasgow to London to relieve a land shortage in London. Land, however, is occupationally mobile to some extent. Much land has a variety of uses – for agriculture, for recreation, for industry, etc. In the UK, land use is strictly regulated by planning regulations. For instance, it is not possible to develop industry in the Green Belt. This restricts occupational mobility of land.

The Mobility of Capital

Some capital is both geographically and occupationally mobile. A typewriter, or a small lathe, or a computer are such examples. But something like an office block is only occupationally mobile, whereas something like a petro-chemical works is broadly immobile (i.e. it has no alternative use). The fact that much capital is both geographically and occupationally immobile means that it is difficult to solve the problem of high unemployment in a region quickly and easily. It takes years to build up the capital necessary to provide jobs for everybody who wants them. One of the major problems of an area like north-east England is that it may have plenty of capital in the form of old factory buildings and old machinery, but these remain unemployed, because demand for the goods they were intended to produce has gone and these pieces of capital are immobile (i.e. have no alternative use).

The Mobility of Labour

In theory, labour should be the most mobile of factors. People can move from area to area to work, and can be trained and retrained for new jobs. In practice, labour is geographically immobile because:

- the financial cost of moving from one area to another is high;
- workers, especially those in rented council houses, may not be able to find housing in another area;
- workers are often reluctant to move away from friends, family and their local area, even if they are unemployed;
- there is very little information in one area about job opportunities in another area – for instance, vacancies for unskilled workers in London are not advertised in Aberdeen.

Labour can be occupationally immobile for the following reasons.

- Workers can become over-specialised. Many jobs require long periods of education, training and experience. So a steel worker cannot suddenly become a shop manager or an electrician.
- Workers have different natural talents. Only a few, for instance, can become professional golfers or university lecturers.
- Institutional barriers, such as laws, qualifications, and trade unions, can prevent workers moving into a particular profession.
- Money (to cover start-up costs) can be a problem for anybody wanting to set up in business by themselves.
- As with geographical mobility, a lack of information can mean that workers don't move from one occupation to another.

Immobility of labour causes unemployment – there may be unemployed workers unable to fill job vacancies because of barriers to mobility. Immobility of labour can also produce differences in wage rates, because the supply of labour may differ between industries and between regions.

Costs (1)

S T U D Y   P O I N T S

1 FIXED COSTS are costs which do not change however many miles a year Joyce travels. Fixed costs are the same whether she travels 1 mile or 30 000 miles a year. Which of the costs shown below are fixed costs? (Assume that servicing and repairs are a fixed cost.)

2 VARIABLE COSTS are costs which increase for every extra mile that Joyce travels. Which of the costs are variable costs?

Copy out the grid and record your answers to questions 3 to 9 in it.

Yearly mileage	Total fixed cost	Total variable cost	Total cost	Average cost
10 000				
20 000				
30 000				
40 000				

3 Calculate Joyce's total fixed costs at an annual mileage of 30 000 miles.

4 Calculate Joyce's total fixed costs if she travels (a) 10 000 miles, (b) 20 000 miles, (c) 40 000 miles a year.

5 Calculate Joyce's total variable costs if she travels (a) 10 000 miles, (b) 20 000 miles, (c) 30 000 miles and (d) 40 000 miles a year.

6 Calculate Joyce's total costs (i.e. total fixed costs plus total variable costs) if she travels 30 000 miles per year.

7 Calculate Joyce's total costs if she travels (a) 10 000 miles, (b) 20 000 miles, (c) 40 000 miles.

8 How much on average did it cost Joyce per mile to run her taxi travelling 30 000 miles over the year? (This is known as the 'average cost'.)

9 How much per mile on average would it have cost Joyce if she had travelled (a) 10 000 miles, (b) 20 000 miles and (c) 40 000 miles over a year?

10 What would be the marginal cost for Joyce travelling an extra mile?

11 The *break even* point is where costs are just equal to the revenue that is earned. So, if Joyce's costs were £10 000 and she received £10 000 in fares, then that would be a break even point for her.

If she carried 5000 passengers in a year, and travelled 30 000 miles, how much would she have to charge on average per passenger to break even?

12 If Joyce travels 20 000 miles a year, carrying 3000 passengers at an average fare of £3, is she going to make a profit or a loss?

13 Last year, Joyce travelled 30 000 miles and carried 4000 passengers at an average fare of £3. Is she making a profit or a loss? What should she do to improve the situation do you think?

Joyce Bigford is a taxi driver. She works 40 hours a week, 48 weeks a year irrespective of the number of passengers she carries. For this, she pays herself a wage of £8000 a year. The costs shown above are based on costs over a year in which Joyce travelled 30 000 miles.

'TV causes major problems to the Central Electricity Generating Board. There can be a great surge in demand for electricity at the end of a popular TV programme when people suddenly begin brewing tea and switching on lights and electric blankets. Power demand can vary by a factor of four during the year and by a factor of two during any one day.' (Source: *Financial Times*, 7 April 1981)

The Central Electricity Generating Board (CEGB) is faced with a major problem. It has to be able to produce enough electricity to meet the maximum demand in a year. For most of the time, demand is considerably lower than this maximum demand. The change in demand is enormous. Between the highest-demand day in winter and the lowest-demand day in summer, demand can vary fourfold.

In order to cope with this, the CEGB has to have a large number of power stations ready and waiting to make electricity. For much of the time, however, particularly during the night and during the summer, many of these power stations lie idle.

All this has a very important effect upon the *cost* of producing electricity. Here, the word 'cost' is being used in the sense of the private cost to the CEGB of generating electricity, as opposed to any of the other definitions of cost found elsewhere in economics.

Fixed and Variable Costs

To start with, much of the cost of generating electricity is a FIXED COST. This is a cost that stays the same whether the CEGB is producing as much electricity as possible or not producing any at all. The major fixed costs of the CEGB are the power stations and the National Grid (the power lines that connect all the country). The CEGB has to pay off the loans it took out to build these installations. It also has to keep them in good repair. Fixed costs are also sometimes called OVERHEAD COSTS.

VARIABLE COSTS are costs that change as output changes. The coal, gas and oil used to generate electricity are variable costs, because the more electricity that is generated in a day, the more fuel that is used. The variable costs of production added to the fixed costs of production equal the TOTAL COSTS of production.

Economists define the LONG RUN in production as being the time period over which there are no fixed costs. In the long run, it is possible to replace electricity power stations, change the National Grid, alter the size of the workforce, etc. The SHORT RUN is the time period when at least one cost is fixed. In the electricity industry, a year would certainly be in the short-run period, because the number of power stations and other installations is unlikely to change significantly over that time.

Total, Average and Marginal Costs

TOTAL COST is the cost of producing all output over a period of time. AVERAGE COST is the cost per unit of production. For instance, the total cost of constructing ten nuclear power stations might be £15 billion. The average cost of each station is £1.5 billion (£15 billion ÷ 10). Average cost can be calculated using the formula:

$$\text{Average cost} = \frac{\text{Total cost}}{\text{Quantity produced}}$$

The MARGINAL COST of production is the cost of producing an additional unit. For instance, if the total cost of producing nine power stations was £14 billion and the cost of producing ten power stations was £15 billion, then the cost of producing the *marginal* unit (i.e. the tenth power station) would be £1 billion. Marginal cost can be calculated by subtracting total costs. For example:

Marginal cost of the 10th
power station =
Total cost of 10 stations
− Total cost of 9 stations.

KEY TERMS

FIXED or OVERHEAD COSTS – the costs of production that do not vary with output.

VARIABLE COSTS – the costs of production that vary directly with output.

TOTAL COST – the cost of producing all output. It is equal to total fixed costs plus total variable costs.

AVERAGE COST – the cost per unit of output. It is equal to total cost divided by total output.

MARGINAL COST – the cost of producing an additional unit of output.

LONG RUN – the period of time over which all costs are variable.

SHORT RUN – the period of time over which some costs are fixed and some costs are variable.

Costs (2)

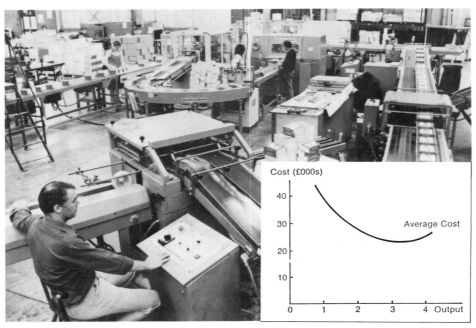

In book printing considerable economies of scale can be made.

Average Cost

If you bought one car battery, you might pay £30 for it. If a car manufacturing company bought 10 000 car batteries, it might well expect to pay considerably less for each battery. This is because buying in bulk should be considerably cheaper than buying individual items. This illustrates just one reason why companies normally find that the more they produce, the cheaper the cost per unit – that is, the lower the average cost.

Figure 32.1

1	2	3	4
Number produced	Average cost (long run) (£000)	Total cost (long run) (£000)	Marginal cost (£000)
0	—	10	—
1	22	22	12
2	14	28	6
3	11	33	5
4	11	44	11
5	14	70	26

It can be seen in Figure 32.1 that as production increases from 1 to 3 units, the average cost (shown in column 2) declines from £22 000 to £11 000. ECONOMIES OF SCALE are said to exist here. A firm experiences economies of scale when its long-run average cost declines as the scale of production increases. Between 4 and 5 units, however, average costs start to increase. Economists say that DISECONOMIES OF SCALE exist at this higher level of output.

The total cost of production can be calculated by multiplying average cost by the number produced. (For example, imagine that you buy 5 apples at an average cost of 10p each. Then the total cost to you would be 50p; that is 5 × 10p.) Total cost increases as production increases, but the increase is not uniform. For instance, it costs £22 000 to produce one unit, but only £28 000 to produce

STUDY POINTS

1 Copy out the graph above carefully.

2 ECONOMIES OF SCALE exist where the long-run average cost of production is falling. Mark on the graph between what levels of output there are economies of scale.

3 DISECONOMIES OF SCALE exist where the long-run average cost of production is rising. Mark on the graph the levels of output where diseconomies of scale exist.

4 The OPTIMAL POINT OF PRODUCTION is the level of production at which average cost is lowest. Mark this point on the graph.

5 The total cost of production can be calculated by multiplying the average cost of production by the total quantity produced. So if 10 were produced at an average cost of £5, then the total cost of production would be £50. Copy the box below. Calculate the total cost of production at output levels between 1 and 4 and record your answers in the box.

Output	1	2	3	4
Total Cost (£000s)				

6 On a new graph, draw a total cost curve, putting 'cost' on the vertical (y) axis and 'output' on the horizontal (x) axis.

7 The *marginal cost* of production is the cost of producing an additional unit of output. Copy the box below. Calculate the marginal cost of the production of the 1st unit, the 2nd unit, the 3rd unit and the 4th unit and record your answers in the box.

Output	1	2	3	4
Marginal Cost (£000s)				

8 Plot the marginal cost curve on the same graph as the average cost curve drawn in Question 1. Plot the marginal cost half way between each level of output, e.g. plot the marginal cost of the first unit at output level ½, the marginal cost of the second unit of output level 1½ and so on.

9 What is the average cost of producing 3½ units?

10 Estimate the average cost of producing 5 units.

11 A manufacturer faces the costs drawn in the above graphs. He is offered a contract to manufacture a fifth unit of production for £40 000. Should he accept the contract and why?

two units. This reflects the economies and diseconomies of scale that may exist.

The marginal cost of production is the cost of producing an additional unit. So the cost of producing the second unit is £6000, the third unit £5000, the fourth unit £11 000. It is calculated by subtracting the relevant total cost figures. For instance, the marginal cost of producing five units (i.e. the cost of the fifth unit) is the difference in the total cost of producing five units and the total cost of producing four units. Notice that the marginal cost at first declines, but then increases as output increases.

A Graphic Presentation

Costs are often shown by means of graphs. Figure 32.2 plots the costs shown in Figure 32.1. Notice the shape of the long run average cost curve. It is downward sloping to start with, reflecting the economies of scale present, and then it moves upwards as diseconomies of scale set in. Notice, too, that marginal costs start to increase, even though average costs are still falling. Average cost will continue to decline so long as marginal cost is below average cost. This is because if the cost of producing an extra unit of output is below the average cost of existing production, then producing that extra unit will lower the average cost. For example, if it costs £100 to produce 4 tonnes of apples, then the average cost is £25 per tonne. If it costs £20 to produce an extra tonne, then total cost would rise to £120 for 5 tonnes and average cost would go down to £24 per tonne. If average cost is rising, then this can only be because the cost of producing the last unit (i.e. the marginal cost) was above the average cost. Hence, the marginal cost curve must always pass through the lowest point of the average cost curve.

Optimum Production

The **OPTIMUM PRODUCTION** of a company is defined as the level of production where average cost is at a minimum – that is, the optimum level is at the lowest point on the average cost curve. It is the 'optimum' point, because it is the most efficient level of production in terms of combining scarce factors of production to produce a given quantity of output.

Figure 32.3

Output	Total cost (£m)	Average cost (£m)	Marginal cost (£m)
0	5.00		
1	6.75		
2	7.80		
3		2.90	
4		2.50	
5		2.40	
6	15.00		
7			4.25

Figure 32.4

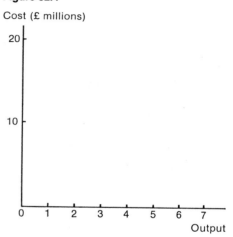

Cost (£ millions)

2 Explain, using numerical examples, the relationship between total, average and marginal costs.

Cost (£000s)

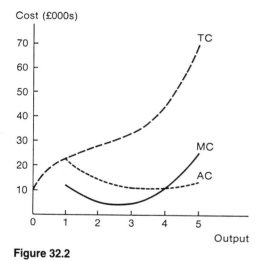

Figure 32.2

K E Y   T E R M S

ECONOMIES OF SCALE – reductions in long-run average costs as the scale of production increases.

DISECONOMIES OF SCALE – increases in long-run average costs as the scale of production increases.

OPTIMUM PRODUCTION – the level of production where average cost is at a minimum.

Data Response Questions
Units 28–32

Unit 28 Rent, Interest and Profit

It's Mac The Nice!

BUILDER John McCarthy is a happy man.

He is making a fortune selling sheltered housing to the elderly.

His homes come with a live-in warden, security systems and an alarm to summon help in an emergency.

In the first six months of this year profits of his firm, McCarthy and Stone boomed by one third to £4 million and John 46, reckons he will show record yield for the full year.

Since McCarthy and Stone started building sheltered houses in 1977 they've provided homes for 3,500 people, whose average age is 74.

John has 57 sites around the country with work starting on another 47 and he has plans to build sheltered homes in Jersey as well as expanding into France, Germany, Holland and Belgium.

How does he decide where to build?

"I just visit a town and count grey hairs," he says.

John is also building a nursing home at Bexhill-on-Sea and wants to start a package tour company for pensioners.

Source: *Daily Mirror*, 21 May 1985

1 What does McCarthy and Stone produce?　　(*1 mark*)

2 (a) What factors of production would the company be likely to use?
   (b) What rewards would be given to those factors?　　(*5 marks*)

3 To what extent could John McCarthy be called an 'entrepreneur'?　　(*4 marks*)

Unit 29 Economic Rent, Costs and Profits

Average house prices in second quarter 1985

Area	Detached house (£)
Greater London	82 830
Outer South East	58 080
East Anglia	46 370
North	39 560

Source: Nationwide Building Society: *House Prices in Second Quarter 1985*

1 Compare house prices in England.　　(*2 marks*)

2 Explain why house prices might vary between regions.　　(*4 marks*)

3 (a) What is 'economic rent'?
   (b) How and why does the economic rent on houses vary between regions?　　(*4 marks*)

Unit 30 Factor Mobility

Skilled jobs galore – but too far away

Jobs for skilled craftsmen are going unfilled in the south because Northerners and Midlanders are reluctant to move, it has been claimed.

Mr Alan Aspinall of the Engineering Industry Training Board, said that some engineering companies in the south were desperate to fill skilled jobs paying up to £15,000 a year.

As well as a need for high technology technicians there was also a need for more traditional craftsmen such as toolmakers, gaugemakers and precision engineers.

Mr Aspinall felt that due to family and housing commitments craftsmen in the north were not easily moved.

The differential in pay between skilled and less skilled work had narrowed in recent years and this also contributed to the situation.

"A craftsman in the north might have to face moving home to find similar work elsewhere or finding alternative work as a milkman, porter or whatever. The differential in pay may be so narrow that he chooses to change professions."

Mr Aspinall, speaking on Radio Two, said that the difference in house prices — which could be 100 per cent more in the south than in depressed areas of the north — was another factor.

Source: *Express and Star*, 20 June 1985

1 What did Mr Aspinall say was true of engineering jobs in the south of England?　　(*1 mark*)

2 Explain carefully *three* reasons why labour was claimed to be immobile in the passage.　　(*6 marks*)

3 What are the costs:
   (a) to the worker
   (b) to firms
   (c) to the economy as a whole
   of the lack of labour mobility from the North to the South of England?　　(*8 marks*)

Unit 31 Costs (1)

James Meade puts his shirt on mail order

WHEN 35 year-old James Meade left the Coldstream Guards, he decided he wanted to set up in business himself. A year at the London Business School convinced him that mail order was one business he could enter at low cost.

He saw a gap in the shirts market. Made-to-measure shirts start at £40 in the small number of up-market tailors' shops in London. Much of that represents the high cost of rent and rates in the most select areas of the Capital. He argued that they would not be able to cut prices to meet mail order competition from a supplier located in one of London's cheapest areas.

Meade's made-to-measure shirts start in price at £23.50, about half of which represents the cost of buying the shirt from the four shirt manufacturers he buys from. The other half pays for the rent and rates on his premises in Brixton, the advertising in the national press and up-market glossies like 'Harpers and Queen' and 'Country Life', interest on bank loans, postage and packing, V.A.T., wages and sundry expenses.

Source: Financial Times, 7 May 1985

1 Explain the nature of James Meade's business. *(2 marks)*

2 How was he able to attract customers to his business? *(2 marks)*

3 Which of his costs are fixed costs and which are variable costs over a time period of a month? *(4 marks)*

4 What would be the marginal cost to the company of selling an extra shirt? *(1 mark)*

5 If the average cost of selling a shirt is £30 and the company sells 15 000 shirts, what will be the total cost? *(1 mark)*

Essay Questions
Units 28–32

1 Wayne Headly is a 25-year old unemployed, unskilled, general labourer in the building trade who lives in a council house in Liverpool with his wife and two small children.
 (a) Give *four* reasons why he is likely to find it difficult to get a skilled bricklayer's job in London. *(8 marks)*
 (b) Suggest *two* ways in which the Government could help Wayne get this job in London. *(4 marks)*
 (c) Wayne is 'discovered' by a pop manager and starts to earn £200,000 from singing. Explain what is meant by 'economic rent' and illustrate how much economic rent Wayne is now earning. *(8 marks)*
2 Jenny Price runs a shoe repair shop in the centre of town.
 (a) What costs is she likely to face in running her business? *(8 marks)*
 (b) Explain the difference between fixed and variable costs. Which of Jenny's costs are fixed and which are variable? *(6 marks)*
 (c) Why is Jenny likely to be able to experience economies of scale? *(6 marks)*

Unit 32 Costs (2)

A company buys a £6000 car for one of its salesmen. Its costs are as follows:

CAR COSTS
Engine capacity 1001–1500 cc

Standing Charges per annum (£)	
Car Licence	100·00
Comprehensive Insurance	277·40
Depreciation form new	745·79
Interest on Capital*	522·05
Garage/Parking	156·00
Subscription — Motoring Organisation	36·50
	1,837·74

Cost per mile (in pence)	
5,000	36·754
10,000	18·377

Running Cost per mile (in pence)	
Petrol	5·465
Oil	0·336
Tyres	0·573
Servicing	0·665
Repairs and Replacements	4·226
Pence	11·265

TOTAL COST	
10,000 miles	£2,964

* Interest on Capital—New Car Value if invested at 8·75% per annum. This element must be adjusted in the case of secondhand vehicle according to the prices paid.
Source: AA.

Source: Daily Express, 17 April 1985

1 Name one fixed cost and one variable cost of running a car over a one year period. *(2 marks)*

2 What are the total fixed costs of the car over a year? *(1 mark)*

3 What is the average fixed cost per mile if the car travels:
 (a) 5000 miles;
 (b) 10 000 miles and
 (c) 20 000 miles a year? *(2 marks)*

4 What is the average variable cost per mile of the car? *(1 mark)*

5 What would be the total variable cost if the car travelled:
 (a) 10 000 miles and
 (b) 20 000 miles? *(1 mark)*

6 What would be the likely marginal cost of travelling one extra mile? *(1 mark)*

7 Calculate the total cost of travelling (a) 5000 miles and (b) 20 000 miles a year. *(2 marks)*

8 Calculate the average cost per mile of travelling:
 (a) 5000 miles;
 (b) 10 000 miles and
 (c) 20 000 miles a year
 and plot the average cost curve on a graph. *(6 marks)*

9 Explain why the average cost falls as mileage increases. *(4 marks)*

Economies of Scale

Steve Plimmer is a chef who owns a restaurant in Wolverhampton. He has been working on his own for a year now and is worried about the financial security of his business. The restaurant is open for 52 weeks a year for 6 days a week. Custom varies from month to month but on average he serves 50 customers per day. Customers spend on average £5 per head.

At current prices, food costs account for half the price of a meal. So, a £5 meal would cost Steve £2.50 in food. In addition, he pays himself an annual salary of £8000. His wife and two part time employees act as waitresses and are paid a total of £11 000 per year. Other overheads include paying off the bank loan on the property, rates, electricity and crockery. These amount to £20 000 per year. On a

daily basis, this means that Steve is faced with these costs:

Food (50 meals)	£125.00
Wages	£ 60.90
Overheads	£ 64.10
Total	£250.00

Steve's restaurant is big enough to seat a maximum of 60 people at any one time.

S T U D Y   P O I N T S

Assume in questions 1 to 7 that the price of a meal per customer averages £5.

1 How much on average does it cost to serve a meal?

2 Which costs are fixed costs and which are variable costs?

3 How much profit does Steve make per day?

4 Custom falls to 40 customers a day.
   (a) What are the total costs facing Steve on the average day?
   (b) How much on average will it cost to serve a meal?
   (c) How much profit will Steve now be making?

5 If Steve could raise the level of custom to 70 customers a day, he would not have to take on any extra staff, nor pay any extra overheads. What's more, he could save 10% on his food bill by buying in bulk.

   (a) What would be his daily cost if he served 70 customers?
   (b) What would be the average cost per customer of providing a meal?
   (c) What would Steve's profit now be?

6 Steve could serve a maximum of 200 customers a day. To do this, he would have to take on extra staff, whose cost per day would work out at £50. He could also buy food in bulk and get a 20% reduction in cost compared to the figures for 50 meals a day.
   (a) What would be his daily cost?
   (b) What would be the average cost per customer?
   (c) What would Steve's profit now be?

7 Explain why the cost per meal declines as more meals are served per day.

8 How could Steve increase the number of meals served per day? Would these measures lead to greater profit?

In Unit 32, economies of scale were said to exist where the average long run cost of production declines as the scale of production increases. Diseconomies of scale exist where the long run average cost of production rises as the scale of production increases. Why is it that this occurs? There are two types of economies of scale: internal and external.

Internal Economies of Scale

INTERNAL ECONOMIES result from the growth in production of the firm itself. Consider the figures in Figure 33.1. Note that costs are expressed here not in pounds, but in an index. (Index numbers were explained in Unit 5.)

Figure 33.1

Annual production of diesel engines	Index of costs
1 000	120
5 000	100
50 000	80
100 000	70
200 000	65

Source: G. Rhys, Heavy commercial vehicles: a decade of change. *National Westminster Bank Quarterly Review* (August 1984)

The figures show that it costs nearly twice as much per diesel engine if only 1000 engines are produced a year then if 200000 are produced a year. There are a number of reasons for this:

- *Technical economies* arise because greater production allows the use of more efficient methods of production or more efficient machines. In the case of diesel engines, a firm producing 200 000 engines a year will be able to make far more use of the division of labour and buy more specialised machines than a firm that only makes 1000 engines a year.

- *Marketing economies* arise because a large manufacturer can buy in bulk and can therefore get lower prices than the small manufacturer. The cost of selling is also lower, because advertising costs can be spread over a larger number of units sold and specialist salesmen can be employed.

- *Financial economies* arise because a small firm making engines is likely to have to pay higher interest rates on loans. The small firm is also likely to find it more difficult to raise money through selling new shares than a larger diesel engine firm would.

- *Administrative or managerial economies* arise because a large manufacturer can employ specialist staff to manage and supervise production, thus cutting managerial costs per unit. Specialist administrative equipment, like computers, can also be used profitably in large firms.

- *Risk-bearing economies* arise when a large firm sells in more markets and has a wider product range than a smaller company. A larger diesel engine manufacturer may sell in several countries rather than just one and may sell a much wider range of engines than a small manufacturer. This helps spread risks so that if one market does badly (e.g. small diesel engines in the UK), the company has other markets to sell into.

Internal diseconomies of scale arise mainly through problems of management. As a firm grows, management finds it more difficult to organise production efficiently. It is much easier to lose control of costs in a large organisation than in a small organisation. Relations with workers, too, can be worse because there may be little contact between management and workers.

External Economies of Scale

EXTERNAL ECONOMIES arise from the size of the industry rather than the firm. As the industry grows in size and there are more firms in the industry, firms in the industry enjoy lower costs for several reasons.

- Labour costs may be reduced. Firms will be able to draw on a pool of skilled labour, trained by firms and government, thus reducing their own training and living costs.

- The necessary infrastructure is more likely to be present. Roads, gas supplies, etc. are more likely to be laid on, if the industry is large rather than small. This helps reduce costs for individual firms.

- Suppliers for the industry will emerge – specialist firms that make or service machinery, or supply components. Because they specialise, these firms are able to produce goods and services far more cheaply than if the main company attempted to produce them on its own.

CHECKPOINTS

1 Explain the difference between internal and external economies of scale.

2 What type of internal economy of scale would each of the following be? Average cost decreases as production rises, because the firm is now able:
   (a) to employ a specialist accountant;
   (b) to buy a specialist machine;
   (c) to sell overseas as well as in the UK;
   (d) to obtain cheaper bank loans;
   (e) to get a larger discount on components that it buys in.

3 Describe the internal economies of scale that a large chain of supermarkets is likely to experience.

4 Explain why diseconomies of scale arise.

COURSEWORK SUGGESTION

Identify the major industry in your local area using either *Regional Trends* (published by HMSO), or data published by your local council. List the firms in that industry that are located in your area and describe those firms. Identify their markets and their sources of supply. Analyse the external economies of scale which they enjoy. Try to assess the extent of the competitive advantage that this gives to these firms in their markets.

KEY TERMS

INTERNAL ECONOMIES – economies of scale that arise due to the growth of a firm.

EXTERNAL ECONOMIES – economies of scale for a firm that arise due to the growth of the industry in which the firm operates.

Profits and Revenue

EUROPEAN FERRIES GROUP PLC.

Group Profit and Loss Account for the year ended 31st December

	1984 £m	1983 £m
Turnover	309.4	322.9
Less net operating charges and exceptional items	264.7	277.5
Profit before taxation	44.7	45.4
Less Tax on profit	9.3	10.4
	35.4	35.0
Less Dividends paid to shareholders, majority interests, extraordinary items and employee profit share	5.3	11.9
Retained profit for year	30.1	23.1

Source: European Ferries Group PLC, Report and Accounts 1984

'Paint manufacturers suffered a severe squeeze in profits last year. Raw material costs grew by about 23 per cent in 1984, while average selling prices for paint rose by only 3 per cent.' (*Source: Financial Times*, 20 March 1985)

Companies need to make profits, if they are to survive in the long term. Firms in the paint manufacturing industry will not have been happy to see PROFITS declining. Profit is the difference between TOTAL REVENUE and *total costs*. Total revenue is the total receipts of a company – in this case, receipts from the sale of paints. So total profit is the difference in the money received by the paint company and the money it has to pay out to produce paint. If the total revenue is less than total costs, the firm would make a *loss*.

The Importance of Profits

The profit that a company makes is used in three ways.

- Part is kept by the company and used for investment. The company may buy new machinery or re-equip a building. If profits are low, a company may well decide to cut back on investment plans.

- Part is paid to the government in taxes.

- Part is paid out as dividends to the shareholders of the company. The *dividend* is the reward to the owners for having allowed the company to use their money or assets and for the risk which that involves.

Profits act as an indicator. If profits are low, as in the paint industry in 1984, then firms in the industry and firms outside will be discouraged from investing in the industry. They will prefer to invest in industries where profits are higher. High profits would attract new investment to the paint industry. More investment would lead to greater output, and probably a fall in paint prices and therefore profits.

STUDY POINTS

1 What was the value of total revenue (i.e. total receipts from sales of tickets etc.) in 1984 for European Ferries?

2 What were the total costs of providing services to the public in 1983?

3 Profit is the difference between total revenue and total costs. Explain why profit before tax fell in 1984 compared to 1983.

4 What does European Ferries PLC do with the profits it makes each year?

5 Why did the amount paid in tax by European Ferries decline between 1983 and 1984?

6 Why did the company pay money to its shareholders in 1983 and 1984?

7 For what do you think the company might use the profit it doesn't pay out to shareholders? (This is its 'retained profit'.)

8 If European Ferries PLC started to make losses, explain:
  (a) why the company would find it difficult to make as large investments in new ships etc. as before;
  (b) why the company would find it difficult to persuade shareholders to buy new shares in the company.

9 How can profits and losses alter the allocation of resources in the economy over a period of time?

Profits would then return to 'normal' levels. So profit acts as an indicator of where to invest.

Profits can also act as an indicator of consumer exploitation. If existing firms can prevent new firms from investing in their industry, they may well be able to keep prices artificially high. Higher prices mean that the company makes bigger profits. Consumers are therefore being *exploited* – being forced to pay more than they might. This will be further discussed in Unit 37.

Revenue

Just as there are different types of costs, so there are different revenues.

- TOTAL REVENUE is total receipts from the sale of all products.

- AVERAGE REVENUE is the revenue received per unit sold. It is the average price received for the product. It can be calculated by dividing total revenue by the quantity sold. If a paint manufacturer sold 1 million cans of paint and received £5 million on the sale, then total revenue would be £5 million and average revenue, or average price per can of paint, would be £5 (£5 million ÷ 1 million).

- MARGINAL REVENUE is the revenue gained by selling an extra unit of production. If a paint manufacturer could sell 1 million cans for £5 million, but could sell 2 million cans for £9 million, then the marginal revenue (i.e. the additional revenue gained from the sale of the second million) would be £4 million.

As sales increase, total revenue should obviously increase too: the more that is sold, the more revenue

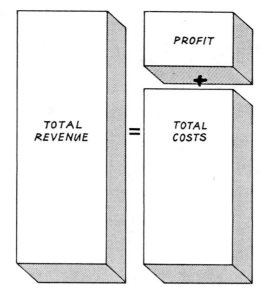

that is gained. But it may well be the case that average revenue would decline as sales increase. This is because a manufacturer may have to give bigger discounts or drop prices to sell more of a product.

CHECKPOINTS

1 Define 'profit'.

2 Calculate the profit earned by a company:
  (a) if revenue were £10 000 and costs were £8000;
  (b) if costs were £2 million and revenue were £2.5 million;
  (c) if revenue were £40 million and costs were £38 000;
  (d) if revenue were £800 million and costs were £900 million.

3 Why would rising costs and falling prices squeeze profits for a company?

4 What would a paint manufacturing company do with its profits?

5 If profits in the paint manufacturing industry are high in comparison with other industries, what might this indicate?

6 Complete Figure 34.1 and then plot total, average and marginal revenue curves on the graph.

Note: Plot the marginal revenue figures half way between the sales figures. For instance, marginal revenue of £12 should be plotted at ½ on the sales axis, £10 at 1½ and so on.

Figure 34.1

Quantity sold	Total revenue (£ m)	Average revenue (£ m)	Marginal revenue (£ m)
0	0	0	—
			12
1	12		
			10
2		11	
			8
3		10	
			6
4			
			4
5			
			2
6	42		

COURSEWORK SUGGESTION

Find out figures for the relative profitability of different sectors of British industry (for instance, those given in the *Bank of England Quarterly Bulletin* for September 1984) over a period of time. Examine how the output of these industries has changed over the same period (using data, say from the *Annual Abstract of Statistics* published by HMSO). Analyse the extent to which profitability is linked to changes in output. Try to explain why profits might act as an indicator of how resources should be allocated in the economy. Decide which industries are the growth industries of the future.

KEY TERMS

PROFITS – total revenue minus total costs.

TOTAL REVENUE – total receipts of a company from the sale of production.

AVERAGE REVENUE – average price received per item sold, i.e. the average price received per sale.

MARGINAL REVENUE – the revenue gained from the sale of an extra unit of output.

The Aims of Firms

CRISTARSIN

This drug should provide a complete cure for 'Hymertarsinonosis', the eye disease which afflicts an estimated 20 million people in the developing world and, if left untreated, usually blinds the sufferer within five years of contracting the disease. Preliminary tests strongly indicate that the drug will be marketable.

Key financial statistics are:

Development costs so far	£25 million
Estimated remaining development costs	£10 million
Estimated sales	£53 million per annum for 15 years
Estimated cost of manufacture and marketing	£50 million per annum
Employment – 100 jobs at our Calcutta plant in India	

MOSTARNOL

This drug has been developed to treat a certain type of cancer. An estimated 100 000 people in industrial countries suffer from this disease which causes pain and in severe cases leads to loss of mobility. Preliminary tests indicate that the drug has a 50–70% chance of reaching the stage where it can be put on general sale. Key financial statistics are:

Development costs so far	£35 million
Estimated remaining development costs	£20 million
Estimated sales	£30 million per annum for 15 years
Estimated cost of manufacture and marketing	£20 million per annum
Employment – 30 jobs at our Dundee plant in Scotland	

SOLITOR

This drug should provide a cure for 'Tomirotosis', a disease which attacks the bone structure and in severe cases leads to death. An estimated 20 000 people suffer from the disease in our first world markets. Preliminary tests indicate that there is an 80–90% chance that the drug will reach the final marketing stage. Key financial statistics are:

Development costs so far	£15 million
Estimated remaining development costs	£15 million
Estimated sales	£20 million per annum for 15 years
Estimated cost of manufacture and marketing	£10 million per annum
Employment – 20 jobs at our London plant	

STUDY POINTS

This can either be done on your own in written form or with a small group as a discussion exercise. The company will only develop one of these three products. Your task is to decide which it should be.

1 What are the costs and benefits of each drug (a) to the company and (b) to society?

2 How much profit will each drug yield (a) to the company and (b) to society?

3 What should be the commercial aims of a company manufacturing drugs?

4 Which one of these drugs would you develop and why?

Profit Maximisation

When a household spends money, it aims to get best value for money. That means that it attempts to maximise the 'utility' or satisfaction from consuming the goods and services purchased. What, then, does a firm aim to do? What are its aims?

To answer this question, we need to know who controls firms and what motivates these decision-makers. The traditional answer is that:

- firms are controlled by their owners, the SHAREHOLDERS of the company;

- the shareholders are only interested in making the most money out of the firm. They make money either by receiving a share of the profits – the *dividend* – or by seeing the firm grow in value and therefore seeing the value of their shareholding grow. Growth in size normally means extra investment, much of which will be paid for out of profits made by the company;

- therefore the company, controlled by the shareholders, will attempt to MAXIMISE PROFITS.

To see what this might mean in practice, consider a firm that produces highly toxic (i.e. dangerous and poisonous) chemicals as a result of its main manufacturing operations. It has to dispose of the chemicals and can do that in two ways. It can either build a recycling plant, which will make the chemicals safe. Or it can buy a ship and dump the chemicals into the sea. The profit-maximising firms will choose the least costly of these options – where the cost is the COST TO THE FIRM. By minimising its costs of disposal, the firm will make the most profit. Therefore if the cost of recycling were £20 million a year, whereas the cost of dumping at sea were £1 million, then the company would choose to dump the chemicals at sea. Note that this might not be the most cost-effective way of disposing of the chemicals from society's point of view. It might be extremely dangerous from an environmental viewpoint to dump highly toxic chemicals at sea. If, as a result of the dumping, £40 million worth of damage is done to the environment, then what was most profitable from the company's viewpoint is highly costly from the viewpoint of society and should be stopped.

Other Aims

Profit maximisation may not, however, be the aim of all firms. For instance, in larger firms, the shareholders are different from the managers and directors of the firm. The managers and directors (i.e. the workers who run the firm) may be far more interested in their own rewards than in the rewards of the shareholders. Directors and managers may be far more interested in receiving big salaries, large company cars and spending time eating expense-paid lunches, than in earning maximum profits for the shareholders. Of course they have to make some profit, otherwise they might lose their jobs. But making enough profit to keep shareholders happy, PROFIT SATISFICING, can be very different from making maximum profits, PROFIT MAXIMISING.

In other companies, those companies owned by the government, there may be other aims. The government may want its firms to make profits, but it may also want them to keep prices down to help keep down inflation. Or it may want to keep unprofitable factories or works open so that workers do not lose their jobs. Keeping prices down, or unprofitable works open, means less profits over all.

CHECKPOINTS

1 What is meant by 'profit maximisation'? Why might a firm aim to maximise profits?

2 A firm could invest in one of the projects in Figure 35.1, all of which involve the same initial investment of £1 million. Which of these should the firm undertake and why?

Figure 35.1

Project	Estimated profit per year	Estimated number of jobs created (+) or lost (−)	Estimated value of exports
	(£)		(£)
A	150 000	+ 600	1 000 000
B	120 000	+ 500	1 200 000
C	160 000	− 100	800 000

3 A firm increases its profits from £30 million to £60 million within a year. Which of the following do you think will make a profit and why:
(a) shareholders;
(b) workers;
(c) consumers;
(d) taxpayers?

4 Explain why the fact that the owners of large companies rarely manage them might lead to profit satisficing rather than profit maximising.

5 Why might firms owned by the government not be profit maximisers?

COURSEWORK SUGGESTION

Arrange to visit three companies, preferably of different sizes. You will need to interview a manager who is well acquainted with the overall policy of the company and its finances. Prepare a questionnaire beforehand that asks questions relating to the goals of the firm and the extent to which the company fulfils these goals. After the interviews, prepare a report on your findings. (This should include a copy of the questionnaire, a description of the responses, an analysis of what the questionnaire revealed about the goals of the three firms, and an evaluation of company performance based upon those goals.)

KEY TERMS

PROFIT MAXIMISATION – making the largest profit possible over a period of time.

SHAREHOLDERS – the owners of a company, of whom each owns a part or share of that company.

PROFIT SATISFICING – making enough profit to satisfy the owners of a company.

Competition

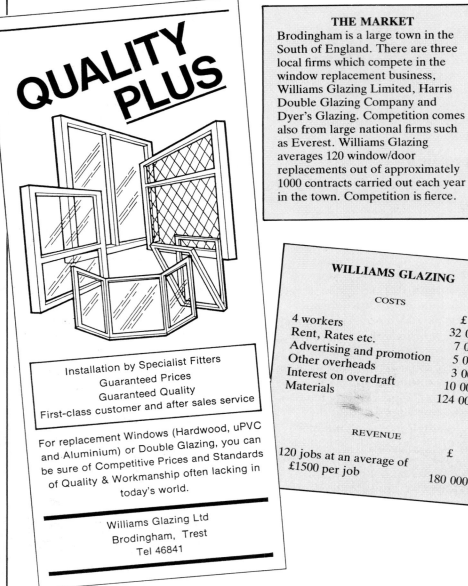

QUALITY PLUS

Installation by Specialist Fitters
Guaranteed Prices
Guaranteed Quality
First-class customer and after sales service

For replacement Windows (Hardwood, uPVC and Aluminium) or Double Glazing, you can be sure of Competitive Prices and Standards of Quality & Workmanship often lacking in today's world.

Williams Glazing Ltd
Brodingham, Trest
Tel 46841

THE MARKET

Brodingham is a large town in the South of England. There are three local firms which compete in the window replacement business, Williams Glazing Limited, Harris Double Glazing Company and Dyer's Glazing. Competition comes also from large national firms such as Everest. Williams Glazing averages 120 window/door replacements out of approximately 1000 contracts carried out each year in the town. Competition is fierce.

WILLIAMS GLAZING

COSTS

	£
4 workers	32 000
Rent, Rates etc.	7 000
Advertising and promotion	5 000
Other overheads	3 000
Interest on overdraft	10 000
Materials	124 000

REVENUE

	£
120 jobs at an average of £1500 per job	180 000

S T U D Y   P O I N T S

For each of the following situations, prepare a short report explaining how and why Williams ought to react.

1 Dyer's Glazing, the smallest of the firms in the area, cut its prices by approximately 10% three months ago. There is no sign that it is going to raise prices again in the immediate future. Orders at Williams have fallen from about 10 a month to about 8 a month.

2 Harris Double Glazing Company has embarked on a large advertising campaign in the local press, on local radio and through the distribution of leaflets. Estimated cost of the campaign to date is £9000 – £4000 more than Williams annually spends. Orders at Williams have fallen from about 10 a month to 9 a month since the campaign started.

3 Everest, the national firm of glaziers, has just introduced a new 'wonder window' which, it is claimed, is 20% more effective at retaining heat than existing windows.

4 Harris Double Glazing Company buys Dyer's Glazing.

The Meaning of Competition

'Competition' and 'competitiveness' are words that are frequently heard on the lips of politicians today. COMPETITION is felt by many to lead to greater efficiency. Therefore, the more competition there is the better. But what does competition mean? Is it really true that greater competition leads to greater efficiency?

Competition is not something that has a precise meaning, because there are degrees of competition. At one extreme, there is PERFECT COMPETITION. In a perfectly competitive industry:

* there are a large number of small producers;

* all these firms produce an identical or HOMOGENEOUS product;

* new firms can set up in the industry and existing firms can sell up and leave the industry if they wish – there are no *barriers to entry or exit*;

* all firms are able to have access to the same information about techniques of production, likely developments in the industry, etc.

Very few industries are perfectly competitive. Probably the best example of such an industry is farming.

At the other extreme is *monopoly* – a market situation where just one firm produces all the output in the industry. Again, like perfect competition, there are very few examples of monopolies in the real world. In between are various types of IMPERFECT COMPETITION. Most industries fall into this category.

The Competitive Process

In a competitive industry, a firm is constantly fighting for its survival, which means successfully selling its products to consumers. The consumer buys those products that give best value for money – value for money means keenest prices, highest quality, latest technology, reliability, etc. If a firm produces goods that are more expensive or lower quality than its competitors, sales decline. Profits will go down too and the company could soon be making a loss. At this point, it will either have to make itself competitive or 'leave the industry' (i.e. stop producing). The successful firm will see its sales and profits climb. This will encourage it to invest, making it even more competitive. It will encourage other firms in the industry to improve their competitiveness to get their share of sales and profits. It will also attract new firms into the industry. This competition serves to keep prices and profits down to a level just high enough to prevent firms from switching their investment into more profitable industries. This level of profits is called **NORMAL PROFITS**.

Competition can take various forms. In a perfectly competitive industry, firms compete mainly on price. The firm with the lowest price gets the sales. In imperfect competition, since firms sell branded goods, they compete not only on price, but also by advertising and promoting their product and by trying to produce better products than their rivals.

Competition and Efficiency

Consider this extract:

'The home computer industry is starting a price war as fears grow that the market will fall sharply and competition from the US and Japan will become much

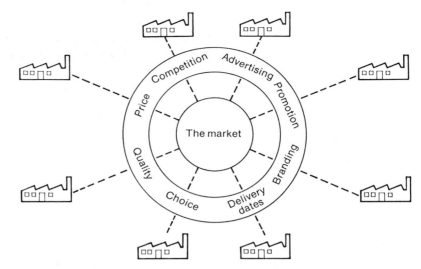

In a competitive market firms compete on price, quality of goods etc. for a share of the market.

tougher.' (*Source: Financial Times*, January 1985)

Economists would argue that competition in the home computer industry has led to efficiency because:

- prices to consumers are as low as possible (shown by talk of a price war);
- the consumer has a wide range of *choice* of products from US and Japanese firms as well as British firms;
- only those firms making the best-value-for-money products will survive.

However, as we shall see in the next unit, competition does not necessarily lead to the highest level of efficiency.

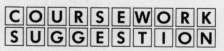

1 How do the following compete in their industries and persuade buyers to purchase their products:
   (a) a farmer selling potatoes;
   (b) a car manufacturer selling small cars;
   (c) a bank selling services?

2 Explain the difference between a perfectly competitive industry and a monopoly.

3 What are 'normal profits'?

4 Explain, giving examples, why competition in industry might benefit the consumer.

COURSEWORK SUGGESTION

Make a list of all the shops in your local area selling groceries. These might include local shops and large supermarkets outside the immediate area. Construct a questionnaire to find out which grocery shops local consumers use and why they use them (e.g. price, opening hours, nearness, range of products, quality of products, etc). Ask five local people to answer your questionnaire. Describe your findings. Analyse how local shops compete for custom. Decide which shops are the most successful at competing and try to explain why this is so.

KEY TERMS

COMPETITION – a process in which firms or the owners of factors of production offer products for sale in the same market to the same customers.

PERFECT COMPETITION – a situation where there is a large number of buyers and sellers in the market, the sellers offering identical products, and where there are no barriers to entry to or exit from the industry.

HOMOGENEOUS PRODUCT – a product where there are no brands and no differences between individual goods.

IMPERFECT COMPETITION – a situation where a few or a large number of sellers offer branded goods for sale, and where barriers to entry to the market may or may not exist.

NORMAL PROFIT – the level of profit needed to keep a firm from switching its resources into the production of other goods and services.

Monopoly

Strong Feelings about the Rules

IN THE UK, the principle of patents goes back for many centuries. A patent gives a person or a company the sole right to make and sell a new product which it has invented. Under current British law, companies which make drugs and medicines can patent new drugs for 20 years. After that, any company can copy the drug and produce it itself.

The big drug companies would like to see patent life increased, say to 25 years, as in the USA. They argue that this is essential if new drugs are to be found in the future.

They point out that the effective life of a patent has decreased over the past twenty years. This is because it now takes much longer to test a new drug and get it approved. Safety standards have become steadily more strict – which, in view of past disasters such as thalidomide, is a development which hardly anybody would quarrel with. A new chemical is patented very early on its development phase. As a result, one recent UK study claims, the average drug brought to the market in the early 1980's had in practice only five years of its patent life left. In 1960, the average was 13 years.

How long a company can sell the drug under patent is an important determinant of how profitable the drug will be. In the early years of sale, costs of advertising and promotion may well be so high as to cause the product to run at a loss. Only later will the company be able to make profits.

At the same time it is argued that whilst spending on research has gone up 9 times (in real terms) since 1960, the average number of new drugs reaching the market each year has fallen from 40 to under 20. Big profits on the drugs which do come to market are needed, it is argued, if the drug companies are to spend large sums of money on research and development on new drugs.

However, the small drug companies see matters in a different light from the big companies. The small companies make their profits by copying existing drugs and selling them at a cheaper price than the large companies. Whilst a drug is still under patent, they can't copy it. So the small drug companies would prefer to see patent lives reduced rather than extended.

Cheaper prices obviously benefit consumers in the short term. But cheaper prices could mean fewer new drugs. It could also mean that the big drug companies are making less profit out of an exploited consumer. Such conflicting ideas means that it is difficult for government to judge whether the big drug companies really do have a case for extending drug patent life.

Adapted from the *Financial Times*, 23 September 1985.

Ford, the motor car company, had refused to allow other companies to manufacture replacement panels for Ford cars. According to the Monopolies and Mergers Commission (the government watchdog which investigates monopolies), this led to:

- higher prices for consumers;
- less INNOVATION (other companies had started the manufacture of part panels to keep down the costs to motorists);
- higher profits for Ford.

Ford, here, was being accused of acting as a MONOPOLIST. A monopolist is a firm that is the only supplier of a product in the market. Ford, by refusing a licence to other manufacturers, was making sure that the only body panels that would fit Ford cars would be made by Ford itself.

Sources of Monopoly Power

A monopolist can prevent competition in the market by preventing new firms from entering the market. Economists say that a monopolist can put up BARRIERS TO ENTRY. A variety of barriers exist:

- *Legal barriers.* This was the source of Ford's monopoly. It had copyright for 15 years over the design of the panels and could legally stop other manufacturers from copying its body panels.

- *Cost barriers.* It may be far too expensive for another firm to set up in the industry. In the car industry, for instance, when it costs £500 million to develop just one car, it is difficult to see a new

STUDY POINTS

Patents give the holder of patent the sole right to make and sell a product. This means that the patent holder is a MONOPOLIST – i.e. is the only maker and seller of the product.

1 Who benefits from the fact that drug companies have a monopoly over a particular drug for the 20 year life of its patent?

2 Who loses out as a result of this 20 year monopoly?

3 The Government proposes to extend patent life from 20 years to 25 years. What would be the advantages of this (a) to drug companies and (b) to consumers? What would be the disadvantages? In your opinion would this change be in the best interests of society as a whole?

4 The Government proposes to abolish all patent rights with regard to drugs (i.e. the Government proposes to abolish the drug companies' monopoly over patented drugs.) What would be the possible economic effects of this? Would it be in the best interests of society?

mass-production car producer suddenly entering the market.

- *Economies of scale.* These may also be a barrier. Given that the larger the firm, the lower the costs of production are likely to be, then it is possible that just one firm may come to dominate the market. That one firm would be the *natural monopolist*, a term discussed in Unit 45. New entrants would not be able to compete on cost grounds with the natural monopolist.

- *Marketing barriers.* These are barriers such as advertising. A monopolist may develop a very strong brand image for its product so that consumers continue to buy the product, even though better products may appear on the market. (A brand is the name of a company's product, such as 'Persil', 'Mars Bar', or 'Montego'.) Or, a monopolist may make it prohibitively expensive, in terms of advertising costs, for a new firm to launch its product.

Monopoly and Efficiency

As we saw above, Ford was accused, as a monopolist, of pushing up prices, earning excess or ABNORMAL PROFIT, and restricting innovation. Consumers were denied a choice of whom to buy from. The Monopolies and Mergers Commission also accepted evidence that higher prices meant that some car owners preferred not to buy the body panels, but to scrap their cars instead. So higher prices led to lower output of replacement panels. All of these are standard criticisms of monopolies. They all add up to lower efficiency in the economy.

But there is some evidence that a lack of competition can lead to greater

efficiency. This would be the case:

- if economies of scale were very large. Economies of scale mean that as more is produced, so the average cost of producing each item goes down. So long as the saving in production costs is greater than the extra or abnormal profit the monopolist might charge, then monopoly will lead to lower prices for customers. For example, if a monopolist could produce an item at £10 less per item than if several firms were producing smaller quantities, but it charged an extra £6 profit per item, then the consumer would still be £4 better off with monopoly production than if there were competition in the industry.

- if being a monopolist encouraged the company to risk its money in research, investment and new products, in the knowledge that it could sell what it produced at a profit. Ford, for instance, argued that if it did not keep its monopoly on body panels, there would not be enough profit coming in to finance research and development on new products.

- if the high profits earned by a monopolist encouraged other firms to develop totally new products to break the monopoly. On a very small scale, the decision by independent manufacturers to offer part panels, instead of the whole panels initially available from Ford, was an example of innovation in the face of a monopolist.

Overall, it is unclear that competition does lead to greater efficiency than monopoly. It is true that consumers may end up with lower

prices and more choice in the short run. If monopoly encourages research, development, investment and innovation, however, then those short-term gains may be far less important than the long-term gains of higher economic growth resulting from an economy dominated by large monopoly firms.

KEY TERMS

MONOPOLY – a situation where there is only one seller of goods and services in a market.

BARRIERS TO ENTRY – factors that prevent firms entering a market to compete with existing firms.

ABNORMAL PROFIT – profit earned that is greater than the profit needed to keep a firm producing in a market.

INNOVATION – the development of new products or new techniques of making products.

Data Response Question
Units 33–37

Unit 33 Economies of Scale

BL may make more Hondas

The Government go-ahead to Austin Rover to develop its own cars and engines hinges on a new deal with the company's Japanese partner, Honda.

The plan is for Austin Rover to fill up space on its Longbridge and Cowley production lines by making Honda cars alongside its own models.

Details of a fresh agreement between the British and Japanese car companies are expected to be revealed later this week or early next week by Industry Secretary Norman Tebbit.

Final 'delicate' negotiations are taking place to work out which Honda models Austin Rover will manufacture.

The plan, to be presented to the House of Commons, is likely to push up production from around 440,000 to nearly 700,000 a year.

Austin Rover and Honda are already geared to produce in both countries Rover and Honda versions of Project XX, the executive car jointly developed by British and Japanese engineers.

The Longbridge factory recently recruited 400 extra workers following a deal to make Honda five-speed gearboxes under licence.

Source: *Express and Star*, 5 June 1985

1 Describe the nature of the 'deal' between Austin Rover and Honda cars. (*2 marks*)

2 Why is Austin Rover likely to experience lower costs as a result of the deal? (*3 marks*)

3 What economies of scale are likely to result? (*5 marks*)

Unit 34 Profits and Revenue

PIPER'S GO BANKRUPT

Piper's, the Midland steel manufacturing firm, has declared itself bankrupt. The company has not made a profit since 1984. A spokesman for the company blamed falling sales of British made cars for the 20% fall in total revenue last year. This, combined with increased costs, meant that Piper's lost any chance of being able to survive the current recession in the industry as a whole.

1 What do Piper's produce? (*1 mark*)

2 What difficulties has the company got itself into? (*4 marks*)

3 Assume you were the managing director of Midco, a firm in direct competition with Piper's in the steel industry. What would be your reaction to a request from a manager to increase the company's investment by 20% and why? (*5 marks*)

Essay Questions
Units 33–37

1 (a) What is meant by 'profit'? (*6 marks*)
  (b) What does a firm do with its profits? (*8 marks*)
  (c) How can profits allocate resources in an economy? (*6 marks*)

Unit 35 The Goals of Firms

Profits and the post

It's difficult for publicly-owned bodies to win with this Government. Show a loss and they have to put up their prices and cut their services; show a profit and Mrs. Olivia Twist Thatcher wants a higher one — whereupon they have to put up their prices and cut their services.

The Post Office is a prime example. Already making over ten million pounds a month profit, it has been ordered to become more viable. Viable in the Thatcher vocabulary, means make more money.

The result is a cost-slashing operation which will close over a thousand post offices — one in twenty — in the next three years. Already hundreds of urban post offices have shut down, producing in the communities affected that impotent, fuming resentment that is so much a product of Thatcherism.

A post office is really part of the social services. Which is what all the fuss is about. As post offices close, more old and infirm people wishing to collect their pensions, purchase a game licence or post a parcel are faced with a long trek to somebody else's high street.

Source: Daily Mirror, 11 February 1985

1 What type of business organisation is the Post Office? *(1 mark)*

2 What are (a) the costs and (b) the benefits of the plan to close over a thousand post offices on (i) consumers, (ii) taxpayers, (iii) workers? *(6 marks)*

3 Should the Post office aim to maximise its profits? Explain your answer carefully. *(5 marks)*

2 One supermarket chain opens a new branch in a shopping centre where another supermarket chain already has a store.
  (a) Suggest *five* ways in which these two shops might compete for custom. *(10 marks)*
  (b) The two supermarket chains merge to form the largest supermarket chain in Britain. As a result, one of the two stores in the shopping centre is closed. What might be (i) the benefits and (ii) the costs to the consumer of this happening? *(10 marks)*

Unit 36 Competition

Servis succumbs in a competitive market

SERVIS, BRITAIN'S third largest washing machine maker, has gone out of business.

At first sight, it might seem surprising that a company like Servis should have got into difficulty. Sales in the domestic appliance industry have grown steadily over the last three years and prospects for the future look good.

But the problem is that there are too many companies chasing after too little business. Many appliance manufacturers invested heavily in the 1970s. According to one UK producer, there is roughly 50% too much washing machine making capacity in Europe, and about 25% in the UK.

Inevitably price competition is extremely keen. Average selling prices are said to have risen by less than half the rate of inflation since 1979, meaning that companies have had to cut costs in order to survive. Servis, a small manufacturer, couldn't cut costs enough.

Adapted from the Financial Times, 7 March, 1985

1 What is the 'domestic appliance industry'? *(2 marks)*

2 Why did Servis go bankrupt? *(4 marks)*

3 Has competition in the industry led to greater efficiency? *(4 marks)*

Unit 37 Monopoly

BR plans overhaul of taxi provision

BRITISH RAIL is to change its policy on taxi services at more than 325 commuter stations. Up till now, British Rail has tended to give a single taxi company an exclusive franchise to serve a particular station.

At Brighton station, for instance, only taxis from Brighton Stream-line Taxi-Cab company are allowed to pick up passengers. Taxi companies then have to pay a "small sum" for the franchise.

However, a report from the government consumer watchdog, the Office of Fair Trading, has stated that British Rail has been operating in a manner "likely to restrict and distort competition" by granting these franchises.

BR's decision to drop the franchises will allow more taxi operators to compete for business at most stations and could mean more taxis available at peak hours.

Adapted from the Financial Times, November 1982 and February 1983

1 Explain what is meant by an 'exclusive franchise', and why British Rail operated such a franchise with regard to taxis. *(4 marks)*

2 Why did the franchise system 'restrict and distort competition'? *(3 marks)*

3 What advantages would the removal of the franchise have for consumers? *(3 marks)*

The Size of Firms

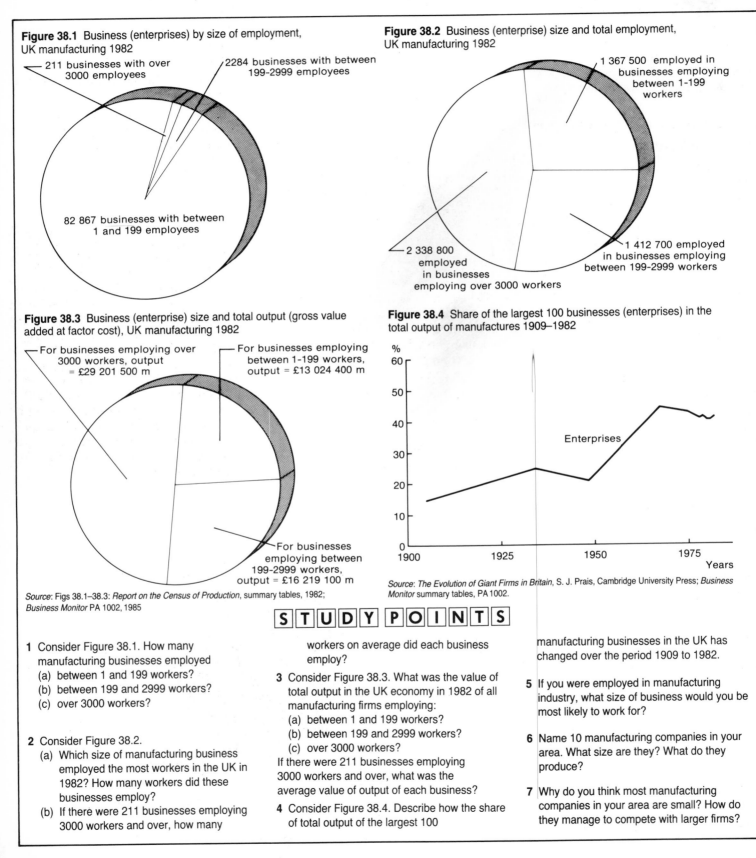

Figure 38.1 Business (enterprises) by size of employment, UK manufacturing 1982

211 businesses with over 3000 employees

2284 businesses with between 199-2999 employees

82 867 businesses with between 1 and 199 employees

Figure 38.2 Business (enterprise) size and total employment, UK manufacturing 1982

1 367 500 employed in businesses employing between 1-199 workers

2 338 800 employed in businesses employing over 3000 workers

1 412 700 employed in businesses employing between 199-2999 workers

Figure 38.3 Business (enterprise) size and total output (gross value added at factor cost), UK manufacturing 1982

For businesses employing over 3000 workers, output = £29 201 500 m

For businesses employing between 1-199 workers, output = £13 024 400 m

For businesses employing between 199-2999 workers, output = £16 219 100 m

Source: Figs 38.1–38.3: *Report on the Census of Production*, summary tables, 1982; *Business Monitor* PA 1002, 1985

Figure 38.4 Share of the largest 100 businesses (enterprises) in the total output of manufactures 1909–1982

Enterprises

Source: *The Evolution of Giant Firms in Britain*, S. J. Prais, Cambridge University Press; *Business Monitor* summary tables, PA 1002.

STUDY POINTS

1 Consider Figure 38.1. How many manufacturing businesses employed
   (a) between 1 and 199 workers?
   (b) between 199 and 2999 workers?
   (c) over 3000 workers?

2 Consider Figure 38.2.
   (a) Which size of manufacturing business employed the most workers in the UK in 1982? How many workers did these businesses employ?
   (b) If there were 211 businesses employing 3000 workers and over, how many

workers on average did each business employ?

3 Consider Figure 38.3. What was the value of total output in the UK economy in 1982 of all manufacturing firms employing:
   (a) between 1 and 199 workers?
   (b) between 199 and 2999 workers?
   (c) over 3000 workers?
If there were 211 businesses employing 3000 workers and over, what was the average value of output of each business?

4 Consider Figure 38.4. Describe how the share of total output of the largest 100

manufacturing businesses in the UK has changed over the period 1909 to 1982.

5 If you were employed in manufacturing industry, what size of business would you be most likely to work for?

6 Name 10 manufacturing companies in your area. What size are they? What do they produce?

7 Why do you think most manufacturing companies in your area are small? How do they manage to compete with larger firms?

Firms

Consider Figures 38.1–38.3. They show that nearly all firms in manufacturing industry are small, employing less than 200 workers. Yet these firms produce only a very small part of manufacturing output. 50% of all output is produced by just 211 firms. This unit considers why some firms are small and some are large.

Reasons for the Existence of Large Firms

Large firms enjoy many advantages over small firms. They may enjoy *economies of scale*. Lower costs may mean lower prices and increased competitiveness. Large firms may find it not only cheaper to obtain loans (a financial economy of scale), but also easier to obtain credit and new equity capital than smaller firms. Hence they find it much easier to expand than smaller firms. For these reasons, one would expect to see large firms growing at the expense of small firms. Large firms should be far more competitive than smaller firms and should therefore force smaller firms out of the market. This has happened to some extent. Figure 38.4 shows how the share of total output of the top 50 manufacturing companies has grown in the UK this century. But, as Figure 38.1 shows, there is no shortage of small firms, even if they are producing a smaller proportion of total output than, say, 50 years ago.

Reasons for the Existence of Small Firms

Small firms continue to exist for a number of reasons. First, there is a ready supply of entrepreneurs who want to work for themselves, who see a gap in the market and are prepared to risk their money and time in a venture.

Second, many markets are too small to accommodate large firms. Many markets are localised, perhaps because it is not possible to transport goods cheaply over long distances or because there are special tastes in the local market (e.g. local sausages). Where market demand is small, small firms tend to predominate.

Third, small firms may be more flexible than large firms. They may be willing to supply highly specialised products in small quantities to larger businesses. Large businesses like the speed, flexibility and cheapness of this and buy from small firms.

Fourth, small firms can often pay workers less than larger firms. Unions tend to be weak and there is a history of low pay in small businesses. This helps reduce costs and allows small business to compete.

Fifth, in some industries, optimum production (i.e. where the average cost of production is lowest) is achieved at very low levels of output. This is true of many personal services, such as hairdressing. Without the advantages of lower costs due to economies of scale, there is no reason for firms to grow and outcompete smaller firms.

Lastly, small firms in some industries have combined to share costs such as advertising, research and development. Examples of this are the Spar and Wavy Line chains of independent shops, which pool advertising and other services. Here small businesses can enjoy greater economies of scale than would otherwise be the case.

So small firms will continue to exist, but if past trends are anything to go by, they will produce less as a proportion of total output over time.

C·H·E·C·K·P·O·I·N·T·S

1 Using Figures 38.1–38.4, describe the importance of small firms in the economy.

2 Why might economies of scale give larger firms a competitive advantage over small firms?

3 Account for the continued existence of small firms.

4 Why are hairdressing firms and painting and decorating firms usually small, whereas car manufacturers and banks are usually large?

C·O·U·R·S·E·W·O·R·K
S·U·G·G·E·S·T·I·O·N

Arrange to interview the owners of two small firms in your local area. Devise a questionnaire prior to the interview which asks why these small firms are able to exist despite their small size. Also ask whether or not the firms are likely to expand in the future, and why they might want to do this. After the interviews, write up your findings and compare the position of the two firms in your survey. Try to assess the chances of survival and growth for these firms in the future.

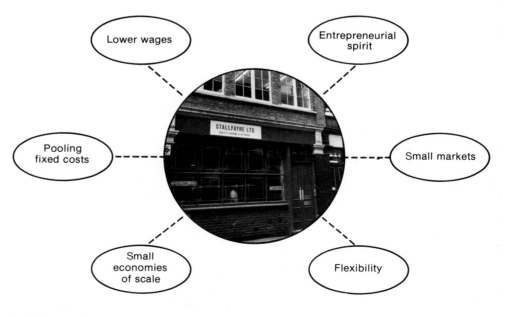

Small firms continue to survive for a variety of reasons.

The Growth of Firms

MAKER'S

Business Activity
A small oil company which also has some interests in forestry.

Recent History
Formed only ten years ago, this company had some lucky finds in the North Sea. It has recently started investing money in forestry.

Likely willingness to be taken over
A favourable response is expected from a good offer.

Recent financial statistics:	1984	1985	1986	1987
Turnover (£ millions)	30.6	35.4	37.4	42.2
Profits (£ millions)	0.2	0.22	0.24	0.26
Assets (£ millions)	4	4.1	4.2	4.3
Share Price (pence)	150	145	138	132
Number of shares issued (millions)	30	30	30	30

BAKER'S

Business Activity
Mainly a printing company with a small interest in paper making.

Recent History
Baker's has proved a solid, dependable, if somewhat unexciting company over its 50 year history. It has recently undertaken an ambitious investment programme designed to automate much of its production.

Likely willingness to be taken over
Initial soundings indicate that management and major shareholders would be receptive to a fair offer.

Recent financial statistics:	1984	1985	1986	1987
Turnover (£ millions)	5.2	5.6	6.3	7.0
Profits (£ millions)	0.1	0.1	0.2	0.22
Assets (£ millions)	1.0	1.1	1.3	1.6
Share Price (pence)	22	24	30	50
Number of shares issued (millions)	5	5	5	5

MILLINER'S

Business Activity
Mainly a book publishing firm but also owns a chain of 30 bookshops nationwide.

Recent History
Founded 153 years ago, this is a well established, old fashioned publishing company. Poor profitability prompted a major change in management three years ago.

Likely willingness to be taken over
Management likely to advise shareholders against almost any offer made.

Recent financial statistics:	1984	1985	1986	1987
Turnover (£ millions)	10.2	10.3	9.6	9.5
Profits (£ millions)	0.1	0.1	0	−0.2
Assets (£ millions)	3.2	3.3	3.5	3.8
Share Price (pence)	26	22	18	14
Number of shares (millions)	10	10	10	10

TAYLOR'S

Business Activity:
Mainly a book publishing firm with interests world wide. Also owns a UK national newspaper, magazines and a large newsagent chain in North West England.

Recent History:
Started 15 years ago by the dynamic Martin Taylor as a printing company, it grew rapidly in the book publishing field, acquiring several much larger firms. It recently took over the Mixwell newspaper company which owned a national newspaper and a valuable chain of over 1000 newsagents.

STUDY POINTS

Taylor's wishes to acquire a small company to expand its interests. It has over £20 million in cash reserves, so price is no object with regard to the three firms described. You are the director of Taylor's.

1 If your company were to take over just one firm, which of the three should it take over? Explain your reasons carefully.

2 What is the opportunity cost of buying any of these firms?

3 What is the maximum price that your company should pay for the chosen company? Explain your reasoning.

'Beecham's, the maker of toiletries like Silvikrin hair shampoos and Badedas bath additives, is to take over British–American Cosmetics which includes names like Tweed, Tramp and Juvena. The purchase caps a 20 year strategy of expanding into the perfumes and fragrances business.' (*Source: Financial Times*, 19 December 1984)

Beecham's was originally a pharmaceutical company making drugs and medicines such as 'Beecham's Powders'. Why should it want to grow? Why might it want to get involved in new markets? There are a variety of possible reasons:

- Growth could well lead to higher profits and higher share values, simply because more is being sold. Beecham's is likely to make more profits than a small chemist firm, because its turnover is so much larger.

- Growth could take the form of DIVERSIFICATION. This is where a company like Beecham's moves into a different market from its original activities. Being in two markets reduces *risk*. If one market does badly (like the pharmaceutical market for Beecham's), then the firm can fall back on the profits being made in the other market (the cosmetics market in our example).

- Growth could lead to a reduction in costs. This would arise if growth leads to further economies of scale being exploited. Lower costs could lead to higher profits.

- Growth could lead to greater control over the market. The bigger the share of the market that a company has, the more likely it is to be able to exploit monopoly powers – fixing high prices and earning high profits.

Methods of Growth

There are two main ways in which a firm can grow. *Internal Growth* is achieved by the firm expanding on its own. The firm invests and increases its production and sales. A firm can also grow by taking over or merging with other firms. This is known as growth by AMALGAMATION. A MERGER occurs when two companies of similar size agree to come together to form just one company. A TAKE-OVER usually refers to the situation where one firm attempts to buy another firm against the wishes of the directors of the second firm, or where a large company buys a small one. Beecham's purchase of British–American Cosmetics was an example of a large company buying up a smaller company.

When two companies do come together, *integration* is said to take place. There are three major types of integration or merger:

- HORIZONTAL INTEGRATION occurs when two firms producing similar goods and services amalgamate. For instance, Beecham's take-over of British–American Cosmetics is an example of horizontal integration, because Beecham's already has a toiletries and cosmetics business.

- VERTICAL INTEGRATION occurs when a company amalgamates either with a company it sells products to (*forward integration*), or with a company it buys products from (*backwards integration*). For instance, if Beecham's were to buy a chain of chemists selling medicines and cosmetics to consumers, that would be an example of forward vertical integration.

- CONGLOMERATE MERGERS occur when a firm amalgamates with another company that has little or nothing to do with its existing activities. If a sweet manufacturer were to buy a chain of furniture shops, or an oil company were to buy a computer company, these would be examples of conglomerate mergers.

A merger could well lead to higher growth and higher profits for the two companies concerned. This need not be the case, however:

- if the amalgamation of the two firms did not result in greater economies of scale than were enjoyed by the two firms producing on their own;

- if diseconomies of scale resulted – for instance, because the two sets of management failed to work well together or because managers from one firm were appointed to positions in the other firm, despite knowing little about the other firm's business.

CHECKPOINTS

1 Explain why a company might want to grow in size.

2 What is the difference between (a) the internal growth of a firm and external growth; and (b) a merger and a take-over?

3 Explain what type of integration the following represent:
   (a) a brewery merging with a chain of off-licences;
   (b) a furniture maker merging with another furniture maker;
   (c) an oil company merging with a chain of supermarkets;
   (d) a car manufacturer merging with a steel manufacturer.

COURSEWORK SUGGESTION

Investigate a merger currently in the news. Describe the companies involved. Analyse why the merger is taking place. Evaluate whether the merger will lead to greater efficiency in the economy.

KEY TERMS

DIVERSIFICATION – Moving into a new and different market.

MERGER, AMALGAMATION or TAKE-OVER – a situation where one company is joined to another company.

HORIZONTAL INTEGRATION – the merger of two firms that produce similar goods and services.

VERTICAL INTEGRATION – the merger of one firm with another firm that either supplies it with products or buys from it.

CONGLOMERATE MERGER – a merger between two companies whose markets are unrelated.

Business Finance

Figure 40.1 Sources of capital funds (£ m) for industrial and commercial companies 1979–1984

	1979	1980	1981	1982	1983	1984
Retained profit	24 328	18 618	20 569	18 236	26 771	33 019
Bank borrowing	3 981	6 340	5 847	6 568	1 552	7 967
Ordinary shares	879	900	1 660	1 033	1 872	1 127
Debentures and preference shares	−22	523	738	245	608	249
Other	3 167	2 590	3 069	3 175	3 733	1 350
Total	32 333	28 971	32 621	29 257	34 536	43 712

Source: CSO, *Financial Statistics*, August 1984 and August 1985

Figure 40.2 Gross domestic product at factor cost: at 1980 prices

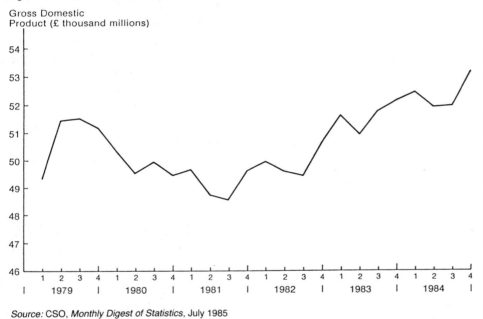

Source: CSO, *Monthly Digest of Statistics*, July 1985

STUDY POINTS

Look at Figure 40.1 and Figure 40.2

1 Explain what is meant by 'capital' for a company.

2 What is the most important way in which companies obtain funds for new investment?

3 What is the cost to a company of (a) borrowing money from a bank, (b) issuing ordinary shares?

4 What is the opportunity cost to a company of using retained profits for investment?

5 Describe how the different sources of capital funds have changed over the period 1979 to 1984.

6 (a) Gross Domestic Product is a measure of the value of total output in the economy. What happened to output over the period 1979 to 1984?

(b) How do you think these changes in output will have affected the profits of companies producing goods and services?

(c) Why do you think company bank borrowing was at a high level between 1980 and 1982?

7 A government wishes to increase investment in the economy. Which of the following measures would most help promote this in your opinion and why? (a) lowering interest rates, (b) making it easier for firms to issue new shares, (c) increasing total spending in the economy.

Financing Investment

'United Biscuits in £98m rights issue' read the headline from the *Financial Times* for 14 March 1985. The company needed more money to finance investment, much of which was to be used to promote just one product in the United States – a cookie (or biscuit) with a 'hard crust and soft centre'. Firms pay their day-to-day running costs, such as wages or raw material costs, from the revenue or turnover they receive from selling their products. But they also need money to finance investment – perhaps to start up a new product or company or to buy new factories and machinery, or to fund research and development. This unit considers the sources of such money for companies.

Retained Profit

Figure 40.1 shows that the major source of new funds for companies is **RETAINED PROFIT**. This is money that the company has made in profits and instead of being given out to shareholders in dividends, it is kept back by the company for investment. The more profit a company makes, the more funds it has to keep back for investment purposes.

Borrowing Money

The next most important source of funds is borrowing. There are many ways in which a company can borrow money. It can borrow:

● from a *bank*. A company may have a loan, where money is borrowed from the bank and paid back in regular instalments. Or it may have an overdraft, where it borrows money and repays it as and when it wants, through its current account with the bank. The big banks (e.g. Barclays and Lloyds) lend a large amount to British industry. There are also industrial banks, which specialise in lending to industry. Foreign banks also lend money to British industry, often in foreign currencies to finance investment abroad.

- from the *money markets*. Firms can go to a financial centre like London and borrow money from a wide variety of institutions, such as pension funds and insurance companies. One form of such borrowing is DEBENTURES or LOAN STOCK. The company issues certificates in small amounts called debentures or stocks. In return for money, the company promises to pay regular interest and repay the borrowed money at some specified time in the future (the REDEMPTION date). The advantage to the borrower is that these certificates can be sold to another saver, often through stock markets such as the London Stock Exchange, before the time when the stock is due to be repaid or *redeemed*. The new owner then receives interest and the right to be repaid the money originally lent on the redemption date.

- from FINANCE HOUSES and other financial institutions. Firms can buy goods on HIRE PURCHASE or rent them on a LEASING agreement. With hire purchase, the goods are hired and only become the property of the company when the last instalment is paid. Both hire purchase and leasing are really a way of borrowing money, because the company is able to use the goods without having to pay their full cost at the start in order to acquire them. Finance houses are banks that specialise in providing hire purchase and leasing services.

- from the *government*. The government provides a number of ways in which firms can borrow money cheaply. Recently, the government has been particularly keen to help small firms.

Equity Capital

A company can gain further money by selling new shares in the company. This was what United Biscuits was doing in the extract above. It is known as adding to the EQUITY CAPITAL of the company. This simply means that the value of the company or what it could be sold for increases. For instance, if a company was worth £10 million (i.e. its equity capital was £10 million) and it sold an extra £2 million worth of shares, then the new value of the company would be £12 million. In return for buying the new shares, the new shareholders would be entitled to a share of the profits. The issuing of new share capital will be discussed further in Unit 42.

Grants

Companies can also obtain grants for new investment, mainly from the government. Firms receiving grants usually receive them for:

- investing in high unemployment areas of the UK (see Unit 73 for further details);

- investing in new technology;

- restructuring and running down older industries.

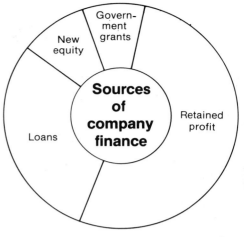

Firms obtain finance for investment from four main sources.

CHECKPOINTS

1 Why do firms need finance?

2 What is meant by 'retained profit'? Why is retained profit so important for investment in the UK?

3 Compare the different ways of borrowing money for a company.

4 What is meant by 'raising new equity'?

5 What might a firm receive a grant for?

COURSEWORK SUGGESTION

Arrange to interview the financial directors (or equivalent) of two local firms, one a small firm, the other a medium to large firm. Draw up a questionnaire that seeks to find out what the sources of finance for the two firms are and what problems they encounter in finding finance for new investment. Also find out whether each company has had to abandon investment plans because of a lack of finance. Describe your findings. Compare and contrast the sources of finance and the difficulties encountered in obtaining finance for the two firms. Discuss whether or not a lack of finance has been a source of lack of investment.

KEY TERMS

RETAINED PROFIT – profit not distributed to shareholders, but kept back for investment purposes.

DEBENTURE or LOAN STOCK – a fixed interest security issued by a company in return for a loan of money. The certificate can be sold and resold, if desired.

REDEMPTION – paying back.

FINANCE HOUSE – a bank that specialises in hire-purchase loans.

HIRE PURCHASE – a form of borrowing where the good being purchased is the property of the lender up to the final payment, when it becomes the property of the borrower.

LEASING – renting.

EQUITY – the monetary value of the shareholdings in a firm at a particular moment in time.

Sole Proprietorships and Partnerships

SPENCERS

Name of business: Spencer's

Owner: John Spencer

Activity: Retailing – general hardware

Assets: Stock £7500, house £35 000, car £2000, cash £7000, other £2000.

Location: On a parade of small shops in a suburb of Wolverhampton.

Financial statistics for last year:

New stock	37 000	Sales	50 000
Rent, rates	3000		
Other	2000		
Surplus	8000		
Total	50 000	Total	50 000

History: John Spencer moved into the hardware business after 15 years in the army. The shop has now been established 10 years. Premises are rented. John's wife, Mary, helps out when needed. Trade has always been steady.

STUDY POINTS

It has come to the notice of John Spencer that the hardware shop on a similar parade of shops only one mile away is up for sale at a price of £10 000 plus stock. The premises are rented. Last year, the financial statistics for the shop were:

	£		£
New stock	31 000	Sales	40 000
Rent, rates	2 000		
Other	2 000		
Surplus	5 000		
Total	40 000	Total	40 000

1 If John Spencer were to buy the shop, what would be the implications for him in terms of: (a) staff? (b) total costs of the business? (c) surplus?

2 What is the maximum price he should offer for the business (excluding stock)?

3 Assume that £10 000 worth of stock would be sold with the shop. Where should John Spencer obtain the money from to purchase the business? (Note that Mr. Spencer has a good record with his local bank, but would have to pay 20% interest a year on a loan, and the bank would take his house as security. An older brother lent him the money to start off the business ten years ago, and

might be prepared to lend him money again. An unemployed friend with savings of £4000 would be interested in going into partnership with him.) Explain carefully the reasons for your choice.

4 What would happen if, having bought the business, trade in both shops declined so that the surplus turned into a loss of £10 000 in one year?

Sole Proprietorships

'Britain created more new jobs in 1984 than in any year since 1978. Since March 1983, the total number employed has climbed by over 600 000. Many of these people have been setting up a business for themselves – about an extra 200 000 in 1984.' (*Source*: Department of Employment, *Employment News*, April 1985)

The simplest and commonest form of BUSINESS ORGANISATION in the UK is a SOLE PROPRIETORSHIP, and many of the 200 000 new businesses set up in 1984 will have been sole proprietorships. These are businesses owned by one person only. That person, however, may employ other workers. The owner usually works in the firm and is responsible for its day-to-day running. The owner will receive all the profits made by the firm. He or she is totally responsible for any debts the business runs up. This is known as having UNLIMITED LIABILITY. For instance, if a sole proprietor goes bankrupt owing £150 000, then not only can all the assets of the business be sold – shop or factory, machinery, etc. – but all the proprietor's personal possessions – house, car etc. – can also be sold. Sole proprietorships are common in many service industries, such as hairdressing, retailing (shops) and the tourist industry.

People going into business choose sole proprietorships as a form of business organisation because:

- it is simple to set up, and there is no need to obtain special legal documents;
- the owner can have complete control of the business if he or she wishes;
- there is no legal requirement to publish accounts.

However, the disadvantages include:

- unlimited liability;
- great difficulty in obtaining finance. Many firms are started from moneys raised by the sale or mortgaging of personal possessions, like houses, or money borrowed in the family. Banks are less likely to lend to small firms than large firms, because small firms are far more likely to go bankrupt. Access to finance through the City of London money market is out of the question, because the firm is too small.
- the fact that the firm may find it difficult to compete with larger firms, if larger firms enjoy greater economies of scale.

Partnerships

ORDINARY PARTNERSHIPS are unlimited liability businesses with between two and twenty partners or shareholders. They are commonly found in professions such as medicine, accountancy and the law.

The advantages of a partnership are that:

- it is cheap and easy to form, just requiring a legal contract called a Deed of Partnership;
- having more than one owner should increase the amount of money that can be raised for investment in the business;
- there is no need to disclose publicly the accounts of the business;
- partners who do not work in the business can have *limited liability* (the advantages of which are discussed in Unit 42) – this sort of partnership is known as a *limited partnership*;
- having more partners and more business is likely to help exploit potential economies of scale.

The disadvantages include:

- unlimited liability for ordinary partners;
- twenty partners might still be far too few to exploit economies of scale fully;
- partners have to trust each other, because one partner can sign a contract binding on all partners;
- the partnership lacks continuity, because if one partner leaves, the whole partnership is dissolved and a new one has to be formed by the remaining partners.

1 Explain who (a) owns; (b) controls; and (c) is responsible for any debts in a sole proprietorship and a partnership.

2 Why do sole proprietorships often find it difficult to raise money for investment?

3 Two workers are considering becoming self-employed and setting up their own business. What would be the advantages of them setting up as a partnership rather than setting up as two sole proprietorships?

4 What is the difference between an ordinary partnership and a limited partnership?

COURSEWORK SUGGESTION

Contact a sole proprietorship or a partnership. Describe the business by stating who owns it, who runs it, what it produces and sells, who is responsible for profits and losses, and how the business is financed. Describe, too, how it was initially started. Analyse the success of the business and the problems facing it. Assess the extent to which these problems could be overcome and success increased, if the business were to become larger and perhaps change its form of organisation.

KEY TERMS

BUSINESS ORGANISATION – an organisation established with the purpose of producing and selling goods and services.

SOLE PROPRIETORSHIP – a one-person business with unlimited liability.

UNLIMITED LIABILITY – a legal obligation on the owners of a business organisation to pay all debts of the business. Even their own personal wealth may be claimed.

ORDINARY PARTNERSHIP – an unlimited liability business where between two and twenty partners own, control and finance the business.

Joint-stock Companies

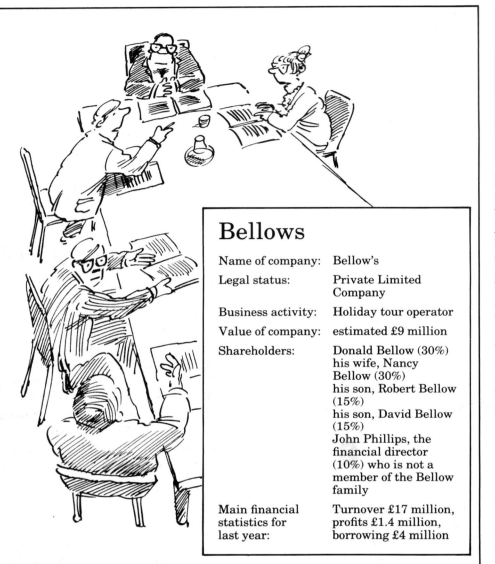

Bellows

Name of company:	Bellow's
Legal status:	Private Limited Company
Business activity:	Holiday tour operator
Value of company:	estimated £9 million
Shareholders:	Donald Bellow (30%) his wife, Nancy Bellow (30%) his son, Robert Bellow (15%) his son, David Bellow (15%) John Phillips, the financial director (10%) who is not a member of the Bellow family
Main financial statistics for last year:	Turnover £17 million, profits £1.4 million, borrowing £4 million

STUDY POINTS

The board of Bellow's is meeting today to consider a £3 million expansion plan. Based mainly in London and the South East, it is proposed that new travel agents should be set up in the South West and the Midlands. It is estimated that profits would increase by £0.5 million per annum. Finance for the expansion can only come from one of two sources. A bank loan would cost 17% per annum in interest. Or the company could go public. The professional fees for a flotation would be £300 000. It is likely that a successful flotation would require existing shareholders to sell some of their shares, so that the Bellow family would own no more than 60% of the shareholding.

1. What would be the cost to the company of borrowing the money?

2. Why might their bankers be reluctant to lend them the £3 million?

3. What would be the cost to the company if new shares were issued?

4. What would be the implications for the existing shareholders of a share flotation in terms of (a) dividends, (b) control of the company, (c) the ability of shareholders to sell their shares.

5. Should the board decide against the expansion plan, borrow the money or go public and issue new equity?

'Barker & Dobson, the confectionery group, yesterday announced pre-tax losses of £2.8m. Mr John Fletcher, the new chairman of the company said that the cause of the loss was "a complete loss of control of gross margin". No final dividend will be paid. The results are a bitter disappointment to shareholders.' (Adapted from the *Financial Times*, 21 June 1985)

Barker & Dobson is an example of a public limited company (PLC), one of the two types of JOINT-STOCK COMPANY. Joint-stock companies are the most important form of business organisation in the UK. There are more sole proprietorships and partnerships, but joint-stock companies are bigger and produce a larger proportion of total output.

Joint-stock companies are owned by shareholders. By law, there must be at least two shareholders in the company. These shareholders elect a board of directors and a chairman. In the extract, it mentioned that Mr John Fletcher was the new chairman of Barker & Dobson. The Board of Directors appoint managers to run the day-to-day business of the company. At least some of the directors are likely to work full-time for the company, but others may be part-time directors. Shareholders, unless they also happen to be directors and managers, do not have a direct say in how the company is run. As was mentioned in Unit 35, this could result in the interests of shareholders and managers conflicting.

There are two types of joint-stock company:

- A PRIVATE LIMITED COMPANY is usually the smaller of the two types. It can range from a small family business, with just a few shareholders, to much larger companies. The shares of the company are not freely available for purchase by the general public.

- A PUBLIC LIMITED COMPANY (or PLC) is a company whose shares must be freely available for purchase by the general public on a stock exchange like the London Stock Exchange. The company must have £50 000 worth of capital when it is formed.

Finance

Joint-stock companies are in a much better position than sole proprietorships or partnerships to raise money for expansion. The larger the company, the greater the number of sources of finance. Not only can these companies borrow relatively easily from banks, finance houses, etc., but PLCs have the additional advantage of access to stock exchanges. They can issue debentures. They can also issue two types of shares in the company:

- *preference shares* – shares which carry a fixed rate of dividend (say 5%), a dividend which must be paid before ordinary shareholders receive their dividends;
- *ordinary shares* – shares where the dividend earned varies according to the amount of profit made: if the company makes a large profit, dividends should be high and vice versa.

If a company votes to raise money through the issue of new equity, it will offer shares for sale to the public, probably acting through a bank or merchant bank. Once the shares have been sold, they will become tradable on a stock exchange. Shareholders can sell their shares, if they want to. This makes the share in PLCs far more attractive than those in a private limited company, where there is no open market for the shares.

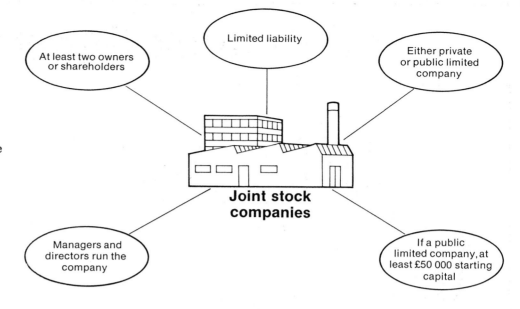

Joint stock companies

- At least two owners or shareholders
- Limited liability
- Either private or public limited company
- Managers and directors run the company
- If a public limited company, at least £50 000 starting capital

Advantages and Disadvantages

Joint-stock companies have advantages in that:

- they have access to wider sources of capital than sole proprietorships and partnerships – this is particularly true of PLCs;
- because they tend to be larger, they can enjoy economies of scale;
- shareholders have LIMITED LIABILITY.

They also have disadvantages, in that:

- accounts have to be made available to the public;
- it is very expensive to form a PLC;
- the original founders of the company are likely to lose control of it, as their shareholding is diluted and this may discourage owners of firms from going public.

CHECKPOINTS

1. What is a joint-stock company?
2. Explain the difference between a shareholder, a director and a manager of a company.
3. What are the advantages and disadvantages of a private limited company rather than a partnership as a form of business organisation?
4. How can a public limited company raise money for expansion?
5. Explain the difference between a preference and an ordinary share.

COURSEWORK SUGGESTION

Investigate the activities of a large public limited company which has a factory, offices, shops and other premises in your locality. Write to the headquarters of the company and obtain a copy of its *Company Report and Accounts*. Request any other material which might be of help to your project. In a written report, describe and analyse the structure of the company, its activities and how those activities are financed. Consider to what extent the shareholders do control and should control the company.

KEY TERMS

JOINT-STOCK COMPANY – a company that has an independent legal existence from its shareholders and where shareholders have limited liability.

PRIVATE LIMITED COMPANY – any joint-stock company that is not a public limited company.

PUBLIC LIMITED COMPANY – a joint-stock company that must have £50 000 capital when founded, and must allow its shares to be traded freely (e.g. on a stock exchange).

LIMITED LIABILITY – a legal safeguard that allows shareholders to be liable for their company's debts only up to and including the value of their shareholding.

Co-operatives

The Mondragon Co-operatives

MONDRAGON is a town in the Basque region of Spain. In 1956, inspired by a local Catholic priest, workers set up a co-operative called ULGOR to produce domestic appliances such as washing machines and refrigerators. Today, there are 85 similar manufacturing companies with total sales of £525 million and 18,000 worker-owners. These independent but associated co-operative companies vary in size from 20 workers to one of 3,400, with an average workforce of around 200. They produce a wide range of goods, from electrical cookers, through machine tools, to high technology components. In addition, there are co-operatively owned banks, six agricultural co-operatives, 14 housing co-ops, plus 43 co-operatively owned schools and colleges, a social security and pensions co-op, a medical and hospital services co-op and a consumer co-op.

Central to the success of these co-operatives has been the Caja Laboral Popular (CLP, the bank controlled by the co-operatives). Their role begins when a group of workers wants to set up a co-op. The CLP helps with a feasibility study which may take up to two years, helps design and develop the plant, and trains or supplies a manager.

The bank provides 75% of the cost of setting up a new co-op by means of a ten year loan at cheap interest rates. The government provides a 12½% low interest rate loan for job creation. The other 12½% comes from the workers themselves. This currently averages £2,600 per worker and is not regarded as a problem. It can be paid by a deduction from wages over a two-year period on an interest free basis, or it may be borrowed as a personal loan from the bank over five years.

Each co-op is set up on the same principles. Each worker must be a member of the co-op, with one vote, and no one else may become a member. Policy decisions of the co-op are taken democratically through a general meeting, or through a board of the company which has been elected. Managers then carry out those decisions. The ratio between the highest and lowest wages is 3:1, the lowest wage usually being set above the rate for the same work in the locality.

Profits are distributed to a social fund to benefit the local community (10%), to the co-ops collected reserves (20%) and to the workers themselves in proportion to their wages (70%).

Workers are not allowed to withdraw their share of the profits before they retire, but have to re-invest it to expand the co-op and create jobs. They receive a fixed 6% per annum interest on their total profits to date as well as their wages. If a worker leaves to join a private company, he loses one fifth of his total profits.

If a co-op gets into financial difficulties, the co-op bank, the CLP, will help with advice. The bank's experts may recommend a range of measures to the general meeting of worker-members – from replacing the managers to changing the production techniques or even changing the product entirely. If workers do have to be lost, the worker is guaranteed 80% of wages whilst no alternative employment is available. But unemployment is unlikely to last long because other co-operatives which are expanding will take on workers no longer required by co-ops in difficulties.

The Mondragon co-operatives are probably the most well known and most successful of co-operative experiments in Europe. If it can be successful in Spain, why should it not be an answer to many of our industrial problems in the UK?

Adapted from the *Financial Times*, 14 December 1982

STUDY POINTS

Read the above extract carefully. Assume you are a worker member of the Caja Laboral Popular, the co-op bank, and have been asked to prepare a report on the setting up of a new co-operative making electrical components for the Spanish car industry. It is proposed that the co-operative should start off with fifty worker employees and that it will cost £1.2 million to set up the co-op. A manager–worker will be appointed at a salary of £21 000 per annum. In your report:

1 Explain who will provide the £1.2 million needed to start the company. Calculate how much each agency will need to provide.

Calculate how much each worker will need to contribute. How can each worker pay this initial sum?

2 Explain who will make the decisions in running the co-op. What is the role of the worker–owners? What might be the role of a board? How many should be elected onto the board? Who, in your opinion, would be best elected onto the board? What is the role of the manager?

3 What will the wages of the workers be? What will be their share of the profits? (Take as an example a worker who has worked for the

co-op for ten years and has accumulated £10 000 in profits).

4 Explain the advantages of worker co-operatives. For instance, why might worker co-operatives improve industrial relations in a place of work and lead to no strikes? Why might workers prefer to work in a worker co-op rather than an ordinary private company? Why might worker co-ops lead to a fairer distribution of income? Why might worker co-ops benefit the local community, and the unemployed?

Types of Co-operatives

The word 'co-operative' comes from the verb 'to co-operate', which means to join together to do something. CO-OPERATIVES differ from ordinary companies in that the main aim of the company is not necessarily to make as much profit as possible for the shareholders. There are two main types of co-operative in the UK; producer co-operatives and consumer co-operatives.

Producer Co-operatives

Producer co-operatives are businesses owned by some or all of the workers in the firm. The aim of the co-operative movement is to run the business for the sake of the workers and not for the shareholders, who may have nothing to do with the firm except own shares. The workers have to provide any money or financial capital to set up the business. They then have to find some way of making decisions – for instance, by appointing managers or, if a company is small, by voting on important issues. They also have to decide how to distribute the profits of the co-operative, although these will almost certainly go to the workers, since they are the shareholders of the company. Workers do have the advantage under law of having limited liability.

The main advantage of a worker or producer co-operative should be that there is no conflict of interest between workers and shareholders, since workers are the shareholders. So there should be no strikes, and workers should have a strong incentive to work. Worker co-operatives are extremely rare in the UK. This is because:

- workers find it difficult to raise enough money to set up and then finance the growth of firms;
- workers often lack the necessary management experience to make a company successful.

Probably the most successful example of worker co-operatives is in the Mondrian region of Spain, where there are a number of very successful co-operatives, ranging from a bank to the largest washing-machine manufacturer in Spain.

Consumer Co-operatives

Consumer or retail co-operatives are co-operatives set up with the aim of helping consumers. The first such co-operative in the UK was set up in 1844 in Rochdale by 28 weavers, who wanted to sell food more cheaply than in the local shops.

Some of the Original Rochdale Principles

1. *Voluntary and open membership.*
2. *Democratic control – one man, one vote.*
3. *Payment of fixed interest on capital.*
4. *Surplus allocated in proportion to members' purchases – the dividend.*
5. *Education facilities for members and workers.*

The co-operatives are owned by members of the general public, who can own between £1 and £5000 of shares. Interest is paid on the shares. Unlike limited companies, shares can only be sold back to the co-operative, and each shareholder (or 'member') is only entitled to one vote at shareholders' meetings, however many shares are held. Shareholders elect a management committee (like the board of directors in a PLC), who in turn appoint paid full-time managers to run the co-operative society on a day-to-day basis. Profits are distributed not to shareholders, but to shoppers, according to how much they spend at the co-op. Many co-ops now pay this in the form of stamps. Co-operatives finance their investment mainly through retained profits and loans of various sorts.

The co-operative ideal has to a great extent diminished over the past twenty years. Co-operatives have found that larger PLCs, such as Sainsbury's, have been able to exploit economies of scale and often sell produce more cheaply and in greater variety. If co-operatives can no longer guarantee to have the cheapest produce, what is their role in the economy? Co-operatives have responded in part by joining together in larger and larger societies, to exploit the economies of scale needed to reduce prices. However, there are still over 200 co-operative societies in Britain, many of which are very small. As they get larger, they lose their local roots, and it becomes more difficult to maintain the original aim of having shops controlled by the people who shop there. It is difficult to see how co-operatives are going to be very different from other companies in the future.

C H E C K P O I N T S

1 Explain how a typical producer co-operative is owned, financed and controlled.

2 Explain the role of the shareholder, the consumer and the management committee in a typical retail co-operative society.

3 In what ways does a typical retail co-operative society differ from a public limited company?

4 Why have retail co-operatives to some extent lost their traditional role in the economy?

C O U R S E W O R K S U G G E S T I O N

Write to your local retail co-operative society and ask for its latest *Report and Accounts*, together with any other material which might be of help to you. Describe and analyse the ownership, finance, control, location and activities of the society. Try to assess the extent to which the co-operative aim is being upheld by the society in your local economy.

K E Y T E R M S

CO-OPERATIVES – firms that exist either for the benefit of their worker–owners (*worker* or *producer co-operatives*), or for the customers they sell to (*consumer* or *retail co-operatives*).

Data Response Questions
Units 38–43

Unit 38 The Size of Firms

Welcome niche for beer drinkers

THE STORIES of ruin and wretchedness surrounding 28 small independent breweries that failed in the last two years are enough to freeze the blood of any bright-eyed entrepreneur.

"There is a growing feeling that only companies which produce at least 25 barrels a week will survive," says Brian Glover, author of Small Beer, a volume about them to be published next year. "The rest will perish," he adds.

Nevertheless, this last year has seen a brewery set up for every one that closed down — and more. There are now about 120 pure wholesaling small independents in the UK and more than 70 pub breweries.

Despite their problems the new small independents have found a niche in the British beer market. Apart from keeping larger breweries on their toes by scotching local monopolies, they have also won the heart of the beer drinkers pressure group, CAMRA (Campaign for Real Ale). Prices are down through healthy competition in West Country, Midlands and South-East strongholds. They have also managed to cling on through providing a better service to the free trade — bringing supplies out, day or night, and learning how to market their beer.

Source: Financial Times, 15 May 1985

1 Describe how small independent breweries have grown over the period 1983–5. *(2 marks)*

2 How do small breweries manage to compete with the large national breweries? *(5 marks)*

3 Suggest *three* reasons why so many small breweries have gone out of business. *(3 marks)*

Unit 39 The Growth of Firms

Intasun to buy Global Tours

BY ARTHUR SANDLES

INTASUN LEISURE is to buy Global Tours. The deal takes Intasun into the coach tour business and the booming market in overseas visitors. The price is expected to be between £3m and £6m.

Once among Britain's biggest tour companies, Global's share of the mass market to the Mediterranean has shrunk in recent years. At present it is thought to hold about 2 per cent of the total business compared with Intasun's 15 per cent and more than 20 per cent held by Thomson's, the market leader.

Global is, though, one of Britain's biggest coach tour operators, taking Britons on European trips and bringing Australians, New Zealanders and some Americans into the UK and on to Continental tours.

Global is also strong in the Irish package tour market, where Intasun's hold is tiny. At the same time, Intasun acquires Golden Circle, a company which specialises in holidays for the retired, competing directly with Saga Holidays, and a winter sports operation, Global Ski. Until now, Intasun has been active only in winter sports for schools.

A spokesman for Global said last night that Global's comparatively small air holiday operation meant that it could not compete effectively in package tours.

Mr Peter Woodward, Intasun finance director, said the deal made "very good sense" for Intasun Global's overhead burden could be reduced considerably by the use of Intasun's computer and flying resources. It also meant that Intasun would break into the self-catering market.

Source: Financial Times, 24 April 1985

1 As companies, what do Global Tours and Intasun produce? *(1 mark)*

2 What type of merger is taking place? *(1 mark)*

3 Why did Global Tours find it difficult to compete in its market? *(3 marks)*

4 Why might Intasun have decided to buy Global Tours? *(5 marks)*

Unit 40 Business Finance

The Business Development Loan

The Business Development Loan is a simple form of finance for all types of businesses and professional practices. It is available in amounts from £2,000 up to £250,000 and for periods between 1 and 20 years. Repayment is by monthly instalments unless an arrangement is made for repayments of capital to be postponed for an initial period.

Why Choose a Business Development Loan?

The Business Development Loan has been specially designed to meet the needs of new and expanding businesses or practices:

☐ It is **simple to arrange**, so you can quickly implement your business plans.

☐ The loan can be used **for any capital expenditure** such as the purchase of property, plant, machinery, vehicles or to buy the business or practice itself. It can even be used for additional permanent working capital. This means that the finance of such major items is kept separate from your day to day requirements which makes for better control of the financial side of your business.

☐ The **fixed term** is matched to your individual requirements and agreed at the outset.

☐ The **fixed interest rate** means that you know the cost of borrowing in advance and that it will not change however market interest rates may fluctuate.

☐ The **fixed repayments** mean that you know in advance how much you will have to pay in each instalment so you can accurately plan your cashflow and budgeting.

☐ The **option to defer repayment of capital** allows the repayments to reflect the flow of income generated by the asset which you have purchased.

Source: National Westminster Bank

1 How much can a company borrow through a Business Development Loan? *(1 mark)*

2 For what might a company use a Business Development Loan? *(2 marks)*

3 How is the loan repaid? *(2 marks)*

4 What is the cost to a company of a loan compared to issuing new equity capital to finance investment? *(5 marks)*

Data Response Questions for **Units 41** and **42** can be found on *page 220*.

Unit 43 Co-operatives

Co-op sales top £2 billion mark

The CWS (Co-operative Wholesale Society) announced sales of £2 billion last year, results which enabled the society to increase its dividend payment by £1.5 million.

The CWS is the buying arm of 200 retail co-operative societies in the UK. In return for buying from CWS, an individual retail society gets a dividend payment in the same way as an ordinary shopper gets a dividend by shopping at his or her local co-op.

The CWS is also a major manufacturer of everything from food to shoes. It runs dairies, a property business as well as a funeral business which buries one person in four in Britain.

Source: The Guardian, 2 May 1984

1 What does the Co-operative Wholesale Society produce? *(3 marks)*

2 Who gets the profits made by the CWS and why? *(4 marks)*

3 What is the difference between the CWS and an ordinary retail co-operative society? *(4 marks)*

Essay Questions
Units 38–43

1 Two chocolate confectionery manufacturers merge to form one company.
(a) Suggest *four* reasons why this might have happened. *{8 marks}*
(b) What type of merger is this? *(2 marks)*
(c) What might be the effects of this merger for (i) consumers and (ii) the workers of the two companies? *(5 marks)*

2 'Workers trying to set up in business often find that the most important obstacle is the finance to start the business'.
(a) Describe where a woman wanting to set up a small engineering firm could raise the money to start it. *(5 marks)*
(b) What form of business organisation might she choose for her firm and why? *(5 marks)*
(c) Why do small businesses find it difficult to obtain finance? *(5 marks)*

Public-sector Enterprises

Figure 44.1 British Rail selected statistics

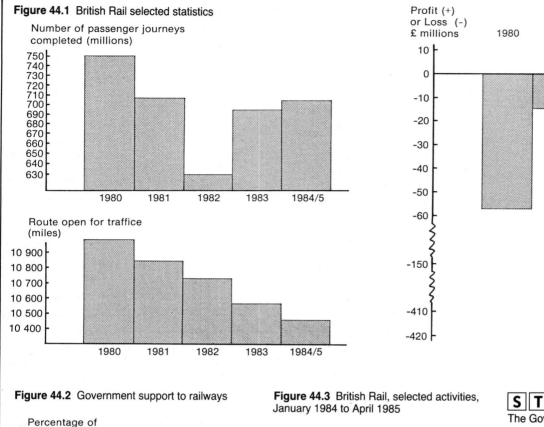

Number of passenger journeys completed (millions)

Route open for traffice (miles)

Profit (+) or Loss (–) £ millions

Figure 44.2 Government support to railways

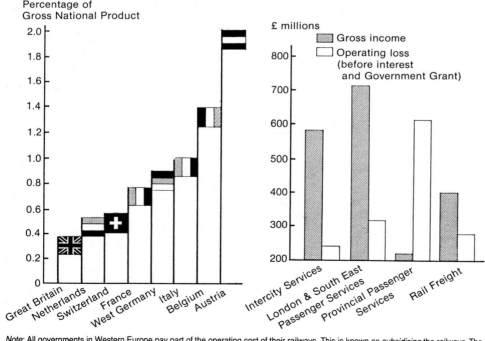

Percentage of Gross National Product

Great Britain, Netherlands, Switzerland, France, West Germany, Italy, Belgium, Austria

Figure 44.3 British Rail, selected activities, January 1984 to April 1985

£ millions

Gross income
Operating loss (before interest and Government Grant)

Intercity Services, London & South East Passenger Services, Provincial Passenger Services, Rail Freight

The Government proposes to privatise British Rail. Draw up a report giving the likely consequences of such a move. For instance:

1 Would there be any private companies who would want to buy British Rail?

2 What might be the effect on the number of railway lines in the country and on the number of services?

3 What are the likely effects on consumers?

4 What would be the private and social costs and benefits of such a move?

5 How much should British Rail be sold for and what should be done with the money received?

Note: All governments in Western Europe pay part of the operating cost of their railways. This is known as *subsidising* the railways. The graph shows how much of the total income of a country was spent on railway subsidies in 1984/5. Profits and losses of British Rail shown in Figure 44·1 *include* this subsidy. In 1984/5, the Government provided £1209.9 million in subsidies. Without this, British Rail would have made a loss of £1629.8 million over that period. Figure 44·3 shows the losses of parts of British Rail *before* Government subsides/grants are included.

Source: British Rail, Annual Report and Accounts, 1984/5

State Output

The public sector (i.e. the state) produces a significant proportion of total output in the UK. Some is produced by various government departments: for example, health care by the Department of Health and Social Security, or education by local authority education departments. Some is produced by businesses owned by government.

Public Corporations

The most important type of business organisation in terms of tonnes of output in the public sector is the PUBLIC CORPORATION (also called NATIONALISED INDUSTRY). Nationalised industries include the Central Electricity Generating Board, the National Coal Board, the Post Office, the British Steel Corporation and British Rail. Each public corporation is established by an Act of Parliament. The only shareholder in the corporation is the government. It appoints a Board of Directors to run the corporation on its behalf. Each public corporation is given a set of targets by the government, and the Board is responsible for achieving those targets. The Board is free to choose how to organise the business, but most Boards are either organised on a regional basis (like the electricity boards) or on a product basis (like British Steel). The person directly responsible for the public corporation in government is the relevant government minister. For instance, the Minister for Energy is responsible for the National Coal Board. This minister is responsible to Parliament itself.

Three bodies can act as watchdogs on the activities of public corporations:

- Each corporation has a CONSUMER COUNCIL. This is a body made up of typical consumers of the products that the corporation sells. The Gas Corporation Consumer Council, for instance, is made up of personal customers and of repreentatives from industry. Councils have the power to comment and advise on corporation policy, but they do not have the power to change it. For this reason they tend to have rather a weak influence.

- The *Select Committee on Nationalised Industries* is a group of MPs in parliament whose job it is to look into the affairs of public corporations and check that they are doing their job properly. Again, they have no power to alter policy, but they can and do criticise corporations publicly, when they feel it is necessary.

- The government may also ask the *Monopolies and Mergers Commission*, an investigating body responsible to the Office of Fair Trading, to look into the affairs of corporations, if it feels that they are exploiting their monopoly position.

Public corporations are financed from retained profits, borrowing from banks and other financial institutions in the UK and abroad, by government loans and by injections of new share capital by government. The government is entitled to a dividend on any profit saved.

The arguments for and against nationalised industries are considered in the next unit.

Other Government-owned Businesses

The government also owns shares in a number of other businesses in the UK, such as British Leyland and British Petroleum. These companies, however, are public limited companies, and as such conform to the legal requirements of joint-stock companies.

Municipal Enterprises

Local authorities often own businesses of their own. Examples of such MUNICIPAL ENTERPRISES include bus companies, golf courses, crematoriums, and sports complexes. The local authority has to finance any investment and receives profits or pays the losses resulting from the trading activity of the enterprise.

The local authority controls the enterprise by appointing a Trading Committee, made up of unpaid councillors. This committee, in turn, appoints full-time staff to carry out the day-to-day running of the enterprise.

CHECKPOINTS

1. Name eight public corporations.
2. What is a 'public corporation'?
3. What roles do the consumer council of the corporation, the Select Committee on Nationalised Industries, and the Monopolies and Mergers Commission play in influencing the policy of a public corporation?
4. What are the differences between the management and finance of a public corporation and that of a public limited company?
5. What is a 'municipal enterprise'? What municipal enterprises exist in your local area?

COURSEWORK SUGGESTION

Investigate a municipal enterprise in your local area. Describe its organisation and activities. Analyse its financial affairs. Try to evaluate the extent of the social profit or loss it generates for the local community.

KEY TERMS

PUBLIC CORPORATION or NATIONALISED INDUSTRY – an enterprise wholly owned by the state.

NATIONALISED INDUSTRY CONSUMER COUNCIL – the consumer watchdog of a nationalised industry.

MUNICIPAL ENTERPRISE – a business owned by a local authority.

Nationalisation and Privatisation

Figure 45.1 Nationalisation and privatisation

Post Office and Telephones	Set up as government department in 1840. 51% of British Telecom privatised in 1984	Privatised for political reasons
British Airways	Nationalised in 1946. Privatisation expected 1987	Nationalised and privatised for political reasons
National Coal Board	Nationalised 1947	Nationalised for political reasons
British Rail	Nationalised 1948	Nationalised for political reasons
Electricity	Central Electricity Generating Board created between the wars. Rest of industry nationalised in 1949	CEGB created to gain economies of scale and prevent monopoly. 1949 nationalisation for political reasons
Gas	Already mostly owned by local authorities, nationalised in 1949. Privatisation expected in 1986	Nationalised and privatised for political reasons.
British Steel	Nationalised in 1951, privatised in 1953 and renationalised in 1967	Nationalised and privatised for political reasons
Rolls-Royce	Nationalised in 1971	Nationalised because the company went bankrupt and was too important (for defence and employment reasons) to be allowed to cease trading
British Leyland	Nationalised in 1975. Jaguar privatised in 1984	Nationalised because the company was going bankrupt and was too important for employment reasons to be allowed to cease trading

Public assets due for privatisation in the future include the rest of British Telecom, National Bus, Land Rover, Rolls-Royce, Unipart, British Airways, British Nuclear Fuels and the Naval war shipbuilding yards.

STUDY POINTS

Look at Figure 45.1

1 When were most major industries nationalised (i.e. bought by the government from the private sector)? When has there been most privatisation (i.e. selling by the government to the private sector)?

2 Why were most industries either nationalised or privatised?

3 Many industries that were nationalised became monopolies (i.e. sole sellers of a product to the consumer or to other firms). Which nationalised industries were or are monopolies?

4 Other industries faced competition, usually from foreign firms. Which were these?

5 It is argued that one of the major reasons why firms should be privatised is that this will increase the level of competition in the industry and thus increase efficiency. Take any nationalised industry. State how privatisation could lead to more competition and what forms this competition might take. What benefits might result from this for the consumer? To what extent is there a danger that privatisation might lead to greater profits for the company and higher prices for the consumer?

'The Cabinet yesterday formally approved proposals for the privatisation of the British Gas Corporation.'

'The Government intends to offer for sale later this year the whole of its remaining 48.8 per cent shareholding in Britoil, the oil production and development company initially privatised in November 1982.'
(*Source: Financial Times, 3 May 1985*)

These two extracts are discussing the PRIVATISATION of two companies – that is, the companies are to be sold by the government to the private sector. This privatisation is part of a much wider policy of the Conservative government in the early 1980s of selling nationalised industries to the private sector and of replacing government-provided goods and services by private sector provision. Between 1945 and 1979, however, successive governments *nationalised* selected companies and industries. Figure 45.1 shows this history of NATIONALISATION and privatisation. Why was there this change of policy from 1979? Is this change right? This unit considers these important questions.

Efficiency

The nationalisation versus privatisation debate centres round the economic concept of *efficiency*, although other factors also come into play. Economists who support the nationalisation of industries such as rail, coal, steel and electricity put forward the following arguments.

- One nationalised industry is able to exploit economies of scale far better than several smaller competing firms. For instance, having one railway company with one set of tracks between two stations would be less costly than having two competing companies with two sets of tracks. This should reduce prices to the consumer.

- Without nationalisation, the customer risks being exploited, given that many industries are **NATURAL MONOPOLIES**. As seen in Unit 37, a monopoly exists in an industry where there is just one firm in the market – i.e. there is no competition in the market. The monopoly firm can therefore charge whatever prices it likes, and the consumer will have to pay those prices, or not buy the goods or services. A natural monopoly is one where the economies of scale are such that it is likely that one firm will grow and grow until it comes to dominate the whole market. If the consumer is not to be exploited by this monopolist, the government has to control the situation and it can obviously do this if it nationalises the company.

- Nationalisation improves performance. Many of the present nationalised industries performed badly in the past, in the hands of the private sector. After the Second World War, for instance, both the railways and the coal mines were in a very poor state, due to lack of investment. Nationalisation meant that more money could be put into these vital industries. Similarly, in the 1970s, both Rolls-Royce and British Leyland went bankrupt. The government nationalised both firms to prevent massive job losses and the destruction of firms of national importance.

- Nationalisation of the basic industries, such as coal and steel, helps the government control the economy more easily.

- Nationalisation helps preserve national defence interests.
- Nationalisation is 'socially' right. Firms should be owned by all the people, not just the lucky few who can afford it. They should be run for the benefit of everybody in society, not just for the benefit of a few shareholders. Social costs and social benefits have to be taken into consideration when making decisions, not just the firm's private costs and benefits.

Economists who are in favour of privatisation present the following arguments.

- Nationalisation often leads to higher costs and higher prices for consumers. This is because nationalised industries lack any real competition. Without the pressures of competition, workers and managers allow costs to rise.
- Privatisation leads to more *choice*. Nationalised industries only provide a narrow range of choice between products for consumers. Having competing firms provides far greater choice and that choice benefits the consumer.
- Privatisation leads to an improved *quality* in goods and services. Again, the argument is that this is the result of greater competition.
- Private firms are much more sensitive to the demands of consumers than nationalised industries, which can sell anything because they are monopolists. Private firms are far more likely to innovate and develop new desirable products than nationalised industries.

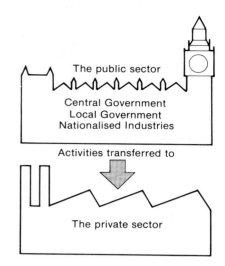

Privatisation means selling nationalised industries to the private sector and replacing government provided goods and services by private sector provision.

C H E C K P O I N T S

1 Only one major industry was denationalised between 1945 and 1979. What was it?
2 List the companies that have been privatised since 1979.
3 What are the arguments in favour of nationalisation?
4 Explain why privatisation could lead to higher prices for the consumer, rather than lower prices.
5 Assume that the Post Office is to be privatised. What benefits might this bring about to the consumer? What might be the costs?

C O U R S E W O R K S U G G E S T I O N

Find out about the privatisation of British Telecom (or indeed any recent example of privatisation). Describe the activities of the corporation before privatisation. How was the corporation privatised? Describe the activities of the company since privatisation. Analyse the changes that have occurred so far as the consumer is concerned. Try to decide whether or not the consumer has benefited from privatisation so far, and whether or not he or she is likely to in the future.

K E Y T E R M S

PRIVATISATION – a change in the production of goods and services from the public sector to the private sector. It often refers to the sale of government-owned firms to the private sector.

NATIONALISATION – the purchase of a private company by the public sector.

NATURAL MONOPOLY – a monopoly situation that arises because only one firm can fully exploit all the economies of scale existing in the industry. Electricity is an example of a natural monopoly, as it would not be very efficient to have two companies supplying the same area, as this would result in two sets of cables, pylons, transformers, etc.

The Location of Industry

The company

Wilsons is a medium sized company in the light engineering industry. Established for over 150 years at its site in Wimbledon in London, it has outgrown its factory premises and is seeking a new location. Four sites have been proposed. One is just half a mile away. The others are in other parts of the country. Much of the firm's business is done with firms in the South of England and on the Continent. Moving to another area of the country would increase transport costs, both for raw materials and for transport of finished products. These increased costs are likely to be offset by cheaper labour costs and site costs.

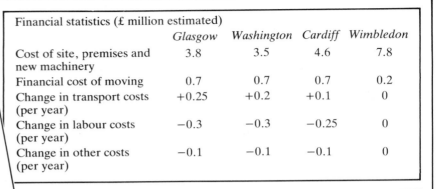

Financial statistics (£ million estimated)				
	Glasgow	*Washington*	*Cardiff*	*Wimbledon*
Cost of site, premises and new machinery	3.8	3.5	4.6	7.8
Financial cost of moving	0.7	0.7	0.7	0.2
Change in transport costs (per year)	+0.25	+0.2	+0.1	0
Change in labour costs (per year)	−0.3	−0.3	−0.25	0
Change in other costs (per year)	−0.1	−0.1	−0.1	0

Report on staff reaction to a move

Last month, a detailed questionnaire was circulated to all salaried staff, and Grade III and above, manual workers, concerning the proposed move. It is obvious that there will be strong resistance to any move away from Wimbledon and that the company stands to lose many of its key personnel. This could impose severe costs to the company, especially if suitable staff cannot be recruited in the new location.

Glasgow
Renovated premises in the industrial heartland of Glasgow. The factory building is 10% larger than required and adjoining land would allow a doubling of capacity if needed.

Washington New Town
New purpose-built premises on an industrial park with enough land to increase production potentially by 50%.

Cardiff
New purpose-built premises on an industrial park with enough land to increase production by a potential 20%.

Wimbledon
An existing factory with no further room for expansion.

STUDY POINT

1 Which of the four sites should the board of Wilsons choose to move to? Write a 200 word report explaining your decision.

£200 million is a great deal of money to spend on a shopping and leisure centre. Why are the property developers prepared to spend this amount? Why are they looking at Essex? And what is the significance of the M25?

Businesses locate themselves in a particular area for a variety of reasons, which include:

- *Proximity to their markets.* Essex is a large centre of population and is next to an even larger centre – London. The building of the M25 motorway means that shoppers can travel longer distances more quickly, so they will be attracted to a large shopping centre near the motorway. The new shopping centre will, itself, attract firms making goods for sale there. This is because their transport costs will be lower compared with firms situated in, say, Glasgow. They will also be able to see more quickly and easily the sorts of products that people in Essex want to buy. Some firms, like hairdressers, will have no option but to set up near their market.

- *Proximity to raw materials.* Some industries, like coal mining, have to be sited where there are raw materials. Others, like the steel industry, are sited near their raw materials, because the cost of transporting raw materials is high.

- *Availability of suitable labour.* Building a shopping complex in Essex will not be worth while if there are no workers available to work in the complex. There is unlikely to be a problem in this case. But firms do locate themselves on the basis of being able to get the right workers in an area. One of the reasons why many micro-chip firms have located themselves along the M4 motorway is because most of the key workers in this still small industry live in the area.

- *Cost.* Building a complex in Essex will not be cheap, but the land will certainly be cheaper than if the developers wanted to build the shopping centre in central London. The costs of land, of buildings, of training workers, etc. will all play a part in the decision of a firm as to where to locate.

- *External economies of scale.* (These were discussed in Unit 33.) If an industry has grown up in an area such that the infrastructure, the labour force and the suppliers are now better suited than in other areas, then that will attract other firms in that industry to the area.

- *Inertia.* Firms, especially small ones, dislike moving. So a firm based in London will tend to stay in London, even if costs are cheaper in, say, Glasgow. This is known as *industrial inertia*. It helps to explain, in part, why firms continue to grow in the south of England, despite the very high costs of staying in the region.

- *Other factors.* These include climate (one of the main reasons for the growth of the cotton industry in Lancashire was the wet climate, which helped in the manufacture of cotton) and safety (nuclear power stations cannot be sited near large centres of population).

- *Government policy.* The government has attempted to alter the location of industry through its *regional policy* (this will be discussed in Unit 73).

The geographical location of industry is discussed further in Unit 67.

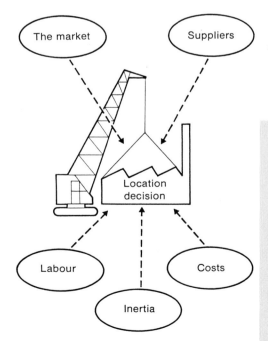

A business has to take into account many factors when deciding where to locate new premises.

CHECKPOINTS

1 Explain the factors that influence where a firm locates itself.

2 Explain what would be the most important factors the following would take into consideration when deciding where to locate:
   (a) a garage selling petrol;
   (b) a car assembly company;
   (c) a local authority building a sports complex;
   (d) an oil terminal.

3 Explain why:
   (a) steel works in the UK tend to be situated on the coast;
   (b) hypermarkets and superstores tend to be situated outside town centres;
   (c) nuclear power stations are sited away from large centres of population.

4 What is meant by 'industrial inertia'? Explain why inertia occurs.

COURSEWORK SUGGESTION

Undertake a street survey of a part of your local area. Mark on a map the location of all the businesses in the area chosen. Explain briefly why you think those businesses might have located themselves there. Then arrange to interview the owners/managers of two of the businesses in your survey. Find out why they are located in their present position. Assess the costs and benefits to the firm and to society as a whole of that location.

The Social Costs of Production

Figure 47.1 Derelict land: by region and by cause of dereliction, 1982

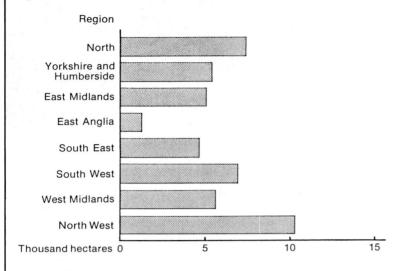

Region

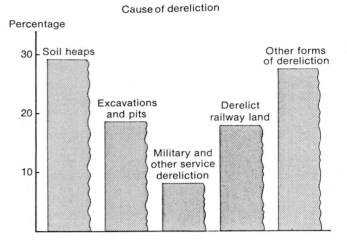

Cause of dereliction

Figure 47.2 Air pollution: by source (Sulphur dioxide: emissions from fuel combustion, U.K.)

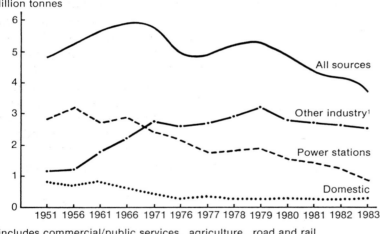

[1]includes commercial/public services, agriculture, road and rail transport, and refineries

Figure 47.3 Noise – complaints received by Environmental Health Officers: by source

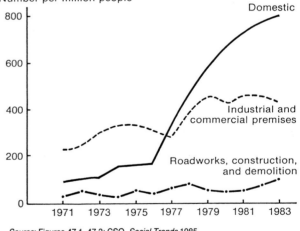

Source: Figures 47.1–47.3: CSO, *Social Trends* 1985

STUDY POINTS

Consider Figure 47.1.

1 What is meant by 'derelict land'?

2 Give *two* examples of derelict land in your local area.

3 Why does land become derelict?

4 According to the statistics for 1982 what was the single most important cause of dereliction? Which industry has been mainly responsible for this?

5 Which area of the UK had the least derelict land? Why do you think this was the case?

6 Derelict land is part of the *cost* of production in an economy. Some costs are paid by producers, and these are known as *private costs*. But some costs are paid for by the rest of society. These are known as **EXTERNALITIES**. The total costs of production (i.e. private costs plus externalities) are known as the *social costs* of production. Make a list of the costs of production of railway services. State which are private costs and which are externalities.

Consider Figures 47.2 and 47.3.

7 What costs of production are shown in the data for (a) electricity power stations and (b) industry in general. Are these private costs or externalities for the companies involved and why?

8 What are the private costs of owning a motor car? What externalities does the motorist impose upon the rest of society?

9 Should the government force all firms to eliminate all forms of pollution they create? What would be the costs and benefits of this?

Costs and Benefits

In Unit 3, a distinction was made between *private* costs and benefits and *social* costs and benefits. Private costs and benefits are the costs and benefits paid and received by the individual, firm, area, country, etc. which engages in a particular activity. Take, for instance, a firm making cars. Its private costs are the money costs it has to pay for raw materials, components, workers, etc. The social costs and benefits of an activity, however, are all the costs and benefits paid and received. The firm making cars, for instance, might cause a noise problem for residents in the area of the factory. This is not a private cost for the company, because it does not have to pay anything. But it is a social cost, because local residents have to bear this cost of production.

The difference between social costs and benefits and private costs and benefits is known as an EXTERNALITY — i.e. private costs + externalities = social costs. Of what interest is this to economists and indeed to anybody?

Misallocation of Resources

Consider this extract:

'In December 1984, there was a leak of poisonous gas from a Union Carbide plant at Bhopal in India. At least 2000 people died. At least 200 000 people were sufficiently affected to be treated for a variety of disorders including eye and respiratory problems.'

The extract refers to a plant in India making pesticides to spray on crops. It was owned by a US company, Union Carbide. The accident that occurred was one of the worst disasters of its kind. The private costs of production for Union Carbide included the cost of equipment, raw materials, labour, etc. The social cost turned out to include the death of 2000 people and damage to the health of at least 200 000 others. This represented the externality of production for Union Carbide (although the company will have to pay compensation to the victims of the disaster).

This is a spectacular example of how resources can be misallocated in society. An individual firm bases its decision on what to produce and how to produce it on its private costs and benefits. It is not interested in any externalities. So if private costs and benefits differ widely from social costs and benefits, then firms can operate in a way that is harmful to society and yet still make a profit for themselves. The *New York Times* reported that the Bhopal plant was not as technologically advanced as a similar plant in the USA. *The Guardian* reported that the local company relied upon workers' eyes watering to reveal a leak, rather than upon the sophisticated computer system available at Union Carbide's West Virginia plant. This makes sense from a private viewpoint. Any victims of an accident in the USA would receive far more compensation than victims in India. Therefore there was less point in installing costly and sophisticated safety devices. But the social cost of this decision was enormous. From the profit-making point of view of the company, resources might have been correctly allocated, but they were badly misallocated from a social viewpoint.

Pollution is only one of the externalities caused by the operation of firms. Others include:

- *The destruction of the environment.* Coal mining in Britain has a long history of spoiling and destroying the local environment.

- *The build-up of social pressures in society.* Firms need to sell in order to make a profit. In part, they succeed in selling by pressurising consumers to buy through advertisements and other promotions. But this means that

consumers who have no income or little income (e.g. the unemployed) may feel left out because they cannot buy. This may, in turn, cause an increase in crime, suicide and other forms of antisocial behaviour.

CHECKPOINTS

1 Using an example, explain what is meant by an 'externality'.

2 A garage seeks to set up on waste ground opposite a row of houses. What externalities might the garage produce for local residents?

3 The Central Electricity Generating Board decide to build a nuclear power station on the coast of East Anglia. What externalities might this power station produce?

4 Why need a company not take into account the externalities it produces when making its decisions?

5 Explain why the 'cost' of a life in India might be less than the 'cost' of a life in the USA.

COURSEWORK SUGGESTION

Examine a local environmental issue. Describe the background to the issue. Analyse the private costs and benefits and the social costs and benefits involved. Try to decide how the issue should be resolved in order to maximise the level of social profit.

KEY TERM

EXTERNALITY — social costs minus private costs, i.e. that part of costs that is not borne by the individual consumer, producer, etc. whose activities have given rise to it.

Data Response Questions
Units 44–47

Unit 44 Public Sector Enterprises

Switched-on customers hit at MEB

Complaints against the Midlands Electricity Board are soaring, a consumer watchdog said today. The number of dissatisfied customers going to the Midlands Electricity Consultative Council has risen by nearly a quarter.

Figures in the council's annual report show that 1,710 complaints — a leap of 22 per cent — were received in the year ending March 31.

The council said: "This increase represents a serious trend which will need to be carefully monitored. If continued it would represent a doubling of the number of cases handled in just three years."

The council, an independent body set up to protect the interests of electricity consumers, dealt mainly with complaints about accounts.

Members felt that many of the complaints should have been settled by board staff.

Source: Express and Star, 11 July 1985

1 What is the Midland Electricity Consultative Council? *(3 marks)*

2 What has the Council complained of in its report? *(2 marks1)*

3 Why does the Midland Electricity Board have such a council when firms like the Midland Bank, Tesco's or ICI do not? *(5 marks)*

4 Would the Midland Electricity Board need such a council if it were privatised? Explain your answer carefully. *(5 marks)*

Unit 45 Nationalisation and Privatisation

Back in the old routine

FOR THE year to March, British Telecom registered a record profit of £1,480 million as compared to £990 million the previous year.

This profit is £130 million more than the optimistic forecast that was made when the company was first privately floated — due in no small way to the large increases in telephone charges.

When BT was hived off, the public were told that a more efficient running would provide the customer with a better service, and that in certain areas competition would be beneficial.

Like the gas and electricity services, BT had previously been a useful set-up for backdoor taxation, as the public were constantly being charged higher tariffs regardless of whatever profits were made.

Now Sir George Jefferson, chairman of BT, tells us that there will be no increase in prices before November, for which, presumably, we are supposed to be grateful.

Admittedly BT must continue to be a pioneer in the telecommunications field, but is the public expected to finance such expensive aspirations?

Are we, under privatisation, to return to the old nationalised maxim of regularly increased charges regardless of profit margins?

The Government has ordered BT to limit its rises to a figure below the inflation rate, which sounds fair enough. But if the profits are so massive, why should there be any increase at all? Indeed, why should there not be a decrease?

Source: Express and Star, 20 June 1985

1 What was the increase in BT profits between 1983/4 and 1984/5? *(1 mark)*

2 What is meant in the article by:
(a) 'privately floated'
(b) 'back door taxation'? *(4 marks)*

3 In what ways have consumers (a) benefited and (b) lost out due to the privatisation of BT? *(5 marks)*

Unit 46 The Location of Industry

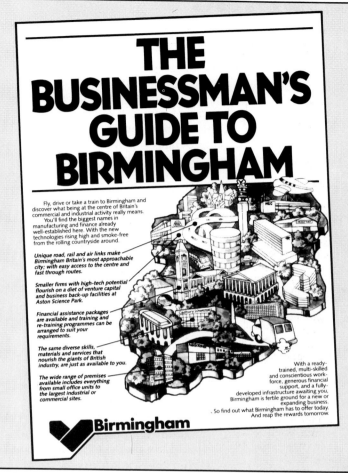

THE BUSINESSMAN'S GUIDE TO BIRMINGHAM

Fly, drive or take a train to Birmingham and discover what being at the centre of Britain's commercial and industrial activity really means.

You'll find the biggest names in manufacturing and finance already well-established here. With the new technologies rising high and smoke-free from the rolling countryside around.

Unique road, rail and air links make Birmingham Britain's most approachable city; with easy access to the centre and fast through routes.

Smaller firms with high-tech potential flourish on a diet of venture capital and business back-up facilities at Aston Science Park.

Financial assistance packages are available and training and re-training programmes can be arranged to suit your requirements.

The same diverse skills, materials and services that nourish the giants of British industry, are just as available to you.

The wide range of premises available includes everything from small office units to the largest industrial or commercial sites.

With a ready-trained, multi-skilled and conscientious work-force, generous financial support, and a fully-developed infrastructure awaiting you, Birmingham is fertile ground for a new or expanding business. So find out what Birmingham has to offer today. And reap the rewards tomorrow.

Birmingham

Source: Financial Times, 25 January 1985

1 Who is the advertisement aimed at? *(1 mark)*

2 What attractions does Birmingham offer according to the article? *(3 marks)*

3 Which of these attractions might particularly influence a firm:
(a) supplying parts to the motor industry?
(b) distributing goods all over the country?
(c) engaged in promoting other firms' products? *(6 marks)*

Unit 47 The Social Costs of Production

Battle to beat killer clouds costs billions

DEADLY acid rain is turning the air sour for the money-making industries of North America.

Clouds laden with sulphur dioxide and nitrogen oxide from factory chimneys are killing national forests from the maple woods of Quebec, to the redwood forests of California.

From ROSS MARK in Washington

According to a congressional survey, acid-rain damage to crops, forests and fisheries adds up to ten billion pounds a year on the whole continent.

America's Environmental Protection Agency alone will spend £50 million this year on acid-rain research.

The congressional survey also blames the chemical emissions for unusually high rates of birth defects and cancer.

One study showed that during the last five years, residents of industrial suburbs, particularly near chemical plants, suffered a 21 per cent higher incidence of cancer than the national average.

Some smelting and chemical plants are being forced to close down because they cannot afford to clean up and produce economically.

Mr David Stockman, White House director of the budget, told Congress: "It will cost something like 6,000 dollars a pound if we clean up to the point of preserving our fish."

Source: Daily Express, 3 April 1985

1 What pollution is being produced by US industry? *(4 marks)*

2 How much is pollution costing the US economy? *(2 marks)*

3 To what extent should pollution by industry be controlled? *(4 marks)*

Essay Questions
Units 44–47

1 'The Government plans to sell off the whole of the electricity industry to the private sector'.
(a) Give *four* reasons why the Government might want to sell off the electricity industry. *(8 marks)*
(b) How might the consumer be affected by this privatisation? *(6 marks)*
(c) How could the industry be privatised without creating a private sector monopoly? *(6 marks)*

2 (a) Give *five* reasons why a firm making cars might decide to open a new factory in one place rather than another. *(10 marks)*
(b) What would the costs and benefits to the local economy of the establishment of such a factory in the area? *(10 marks)*

National Income

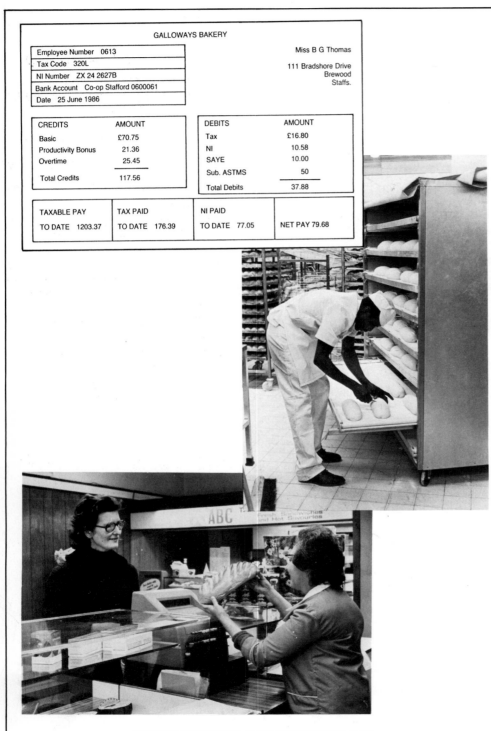

GALLOWAYS BAKERY

Employee Number	0613
Tax Code	320L
NI Number	ZX 24 2627B
Bank Account	Co-op Stafford 0600061
Date	25 June 1986

Miss B G Thomas
111 Bradshore Drive
Brewood
Staffs.

CREDITS	AMOUNT		DEBITS	AMOUNT
Basic	£70.75		Tax	£16.80
Productivity Bonus	21.36		NI	10.58
Overtime	25.45		SAYE	10.00
			Sub. ASTMS	50
Total Credits	117.56		Total Debits	37.88

TAXABLE PAY	TAX PAID	NI PAID	
TO DATE 1203.37	TO DATE 176.39	TO DATE 77.05	NET PAY 79.68

S T U D Y P O I N T S

1 What is the link between these three illustrations?

2 Use these illustrations to show how money flows round the economy.

3 Construct a circular flow diagram showing the transactions in the three illustrations.

4 What would be the effect if the Government imposed a 10% tax on the sale of bread?

'GNP to rise by 3% next year.'

GNP or gross national product is a measure of *national income*. It measures the value of the goods and services produced over a period of time by an economy, which must also equal what is spent and earned in the economy as a whole.

National income can be measured in a number of different ways:

- GROSS DOMESTIC PRODUCT (GDP). This is the value of all the goods and services produced over a period of time within a country.

- GROSS NATIONAL PRODUCT (GNP) is GDP plus what is called 'net property income from abroad'. The citizens and organisations of one country may own assets such as firms or land in another country or may have lent money to another country. These assets will earn interest, profits and dividends, which can then be brought back to the home country to spend, and so they are part of the income of that country. UK *net property income from abroad* is the difference between income earned abroad and what the UK has to pay to foreigners who own assets in the UK.

- NATIONAL INCOME is GNP minus an allowance for *depreciation*. Over a period of time, the value of the existing stock of capital in an economy – the machines, buildings, etc. – declines through wear and tear. So depreciation needs to be taken away from the gross income of the economy to get at the true value of what the country has earned after allowing for the wear and tear of the nation's stock of physical wealth.

The Circular Flow of Income

The CIRCULAR FLOW OF INCOME is a way of showing how income circulates in the economy. Figure 48.1 shows a simple economy with no government sector and no foreign trade. There are only households and firms in the economy. Households spend money on goods and services produced by firms. What households spend must equal exactly the value of what firms have produced for sale – i.e. national expenditure must equal national output. Households get the money to buy these goods and services by supplying the factors of production they own to firms. Households earn their income by working for firms, hiring out the land and the machines they own, etc. So income must equal expenditure. Hence:

National Income = National Expenditure
= National Output.

In the real economy, this is still true. Matters are complicated, however, because there is a government sector and there is foreign trade. In Figure 48.1, it was assumed that households spent all their income on the output produced by firms, and that firms produced only goods and services for consumers. In Figure 48.2, this assumption is relaxed because:

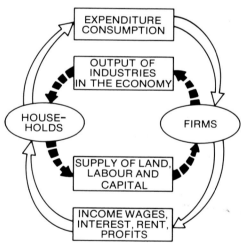

Figure 48.1

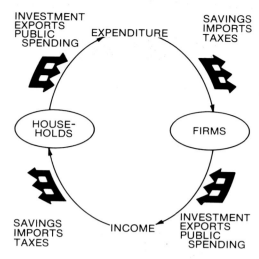

Figure 48.2

- Money is added to the circular flow, because firms – as well as producing goods for consumers – also *invest*. Governments spend money on public expenditure programmes and foreigners buy exports. Investment, government (public) spending and exports are known as *injections* into the circular flow of income.

- Money leaks out of the circular flow because both households and firms have to pay taxes to the government; money is spent on imports (i.e. goods and services not produced by UK firms); and firms and households do not spend all their income, but save some of it. Savings, taxes and imports are known as *leakages* or *withdrawals* from the circular flow.

At any point in time, money going into the circular flow must equal the money leaving it – i.e. injections must equal withdrawals. But the amount of money going round the circular flow of income can and does change over time. National income tends to grow.

What this might mean to the ordinary citizen is discussed in Unit 65.

CHECKPOINTS

1 What is the difference between GDP, GNP and national income?

2 Figure 48.3 shows national accounts. Copy out the table and fill in the missing figures.
Figure 48.3

	£ billion		
	1985	1986	1987
Gross domestic product	100	102	105
Net property income from abroad	+4		
Gross national product		107	
Depreciation	–6	–5	–7
National income			104

3 What will happen to the income in the circular flow:
(a) if investment expenditure increases;
(b) if government spending declines;
(c) if saving increases;
(d) if exports decline?

COURSEWORK SUGGESTION

Consider a small part of the circular flow of income. Take your household and the employers for whom members of your household work. Show to whom money is paid from your household (e.g. your local shop). Try to show how those firms pass on that money to other firms or back to households. Find out how the employers receive money to pay for the wages, salaries, interest, etc. earned by your household. Show how the government and the foreign sector fit in to all this. Explain why the circular flow of income in the real world is much more complex than the simple textbook model. Try to assess the extent to which income tax cuts by the government might help to increase income in the circular flow and create jobs.

KEY TERMS

NATIONAL INCOME – the value of income, output and expenditure of an economy over a period of time.

GROSS NATIONAL PRODUCT – the value of national income, not including the value of wear and tear (or *depreciation*) on the capital stock of the economy.

GROSS DOMESTIC PRODUCT – the value of all goods and services produced within an economy over a period of time.

CIRCULAR FLOW OF INCOME – a term used to describe the flow of money round the economy as it passes between consumers and producers.

Output

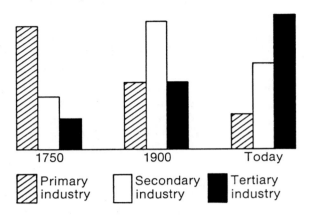

Figure 49.1 The change in the composition of output, 1750 to the present day

1750   1900   Today

Primary industry   Secondary industry   Tertiary industry

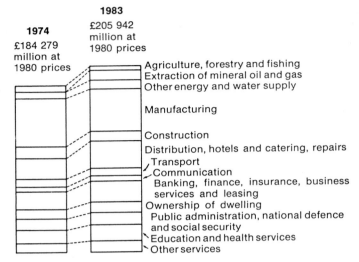

Figure 49.2 Value of national output by industry (value added, Gross Domestic Product at factory cost), 1974 and 1983

1974
£184 279 million at 1980 prices

1983
£205 942 million at 1980 prices

Agriculture, forestry and fishing
Extraction of mineral oil and gas
Other energy and water supply

Manufacturing

Construction
Distribution, hotels and catering, repairs
Transport
Communication
Banking, finance, insurance, business services and leasing
Ownership of dwelling
Public administration, national defence and social security
Education and health services
Other services

Source: CSO, *United Kingdom National Accounts*, 1984

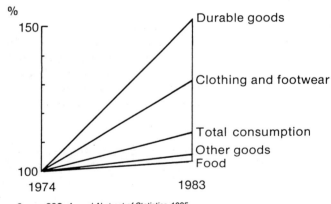

Figure 49.3 Increase in spending: 1983 consumers' expenditure, as a percentage of 1974

%

150

Durable goods

Clothing and footwear

Total consumption
Other goods
Food

100
1974   1983

Source: CSO, *Annual Abstract of Statistics*, 1985

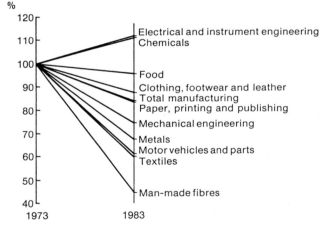

Figure 49.4 The decline in manufacturing output: 1983 output as a percentage of 1973

%
120
110
100
90
80
70
60
50
40
1973   1983

Electrical and instrument engineering
Chemicals
Food
Clothing, footwear and leather
Total manufacturing
Paper, printing and publishing
Mechanical engineering
Metals
Motor vehicles and parts
Textiles
Man-made fibres

Source: CSO, *Economic Trends Annual Supplement*, 1985

S T U D Y   P O I N T S

Read the section on 'Primary, Secondary and Tertiary Industry' in the text. Look at Figure 49.1

1 How has the composition of output in the UK economy changed?

Look at Figure 49.2

2 Make a list of primary, secondary and tertiary industries.

3 Estimate the proportion of total output in the economy in 1983 produced by each of the three sectors of industry.

4 How has the output of each of the sectors changed in size between 1974 and 1983?

Look at Figure 49.3

5 Why might you expect from Figure 49.3 that manufacturing output should have gone up over the period?

Look at Figure 49.4

6 How has output in manufacturing industry changed between 1974 and 1983?

7 What are the likely effects on jobs and incomes in the UK of the falling output in manufacturing (called 'de-industrialisation') shown in Figure 49.4?

Primary, Secondary and Tertiary Industry

The factors of production – land, labour and capital – are combined to produce goods and services. Choices have to be made about what to produce. What do the economic decision-makers in the UK economy choose to produce?

The value of total production in the economy is known as total OUTPUT. This can be measured by calculating the value of production in the three sectors of the economy.

- The PRIMARY sector of the economy is where raw materials (i.e. the factor of production called land) are being mined, grown, collected or cut down. Coal mining, agriculture and North Sea oil production are the three most important primary industries in the UK.

- The SECONDARY or *manufacturing* sector of the economy turns raw materials into goods – everything from steel bars and tanks to flower pots and yoghurt.

- The TERTIARY or *service* sector of the economy produces services ranging from education to prisons to tourism to defence.

Changes Over Time

The economy changes over time. The UK economy has developed in a broadly similar way to other developed economies round the world. Three hundred years ago, it was still an economy that was essentially agricultural. The primary sector of the economy was the most important wealth-creating sector of the economy.

Then came the Industrial Revolution, which started about 200 years ago. A series of important inventions led to the development of new manufactured products and new cheaper ways of producing those products. People moved to towns and cities to work in the new factories. Manufacturing became the most important sector of the economy. During the twentieth century, it has been the tertiary or service sector of the economy that has seen the fastest growth. With rising incomes, consumers spend a larger and larger proportion of their incomes on services such as health, education and financial services. This process is shown in Figures 49.1–49.2.

Deindustrialisation

Manufacturing industry may have been shrinking as a *proportion* of total output, but the demand for manufactured goods has grown as household incomes have increased. Figure 49.3 shows how spending on a variety of manufactured goods has risen in the UK.

Yet Figure 49.4 shows that manufacturing output has actually declined in recent years. Output over the period 1973–83 has fallen for nearly all manufacturing industries. If the British consumer is spending more on manufactures, but British industry is producing less, it can only be the case that Britain's imports of manufactured goods from abroad have increased.

The fall in manufacturing output in the UK is a very worrying trend. It is known as DEINDUSTRIALISATION – losing industry. It is worrying because less industry means fewer jobs. Nearly 3 million jobs were lost in manufacturing between 1971 and 1985. It is also worrying because less industry means lower income. While foreign countries grow better off, in part by selling their products to the UK, Britons see their incomes growing at a much slower pace.

K E Y T E R M S

OUTPUT – that which is produced by the factors of production.

PRIMARY INDUSTRY – industry that extracts raw materials from the earth, such as coal, fish or wheat.

SECONDARY INDUSTRY – industry that processes primary products into manufactured goods.

TERTIARY INDUSTRY – industry that provides a service, such as banking, hairdressing or retailing.

DEINDUSTRIALISATION – the process whereby an economy loses established industries, which are not replaced by new industries.

The Standard of Living

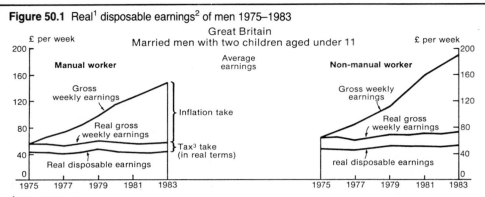

Figure 50.1 Real[1] disposable earnings[2] of men 1975–1983

Great Britain
Married men with two children aged under 11

[1] At April 1975 prices.
[2] The husband's earnings *plus* family support. Family support is the value of family allowance or child benefit, which replaced family allowance from April 1977.
[3] Income tax *plus* national insurance contributions.

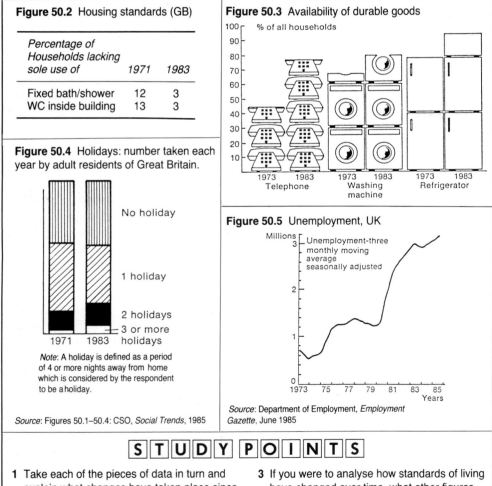

Figure 50.2 Housing standards (GB)

Percentage of Households lacking sole use of	1971	1983
Fixed bath/shower	12	3
WC inside building	13	3

Figure 50.4 Holidays: number taken each year by adult residents of Great Britain.

No holiday
1 holiday
2 holidays
3 or more holidays

1971   1983

Note: A holiday is defined as a period of 4 or more nights away from home which is considered by the respondent to be a holiday.

Source: Figures 50.1–50.4: CSO, *Social Trends*, 1985

Figure 50.3 Availability of durable goods

% of all households

1973 1983   1973 1983   1973 1983
Telephone   Washing   Refrigerator
               machine

Figure 50.5 Unemployment, UK

Millions

Unemployment–three monthly moving average seasonally adjusted

1973 75 77 79 81 83 85
Years

Source: Department of Employment, *Employment Gazette*, June 1985

STUDY POINTS

1 Take each of the pieces of data in turn and explain what changes have taken place since the early 1970s.

2 Have these changes resulted in an improvement or a deterioration in people's standard of living on average? Explain your answer carefully.

3 If you were to analyse how standards of living have changed over time, what other figures might you want to consider apart from those shown above?

4 What do you expect to happen to living standards over the next fifteen years and why?

Is the UK better off today than it was 20 or 50 or 200 years ago? How is the UK doing compared to countries such as France, the USA or Japan? These are important questions and they relate to the measurement of a country's **STANDARD OF LIVING**. There is no precise measure of a country's standard of living, but economists produce a variety of statistics which help provide answers.

National Income

The set of statistics most commonly linked to measurement of the standard of living is national income. At first sight, this makes a lot of sense. If your income were to go up by £10 a week, surely your standard of living would improve? Unfortunately, the answer is 'not necessarily'. National income statistics have a number of important limitations.

- National income statistics only measure the value of goods and services sold, or incomes actually paid in the economy. Much 'expenditure' and 'income' goes unrecorded. Housewives, for instance, produce goods and services, but they do not receive a wage for that. DIY is another example. If you pay a decorator to paint your house, that will be recorded as part of national income. If you do it yourself, it will not be recorded. The end product – a painted house – is the same, however. Changes in the amount of unrecorded output, expenditure and income can have a very important effect on the standard of living, but they will not show up on national income statistics.

- National income statistics measure the value of income, including the inflation element. This inflation element must be taken out of the statistics, if any sensible comparison is to be made.

- National income may grow, but that does not necessarily mean that everybody will be better off. Some groups in society may be a great deal better off, and others may actually be worse off. National income only shows how the economy *as a whole* is doing.

- Income may grow, but so too may population. So it is far better to consider income per head of the population if any comparison is to be made.

- National income statistics do not show any improvements in the quality of products. National income may stay the same over time, but if the quality of products is rising, then the standard of living should be improving too.

- Goods and services may be produced, but they do not necessarily help increase the standard of living of the population. Cigarettes, for instance, arguably lead to a lowering of the standard of living for smokers and non-smokers, but they are included in national income.

- The social costs of production – pollution, stress, crime, etc. – are not recorded as part of national income, yet they need to be included in a measure of the standard of living.

Consumption and Ownership Statistics

An alternative way of judging living standards is to consider consumption and ownership patterns. This is particularly useful in developing countries, where national income figures are even less reliable as a measure of the standard of living than in developed countries. Consumption and ownership statistics might include:

- the number of households that own a cooker, television set, refrigerator, car etc;

- the number of patients there are per doctor;

- the number of children per thousand of the population who die each year;

- the average food intake per person;

- the proportion of the population that can read or write.

These statistics should give an indication of what proportion of the population is enjoying a minimum standard of living.

Social and Environmental Statistics

A further way of judging living standards is to look at social and environmental indicators, such as:

- the crime rate;

- whether there are free elections in the country;

- the amount of pollution there is in the country;

- the suicide rate.

Conclusions

By considering these different measures, it is possible to have some idea of how standards of living have changed over time, but it is not possible to come up with a precise measure. Ultimately, any answer must be based on a value judgement of how to weigh all the different components that go to make up a country's standard of living.

C H E C K P O I N T S

1 From the figures in Figure 50.6, calculate for the period 1990–2000:
   (a) the change in national income (at current prices) in pounds;
   (b) the percentage change in national income (at current prices);

Figure 50.6

Year	1990	2000
National income (£ million)	9000	11000
Population (million)	9	10
Price level (1990 = 100)	100	110

   (c) the change in national income per head of the population (at current prices);
   (d) the percentage change in prices.
   To what extent has the standard of living improved over the period 1990–2000?

2 Does a growth in DIY activity in an economy indicate an increase in the standard of living or a decline? Why?

3 Why might an increase in (a) cigarette consumption; (b) butter consumption; (c) consumption of alcoholic drink lead to a rise in national income, but a decline in the standard of living?

4 Why are social and environmental factors important in the standard of living of a population?

C O U R S E W O R K S U G G E S T I O N

Compare changes in the standard of living for the UK economy with that of a particular individual or household. Interview an older person or persons, such as your grandparents. Ask them questions about the standard of living as they remember it in a particular year (e.g. 1950) and their standard of living today. Gather statistics from sources such as the *Annual Abstract of Statistics*, *Social Trends* and *Economic Trends Annual Supplement* (all published by HMSO). Social history books of the period might be of help, too. Compare the way in which living standards have changed for the person you have interviewed and for the nation as a whole. Try to assess the extent to which both are better off now than in the past.

K E Y T E R M

STANDARD OF LIVING – how well off an individual or a nation is at a point in time. One important, but imperfect measure of the standard of living is the level of national income.

NEW NO-PENALTY WITHDRAWALS

Cashpoint Deposit Account

Lloyds Cashpoint

Home Improvement Loans

NatWest eurocheques   NatWest

MORTGAGE SERVICE.

Don't be kept hanging around for a mortgage.

BARCLAYS

The benefits of a cheque account.

A cheque account allows you to move money from one place to another without having to handle any cash. Your salary can be paid directly into your account and then whenever you want cash or need to pay a bill you just write out a cheque.

A husband and wife can pool their resources and open a 'joint account.' This means that either partner can sign cheques on the same account.

A cheque account will make moving your money around a lot simpler. For instance, if you've got to send money to a friend or relative, or if you want to buy something through the post, you no longer have to take the risk of putting cash in the post or making the trek to the nearest post office to buy a postal order.

You just send a cheque. You don't have to worry about carrying large amounts of money about. Once you open a cheque account your money is safe.

A cheque account will help you to control your spending because a cheque book is usually less likely to burn...

Lloyds Bank services for new students.

- FREE BANKING
- £8 CREDIT
- £200 OVERDRAFT
- CHEQUE BOOK AND CARD
- CASHPOINT CARD
- STANDING ORDERS
- REGULAR STATEMENTS

A thoroughbred amongst banks

BARCLAYS TAKE-AWAY BANK

STUDY POINTS

1. What do you think are the main functions of a bank?

2. Who are the main customers of a bank?

3. Explain how a bank acts as an *intermediary*, i.e. linking its customers together.

4. How do banks make a profit?

5. In what ways are building societies similar to banks?

6. Where, apart from banks and building societies, can you borrow and lend money?

7. Are the activities of banks beneficial to the economy? In what ways?

High-street Institutions

Most adults in the UK today have a bank or building society account of some sort. This was not true 50 years ago. The growth of *financial institutions*, such as banks, has come about because the increase in real incomes has meant that customers have demanded more and more sophisticated financial services.

Banks, building societies and other financial institutions are *financial intermediaries*. What this means is that they specialise in acting as go-betweens amongst customers. Customers fall into three main categories: ordinary people ('personal customers'), firms and government. There are three main services which these go-betweens supply:

- as *borrowers*, they enable customers to keep money in a safe place, and to earn interest on their savings;
- as *lenders*, they enable customers to borrow money to finance spending;
- as *transferrers of money*, they enable customers to pay bills, and get money from place to place and from customer to customer.

Most financial institutions aim to make a profit. They do this by charging for transfers of money and by lending out money at higher rates of interest than those at which they borrow.

Probably the most important high-street financial institutions are BANKS. They borrow money from customers either through *current accounts*, which pay customers no interest, but do give them facilities for issuing cheques and other ways of transferring money; or through *deposit accounts* which give interest on savings. They lend to customers through loans or overdrafts. Customers use their bank most often to transfer money through the *cheque* system.

Some banks, often called *secondary banks* or *finance houses*, specialise in providing credit loans and hire-purchase agreements. They also accept savings and many provide a limited cheque system.

Building societies specialise in providing loans for property (these are called mortgages). Almost all the money to finance these loans is borrowed from ordinary customers through their branch network.

The London Money Markets

Very large borrowers, such as governments and financial institutions, themselves borrow and lend money on the LONDON MONEY MARKETS. For instance, Barclays Bank may borrow £200 million from other banks and use this money to lend to the government. Or the Halifax Building Society may have borrowed £50 million more from customers than it can lend in mortgages. Rather than let that £50 million do nothing, it will lend the money on the London money markets to earn interest.

Some of the main institutions in the London money markets are:

- *The Bank of England.* Owned by the government, it is responsible for policing the money markets and making sure that banks and other institutions act properly. It is responsible for the implementation of monetary policy (discussed in Unit 70). It is the government's banker, and is responsible for handling the government's revenue and spending as well as its borrowing. It is responsible for issuing new notes and coins. As the bank to other banks, it is the 'lender of the last resort', willing to lend money to the banking system to prevent banks going bankrupt.

- DISCOUNT HOUSES. These are specialist institutions that borrow money for as short a period as 24 hours and lend it out to governments and other financial institutions on a slightly broader basis. They hold a crucial role in London, because they are the only institutions allowed to borrow money from the Bank of England in its role as lender of the last resort.

- The STOCK EXCHANGE. This is probably the most famous institution in the City of London, although it is not the most important. It is a place where stocks and shares are bought and sold, and it provides a market for long-term borrowing. It is important for the government, because the government borrows a great deal of money via the Stock Exchange. It is also important for companies since the existence of a market for second-hand shares allows companies to issue new shares more easily.

CHECKPOINTS

1 What is a 'financial intermediary'?
2 Why would a firm use a bank?
3 Compare the activities of finance houses and building societies.
4 What are the functions of the Bank of England?
5 How do you think a discount house makes a profit?
6 What is the role of the Stock Exchange?

KEY TERMS

BANK – a financial institution that specialises in borrowing, lending and transferring money.

LONDON MONEY MARKETS – the term used to describe the market for money borrowed and lent by and between banks, finance houses, discount houses, the Bank of England and other financial institutions.

DISCOUNT HOUSES – financial institutions that borrow and lend at very short notice on the London money markets.

THE STOCK EXCHANGE – a market for new and second-hand government stock and for second-hand shares.

COURSEWORK SUGGESTION

Research one financial institution. Describe its activities. Assess the role that it plays in the economy. Try to evaluate the extent to which it secures a better allocation of resources in the economy.

The Creation of Credit

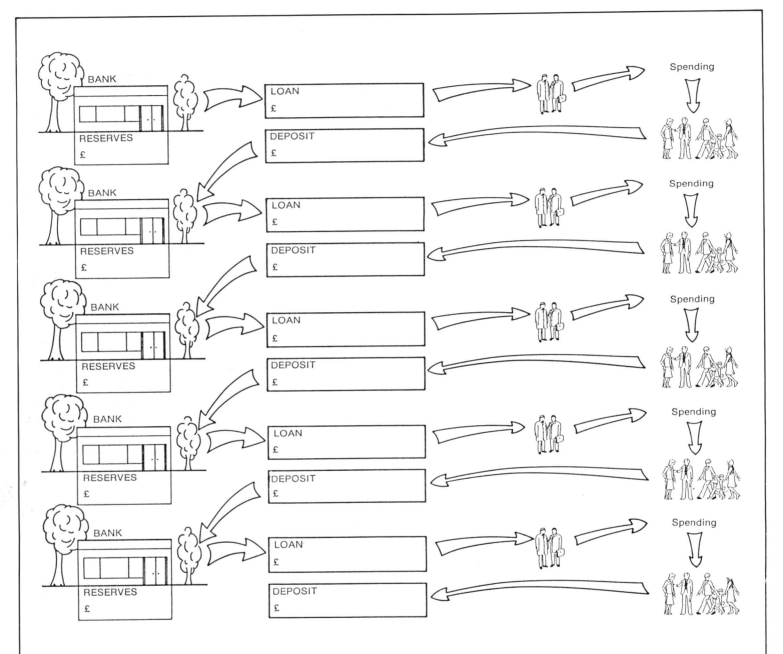

STUDY POINTS

Assume that there is only one bank in the economy. Any money which the bank lends out is eventually redeposited in the bank by other customers. The government of the country has ordered that the bank must keep a fixed percentage of its total deposits in the form of notes and coins. A customer enters the bank and opens an account with £100 worth of notes and coins.

1 Copy out the diagram above and fill in the £ figures, assuming that the bank has to keep 50% of its deposits in cash. If the process carries on until the bank can lend out no more money, how much cash will it have in its vaults? How much money will it have lent out in total? How much money will the bank have deposited with it?

2 What would your answers be to Task 1 if instead of keeping 50% of deposits in notes and coins the bank has to keep: (a) 25% and (b) 10%.

Credit Creation

How much money have you got in the bank? How much money does the bank have available to repay you and all the other customers it has borrowed from? It may come as a surprise to know that for every £1 deposited in a bank, the average bank has only got about 1p in cash. If everybody wanted his or her money back at the same time, the bank would go bankrupt, however big it was and however well run it was. Why is this the case and of what importance is it?

Imagine a customer depositing £100 in notes into a bank account. The bank knows from past experience that the customer is unlikely to want to withdraw that £100 in total in the near future. Assume that past experience shows that on average only £1 is withdrawn on any one day for every £100 deposited with the bank. That means that the bank can safely lend out the other £99. It earns interest on the money lent and therefore it makes a profit on the transaction.

Therefore £99 is lent out. What will the borrowers of that money do with it? They may well spend it, and then the firms or individuals who receive the money are likely to redeposit part or all of that money in a bank account. If they deposit all of the £99, the bank finds itself again in a position to lend out more money, because it need only keep 1% of the £99 to satisfy customer demands for repayment. So the bank keeps 99p and lends out £98.01.

This process of depositing and lending goes on for as long as customers have too much cash and prefer to deposit it in the bank. In our example, the bank ends up with deposits of £100 + £99 + £98.01 + £97.03 + £96.06 + £95.10 + . . . which added up comes to no less than £10 000. This process is what is known as CREDIT CREATION. Banks have the power to increase the amount of bank money (not by the manufacture of notes and coins of course, because

only the Bank of England and the Royal Mint can do that) in circulation.

It is important to realise that when it is said that banks can create money, it is not their own money they are creating. They are creating money for their customers to borrow and lend. If the banks did not lend money, then their lenders could not spend it, and so other customers could not receive money to put back into the banks.

It is also important to realise that banks can only create a limited amount of money. The limits to this creation are fixed by the sorts of assets that banks have to keep when they borrow new money from their customers. For instance, if the banks have to keep £1 in every £100 deposited in the form of notes and coins in order to satisfy the day-to-day cash needs of their customers, then they cannot borrow £10 000 million from their customers and only have £10 million in cash. If they only have £10 million in cash, then they can only borrow a maximum of £1000 million from their customers. Any more and they are threatened with bankruptcy, if they cannot repay customers their money on a day-to-day basis.

Two ways in which money is created – the Royal Mint coining money and banks lending money which will be redeposited as new money with the banking system.

CHECKPOINTS

1 What does the term 'bankruptcy' mean?

2 Why would any bank go bankrupt, if all depositors with the bank wanted to withdraw their money from the bank on the same day?

3 Explain why £1000 lent out by the banking system is likely to return to the banking system as deposits.

4 How can the banking system create credit?

5 What limits the amount of money that the banking system can create?

COURSEWORK SUGGESTION

Using figures from the latest copy of the *Bank of England Quarterly Bulletin*, describe the balance sheet of the UK clearing banks. From textbooks or other material, find out what legal requirements exist for the clearing banks to hold particular types of assets. From this, explain what limits there are to the banking system's ability to create credit.

KEY TERMS

CREDIT CREATION – the ability of the banking system to create new deposits and loans, and hence to increase the money supply.

Data Response Questions
Units 48–52

Unit 48 National Income

National income, 1983 (£ billions)

Gross domestic product	257.5
Net property income from abroad	1.9
Capital depreciation	36.5

Source: CSO, *United Kingdom National Accounts*, 1984

1 Calculate (a) gross national product and (b) national income in 1983. *(2 marks)*

2 Explain what is measured by gross domestic product. *(3 marks)*

3 (a) What is meant by capital depreciation?
  (b) Why should it be subtracted from the nation's gross income to measure better the value of its income? *(5 marks)*

Unit 49 Output

Share of manufacturing in GDP[1] (%)

	1960	1973	1983
Canada	23.3	20.2	15.9
US	28.6	24.9	21.1
Japan	33.9	35.1	30.5
France	29.1	28.3	25.3
W. Germany	40.3	36.3	31.8
Italy	28.5	30.0	27.1
Netherlands	33.6	26.8	17.0
Norway	21.3	21.5	13.7
UK	32.1	28.5	21.0

[1] Value added in manufacturing as percentage of current price GDP.
Source: The Treasury, *Economic Progress Report*, June–July 1985

1 (a) Which country's economy had the largest share of manufacturing in GDP in (i) 1960, (ii) 1973 and (iii) 1983?
  (b) What was the share of manufacturing in GDP in the UK in 1983? *(2 marks)*

2 What has happened to the importance of manufacturing in total output over the period 1960 to 1983 for the countries in the data? *(2 marks)*

3 Suggest reasons why there has been this change over time. *(5 marks)*

4 Which two countries have seen the largest change in the share of manufacturing in GDP over time? *(1 mark)*

Unit 50 The Standard of Living

Is society becoming richer and richer?

Most people believe that the gross national product – the national income – provides a good measure of changes in our economic performance. But if we are to decide whether people are better off now than, say 30, 50 or 100 years ago we must look at other more powerful measures of change.

National income is a poor measure of changes in standards of living for a number of reasons. For instance, over the past 30 years national income has risen due to the fact that more women have gone out to work. But the loss of services produced in the home as a result has not been deducted from national income because they were never included in the first place.

Or take defence spending. Does rising spending on defence indicate that the country is better off or in fact that it is worse off because we feel more threatened by other countries?

National income also includes those expenditures needed to help us work – motorways, cars, buses to transport goods and people, banks to provide finance for business, inspectors and equipment to control pollution. But these don't add to our standards of living. They are part of the cost of producing.

Our industrial society is becoming richer and richer, but isn't it true that pre-industrial society was just as well off and catered better for man's basic spiritual and biological needs?

Adapted from *The Guardian*, 19 December 1984

1 What is meant by:
  (a) 'national income';
  (b) 'standard of living'? *(4 marks)*

2 Explain in your words why, in the author's opinion, national income is not a good measure of the standard of living. *(2 marks)*

3 Describe two ways in which people might have been better off in a pre-industrial society than today. Describe two ways in which they might have been worse off. *(4 marks)*

Unit 51 The Financial system of the UK

Building societies are beginning to suffer

Building societies are now beginning to suffer from the same sort of competitive pressure that they themselves have placed on the banks over the past twenty years.

The big banks are now offering much higher rates of interest on deposits and have increased the amounts offered as mortgages. Over the past year, all the clearing banks have followed Barclay's lead and started opening branches on Saturdays.

The building societies on the other hand, although opening on Saturdays, have been forced to cut back on the number of new branches they are opening. At the same time, the building societies have been challenging the banks' cash transmission services by the establishment of automated teller machine networks such as *Link*.

The competition should become even fiercer once building societies are allowed to offer personal loans to customers.

Adapted from *The Financial Times*, 7 October 1985

1 Describe *four* ways in which banks and building societies are competing. *(3 marks)*

2 Explain *two* ways in which banks and building societies act as financial intermediaries according to the article. *(4 marks)*

3 Suggest *two* ways in which competition between banks and building societies might be increased even further in the future. *(4 marks)*

Unit 52 The Creation of Credit

Run on the Middlewhich Bank

The Middlewhich Bank had to close its doors today as depositors continued to withdraw funds from the troubled bank. Rumours that the bank might have had debts running to hundreds of millions of pounds as a result of lending to small North Sea oil exploration companies prompted the bank's small depositors to remove their savings from the bank. Unless an aid package is forthcoming from some of the major banks or from the Bank of England, the Middlewhich is likely to have to declare itself bankrupt within the next few days.

1 What problems face the Middlewhich Bank? *(3 marks)*

2 Why has the Middlewhich Bank not got enough cash to repay all its depositors immediately? *(3 marks)*

3 Using the Middlewhich Bank as an example, explain briefly the process of credit creation by banks. *(4 marks)*

Essay Questions
Units 48–52

1 'Service output grew faster than manufacturing output in the 12 months to December'.
 (a) Explain, giving *four* examples, what is meant by 'manufacturing' industry. *(6 marks)*
 (b) What is 'service output'? *(4 marks)*
 (c) What factors have led to a faster growing service sector in the UK economy in recent years? *(10 marks)*

2 (a) Describe *three* services that a bank offers to its customers. *(9 marks)*
 (b) What does a bank do with the money that its customers lend to it? *(6 marks)*
 (c) Explain *two* ways in which the commercial banks have dealings with the Bank of England. *(5 marks)*

The Money Supply and the Rate of Interest

PREFERENCE SHARES

CERTIFICATE No.	TRANSFER No.	DATE	NUMBER OF PREFERENCE SHARES
A 2112	T 21121	7 SEPTEMBER 1984	**600**
			OF £1 EACH

European Ferries Group Plc

(Incorporated in England under the Companies Acts 1948 to 1961, No. 1810102)

This is to Certify that the undermentioned is/are the Registered Holder(s) of the number of 5 per cent Redeemable Non-Cumulative Preference Shares of £1 each fully paid in the above Company stated below, subject to the Memorandum and Articles of Association of the Company.

A summary of the rights of the Preference Shares is printed overleaf.

HOLDER(S)

ALAIN GEORGE ANDERTON ESQ
8 BROMLEY GARDENS
CODSALL
WOLVERHAMPTON
STAFFS   WV8 1BB

MRS MARIE-NICOLE ANDERTON

NUMBER OF PREFERENCE SHARES

**SIX HUNDRED SHARES

Given under the Securities Seal of the Company

002146

Lloyds Bank Limited
EXCHANGE BRANCH
EXCHANGE BUILDINGS LIVERPOOL L2 3UP
30-93-13
11-24
OR ORDER
PAY
Z DAVIS

Midshires Building Society

High Return Account

bank giro credit

		Notes	£50	
Date			£20	
Cashier's stamp and initials	Paid in by		£10	
	Address		£5	
			£1	
		Coins	£1	
	Destination Branch Code number		50p	
	Bank		20p	
			Silver	
	Branch where account is held		Bronze	
		Total Cash £		
A/c		Cheques, etc (sub total)		
Cash		No of Cheques		£
Cheques etc	Account (Block Letters) & A/c No			
£	NWB1450 Rev May 81-1 Please do not write or mark below this line			

?0

1 If something is to be called 'money' what distinguishes it from items which are not money? (Or as economists would ask, what are the *functions* of money?)

2 Which of the items shown in the illustrations could be called 'money' and why? To help you answer this question draw up a grid with 4 vertical columns and 6 horizontal divisions. In the left-hand column list the 6 different items shown above. Above each of the other columns write a *function* of money. Fill in the grid by giving a mark out of 3 for how well each item fulfills each function. For instance, if you think that notes and coins are a very good medium of exchange, you would record a 3 in the appropriate section of the grid.

3 What would be the costs to the economy if there were no money in circulation?

Assets other than Money

It was argued in Unit 8 that money had to be able to fulfil three functions: it had to be a medium of exchange, a measure of value and a store of value. In the UK today, money is often thought to be notes and coins. But notes and coins form only a very small part of the MONEY SUPPLY – the total stock of money in the economy. This is because there are other assets, apart from notes and coins, that act as money.

Current Accounts

Far more important than notes and coins is money deposited in current accounts at banks. A current account is one where the customer is able to deposit and withdraw money without giving any notice. If a customer has £20 000 in a current account and wishes to withdraw it all in cash, the bank has to release the money immediately. Current account holders are given a *cheque book*, and they can use cheques to withdraw money from their account. Money in a current account is money because:

- it is a medium of exchange – cheques are acceptable means of payment for most transactions;
- it is a measure of value just like notes and coins;
- it is a store of value – money put into a current account can be used at a later date to purchase goods and services.

Note that cheques themselves are *not* money – it is the money behind the cheque in the current account that counts as money.

Money in deposit accounts at banks can also be counted as money. A deposit account is aimed at savers. Interest is paid on money in the account, but notice of withdrawal from the account has to be given, if the saver is not to lose interest. Deposit money is not a direct medium of exchange like current account money, because no cheque service is provided. But the money is easily available to change into either current account money or notes and coins. Bank deposit money is also a good measure of value and store of value. So bank deposit money performs the functions of money almost as well as notes and coins and current account assets. So, too, do a variety of other assets, including deposits in building societies and the national Savings Bank.

Therefore the question 'what is money?' is not easy to answer. What we find is that a variety of assets, ranging from notes and coins through to bank accounts and building society accounts through to other financial assets, perform the functions of money to varying degrees. The government currently calculates no less than five different measures of the money supply. These, roughly defined, are:

- M0, which consists mainly of notes and coins;
- M1, which is M0 plus money in current accounts at banks;
- M2, which is M1 plus any deposits (e.g. in building societies) that can be withdrawn with cheques, and small deposits in bank deposit accounts;
- M3, which is M1 plus money in bank deposit accounts;
- PSL2, which is M3 plus money in building society, National Savings Bank and other similar accounts.

The Money Supply and the Rate of Interest

If an individual, company or government wishes to obtain extra money, it can do so by borrowing that money. The price it has to pay for that is interest on the loan. So the price of money is the rate of interest. Like any price, if the supply of money increases, then the price or the rate of interest will go down. This is because, with more money to lend, the banks have to lower their rates of interest to encourage more customers to borrow. If, on the other hand, the supply of money decreases, then interest rates will go up. This important relationship will be discussed further in Unit 70.

1 What are the functions of money?

2 Explain why notes and coins perform the functions of money.

3 Why is money in current accounts at banks considered to be money?

4 Explain why gold no longer performs the functions of money in the British economy today.

5 Why are credit cards not money?

6 Explain the difference between M0 and PSL2.

7 What would you expect to happen to the rate of interest, if the money supply increased? Why?

COURSEWORK SUGGESTION

Using statistics from past issues of the *Bank of England Quarterly Bulletin* (published by the Bank of England) and *Financial Statistics* (published by HMSO), examine changes in the various definitions of the money supply since the mid-1960s. Describe the different measures of money supply. Analyse their change over time. Evaluate the extent to which assets used in broader measures of the money supply, such as PSL2, can really be seen as money.

KEY TERMS

MONEY SUPPLY – the total stock of money available in the economy at a point in time. Because there are various assets that act as money or near-money, there are a number of different definitions of the money supply, including M0, M1, M2, M3 and PSL2.

Public Expenditure (1)

Figure 54.1 Public expenditure by programme

Defence	
Overseas aid and other overseas services	
Agriculture, fisheries, food and forestry	■ 1975/6 □ 1984/5
Industry, energy, trade and employment	
Transport	
Housing	
Other environmental services	
Law, order and protective services	
Education and science, arts and libraries	
Health and personal social services	
Social security	
Other	

% of total government spending

Source: The Treasury, *Economic Progress Report*, Nos. 131 and 174

STUDY POINTS

1 Which was the costliest public expenditure programme in 1984/85? Which was the least costly?

2 If total public expenditure was £100 billion in 1984/85, how much would the social security programme have cost?

3 Which public expenditure programme would include spending on:
(a) nurses' pay
(b) school text books
(c) a police van
(d) a new motorway
(e) YTS
(f) repairs on a flat
(g) unemployment benefit
(h) a public park?

4 What have been the benefits, if any, of the change in defence spending over the period 1975/76 to 1984/85? What has been the opportunity cost of this change?

5 What has happened to the percentage spent on education over the period? Why might this have happened?

6 Which public expenditure programmes have increased their share of the total budget over the period 1975/76 to 1984/85? Explain why there might have been this increase.

7 If the government could increase public expenditure by £100 million, what should it spend the money on and why?

8 If the government had to cut public spending by £100 million, what should it cut and why?

Public and Private Sectors

The **PUBLIC SECTOR** is that sector of the economy owned and controlled by the 'state' or by 'government'. The **PRIVATE SECTOR**, by contrast, is the part of the economy directly owned and controlled by private individuals. The public sector is made up of four main parts:

- *Central government* – run by Parliament sitting in Westminster. The Prime Minister is the most important single figure here.

- *Local government* – counties, boroughs, parishes, etc. Local government is controlled by local councillors.

- *Nationalised industries* – companies owned in whole or in part by the government, such as British Rail or British Coal.

- *Other bodies* – such as the BBC and the water boards, which are public bodies, but are not directly owned or controlled by central or local governments.

Public-sector nationalised industries and the private sector both, for the most part, allocate resources via the market mechanism (this was discussed in Units 9–13). In the market place, goods and services are offered for sale and are then purchased by buyers who demand those goods and services. Consumers with no money to spend will not be allocated goods and services. The more money an individual has, the more goods and services he or she is able to buy.

Public Expenditure

Most public-sector goods and services are not allocated in this way. They are allocated on the basis of *need*. Figure 54.2 gives a breakdown of **PUBLIC EXPENDITURE** – spending by local and central government. Taking health as an example, everybody in the UK is entitled to receive 'free' medical treatment. It is free in the sense that the consumer does not have to pay for it when he or she receives medical treatment (although there are a few exceptions to this, such as prescription charges). But the citizen does pay for it through the taxes that he or she pays.

In this system, it is the government that decides how to allocate resources. It has to decide, for example, whether to spend £1 million on treating old people or £1 million on heart transplants; £100 million on strike aircraft or £100 million on nuclear submarines. Under this system, individual consumers cannot buy themselves better defence or better roads in the way that they can buy better cars or better houses, if they have the money. They can influence how governments spend money, but they do this through political means – such as voting for a particular party in an election – rather than economic means.

The government has to make very hard choices. Like an ordinary citizen, it would prefer to be able to spend more and more money – a policy which would be certain to make it popular with the electorate. But for many reasons discussed elsewhere in this book, it cannot do that. Every pound spent in one way has an opportunity cost – (i.e. some other item which could have been bought with that pound, but which now cannot be bought). In other words, the government is faced with exactly the same problems as the individual – how best to allocate the scarce resources at its disposal.

CHECKPOINTS

1 Explain the difference between the public sector and the private sector.

2 Name five services offered by central government and five services offered by local government.

3 A government has an extra £1000 million to spend. It has decided that it will spend it either on new motorways or on improving education in secondary schools. What would you advise it to do and why?

4 (a) Who is entitled to receive from the government: (i) education; (ii) prescriptions for medicines; (iii) electricity?
   (b) Which of these three items are free to the consumer, which are subsidised (i.e. the government pays part, but not all of the cost), and which does the consumer have to pay for in full?
   (c) Who has to pay, if the government provides services free of charge to the consumer?

Figure 54.2 Breakdown of public expenditure

Programme	Main responsibility	Examples of spending
Defence	Central government	Army, navy and air forces
Overseas aid and overseas services	Central government	Foreign aid to poor countries Contributions to EEC
Agriculture, fisheries food and forestry	Central government	Financial help to farmers, fishermen and foresters
Industry, energy, trade and employment	Central government	Investment grants, training schemes such as the Training for Skills
Transport	Local government	Roads, subsidies for bus and rail services
Housing	Local government	Council housing – repairs, renovation and new building
Other environmental services	Local government	Parks, sports centres, refuse collection
Law, order and protective services	Local government	Police, firemen, ambulances, prisons
Education and science	Central and local government	Universities, polytechnics, schools, scientific research
Arts and libraries	Central and local government	Subsidies to theatres, libraries
Health and personal social services	Central and local government	National Health Service Social Services departments
Social security	Central government	Unemployment benefits, pensions, supplementary benefits
Government lending to nationalised industries	Central government	Lending to British Rail, British Coal
Other	Central and local government	Help for Scotland, Wales, Northern Ireland Civil servants

Note: Central government pays for a large part of local government spending by providing grants to local authorities. This grant is known as the *Rate Support Grant*.

KEY TERMS

PUBLIC SECTOR – the sector of the economy owned and controlled by the state or government.

PRIVATE SECTOR – the sector of the economy owned and controlled by private individuals and organisations.

PUBLIC EXPENDITURE – spending by the government on programmes such as defence and social security.

COURSEWORK SUGGESTION

Describe the changes in government expenditure over the past ten years. Analyse why expenditure has changed – both total expenditure and expenditure on particular programmes. Analyse also the impact of these changes on particular groups in society, such as workers, the sick, school pupils and taxpayers. Consider whether the government has made the right changes in public spending. A good source of statistics and facts is past copies of the *Economic Progress Report* (published by the Treasury).

Public Expenditure (2)

Public Goods

The government plays a very important role in the economy. Nearly half of all income generated in the UK is spent by the government, and the government is the single most important employer in the country. Why should the public sector be so large? Why should the government provide education and roads, but not televisions and apples?

One reason is that the market mechanism – where goods and services are bought and sold for money – cannot provide certain important goods and services. Look at Figure 55.1.

Figure 55.1

Year	Average prison population
1973	36 774
1978	41 796
1983	43 462

Source: CSO, *Annual Abstract of Statistics*, 1985.

The number of people sent to prison has been rising in recent years. How are these extra prison places to be provided and who is going to pay for them? The market mechanism will not provide them. For example, if you are robbed and the thief is caught, would you then pay the £5000 a year needed to keep that person in prison? If you would not pay, who would? The only sensible way is for the government to take a small amount of money from each citizen in taxes to pay for a service which few or no individuals would pay for themselves.

A prison is an example of a PUBLIC GOOD. Other examples are the army, the police, lighthouses and the judiciary (judges, magistrates, etc.). Public goods have two essential features:

● Once the good is provided, it benefits everybody, whether or not an individual has paid for the good. For instance, once a thief has been sent to prison, everybody benefits.

S T U D Y   P O I N T S

All these photographs are examples of public expenditure.

1 Identify which services are provided in each case.

2 Which of these services would the private sector *not* provide if the government did not: i.e. which services would never be produced by a private firm and then sold to customers? Why is this the case?

3 (a) Which services can be and are provided by the private sector?

(b) Give examples of private sector firms and institutions which provide these services in the UK or abroad.

(c) Are these services better provided by the public sector or by the private sector? List all the arguments for and against in each case.

- It is impossible to prevent somebody benefiting from the good, once it has been provided. For instance, once the defence of the UK has been provided, an individual citizen cannot fail to benefit from that provision.

An ordinary private good is different. If a consumer buys a television, that television set will not benefit everybody in the country – it will only benefit the owner and the people he or she allows to watch the set. So the owner can prevent others from enjoying the benefits of the set.

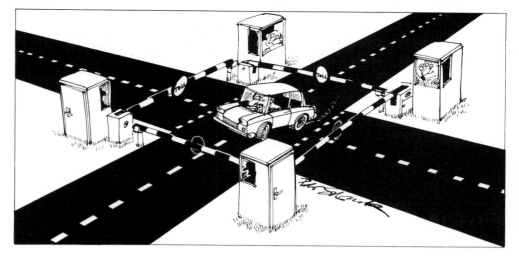

Merit Goods

Public goods, such as defence and law and order, account for only a small part of total public spending. Another important justification for government spending is that otherwise the market would not provide enough of a particular good or service. Take education, for example. If everybody in the UK is to prosper in the future, it is essential that the country should have a well-educated work force. It is also important that citizens are educated to play a responsible role in society. People who cannot read and write, or who cannot use numbers, or who do not understand basic economic issues are going to be a drain on society rather than an asset. But what if all parents had to pay for their children's education and all schools were private? Many parents would not be able to afford or might not want to afford to send their children to school. Fewer children would receive a proper education. Not only would those children be harmed, but everybody else in society would be affected indirectly for the worse.

Products that free market forces would underprovide are known as MERIT GOODS. Examples are roads (imagine the consequences of paying a toll for each section of road you want to use), health services (what if people were walking the streets with contagious diseases, because they could not afford treatment?), and education.

Equity, Efficiency and Control

There are three other important reasons why governments spend money.

- *Equity* – government spending is used to help those in need in society, such as the old, the sick and the unemployed. This aspect is covered in Unit 74. (Note that the word 'equity' has other meanings, including the one explained in Unit 40.)

- *Efficiency* – the government may be able to provide better-quality goods and services at a cheaper price than the private sector. This was considered in Unit 45.

- *Control* – the government may use public spending to improve the general state of the economy. Reducing unemployment, lowering inflation and eliminating externalities are a few examples. This is considered in Units 68–73.

1 What is the difference between a public good and a merit good?

2 Why is a lighthouse an example of a public good?

3 Why is government spending on vaccinating all children against diphtheria an example of a merit good?

4 Why is it better for the government to provide a network of 'free' roads rather than for the private sector to provide it?

5 How are 'free' services such as education and health paid for? How is private education and private health care paid for?

6 Explain why governments provide goods and services.

COURSEWORK SUGGESTION

Describe the way in which a merit good, such as education or health services, is provided in the public sector and in the private sector. Describe what services are offered and their quality, who supplies these services, and how they are paid for. Analyse what would happen if all these services were provided by just the private sector or just the public sector. Consider the advantages and disadvantages of these options.

KEY TERMS

PUBLIC GOOD – a good that has to be provided by government. Once provided, it is impossible to prevent others from benefiting equally.

MERIT GOOD – a good that would be under-consumed, if left to free market forces.

Taxation

Why Tax?

A tax is a levy paid by citizens and organisations to their government. There are several reasons why the government imposes taxes:

- To raise money to pay for public expenditure. Figure 56.1 shows that most public spending is paid for by taxes. The rest is paid for by royalties on North Sea oil; national insurance contributions; 'other' sources, such as profits from nationalised industries or rents from council houses; and government borrowing.

- To affect economic behaviour. For instance, taxes on cigarettes discourage smoking. Taxes on petrol encourage motorists to economise on fuel.

- To help redistribute income between different individuals and between different sectors of the economy. This is considered further in Unit 74.

- To help control the economy. This is considered further in Units 68–73.

The Main Taxes in the UK

Taxes are either direct or indirect. A DIRECT TAX is a tax levied directly on an individual or organisation. Today, direct taxes are mainly taxes on income or wealth. An INDIRECT TAX is a tax on a good or service. All major taxes except local authority rates are paid to central government. Local authority rates are taxes levied by local government to pay for its spending. The main taxes in the UK and their importance in terms of revenue are shown in Figure 56.1.

- *Income tax* is the most important tax in the UK. It is a direct tax on a person's income. An individual is allowed to earn a certain sum free of tax; this is called TAX ALLOWANCE. A single person is allowed, for instance, to earn well over £2000 a year free of tax. Money earned on

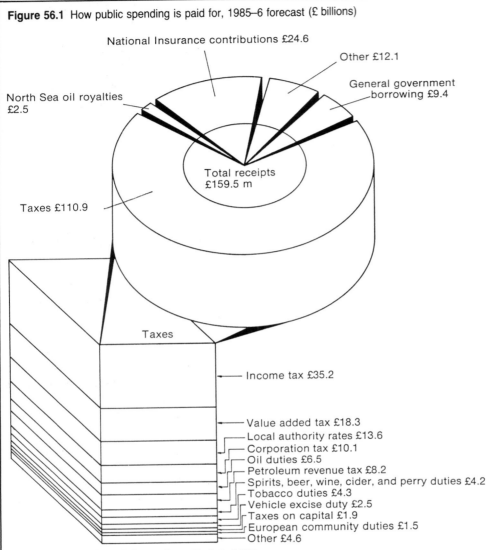

Figure 56.1 How public spending is paid for, 1985–6 forecast (£ billions)

National Insurance contributions £24.6

Other £12.1

General government borrowing £9.4

North Sea oil royalties £2.5

Total receipts £159.5 m

Taxes £110.9

Taxes

Income tax £35.2

Value added tax £18.3
Local authority rates £13.6
Corporation tax £10.1
Oil duties £6.5
Petroleum revenue tax £8.2
Spirits, beer, wine, cider, and perry duties £4.2
Tobacco duties £4.3
Vehicle excise duty £2.5
Taxes on capital £1.9
European community duties £1.5
Other £4.6

Source: The Treasury, *Economic Progress Report*, March–April, 1985

STUDY POINTS

Look at Figure 56.1.

1 How much did the government expect to raise in taxes in 1985/6?

2 What proportion or percentage was this of total government income?

3 If there were 55.45 million inhabitants of the UK in that year, how much on average did each man, woman and child pay in tax?

4 What is a 'royalty'? Why do you think the government earns royalties in North Sea Oil?

5 What was the largest tax in terms of revenue?

6 Which taxes do you pay at the moment?

7 Which additional taxes are you likely to pay when you start working?

8 What does the government do with its taxes and other income?

9 The government wishes to cut taxes. How could it raise the money to do this?

10 If the government were to cut taxes by £10 billion, would this lead to an increase in welfare in the economy? To answer this, consider the costs and benefits to society of such a move.

top of the allowance is taxed at 30%. So if a worker earning £10 000 a year had a pay increase of £1000, £300 of that £1000 would go to the government in income tax. At higher levels of income, the taxpayer has to pay higher rates of tax. The top RATE OF TAX is 60%.

- *Value added tax* (VAT) is an indirect tax levied on most goods and services at a rate of 15%. If an item were priced at £1.15, 15 pence of that would be VAT and £1.00 the cost of the good. Some important items are zero-rated (i.e. there is no VAT charged on them). These include food, children's clothes, books, newspapers, public transport, and coal, gas and electricity.

- *Local authority rates* are an indirect tax on property. How much the owner of a house or factory pays depends upon how much the property could be rented out for.

- *Corporation tax* is a direct tax on the profits of companies.

- *Oil duties and petroleum revenue duty* are indirect taxes on North Sea oil production, and oil sold in the UK.

- *Duties on drink and tobacco* are indirect taxes. They are paid on quantity rather than value. For instance, the duty on a bottle of wine is the same whether the bottle costs £2 or £200. This contrasts with VAT, where VAT on a £200 bottle would be one hundred times as much as on a £2 bottle.

- *Vehicle excise duty* is the indirect tax on owning a car, often called car tax.

- *Taxes on capital* are direct taxes. *Capital gains tax* is a tax mainly on profits made when stocks and shares are sold at higher prices than

they were bought for. *Inheritance tax* is a tax on money left by people who die. If your uncle were to die owning £100 000, then tax would have to be paid on that.

- *European Community duties* are an indirect tax on goods coming into the country from outside the EEC European Community. This money is paid to the European Community.

- *National insurance contributions.* There is some debate about whether these are taxes or not. All other taxes are paid into one fund (known as the 'Consolidated Fund') and used to pay for public spending. National insurance contributions, however, are paid into the national insurance fund and used only to pay for national insurance benefits (such as state pensions and unemployment benefits) and a small part of the National Health Service. National insurance contributions are paid by workers and their employers, and are calculated as a percentage of wages.

CHECKPOINTS

1 Explain the difference between (a) taxation and government borrowing; and (b) direct and indirect taxes.

2 Which taxes (a) do you pay and (b) do your parents pay at the moment?

3 Compare how income tax and VAT are calculated.

4 What is (a) an allowance and (b) a tax rate?

5 Which taxes are paid to (a) local government and (b) the Common Market?

6 Explain why governments impose taxes.

COURSEWORK SUGGESTION

Find out and describe in detail how taxes have changed over the past ten years. Explain why they have changed. Assess whether or not these changes have been desirable, and whether or not a different structure of taxation might have been more beneficial. Useful sources of statistics would be past copies of the *Economic Progress Report* (published by the Treasury) and the *Annual Abstract of Statistics* (published by HMSO).

KEY TERMS

DIRECT TAX – a tax levied directly on an individual or organisation.

INDIRECT TAXES – a tax levied on a good or service.

TAX RATE – the percentage paid in tax.

TAX ALLOWANCE – a sum on which no tax is paid.

Data Response Questions
Units 53–56

Unit 53 The Money Supply and the Rate of Interest

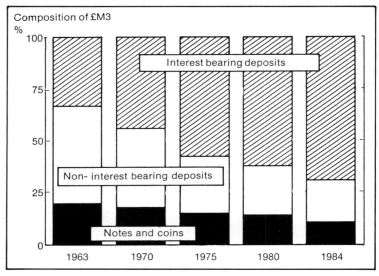

Source: *Financial Times*, 16 September, 1985

1 What is £M3? *(2 marks)*

2 How has the composition of £M3 changed over time? *(4 marks)*

3 Suggest *two* reasons why there might have been this change in composition. *(4 marks)*

Unit 54 Public Expenditure (1)

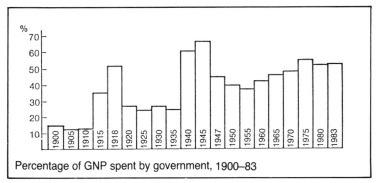

Percentage of GNP spent by government, 1900–83

Source: Barclays Bank Review, May 1980; CSO, United Kingdom Accounts, 1984

1 What percentage of GNP was spent by government in (a) 1900, (b) 1930, (c) 1960, (d) 1983? *(2 marks)*

2 Describe the change in government spending as a percentage of GNP this century. *(2 marks)*

3 Why did public expenditure as a percentage of GNP rise so much between 1915 and 1918, and 1940 and 1945? *(1 mark)*

4 GNP in 1983 was £261 billion. What was the approximate total value of government spending in millions of pounds in that year? *(4 marks)*

5 Give *two* reasons why public expenditure might have risen over the period 1955 to the present day. *(4 marks)*

Essay Questions
Units 53–56

1 (a) Describe *four* ways (apart from education) in which government spends money in your local area. *(8 marks)*

(b) Explain how you and the rest of society will benefit from the education you have received so far. *(8 marks)*

(c) To what extent can education be described as a public good? *(4 marks)*

2 (a) Name one tax which you pay at the moment and describe how much you pay in that tax. *(5 marks)*

(b) Name one tax which you are likely to start paying once you start full-time work and describe how much you are likely to pay in that tax. *(6 marks)*

(c) Explain *three* reasons why government raises taxes. *(9 marks)*

Unit 55 Public Expenditure (2)

Big losses – but city's all-night buses to stay

Public transport chiefs have refused to take Birmingham's all-night buses off the road, despite mounting losses. The ruling comes in the face of a warning that the £500,000-a-year being lost by the 16 services is likely to continue to climb.

A survey has revealed that some all-night buses, which operate hourly out of the city, are carrying fewer than five passengers.

Losses during June varied between £2,065 and £4,330, a report to West Midland County Council's public transport committee said yesterday.

But Labour councillor Terry Donovan said: "The withdrawal of this service would be a backward step."

And Councillor Renee Spector said: "The services may be carrying fewer passengers, but they are still important to city centre workers who have jobs with unsocial hours."

Drain

Tory opposition spokesman, Councillor Jack Ledbetter, said: "There is no point in throwing money down the drain.

When the services were introduced they were well used, but they have been losing money for years.

They are now used mainly by merry-makers leaving night clubs and, if they have enough money to spend on that kind of entertainment, they have enough money to get taxis home," he said.

Source: Express and Star, 10 October 1985

1 Approximately how much are the 16 services mentioned in the article losing per year? (*1 mark*)

2 Who is likely to bear the cost of the losses made in the 16 services? (*2 marks*)

3 Who benefits because of the running of these services and how do they benefit? (*4 marks*)

4 Should the 16 services be axed? Explain the reasons for your decision. (*3 marks*)

Unit 56 Taxation

Taxes and social security contributions as a percentage of gross national product at factor cost

Including social security contributions	1972		1977		1982	
	Percentage	Rank	Percentage	Rank	Percentage	Rank
Sweden	49	3	58	1	57	1
Norway	54	1	56	2	56	2
Denmark	50	2	49	3	54	3
Netherlands	48	4	49	4	51	4
Belgium	39	8	46	7	50	5
France	40	7	44	8	50	6
Austria	45	5	47	5	49	7
German Fed. Rep.	42	6	47	6	46	8
United Kingdom	38	11	39	10	45	9
Italy	30	13	35	12	42	10
Finland	38	10	43	9	41	11
Canada	38	9	37	11	38	12
Australia	28	14	34	13	36	13
Greece	28	15	31	15	33	14
Switzerland	25	16	32	14	31	15
United States	31	12	31	16	31	16
Japan	22	17	25	17	30	17

Source: CSO, Economic Trends, February 1985

1 What percentage of GNP at factor cost was paid in taxes and social security contributions in Italy in (a) 1972 and (b) 1982? (*1 mark*)

2 In which country was the percentage paid in tax and social security contributions highest in (a) 1972 and (b) 1982? (*1 mark*)

3 In which country was the percentage paid lowest in (a) 1972 and (b) 1982? (*1 mark*)

4 (a) How does the UK compare to other countries in the proportion of GNP paid in taxes and social security contributions?
   (b) How has the UK's position changed over time? (*4 marks*)

5 (a) What has happened to the proportion paid in tax in most countries over the period 1972 to 1982?
   (b) Give *two* reasons why this change might have occurred. (*3 marks*)

Unemployment

Bill Phillips, aged 62, forced to take early retirement but would like to still have a job.

Jill Butterworth, aged 52, in part-time work but would like a full-time job.

Helen Briggs, aged 24, physically handicapped in a wheelchair, unemployed but wants a job.

Harry Cole, aged 45, general labourer, out of work now for four years.

Mary Roberts, aged 35, children now at school, not actively looking for work at the moment, but would like a job if jobs were easily available.

Jane Onslow, aged 17, on a YTS placement.

Figure 57.1 Unemployment (including school leavers)

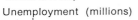
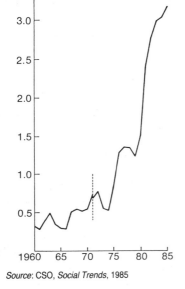

Source: CSO, Social Trends, 1985

Figure 57.2 Unemployment by duration

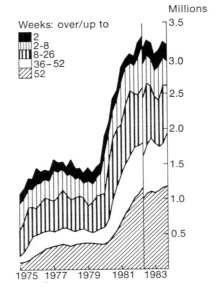

Source: CSO, Economic Trends Annual Supplement, 1984 and CSO, Monthly Digest of Statistics, May 1985

STUDY POINTS

1 Which of the people above would you consider to be unemployed and why?

2 How could the Government attempt to measure the numbers of unemployed people in the UK each month?

3 How does the Government measure the level of unemployment in the UK?

Consider Figure 57.1.

4 How many workers were unemployed in the UK in (a) 1960, (b) 1970, (c) 1985?

5 There is a regular pattern to unemployment over time. What is this?

6 In what years did unemployment fall to a low point compared to surrounding years?

7 In what years did unemployment rise to a high point compared to surrounding years?

Consider Figure 57.2.

8 How many workers were unemployed in each category of time at (a) 1 January 1975 and (b) 1 January 1984?

9 What has happened to the number of workers unemployed for over a year between 1975 and 1984? What are the costs to society of this trend?

'Another 121 552 workers joined the dole queue last month as unemployment rocketed to an all-time high.' (Source: Daily Mirror, 1 February 1985)

This sort of newspaper headline has long been commonplace in Britain. UNEMPLOYMENT rises year after year, and governments seem to be powerless to prevent it. This rise in unemployment is clearly shown in Figure 57.1. In the 1950s and early 1960s, unemployment averaged a little over 300 000. By 1985, it was ten times that level. This unit will consider what we mean by 'unemployment'. Units 58–60 will try to explain why unemployment is a problem and what are the possible causes of unemployment.

Measuring Unemployment

Measuring the level of unemployment is not easy. In the UK, it is measured monthly by the numbers of workers registering for benefits at the Department of Health and Social Security (DHSS). Before 1983, it was measured by the number of jobless signing on at Jobcentres, the government 'job shops'. In other countries, unemployment is also measured through surveys (asking a sample if they are out of work) or through union statistics.

Measuring the number of people unemployed by means of those collecting benefits considerably underestimates the problem. Many workers form part of the HIDDEN UNEMPLOYED. For instance:

'Even by Government estimates there are another 475 000 kept out of unemployment statistics by special measures such as the Training for Skills and the Job Release Scheme.'

Then there are the women at home who would work if jobs were available, but who do not register with the DHSS because they are not entitled to benefits. Young people who stay on longer at school or college, or workers who retire early, but who would like to continue working are two more groups of hidden unemployed. So unemployment in the UK is much higher than the official government statistics would suggest.

Types of Unemployment

Unemployment can be broken down into four main types.

- FRICTIONAL UNEMPLOYMENT will always be present in an economy. It is short-term unemployment caused because many workers who change jobs do not immediately go from one job to the next. They spend a week or a few weeks unemployed. Figure 57.2 shows the length of time workers have been unemployed for. Unemployment up to 8 weeks could

be considered frictional unemployment.

- SEASONAL UNEMPLOYMENT is unemployment caused by changes in demand for workers at different times of the year. Returning to the newspaper extract which told of a 121 552 rise in unemployment:

'This latest rise has staggered Government officials even though January is a traditionally gloomy month for job prospects.'

Increases in unemployment in January are expected, because some industries – such as tourism and the building industry – lay off workers during the winter months.

- STRUCTURAL UNEMPLOYMENT occurs when firms and industries are run down and no new industry steps in to take up the workers made unemployed. One industry that has been shrinking in the UK over the past 30 years is the rail industry. For instance:

'British Rail Engineering announced the axing of another 700 jobs yesterday. They will go over the next two years at the Springburn works in Glasgow.'

Glasgow is already an area of high structural unemployment. These 700 workers will almost certainly be added to the dole queues because even now there are not enough jobs in Glasgow.

- CYCLICAL UNEMPLOYMENT occurs when workers and factories lie idle because there is insufficient spending in the economy to make use of all the factors of production. When commentators say that the economy is in 'recession' or is in a 'slump', they are saying that the resulting unemployment is cyclical.

CHECKPOINTS

1 The television newsreader announces that last month 3 452 322 people were unemployed. How is this figure arrived at? Is it an accurate measure of unemployment?

2 Are young people on Training for Skills really part of the unemployed? Explain your answer carefully.

3 What type of unemployment does each of the following represent:
(a) a hotel worker who is laid off during the winter;
(b) a steel works which is closing permanently where the workers are made redundant;
(c) a worker who spends two weeks unemployed before getting another job;
(d) a car worker who is laid off because orders for new cars are down;
(e) a textile worker who is made redundant in an area of existing high unemployment?

4 To what extent is unemployment in the UK frictional and seasonal?

KEY TERMS

UNEMPLOYMENT – lacking a job while seeking employment. The number of unemployed is measured in the UK by a count of those unemployed who are receiving DHSS benefits.

HIDDEN or CONCEALED UNEMPLOYMENT – workers who are unemployed, but who are not counted as unemployed in the official statistics (e.g. young people on YTS).

FRICTIONAL UNEMPLOYMENT – short-duration unemployment caused as workers move from one job to another.

SEASONAL UNEMPLOYMENT – unemployment caused by changes in demand for workers at different times of the year (e.g. in the building industry, fewer workers are employed in the winter months).

STRUCTURAL UNEMPLOYMENT – unemployment caused by insufficient capital (e.g. factories, offices, machines) in the economy.

CYCLICAL UNEMPLOYMENT – unemployment caused by a lack of demand for goods and services in the economy.

COURSEWORK SUGGESTION

Find out the unemployment figures for your local area or region, both past and present. Try to break down the overall unemployment figure by industry and by duration. Present your findings using graphs, etc. Compare your findings with the national picture. Analyse why the local economy differs from or is the same as the national average. Try to predict likely future trends in unemployment in your area.

Unemployment – Its Consequences

STUDY POINTS

1 (a) Write down *three* points which the father is making about unemployment or the unemployed.
  (b) Are his opinions right or wrong do you think? Explain your reasoning carefully.

2 What are the costs of unemployment to:
  (a) an unemployed person like the boy in the cartoon

  (b) a taxpayer like the father
  (c) the economy as a whole, like the British economy?

3 What would be (a) the costs and (b) the benefits to (i) the unemployed, (ii) taxpayers, (iii) other workers, of a rise in unemployment benefit of £2 a week?

4 Should unemployment benefit be raised today? Explain your answer carefully.

5 The father said that 'if you try, you'll get a job'. Do you think that any worker who has not got a job after eight weeks of being unemployed should have his or her unemployment pay stopped? In your answer, explain the costs and benefits of such a proposal.

- 'The greatest evil of our times'
- 'A great social scourge'
- 'A drain on the nation'

These are some of the phrases used to describe unemployment in Britain today. Why is unemployment so terrible?

The Cost to the Unemployed

The main losers from unemployment are the unemployed themselves. Unemployment is a major cause of poverty. Benefit levels in the UK are high enough to prevent the unemployed from dying of physical hardship, but they do little more. Very few of the unemployed are better off on the dole than in work. So the unemployed are deprived of spending power that they would otherwise have, if they were in employment.

A loss of earnings is only one aspect of the problem of unemployment. Consider this extract:

'The 3.1 million people in Britain without jobs are beginning to have serious social as well as financial problems. They are more likely to fall ill and to drink heavily, according to the Government's statistical evidence published in the 1985 edition of *Social Trends*. There has also been a rapid increase in drug taking. Suicide has been rising. For those in work the picture is more cheerful . . .' (Adapted from *Financial Times*, 10 January 1985)

Social problems, such as heavy drinking, drug abuse and suicide, arise because the unemployed suffer psychologically. Many feel they ought to be working. They feel rejected by society, because nobody wants to employ them. They feel guilty and demeaned by receiving state hand-outs. Many end up feeling that they are to blame for their position. It is these feelings that blight the lives of many unemployed and that add to the already high cost arising from the loss of earnings.

The Cost to Those in Work

The main burden of unemployment falls on the unemployed, but those in work pay a heavy price too. One major way in which those in work have to pay for unemployment is through higher taxes. The unemployed receive benefits – £4600 million worth, according to a study by the Institute of Fiscal Studies published in 1981. More important though, the unemployed pay far less tax than they would if they had been in work – £8260 million less, according to the same study. The result was that in 1981 each unemployed person cost the government £4500. With 23.4 million in work in 1981, that meant that each working person on average was paying £554 a year in extra tax because of unemployment. Today this figure will be much higher, because of inflation.

Those in work, too, may lose out because high unemployment is likely to be associated with a lack of opportunity to work. Employment prospects and wage prospects will be much better in a full-employment, booming economy rather than in an economy where over 3 million people are unemployed. Those in work may also be harmed by social factors. Unemployment, as has been argued above, causes problems of illness, drink, drugs, etc. Increases in crime are linked to unemployment. Those in work have to suffer from these problems of society.

The Cost to the Economy

There is a major cost on a 'macro-economic' level too. The *opportunity cost* of, say, 3 million unemployed is what could be produced, if these workers were in a job. Assume that each worker could produce just £5000 worth of goods and services. The opportunity cost of unemployment is a staggering £15 000 million, or about £265 for every man, woman and child in the UK. In practice, for every two people officially unemployed, there is likely to be another person who forms part of the hidden unemployed. Also, £5000 is likely to be a low figure for the amount that each unemployed worker would produce. If each unemployed worker produced as much as the average worker, then he or she could produce £8000 or £9000 worth of goods and services. With 4½ million unemployed at £9000, the cost of lost output would be £40 500 million, or

about £720 per person in the UK. Whether the figure is £15 000 million or £40 000, or something in between, it is obvious that high unemployment represents a vast waste of *scarce resources* in the economy.

> There's only one think worse than being unemployed at sixteen.
>
> That's still being unemployed at seventeen.
>
> (YTS poster, 1984)

CHECKPOINTS

1 What are (a) the social costs and (b) the economic costs of unemployment to
(i) the unemployed; and
(ii) those in work?

2 What is the opportunity cost of unemployment to the economy as a whole?

3 Calculate the lost output in the economy in each of the following cases:

Number unemployed (millions)	Value of output that each worker could produce on average (£)
3.5	5000
3.75	6000
4.5	4000
5.0	9000

COURSEWORK SUGGESTION

This involves conducting a survey. Contact five unemployed workers who are willing to take part in your survey. Draw up a list of questions concerning the cost of unemployment to an individual person (both social costs and economic costs). Interview each of the five workers. Write up your findings. Explain whether or not you think your sample was representative of the unemployed in the UK today. Decide how important it is that these workers should be found jobs.

Unemployment – Its Causes (1)

The Labour Market

There are two major schools of thought on the causes of unemployment. In this unit, we will consider what is called the 'neo-classical' viewpoint. This viewpoint broadly argues that unemployment is caused by problems in the *labour market*.

The labour market is the market where workers offer themselves for work (workers are *supplied* onto the market) and where employers hire them (workers are *demanded* by employers). Neo-classical economists argue that the market for labour is no different from, say, the market for bananas or the market for clothes. The forces of demand and supply fix a price for labour and this is called the *wage rate*. The same forces also determine how much labour will be bought and sold at any one time. In 1985, for instance, about 24 million people had a job. The problem arises when the number of people who have a job at the existing wage rate (24 million in 1985) is less than the number of people who want a job (about 27 million in 1985). It is then that unemployment occurs (about 3 million in 1985).

In the market for bananas, if bananas are not being bought, then the sellers of bananas have to reduce their prices or not sell their bananas. So too, if workers cannot find a job, it is because wages are too high. Workers have 'priced themselves out of jobs'. Two organisations can be blamed for this.

- The *trade unions* are to blame, because they have forced wages up so that firms cannot afford to take on as many workers as they would if wages were lower.

- The *government* itself is also to blame, because of various Acts of Parliament which keep wages too high. Government wages councils have the power, for instance, to fix minimum wages for a large number of low-paid workers and to fine

---

'Jobs come from customers and nowhere else.' [1]

'Jobs are created when businesses produce goods and services that people want at prices they can afford.' [1]

'The biggest single cause of our high unemployment is the failure of our job market.' [1]

'We all should hang our heads in shame for treating would-be wealth creators with contempt.' [2]

'The Government will reduce the deterrent to taking on workers, by extending to two years in all firms the qualifying period for the right to claim unfair dismissal.' [1]

'Workers have added to unemployment by demanding pay rises which far outstrip productivity, and *unions* by organising crippling strikes.' [2]

'The Chancellor said that the link between pay and jobs was well established, as with the link between high levels of taxation and sluggish economic performance.' [3]

'Our major competitors have paid themselves less, improved their productivity far more, and consequently priced Britain out of the job market.' [2]

'A family man on average earnings might just as well be on the dole. Millions of people are still caught in the "why work" trap. This produces a lack of incentive to work.' [4]

'The biggest sufferers from excessive wage rises are the unemployed.' [1]

Sources: 1 Department of Employment, *Employment News*, number 129, March 1985
2 *Daily Express*, 29 March, 1985
3 *Express and Star*, 26 June, 1985
4 *Daily Express*, 24 April, 1985

S T U D Y P O I N T S

1 What, according to the quotes, are the causes of unemployment?

2 Assume you were the Government. If these were the causes of unemployment, what measures would you take to reduce unemployment?

employers who do not pay these wages. The Equal Pay Act also led to many women losing their jobs.

But this neo-classical view does not see unemployment being caused only by high wages, which lead to a lack of demand for workers by employers. Workers themselves, it is argued, refuse work, because welfare benefits for the unemployed are so high that many workers are better off on the dole than working.

Excessively high wages, welfare benefits and taxes thus cause unemployment. But we know that in a country like West Germany, wages, benefits and taxes are even higher, yet unemployment is much lower. This is because West Germany is a successful economy. In the past, it has created more jobs than the UK because:

- Inflation has been lower. German goods have not been priced out of markets.

- Marginal tax rates are lower. Although Germans are taxed more highly than their UK counterparts, they are taxed less in income on any extra (or marginal) pound that they earn. This encourages Germans to work harder and encourages new firms to be created by the self employed.

- Banks have been more sympathetic to small businesses and their proprietors' demands for financing.

- Investment has been higher because firms have been able to earn higher profits. Higher investment leads to more jobs in the long term.

- There is less government 'red tape', which pushes up labour costs.

To put it another way, the West German economy has been more *competitive* than the UK economy. So now it can afford to pay its workers more, without pushing up unemployment.

To sum up, British industry would *demand* more workers, if wages were lower and if industry were more competitive in international markets. Workers would be prepared to *supply* more labour at lower wage rates, if welfare benefits were cut. The solution to unemployment is to free the labour

market of the barriers – like trade union power, government wage-fixing and welfare benefits – which prevent wages from falling and clearing the labour market of unemployment.

A Diagrammatic Analysis

Figure 59.1 shows the market for labour. With a wage rate of OE, employers want to employ OA workers, but OC workers want a job. So unemployment of AC occurs. If wage rates declined to OF, then full employment would result because:

- employers would take on AB extra workers;

- BC workers would decide that wages were not high enough and would stop looking for a job.

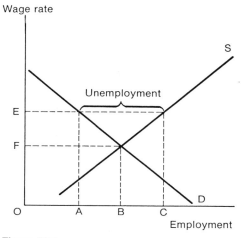

Figure 59.1

Figure 59.2 shows what happens when either trade unions push up wage rates or governments increase welfare benefits for the unemployed. Workers are now only prepared to work for higher wage rates, thus pushing the supply curve for labour from S to S'. The resulting increase in wage rates of EF causes unemployment of AC. Workers could be paid wage rates of OE without unemployment occurring, if the British economy became more competitive. This would increase orders for British goods so that, at any given wage rate, employers would want to employ more workers – i.e. the demand curve would shift to the right. Full employment would be restored, if the new demand curve passed through the point G.

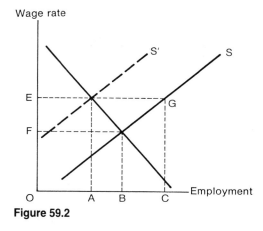

Figure 59.2

CHECKPOINTS

1 A firm employs 100 workers at an average wage of £100 per week. Why might the firm be willing to take on more workers, if the average wage were only £80?

2 Explain what is meant when it is said that workers have 'priced themselves out of work'.

3 Joan Williams is a housewife. Why might a 20% reduction in average wages discourage her from taking on paid employment?

4 Draw a demand and supply diagram and show why unemployment might be caused by too high real wage rates.

5 How do unions force up wages? Does this create unemployment?

6 Why might an increase in the competitiveness of the UK economy reduce unemployment?

COURSEWORK SUGGESTION

You are going to investigate the theory that unemployment benefits cause unemployment. Find out the levels of unemployment benefit, social security benefits, etc. that those out of work can claim. Then, by looking at the local newspaper or by going to your local Jobcentre, find out the rates of pay for different jobs. What sort of workers might be discouraged from taking a job at existing levels of benefits? What would be the costs and benefits to workers, employers and the economy as a whole, if the government were to abolish unemployment benefits?

Unemployment – Its Causes (2)

- 'Michelin to cut 2600 tyre jobs.'
- 'Shell to axe 1000 refinery jobs.'
- 'BSC to close plate mill with loss of 250 jobs.'

Such headlines have become so common in the UK that they rarely make the front page of national newspapers. In the previous unit, we saw that 'neo-classical' economists argue that jobs are lost because wages and benefits are too high, and because industry does not have enough incentives to create new jobs. There is, however, an alternative theory, which is often called 'Keynesian' after John Maynard Keynes, an economist who worked between the two world wars. Keynesian economists argue that unemployment is caused mainly by a lack of demand for goods and services in the economy.

Jobs and Spending

Consider this extract:

'The construction of a Channel tunnel would be beneficial to Kent. In the short run, the impact would be tremendous, with the creation of a large number of construction jobs. It would also lead to a number of permanent jobs and an increase in economic activity.' (Adapted from the *Financial Times*, 17 January 1985)

Money spent on the Channel tunnel would first of all create jobs, because men would be needed to build the tunnel and the roads, railways and buildings associated with it. Then permanent jobs would be created to service the tunnel itself – jobs ranging from painters to customs officials to waitresses. No doubt, too, factories and warehouses would also spring up to take advantage of the new trade to and from the Continent. In this instance, spending (on the building of the tunnel), not lower wages, would create jobs.

Keynesians argue that what is true of the Channel tunnel is true for the whole economy. Jobs will only be created, if there is more spending in

DEMOCRATIC PARTY MANIFESTO

Unemployment

The Democratic Party is committed to reducing unemployment by increasing public spending and reducing taxes. Unemployment is the single most important problem facing the British economy today. It affects every person in our society. We commit ourselves to creating a minimum of 500,000 extra jobs over the next five years. Only if unemployment is reduced can Britain return to prosperity.

JOBS

COSTS OF CREATING ONE EXTRA JOB

Method	Gross Cost to Government* (£000)
Cut in income tax	30–40
Cut in VAT	25
Increase in local authority current spending	15
Increase in construction spending by government	11
Subsidy to private industry for additional employment	5–7
Youth Training Scheme (per place)	1200
Adult Trainiing	2000
Job Release Scheme (early retirement)	2000

* Gross costs do not take into account the sums flowing back to the Government in extra taxes whereas net costs do.

Source: The Daily Telegraph, 29 January 1985

STUDY POINTS

You are a member of the newly elected Democratic Party Government.

1 How do you intend to cut unemployment by 500 000 as promised in your Party Manifesto?

2 What will be the cost of these policies? How will you pay for them?

3 What do you think will be the effect of your decisions on (a) imports coming into the country, (b) inflation, (c) the economic prosperity of those in work, (d) interest rates?

Keynsians see the way forward for the UK through highly paid workers manning sophisticated machines.

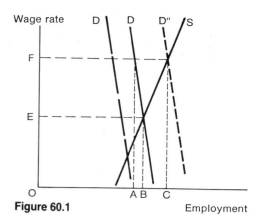

Figure 60.1

the economy. Consumers need to spend more on everything from bread to cars. Firms need to spend more on new up-to-date factories, machines and offices. Governments need to spend more on everything from hospitals to education. Foreigners need to spend more on British goods. Keynesians blame the lack of spending for the doubling of unemployment from about 1.5 million in 1979 to over 3 million in 1982.

- Consumers nearly doubled the proportion of their incomes that they put into savings – and that meant lower spending.
- The government raised taxes, which again reduced spending by taxpayers.
- Firms cut investment plans and reduced stocks to a minimum.
- British goods were priced out of foreign markets, not because British wages were too high, but because the value of the pound soared to nearly $2.50 to the pound in 1980.

Jobs and Investment

Spending more money will not necessarily create many jobs. This is because much of the increase will be spent on goods imported from abroad, and some of the extra spending will trigger off a rise in prices, as companies see the chance to make bigger profits. Britain today could not produce many more goods and services, because the factories and the workplaces have either disappeared or are obsolete (i.e. too old-fashioned). In other words, much of Britain's

unemployment is *structural*. Keynesians argue that the only way to get round this is for the extra spending to be concentrated on investment – producing more factories, more offices, better roads, more education. Only increased investment can get Britain out of the vicious cycle of job losses, which leads to less spending, which leads, in turn, to more job losses. Investment is also the most powerful way to increase the competitiveness of British industry. The way forward for the UK is not through poorly paid workers, but through highly paid workers manning sophisticated machines.

A Diagrammatic Treatment

Keynesian ideas can be shown diagrammatically, as in Figure 60.1. The demand and supply of labour are both inelastic. Keynesians argue that increasing or decreasing wage rates would have little effect either on an employer's demand for labour or a worker's supply of labour. Employers need workers to produce or else they would have to shut down, and workers need a job to earn a living. The figure shows that a massive cut in wages from OF to OE would be needed to get rid of unemployment of AC. What is more, reducing wages might push the demand curve D to the left to D′, as workers could not afford to buy so many goods as before, and more workers would be put out of work. The solution to unemployment is to increase spending, and thereby increase the demand for workers from D to D″.

Data Response Questions
Units 57–60

Unit 57 Unemployment

Hopes rise of fall in the dole queue

BRITAIN'S jobless total will be dropping over the next few months, according to both Government Ministers and Whitehall officials.

The prediction follows a 56,000 fall in the jobless figures in March, which brought the total down to 3,268,000.

Employment Secretary Tom King said this drop was a "significant improvement on recent months."

The number of vacancies is also on the way up again, said Mr King.

The Confederation of British Industry and economic experts have been predicting the Budget, coupled with general economic conditions, will produce more than 300,000 new jobs.

Source: Daily Express, 6 April 1985

1 What, according to the article, was happening to unemployment? *(1 mark)*

2 What was the official level of unemployment in (a) March 1985 and (b) February 1985? *(2 marks)*

3 Why was unemployment likely to have been considerably higher than the official figure? *(3 marks)*

4 Why is the news about the number of vacancies good for the unemployed? *(1 mark)*

5 What 'general economic conditions' could produce more jobs? *(3 marks)*

There is now no national minimum nutritional standard for school meals.

Unit 58 Unemployment – Its Consequences

Jobless 'feed on scraps'

Many poor people in Britain do not have enough money to eat a main meal every day, the Child Poverty Action Group claims today. The group's latest edition of the journal, Poverty, includes evidence that the unemployed are more likely than even pensioners to be short of money for basic food.

The journal finds that there has been no change in the tradition of women depriving themselves for the sake of their husbands and children.

Unemployed men are found to be cutting back on their own food for the sake of their children and there is said to be evidence that single women bringing up children on social security eat better than their married counterparts who have husbands to feed.

Government figures published this month show that an increasing number of children are entitled to free school dinners because of the poverty of their parents. There are now more than a million of these children – a third of those eating school dinners.

"It is therefore particularly scandalous that there is no national minimum nutritional standard for school meals (the old standard was abolished by the present Government in 1981)" says CPAG.

Source: The Guardian, 22 April 1985

1 Summarise in your own words what the article is saying about the unemployed. *(4 marks)*

2 Why are unemployed people likely to be short of food? *(2 marks)*

3 Why might the abolition of the national minimum nutritional standard for school meals have hit unemployed families? *(3 marks)*

4 Explain how (a) firms, (b) other workers and (c) taxpayers are affected because the unemployed cannot afford to buy enough food. *(6 marks)*

Unit 59 Unemployment – Its Causes (1)

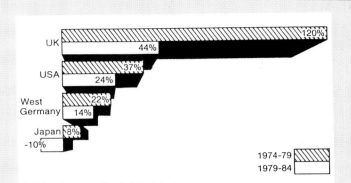

UK 44% 120%
USA 37% 24%
West Germany 22% 14%
Japan 8% -10%

1974-79
1979-84

Note: Local currency; Manufacturing industry
Source: International Monetary Fund

Rise in Unit Labour Costs 1974–79 and 1979–84

THE HIGHER the real costs of labour the lower employment will be, both because employers will be forced to economise on labour and because higher labour costs mean lower profits and competitiveness, less investment and less business.

Competitiveness is sharply affected by unit labour costs – the part of the cost of each item produced that is attributable to labour. This depends not only on wage levels but also on productivity.

Our productivity has been improving and this has helped our unit labour costs to rise at a slower rate in the 1980s than in the 1970s.

But we have to compete not against our own past performance but against other countries.

By that test, we are still not doing nearly as well as we need to. We cannot afford either to relax on productivity or to let wage levels soar.

The biggest factor in our increasing labour costs is the growth of earnings. Despite recession and higher unemployment, those in work have enjoyed on average steadily rising real earnings – by nearly ten per cent altogether since 1979 and by three per cent in the last year alone.

Recent studies have shown that employment could increase considerably if people accepted slightly lower earnings growth.

Source: Department of Employment, *Employment News*, No. 129, March 1985

1 What is meant in the passage by (a) higher labour costs, (b) unit labour costs and (c) wage levels? *(6 marks)*

2 Explain the link, outlined in the passage, between labour costs and unemployment. *(3 marks)*

3 What does the bar chart show and why is it of relevance to the argument in the passage? *(3 marks)*

4 Why, if the argument in the passage is correct, would a reduction in trade union power help reduce unemployment? *(3 marks)*

Unit 60 Unemployment – Its Causes (2)

Firm faces 'mountain' of forms

Bosses at Wolverhampton's Goodyear tyre factory today promised nearly 6,000 people seeking its 350 jobs that every application would be considered. Now they are faced with a mountain of forms after the stampede for work.

More than 5,000 people went to the town's Job Centre yesterday and a further 800 had collected forms by early this afternoon.

About 200 people – some of whom had queued since 2am – were waiting outside the Queen Street entrance yesterday when it opened one and a half hours early at 7.30am.

Today staff gave out 60 forms in the first hour, as interest from the area's 26,733 jobless continued. A dozen people were waiting outside when staff arrived today.

The £150-a-week jobs have been created by a new weekend shift starting next month to meet the booming demand for lorry tyres.

Source: *Express and Star*, 15 October 1985

1 How many jobs are to be created at Wolverhampton's Goodyear factory? *(1 mark)*

2 Why are the jobs being created? *(1 mark)*

3 (a) Briefly outline two different explanations of the causes of unemployment.

(b) To what extent does the experience at Goodyear's support each of these explanations? *(8 marks)*

Essay Questions
Units 57–60

1 'Unemployment last month was 3,456,702 according to official government statistics.'

(a) How is unemployment measured by the Government? *(4 marks)*

(b) What are the costs of unemployment to the unemployed worker? *(8 marks)*

(c) What are the costs of unemployment to the Government and the taxpayer? *(8 marks)*

2 'A 3% fall in real wages could result in an extra 250,000 jobs being created in the economy.'

(a) What is meant by a '3% fall in . . . wages'? *(4 marks)*

(b) Explain why a firm might be willing to take on more workers if it could pay each worker less for working the same time. *(8 marks)*

(c) The Government cuts the real wages of all its workers by 3%. Suggest *two* reasons why this would *not* result in an extra 250,000 jobs being created in Britain. *(8 marks)*

Inflation

Figure 61.1 The Johnson family and their average weekly expenditure

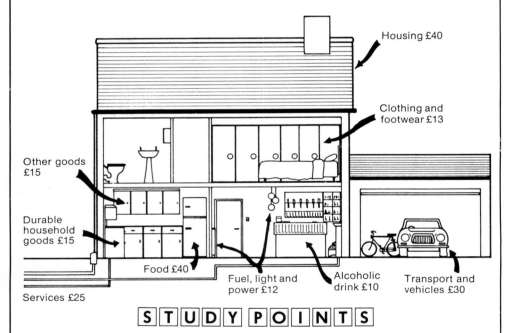

Housing £40

Clothing and footwear £13

Other goods £15

Durable household goods £15

Food £40

Services £25

Fuel, light and power £12

Alcoholic drink £10

Transport and vehicles £30

S T U D Y P O I N T S

1 How much a week does the Johnson family spend?

2 The price of food goes up by 10%. How much would the family need to spend extra in £ s to buy the same amount of goods and services as before?

3 How much extra would they need in terms of a percentage of their total expenditure?

4 The price of alcoholic drink goes up by 20%. How much extra would the family need to spend (a) in £ s and (b) in percentage of total expenditure to buy the same basket of goods as before?

5 The percentage increase in total expenditure that you have calculated in questions 3 and 4 is the *rate of inflation* for the Johnson family. What is the rate of inflation for them if the price of food went up by 20%.

6 The price of food goes up 5% and the price of transport and vehicles by 10%. How much extra would the family need to spend (a) in £s and (b) in percent to maintain their real spending? What has been the Johnsons' rate of inflation?

7 Food prices increase 10%, durable household goods 20% and services by 40%. What is the inflation rate for the Johnson family?

'A rise in inflation was announced yesterday – and the Government fears worse is to come before the situation improves. The Retail Price Index . . . showed that living costs rose by 0.8 per cent between January and February to send the annual inflation level up to 5.4%. (*Source: Daily Express*, 23 March 1985)

What is inflation and how is it measured?

A Definition of Inflation

INFLATION is a *general* rise in prices. In the above extract, it is said that prices or 'living costs' rose by 0.8%. What that means is that on average what would have cost, say, £100 to buy in January 1985 would have cost £100.80 in February 1985. Prices can only change over time, so the inflation rate is always given over a period of time – 0.8% over a month or 5.4% over a year, as in the article.

Inflation Over Time

Figure 61.2 shows how inflation has changed over the period 1955–85. Inflation was not considered a major problem in the UK in the 1950s and early 1960s, but with the rise in inflation from 1973, it became an important issue. The high inflation of the 1970s led to the control of inflation becoming the most important priority of government in the early 1980s.

How Inflation Is measured

The prices of different goods do not go up by the same percentage over a period of time. For instance, the increase in the RETAIL PRICE INDEX – the measure of the level of prices in the UK – of 0.8% described in the article above 'was mainly due to higher mortgage rates and the severe winter weather, which bumped up the cost of fruit and vegetable prices'.

But a 10% increase, say, in mortgage repayments will not increase average prices by 10%, because mortgage repayments are only a small part of the cost of living to many people, and other prices did not go up by as much as 10%. Somehow a way has to be found of averaging out all the individual price rises. This is done by constructing a **WEIGHTED INDEX**. In the case of the retail price index:

- The government finds out the **COST OF LIVING** for the average household. It does this by asking about 7000 households each year to record all their spending over a two-week period. The findings are then averaged out and the spending of the typical or average household is calculated.

- Each month, the government collects about 150 000 prices of some 350 different items up and down the country. The average price of each of the 350 items is calculated.

- The average inflation rate can then

be calculated. Each individual price rise (or fall) is weighted according to how important it is in the typical household's budget. For instance, food represents about 20% or one-fifth of household spending. Therefore, a 10% rise in the price of food would raise average prices by 10% × ⅕ or 2%. Transport and vehicles represents about 15% or $^{15}/_{100}$ of average household spending. So a 20% price rise in transport and vehicles would add 20% × $^{15}/_{100}$ or 3% to the retail price index.

- An index number is then given to the level of prices. This is done by calling the level of prices in one year '100' and comparing how prices have changed before and after that 'base' point. Index numbers were discussed more fully in Unit 5.

The price of a loaf of bread rose 23 times from 1945 to 1985. This is part of a general increase in prices over the period.

CHECKPOINTS

1 **What is meant by inflation?**

2 **How is inflation measured?**

3 **Calculate how much a £100 basket of goods, typical of what is spent in the UK, would cost if the retail price index went up:**
   (a) **by 10%;**
   (b) **by 15%**
   (c) **by 3%;**
   (d) **from 100 to 110;**
   (e) **from 100 to 120;**
   (f) **from 200 to 210;**
   (g) **from 50 to 60.**

4 **Why would a 10% increase in the price of petrol, all other prices remaining constant, *not* lead to a rise in the retail price index of 10%?**

5 **Why is your personal cost of living index almost certainly different from the retail price index?**

UK inflation rate (%)

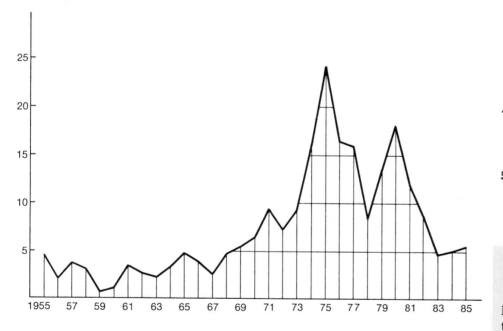

Figure 61.2 UK Inflation rate, 1955–85

Source: CSO, *Economic Trends*, 1985

COURSEWORK SUGGESTION

Describe how prices have changed in the UK over a period of time. Describe how the retail price index is calculated. Analyse what components of the retail price index have risen faster than other components, and how this has affected the cost of living. Assess how different households (pensioner households, one-parent households) have fared over time with rising inflation. What are price levels likely to be in the years 2000 and 2050?

KEY TERMS

INFLATION – a general rise in prices.

RETAIL PRICE INDEX – the measure of the level of prices in the UK.

WEIGHTED INDEX – an index constructed by giving each component of the index a different importance or *weight*.

COST OF LIVING – the money cost of buying a typical basket of goods and services.

The Costs of Inflation

Daisy and Phyllis are two old age pensioners standing in a queue waiting to get their pension. Liz is serving behind the counter in the Post Office.

DAISY: Price of beef's gone up again. Soon won't be able to afford to eat meat no more.

PHYLLIS: And what about that increase in electric bills? Shocking that is. I don't know how they expect us to keep ourselves warm in winter, I really don't.

DAISY: And it's another six months before they put up our pensions. Not that it ever goes up by much. I remember the days when you could buy a loaf for three pence, old pence of course.

(Daisy and Phyllis are served at the counter and get their pensions. They go across to another counter.)

PHYLLIS: Morning Liz. Beautiful morning it is too. Can I have some ordinary envelopes?

LIZ: Which ones do you want? There's these, fifty for seventy nine pence, or these, fifty for eighty-nine pence.

PHYLLIS: What's the difference?

LIZ: I don't really know, but these seventy-nine pence ones are new in. They're made in Spain. Our ordinary ones are made in England. They must have put up the prices because not so long ago they were just seventy-five pence.

PHYLLIS: I'll have the cheapest, luv. Here's the money.

STUDY POINTS

1 How does inflation affect pensions?

2 Daisy could buy a loaf of bread once for three pence. Was she better off at that time than she is today? Explain your answer.

3 Are households always worse off if prices go up? Why or why not?

4 Why might inflation cause a loss of jobs in the UK?

'Inflation up and worse is still to come', reads a newspaper headline. Why is inflation bad and why is a higher rate of inflation worse than a lower rate of inflation? Would a fall in prices be desirable?

The Erosion of Values

One reason why inflation is generally considered to be undesirable is because inflation reduces the PURCHASING POWER OF MONEY – i.e. the value of what can be bought with a sum of money. In 1945, for instance, £1 would have bought 16 pints of beer. Forty years later, that same £1 would only have bought just over 1 pint of beer. Rising prices is not a major problem for many people, because their wages go up even more quickly than prices, leaving them better off. But other people do suffer.

'Millions of people who retire on a decent pension are robbed by inflation. At the present inflation rate of five per cent, anyone retiring on a pension of £115 a week now will find its value sinking to less than £71 in ten years' time.' (*Source: The Daily Mirror*, 1 May 1985)

The pensioners referred to here are pensioners on FIXED PENSIONS – pensions that stay the same from the moment a worker retires. As prices go up, the pensioner can buy less and less with his or her money. The higher the rate of inflation, the more quickly will the real value of the pension go down.

Pensioners are one group who suffer from inflation. Other groups include:

- workers who find it difficult to get pay increases in line with inflation;
- savers who find that the interest rate on their savings is lower than the inflation rate, so that the value of their savings goes down.

The problem of erosion of values can, to a great extent, be solved by INDEX LINKING – increasing pensions, wages, savings, etc. in line with the retail price index. Most welfare benefits are already index linked in the UK, as are state pensions.

Uncertainty

Inflation is also a cost to the economy, because of the *uncertainty* it creates. High inflation means that people find it difficult to keep track of what is the right price to pay for a good. Firms do not know how much they will be able to sell their products for in two years' time. Nor do they know how much it will cost to produce the good. Savers do not know how much their savings will be worth in 20 or 40 years' time. People, firms and governments go to great lengths to avoid uncertainties in their activities – they take out insurance, sign long-term contracts, etc. It is not surprising that they dislike inflation, which creates so much uncertainty about the future.

Unemployment

Some economists (though not all) believe that inflation is a major cause of unemployment. They argue that inflation reduces the competitiveness of British goods. Imports become cheaper, exports more expensive. British goods are then priced out of their markets. That means that there are fewer workers needed in the UK to produce goods and services. Hence inflation causes unemployment. Only by reducing inflation can British industry become more competitive and take on more workers. If this is the case – and it is a controversial theory – then a major cost of the high inflation in the UK in the late 1960s and 1970s is the 3½ million people who are unemployed today.

Pensions have to be increased each year by at least the rate of inflation if pensioners are to be able to buy as much as before.

CHECKPOINTS

1 A pensioner retires on a fixed pension of £5000 a year in 1986. Ten years later, in 1996, prices have doubled. What is the effect of this on the pensioner?

2 Explain why (a) savers and (b) non-unionised workers are particularly vulnerable to inflation.

3 Why do ordinary people not like inflation?

4 Why does inflation create uncertainty? Why is uncertainty an economic cost?

5 Explain the possible link between inflation and unemployment.

COURSEWORK SUGGESTION

Conduct a survey on the costs of inflation to individuals. Interview a pensioner with an occupational pension, a man or woman at home looking after a young family, a businessman and a manual worker. Ask them questions which will reveal the perceived and the actual costs of inflation to these individuals. Analyse your findings and try to assess the extent to which inflation is a cost to society.

KEY TERMS

PURCHASING POWER OF MONEY – what goods and services can be bought with a fixed sum of money.

FIXED PENSION – a pension that remains the same in monetary terms, even when the cost of living increases.

INDEX LINKING – a rise (in pensions, wages, savings, etc.) in line with the retail price index.

The Causes of Inflation (1)

John T. Mayne and Henry Field Junior were the only two survivors of a plane crash on a desert island in the Pacific Ocean ten years ago.

Luckily for them, they escaped the wreck with their wallets intact. Being good upright Americans, they decided that competition and free market forces should rule their dealings. They both had exactly three hundred dollars in their wallets.

John was a great fisherman and set up a firm catching fish. Henry was a farmer and decided to set up a business growing wheat. Each became self sufficient in all commodities apart from wheat and fish.

When it came to fixing prices, John sold 1 fish for a dollar, whilst Henry sold a measure of wheat for two dollars. Each year John sold 300 fish whilst Henry sold 150 measures of wheat.

One day, Henry and John's world was turned upside down by the arrival of George Rex, or GR for short, in his pleasure cruiser. He decided he liked the island so much that he would stay there for a year.

But he did want some fish and some corn – 150 fish and 75 measures of corn to be precise. Henry and John were producing as much as they could already, but each saw an opportunity to up the price of their products. They knew GR had $600 in his wallet.

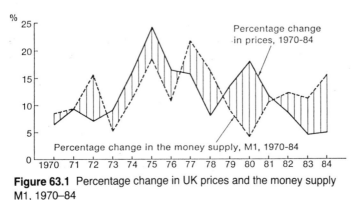

Figure 63.1 Percentage change in UK prices and the money supply M1, 1970–84

Source: CSO, *Economic Trends*, 1985

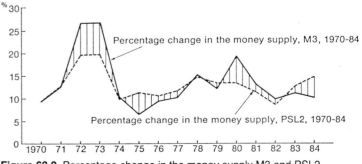

Figure 63.2 Percentage change in the money supply M3 and PSL2, 1970–84

Source: CSO, *Economic Trends Annual Supplement*, 1984; CSO, *Financial Statistics*, August 1985

S T U D Y P O I N T S

1 What was the value in dollars of all the output sold in the desert island economy over a year.

2 What was the total money supply in the economy?

3 If the price of corn relative to fish stayed the same (i.e. 2:1), what is the maximum price that (a) Henry could charge GR for corn and (b) John charge GR for fish?

4 How many fish did that leave for Henry to buy from John? How much would John charge for fish?

5 How many measures of corn did that leave for John to buy from Henry? How much would Henry charge for the corn?

6 What was the value in dollars of (a) total output and (b) the money supply now?

7 What had happened to prices when the money supply increased after GR's arrival?

8 Now look at Figures 63.1 and 63.2. Is there any evidence to suggest that a change in the money supply in the UK leads to a change in prices?

Inflation is a general rise in the price level. In this unit, we will consider what might cause the level of prices in an economy to rise over time. There are three main views or explanations. One, the view covered in this unit, is *monetarist*. Monetarists are economists, politicians, businessmen, etc. who believe that there is a definite link between inflation and the rate of growth of the money supply. The term 'monetarist' has also come to be associated with a whole range of other beliefs, including the belief that free market forces and as little government intervention as possible in the economy will lead to greater efficiency. The other two theories of inflation, covered in the next unit, are *Keynesian*. Keynesian economists believe that, in general, free market forces often lead to a very inefficient allocation of resources and that therefore the state needs to intervene strongly in the economy.

The Monetarist View

Monetarists argue that the only cause of inflation is excessive increases in the money supply. To understand their basic idea, consider this example. In an economy, £1000 worth of notes and coins circulate. Notes and coins are the only form of money. The only good which money buys is red socks. Each year, 2000 pairs of red socks are produced and they are all sold. Once sold, these red socks are never resold. It is obvious that the price of a pair of red socks will be 50p (£1000 ÷ 2000). Now assume that the government prints a further £1000, so that the total money supply is now £2000. The government spends its £1000 on red socks. Then the price of red socks will rise to £1 per pair (£2000 ÷ 2000). Two things have happened as a result of the doubling of the money supply:

- Prices have doubled.
- There has been a redistribution of purchasing power, in this case in favour of the government. This is shown by the fact that the government can buy 1000 pairs of red socks, which previously were bought by the private sector.

The redistribution effects of inflation were discussed in Unit 61. Here, we want to consider the link between money supply and the price level. There would have been no inflation, if the output of socks had doubled along with the money supply. Prices would have remained at 50p per pair.

Monetarists argue that what is true in this simple example is true of the real world. They argue that inflation is caused by increases in the money supply over and above increases in the output of the economy. So, if the money supply rose by 10% and output rose by 3%, then approximately 7% inflation could be expected.

The Evidence

The evidence to support this view of inflation is difficult to interpret for a number of reasons.

- As was shown in Unit 53, there is no clear definition of 'the money supply'. Different measures of the money supply can move in different directions at the same time, so it is often difficult to say whether the rate of growth of the money supply is increasing or decreasing.

- Most monetarists argue that an increase in the money supply leads to higher inflation over a period of time of several years. So inflation in, say, 1988 will be the result of increases in the money supply over the period 1985–8 and possibly before. It is thus very difficult to pinpoint the exact rise in the money supply that led to a particular rise in prices.

Figures 63.1 and 63.2 show how inflation and various definitions of the money supply have changed over the period 1970–84.

C H E C K P O I N T S

1 **What is the monetarist view of the cause of inflation?**

2 **On monetarist assumptions, fill in the missing figures in Figure 63.3 (all figures will be approximate).**

Figure 63.3

Growth in the money supply (%)	Growth in output (%)	Change in prices (%)
10	0	
8	2	
14		13
	4	4

3 **Explain why it is difficult to prove or disprove the monetarist theory of inflation.**

C O U R S E W O R K
S U G G E S T I O N

Describe the pattern of inflation over the past twenty years. Statistics can be obtained from sources such as *Economic Trends Annual Supplement* and the *Annual Abstract of Statistics* (both published by HMSO). Discuss changes in the money supply (figures are available from the same sources). Investigate the extent to which there is any link between changes in the money supply and changes in inflation.

The Causes of Inflation (2)

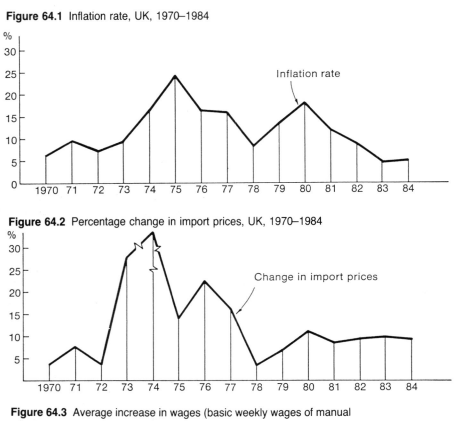

Figure 64.1 Inflation rate, UK, 1970–1984

Figure 64.2 Percentage change in import prices, UK, 1970–1984

Figure 64.3 Average increase in wages (basic weekly wages of manual workers) in the UK, 1970–1983 (per cent)

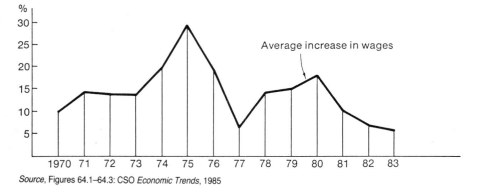

Source, Figures 64.1–64.3: CSO *Economic Trends*, 1985

STUDY POINTS

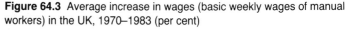

Consider the graphs above.

1 What was the highest annual rate of inflation over the period 1970 to 1984 and in what year did it occur?

2 What was the lowest annual rate of inflation and when did it occur?

3 What is an 'import'?

4 Explain why an increase in import prices can lead to an increase in inflation.

5 If a firm gives a pay increase to its workers, why may it well attempt to increase the prices of its products to customers? Why does this lead to inflation?

6 Look carefully at all three graphs. Do they show, in your opinion, that changes in import prices and pay increases for workers lead to increases in the rate of inflation?

Cost–Push Inflation

Keynesians hold two views of inflation. Some Keynesians argue that inflation is caused by increases in costs. This is known as the COST–PUSH view. A firm faces a number of major costs:

- The major one is often the cost of labour;
- Equally important can be the cost of goods and services purchased from other firms. At least some of these goods and services will be imported from abroad;
- Taxes are yet another cost.

Cost–push economists argue that most firms set prices by calculating how much it costs to make a product, and then adding a MARK-UP to provide a profit. For instance, it may cost £100 to produce a bicycle. The firm will add a 10% mark-up as its profit and sell the bicycle for £110. This method of pricing is known as COST-PLUS PRICING. Obviously, any increase in costs or profits will increase prices. So the argument is that inflation is caused by increases in costs.

What is more, inflation can become permanent, if a WAGE-PRICE SPIRAL is set up. This occurs when an initial increase in prices prompts workers to ask for higher pay rises. These higher wages add to firms' costs and so to even higher prices. This sets off further demands for wage increases, and so it goes on.

There is no doubt that inflation in Britain increased sharply on the two occasions in the 1970s (in 1973/4 and 1978/9) when oil prices shot up. But if the cost–push view of inflation is correct, it needs to be shown that this rise in oil prices increased inflation over a period of time and did not just push up prices on a once-and-for-all basis. Whether this happened is not clear from the evidence available.

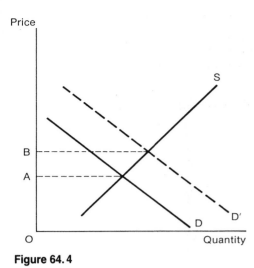

Figure 64. 4

Demand—pull Inflation

The other main Keynesian theory of inflation is the DEMAND—PULL theory. In a normal market, if demand increases, so do prices. This is shown in Figure 64.4. Here, an increase in demand from D to D′ leads to an increase in prices from OA to OB. Some economists argue that the same is true of the whole economy. If consumers try to spend more on consumer goods, or firms try to invest more, or foreigners want to buy more exports, or governments want to increase public spending, then inflation is likely to result.

How much inflation will result depends upon how large the increase in demand is and also on how near the economy is to FULL EMPLOYMENT. Full employment is defined as that level of employment where all available factors or production are fully employed – i.e. no unemployment exists. If the economy is well below full employment, then firms can take on more workers, buy more machines, etc. to produce more goods and services when demand increases. So an increase in demand here should not lead to much inflation. But if the economy is near to or at full employment, then firms will not be able to employ extra factors of production, and therefore they will not be able to produce more goods and services. Thus, an increase in demand at full employment will lead to inflation, but not increased output.

Demand—pull economists argue that inflation could well increase again, if demand rose substantially today, even though there are 3 million people unemployed. It is claimed that this is because, although there are plenty of workers available, there is not enough capital in Britain to produce a large increase in goods and services. Because Britain has failed to invest enough over the past ten or fifteen years, there is a shortage of capital. So an increase in demand today could well spark off a rise in demand—pull inflation.

CHECKPOINTS

1 A firm gives its workers a 10% pay rise. Why might the prices of the firm's products go up as a result?

2 The prices of imported goods, including raw materials, goes up by 20%. Why might this lead to an increase in the price of British goods?

3 A firm wants to take on more workers, but it is situated in an area of the country where unemployment is very low. Why might it have to increase the wages of its workers to do this? What effect might this have on the price of its products?

4 Explain the difference between the cost—push view of inflation and the demand—pull view.

5 Draw aggregate (total) demand and aggregate supply curves on graph paper, using the data in Figure 64.5.

Figure 64.5

Price level (£)	Aggregate demand (£bn)	Aggregate supply (£bn)
10	60	45
12	55	55
14	50	60
16	45	60

(a) What is the equilibrium level of output and prices?

(b) Demand increased by £5 billion at each level of prices. Draw the new aggregate demand curve. What has happened to the equilibrium level of output and prices as a result?

KEY TERMS

COST—PUSH INFLATION – the view that inflation is caused by increases in costs to producers, such as higher wages, higher import prices or higher profit levels.

COST—PLUS PRICING – this occurs when a producer fixes the price of a product by calculating its cost and adding a profit mark-up.

MARK-UP – the percentage that a producer adds to the cost of a product to arrive at the final price.

WAGE—PRICE SPIRAL – a process by which increases in wages lead to increases in prices, which in turn lead to increases in wages and so on.

DEMAND—PULL INFLATION – the view that inflation is caused by more demand in the whole economy than can be supplied at existing prices.

FULL EMPLOYMENT – the level of employment where all factors of production in the economy are fully utilised.

COURSEWORK SUGGESTION

Arrange to interview the finanancial directors (or whoever is responsible for pricing products) of several firms. Draw up a questionnaire beforehand which asks how the firm prices its products. For instance, does it rigidly use a cost-plus mark-up system or are prices set independently of costs? Describe your findings. Compare and contrast the different pricing methods used. Try to decide the extent to which your evidence supports a cost—push view or a demand—pull view of inflation.

Economic Growth

Figure 65.1 Gross domestic product (at constant prices)

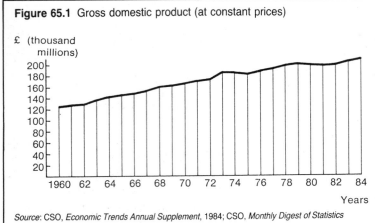

£ (thousand millions)

Years

Source: CSO, *Economic Trends Annual Supplement*, 1984; CSO, *Monthly Digest of Statistics*

Figure 65.2 Economic growth (percentage change in gross domestic product at constant prices)

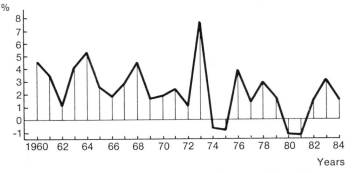

%

Years

Source: CSO, *Economic Trends Annual Supplement*, 1984; CSO, *Monthly Digest of Statistics*

Figure 65.3 Average annual change in real GDP, 1960–1982

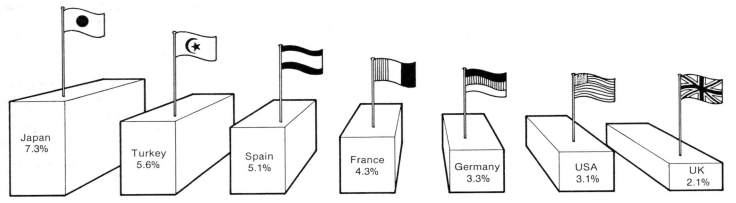

Japan 7.3%

Turkey 5.6%

Spain 5.1%

France 4.3%

Germany 3.3%

USA 3.1%

UK 2.1%

Source: OECD, *Historical Statistics*

STUDY POINTS

Consider Figure 65.1

1 What was the value of gross domestic product (a) in 1960 and (b) in 1984?

2 By how much did gross domestic product increase between 1960 and 1984 (a) in £s and (b) in percentage terms?

3 In what ways might this increase in gross domestic product improve the standard of living of the average Briton?

Consider Figure 65.2

4 In what year did gross domestic product grow the most in percentage terms?

5 In what years did gross domestic product go down compared to the previous year?

6 Why is a high rate of growth in gross domestic product generally considered to be better than a low rate of economic growth?

Consider Figure 65.3.

7 Which country had the fastest average annual rate of economic growth between 1960 and 1982? Which country had the lowest?

8 Assume that Japan and the UK both had GDPs of £100 in 1960. Use your calculator to find out how much their GDPs would be in 1984.

9 Does it matter that the UK had a low growth rate compared to other countries over the period 1960 to 1982? To answer this, consider the costs and the benefits of economic growth.

The Chancellor of the Exchequer said in his 1985 budget speech:

> 'Once again we can look back on a year of steady growth. Output grew by 2½%, with investment up by 6½%. Looking ahead, we are now about to embark on what will be the fifth year of growth, with output in 1985 set to rise by a further 3½%.'

When the Chancellor talked about ECONOMIC GROWTH he was referring to growth in national income, income which was up 2½% in 1984 and forecast to rise by another 3½% in 1985.

Figure 65.1 shows how national income has grown in real terms (i.e. after inflation has been taken out of the figures) over the period 1960–84. The measure of national income used is gross domestic product or GDP (explained in Unit 48). In almost every year, GDP has been higher than in the previous year, so that by 1984 GDP was almost double what it was in 1960.

Figure 65.2 shows the rate of growth of GDP over the same period. Growth averaged about 2½% – in some years it was less, in some years more. Notice that the figures tend to go up and down in a regular pattern. This is known as the TRADE CYCLE. On average, the economy goes into *boom* (i.e. there is high economic growth) every five years. So the economy was going through a boom in 1963, 1968, 1973 and 1979. But between these booms were RECESSIONS – periods of low growth. The economy was going through a recession in 1962, 1966, 1971, 1975 and 1980. In his budget speech in 1985, the Chancellor was claiming that his policies were giving 'steady growth' – i.e. there would be no more recessions with his policies. By the time you read this book, you will probably be able to tell whether he was right, because the economy was due for a recession in 1986 or 1987.

Figure 65.3 shows that since 1960 the UK economy has grown, but it has not grown as fast as its rivals in the world economy. Does this matter?

Growth: Desirable or Not?

Britain's low growth rate is a matter of grave concern. In 1950, the UK was almost the most affluent country in Europe and indeed the world. The average British citizen could spend more money than his or her French, German, Spanish or African counterpart. By 1985, this had changed considerably. Britain now has one of the lowest incomes per head in Western Europe; this means that the average Briton has less money to spend than the average French or German citizen. The basic economic problem is that human wants exceed what can be produced. If Britain fails to grow as fast as other countries, then this problem will become relatively more difficult than in those other countries.

However, a failure to grow quickly is not necessarily bad. We saw in Unit 50 that national income is not the same as the standard of living in an economy. Growth will lead to a lowering of the standard of living, if the advantages of having extra output are more than outweighed by the costs of that output, such as greater pollution, greater stress on workers, etc. During the 1970s, there was a body of opinion that argued that the advantages of being able to consume more goods and services because of economic growth were outweighed by the costs of this production – e.g. in terms of pollution, using up scarce resources of minerals, etc.

Nuclear power can help us meet our energy requirements and achieve growth; but many people are worried about safety.

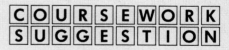

CHECKPOINTS

1 Giving an example, explain what is meant by economic growth.

2 Explain the difference between a 'boom' and a 'recession'.

3 Why does low economic growth present a problem for a national economy?

4 Suppose two countries had identical national incomes of £100 billion in 1985. One country averaged 2% growth over the next 25 years, whereas the other averaged 3% growth. Use a calculator to calculate the national incomes of each country in the year 2010. How much better off is the faster-growing economy in that year?

5 List the possible disadvantages of economic growth.

COURSEWORK SUGGESTION

Consider your local economy (village, town, city or region in which you live). Gather as many statistics as you can to show how that economy has changed over the past 25 years. Useful sources might be your local town hall, central library, and government statistics such as *Regional Trends* (published by HMSO). Evaluate the extent to which economic growth has resulted in an improvement in the standard of living for the local population. What might be the costs and benefits of a high-growth local economy in the future, as opposed to a low or zero-growth economy?

KEY TERMS

ECONOMIC GROWTH – an increase in national income over a period of time.

TRADE CYCLE – changes in a nation's level of economic activity.

RECESSION – a period of higher than average unemployment and lower than average growth.

The Causes of Economic Growth

Motor industry 'faces growing research crisis'

The UK faces a crisis in research and development in the motor industry and other sectors. Mr. Harry Sheron, Managing Director of British Leyland's research, says that this is due to:

- lack of investment;
- not enough Government support;
- a growing shortage of designers, engineers and other technologists;
- an education service which fails to provide enough trained workers.

Mr. Sheron stated that the UK may already be "below the critical level" needed to stay internationally competitive in technology and products. There are few designers left in the UK capable of producing an automatic gearbox, he said. If current trends continue, there will be no engine design capability left in Britain in a decade.

For instance, Jaguar cars has been seeking to expand production and has a new model, the XJ 40, out next year. But it says that it has found difficulty finding qualified engineers at salaries of up to £20,000.

Dr. John Herlock, Vice-chancellor of the Open University, argues that: "What we should be doing is providing double the number of graduate engineers; we produce about half the qualified engineers, as a percentage of the relevant age group, as Japan."

The gap between what the UK and leading developed world competitors are achieving in tons of technological effort is enormous, Mr. Sheron said. "It is likely that total research and development (R and D) spending in the UK motor industry has fallen to below £200m." Only 1% of that is paid for by government.

In the USA in 1983, some $1.07bn. was provided by government for R and D in the motor industry and transportation sectors. When private industry funds are added, total R and D spending in the vehicles industry that year reached $7.19 bn.

Estimates from the University of Sussex's Science Policy Research Unit show that Japanese R and D spending in the sector is about half the US level. West Germany's spending, too, is more than that of the UK's.

Adapted from *The Financial Times*, 6 March 1985

MEMORANDUM   TO THE SECRETARY OF STATE FOR TRADE AND INDUSTRY

I find this report disturbing. For the next Cabinet meeting, I would like a report prepared stating:

* what is happening to Research and Development in our motor industry;

* what are the possible economic consequences of this for growth in incomes and jobs in the UK over the next 10 years;

* what our Government could do to improve the situation and what the costs of this are likely to be.

The Prime Minister

STUDY POINT

1 Imagine you are the Secretary of State for Trade and Industry. Prepare an appropriate response to the Prime Minister's memo.

The Factors of Production

Some 10 000 years ago, world output was extremely small. It consisted mainly of food, simple shelter, wood and other simple necessities of life. Today, the output of just one small economy, that of the UK, is well over £200 billion a year. How has this transformation taken place? What are the likely sources of economic growth in the future?

Long-term growth is generated mainly by increasing the quantity and quality of the factors of production in an economy. Some countries have grown because of their rich resources of *land*. As we have seen, 'land' includes not only land itself, but all natural resources. Saudi Arabia, for instance, has grown because it has been able to exploit its oil reserves. The UK, too, is rich in many natural resources. North Sea oil alone is generally reckoned to be contributing 2–3% a year to the national income of the UK.

Not all countries possess rich natural resources. But *labour* too, can be an important source of growth. A country is likely to produce more, if it has more workers. An increasing population is therefore likely to boost growth, but of course that may not mean that income per head of the population is growing. The main sources of growth per head of the population are:

- an increase in the quality of the workforce;
- a better utilisation of the population.

Increasing the quality of the workforce, through better education, training and experience, increases the value of *human capital* (explained in Unit 20) in the economy and makes workers more productive. Making better use of workers would involve moving workers into more productive industries or bringing into the workforce more women who had wanted to work, but were denied the opportunity by legal, economic and social pressures.

Increasing the stock of *capital* and making more efficient use of it is another important source of growth. Equipping workers with better

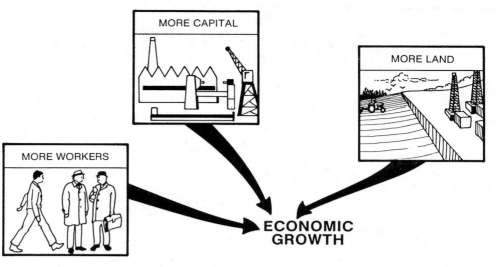

ECONOMIC GROWTH

machines is likely to make those workers more productive – each worker will be able to produce more in the same time. It is perhaps not surprising that Japan, with one of the highest growth rates in the post-war period, should also have one of the best investment records. But investment in itself is not enough to produce growth. If Britain today invested large sums in declining industries, such as shipbuilding and steel making, then that investment would be largely wasted. Since 1945, Japan has not only invested, but has invested in the industries of the future.

Efficiency

Growth can also be stimulated, if more efficient ways are found of combining all the factors of production. For instance, the economy could produce more goods and services:

- if the employment of factors of production like labour were increased. If 1 million unemployed workers were back in work, producing just £5000 of output each, that would add £5000 million to output;

- if there were fewer strikes. These strikes are usually caused by the conflict of interest between the owners of capital who want to earn more profit by paying workers less, and workers who want higher wages;

- if workers and managers worked harder to get the most out of the limited resources available.

1 Draw up a list of ten natural resources.

2 What economic advantage does a country rich in natural resources have over a country with few natural resources?

3 What is 'human capital'? How can an economy improve its stock of human capital? Why is this likely to lead to higher economic growth?

4 How can increased investment lead to increased economic growth?

5 Explain why poor management, poor industrial relations and unemployment can lead to low economic growth.

COURSEWORK SUGGESTION

Consider the British economy as a whole, using the *Annual Abstract of Statistics*, *Social Trends* and the *Economic Trends Annual Supplement* (all published by HMSO). Describe how the UK economy has grown since the Second World War. Investigate various reasons for that growth: e.g. the UK's investment record over the period, increased output of North Sea oil, etc. Evaluate the extent to which a higher investment level might raise the UK's growth rate.

Data Response Questions
Units 61–66

Unit 61 Inflation

THE PRICE OF PASSING YEARS

	Average prices*	
	1945	1985
Daily Express	0·42p	20p
1 loaf bread	1·88p	46p
Packet 10 Woodbine cigarettes	4·38p	68p
1 pint beer	6·25p	85p
1 gallon petrol	9·75p	£2·05p
Average three-bedroom house	£5,625	£31,686

* Decimal value

	Average earnings	Average hours worked	Average hourly earnings
1945	£6·07	49·7	12·21p
1985	£163·40*	44·3**	£3·70

* manual workers
** including overtime

£1 in 1945 is now worth in real terms only 8·1p; in other words, to have the same purchasing power as £1 in 1945 you would need £12·50 in your pocket.

Source: Daily Express, 8 May 1985

1 What was the price of 2 pints of beer in 1945 and 1985? *(1 mark)*

2 Calculate how many times the price of a gallon of petrol has risen over the period 1945 to 1985. *(1 mark)*

3 Which of the goods mentioned in the data has gone up most in price in percentage terms? *(1 mark)*

4 A worker earned £10 a week in 1945. How much would he have had to earn in 1985 to buy the same basket of goods and services? *(1 mark)*

5 Explain whether or not the average manual worker could buy more goods and services in 1985 than in 1945. *(3 marks)*

6 Why would a 10% rise in the price of the Daily Express not add 10% to the general price level? *(3 marks)*

Unit 62 The Costs of Inflation

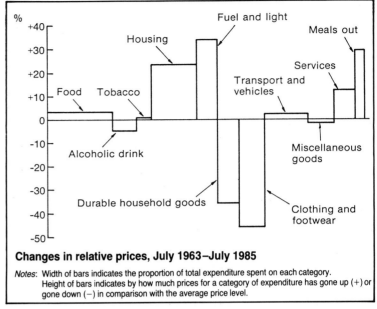

Changes in relative prices, July 1963–July 1985

Notes: Width of bars indicates the proportion of total expenditure spent on each category.
Height of bars indicates by how much prices for a category of expenditure has gone up (+) or gone down (−) in comparison with the average price level.

Source: The Treasury, *Economic Progress Report*, October 1983

1 Prices went up by 6¼ times on average between July 1963 and July 1983. Name *four* categories of expenditure which went up by more than this over the period. *(2 marks)*

2 Which category of expenditure increased *least* in price over the period? *(1 mark)*

3 Which category of expenditure formed the largest proportion of total household expenditure in 1983? *(1 mark)*

4 Pensioners spend a larger proportion than the average on food and fuel and light, and less on durable household goods and clothing and footwear. What is the implication of this on the pensioners' standard of living? *(6 marks)*

The Data Response Question for **Units 63 and 64** can be found on *page 221*.

Unit 65 Economic Growth

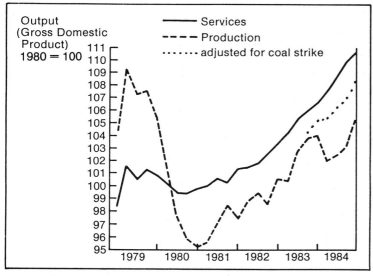

Source: The Treasury, *Economic Progress Report*, June–July 1985

1 What is meant by 'output' in the data? *(3 marks)*

2 Compare how the output of production industries changed over the period 1979 to 1984 with that of service industries. *(4 marks)*

3 From 1983 onwards, the miners took industrial action. How and why did this affect production output? *(4 marks)*

4 (a) Estimate the annual rate of growth of (i) production output and (ii) service output for the period from January 1979 to December 1984, including the effects of the miners' strike.

(b) How would your answer be different if the effects of the miners' strike were ignored and output calculated as if there had been no strike? *(4 marks)*

Unit 66 The Causes of Economic Growth

LABOUR TO MAKE MONEY WORK

A NEW blueprint for putting Britain back to work was unveiled by Labour yesterday.

It aims to slash the record dole queues by putting the country's wealth to use where it can do most good – at home.

Billions of pounds invested abroad since Premier Margaret Thatcher came to power will be brought back to Britain under Labour's scheme.

And a major new national bank will be set up to channel funds – often at cheap rates – to hard-pressed industry.

Yesterday as Shadow Chancellor Roy Hattersley launched his party's radical Investing in Britain scheme, he pledged: "It will work."

He pointed out since 1979 an extra two million men and women had joined the dole queues.

But at the same time £20,000 million of British money – mainly pension funds, insurance schemes and investment trusts – has been invested abroad "creating foreign jobs in foreign factories."

Those sending the cash out of the country were even helped by the taxpayer because they got huge tax concessions.

Under his scheme, big investment groups like pension funds and other major City institutions would have to:

● **CUT the amount they invest abroad or face stinging tax penalties.**

● **INVEST at least some of that money in a newly-created National Investment Bank.**

Even individuals who invested too much abroad – in bank deposits, securities and property other than holiday homes – would face extra tax demands.

The state-owned bank would use the cash it raises for long-term aid to Britain's crisis-torn industries, lending them money at rates that allow them to compete with foreign rivals.

Source: *Daily Mirror*, 15 May 1985

1 Explain carefully what the Labour Party plans to do to help reduce unemployment. *(3 marks)*

2 Why might these plans increase the rate of economic growth in the UK? *(4 marks)*

3 Under what circumstances would these plans *not* lead to more jobs and increased growth? *(3 marks)*

Essay Questions
Units 61–66

1 (a) What is meant by 'inflation'? *(4 marks)*

(b) Describe *two* possible causes of inflation in Britain today. *(8 marks)*

(c) Explain the view that inflation causes unemployment. *(8 marks)*

2 'Growth in national income of the UK slowed to 1.4% last year.'

(a) Suggest *two* reasons why a slow down in the UK's rate of growth of national income is bad for people in Britain. *(6 marks)*

(b) How could growth in national income be increased in the future? *(8 marks)*

(c) To what extent does growth in national income always lead to an increase in economic welfare? *(6 marks)*

Regional Inequalities

Figure 67.1 Regional inequalities, 1983

Region	Unemployment rate (%)	Gross domestic product per head (£)	Average gross weekly earnings: men (£)	Percentage of households with telephone	Infant (0–4) deaths per thousand of the population	Percentage of workforce holding a degree or equivalent
South East	9.3	5155	184.9	75.6	2.4	11.9
South West	11.1	4147	156.2	65.6	2.4	7.7
East Anglia	10.1	4204	157.4	68.2	2.3	7.3
West Midlands	15.5	3814	155.2	63.9	3.0	6.5
East Midlands	11.6	4104	155.0	61.1	2.8	6.5
Yorkshire and Humberside	13.9	3958	158.6	60.6	3.0	6.4
North	17.8	3880	159.3	52.9	2.5	5.9
North West	15.8	4073	160.1	65.8	2.8	7.4
Scotland	14.8	4173	167.5	69.4	2.7	8.4
Wales	15.9	3627	156.3	58.5	2.4	5.9
Northern Ireland	20.7	3156	150.5	45.5	3.2	6.1

Source: CSO, *Regional Trends*, 1984 and 1985

Figure 67.2 Specialisation by region in the UK 1984

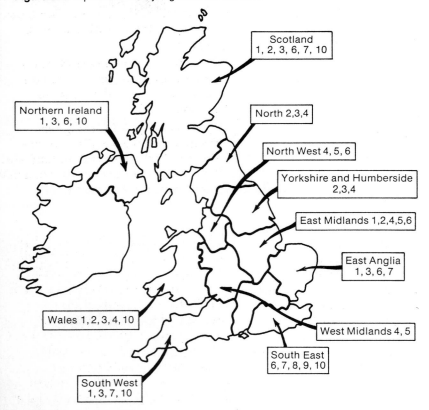

Scotland
1, 2, 3, 6, 7, 10

Northern Ireland
1, 3, 6, 10

North 2,3,4

North West 4, 5, 6

Yorkshire and Humberside
2,3,4

East Midlands 1,2,4,5,6

East Anglia
1, 3, 6, 7

Wales 1, 2, 3, 4, 10

West Midlands 4, 5

South East
6, 7, 8, 9, 10

South West
1, 3, 7, 10

The map shows those regions which have more than the national average percentage of their labour forces employed in a particular sector of industry

Source: CSO, *Economic Trends*, 1985

KEY

1 Agriculture, forestry, fishing
2 Energy and water supply
3 Construction
MANUFACTURING
4 Metals, minerals and chemicals
5 Metal goods, engineering and vehicle industries
6 Other manufacturing
SERVICES
7 Distribution, hotels and catering, repairs
8 Transport and communication
9 Banking, finance, insurance, business services and leasing
10 Public administration and other services

STUDY POINTS

1 Prepare a report on your region. Compare its living standards with other regions.

2 Assess what employment opportunities there are in your region compared to other regions.

3 Evaluate the prospects for your region, remembering that service industries are growing at a much faster rate than manufacturing industry at the moment.

Indicators of Affluence

The UK can be divided into two areas. The South, comprising East Anglia, the South East and the South West, is well off and is likely to continue to grow well. The other area, comprising the rest of the UK, is not as well off and is facing a less certain future. This unit considers in what senses and why the South is better off.

Figure 67.1 shows six different measures of affluence (wealth) for each region of the UK. The South East comes out quite clearly as the most affluent region, whereas Northern Ireland is the poorest region.

Causes

One fundamental reason for this inequality between regions is the location of industry. The South of England has come to have more and better industry than the rest of the UK. This was not always the case. One hundred years ago, the prosperous areas of Britain were in the North. This was where the new industries of the time – manufacturing industries such as steel, textiles, shipbuilding and engineering – had based themselves. The prosperous parts of the UK were situated on the west coast – e.g. Bristol, Liverpool and Glasgow – because our major trading partners were North America and the British colonies. During the twentieth century, manufacturing industry has been in slow decline, as has been shown in Unit 49. Much of the 'new' manufacturing industry, such as motor manufacturing and light engineering, has tended to establish itself in the Midlands and the South. This has left the rest of the UK with declining industries and rising unemployment.

The prosperity of the South was further increased by the growth of service industries in the UK economy. London, the capital of the UK, became a centre for banking and other financial services. It was also the seat of government and this created many

Liverpool was one of the UK's most prosperous cities in the nineteenth century.

new jobs. The South was, and still is, the most important centre of population in the UK. Service industries tend to set up where people live and buy those services. A last important factor has been the growth of trade with Europe and the relative decline in trade with North America and the colonies. This has meant that industry has been attracted to the South to cut down on transport and other costs in its trade with the Continent. The current distribution of jobs, by industry, in the UK is shown in Figure 67.2.

The South has become increasingly prosperous because:

- new industry creates new jobs;
- which creates income;
- which creates a demand for goods and services;
- which creates new industry and jobs.

The North is caught in a vicious circle of traditional manufacturing industry closing down, which leads to lower incomes, less demand for products, and more job losses. The position would be even worse, but for the fact that areas other than the South are slowly losing population as workers move to where the jobs are. The government has helped, too, by offering grants to industry setting up in the poorer regions of the UK.

The REGIONAL PROBLEM has been present now for over 50 years, and with no end in sight to the decline in manufacturing, it could still be here in another 50 years' time.

1 In what ways are regions of the UK unequal in an economic sense?

2 Compare the geographical distribution of industry today with that of 100 years ago.

3 Explain why growing trade with Western Europe has helped pull industry towards the South of England.

4 Land is cheaper, buildings are cheaper and workers' wages are lower outside the South of England. Why, then, is industry still attracted to setting up in the South?

C O U R S E W O R K   S U G G E S T I O N

Compare the region you live in either with Northern Ireland, or the south-east of England, whichever provides the greater contrast. Describe the industry in each region and compare various indices of the standard of living. Explain why the two regions have developed in the way that they have. Assess the costs and benefits of bringing the poorer regions up to the standards of affluence (i.e. wealth) of the richer regions.

K E Y   T E R M

REGIONAL PROBLEM – the fact that different regions of the UK have different employment rates, and therefore different standards of living.

Government Economic Policy

ECHO AND STAR

PRICES
UP
AGAIN

Average annual change in real GDP, 1960–82

Japan 7.3%
Turkey 5.6%
Spain 5.1%
France 4.3%
Germany 3.3%
USA 3.1%
UK 2.1%

In his budget speech in March 1985, the Chancellor of the Exchequer told Parliament:

> 'Today I reaffirm the government's determination to . . . defeat inflation. But the defeat of inflation, essential though it is, is not enough. We must also do what we can to combat the scourge of unemployment. Nor is there any conflict between these two objectives.'

The Chancellor was saying that two major goals of economic policy were:

- to reduce inflation; and
- to reduce unemployment.

The government also has two other major goals of economic policy, namely:

- to increase the rate of economic growth; and
- to ensure that Britain pays its way abroad by exporting (i.e. selling British goods and services to foreigners) at least as much as it imports (i.e. buys goods and services from foreigners). If imports are greater than exports, then the country has to borrow money or reduce its savings. Like any ordinary household, it cannot do that for ever. Exports minus imports is called the *current balance*. If the current balance is positive or 'in the black', then exports are greater than imports and all is well. If the current balance is negative or 'in the red', then imports are greater than exports and Britain could be faced with problems in the future.

In an ideal world, the Chancellor would be steering an economy that had low inflation (a few per cent), low unemployment (0.5–1.0 million perhaps), high economic growth (3–4% per year), and a current balance that was always in a small surplus (say, between £500m and £1000m per year). Are these goals unobtainable or is the Chancellor's belief – that there is no 'conflict' between low inflation and low unemployment – correct?

STUDY POINTS

1 Look at the photographs and the statistics. What economic problems facing the British economy are suggested by them?

2 The government has a responsibility to ensure that the economy is developing in as desirable a direction as possible. Traditionally, four major areas of responsibility have been singled out: the maintenance of a low level of unemployment, price stability (which in practice means low levels of inflation), high economic growth and a balance on foreign trade (i.e. making sure that the UK is paying its way in the world by at least exporting as much as she imports). Explain why (a) high levels of unemployment (b) high levels of inflation and (c) low levels of economic growth can affect you in a negative way?

3 If a government had to choose between a doubling of inflation and a doubling of unemployment, which do you think it ought to choose and why? In order to answer this, consider the costs and benefits of each alternative.

Conflicts of Objective

The Keynesian view of the economy suggests that there will be a conflict between these objectives. To see why, consider the period 1979–82, shown in Figure 68.1. 1979 was a boom year. Unemployment was falling, growth was up, but inflation and the current balance had taken a turn for the worse. A new government was elected in 1979, the Conservative government of Mrs Thatcher. It promised to reduce inflation, reduce unemployment and increase growth in the economy. It introduced tight policies, including rises in interest rates, falls in the rate of growth of the money supply, and rises in taxes. All this, together with lower world growth, helped reduce total demand (or *aggregate demand*) in the economy. With less spending, firms did not produce as many goods and services. So the rate of growth of output fell, but unemployment rose. The current balance improved, in part because of North Sea oil, but also because British industry and British consumers bought fewer imports. Inflation, too, decreased after 1980 as demand in the economy was reduced (i.e. there was less demand–pull

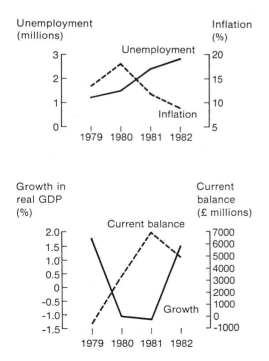

Figure 68.1

inflation) and as costs went down, due to lower wage increases and lower import prices.

Keynesians argue, then, that there is a conflict between high growth and low unemployment, on the one hand, and low inflation and current account surplus, on the other, because high growth leads to more jobs, but also to demand–pull inflation and more imports. Governments either have to accept that there is some trade-off between these two sets of objectives (i.e. low inflation and low unemployment) or they have to devise policies that will reconcile these conflicts.

The Chancellor, as a *monetarist*, did not think a conflict of objectives need be inevitable. His and his fellow monetarists' argument is this. The first priority of a government must be to control inflation. If it fails to control inflation, then Britain will become uncompetitive with the rest of the world. British goods will not sell as well abroad and imports will come flooding in. This will lead to a current account deficit. British jobs will disappear as orders for British goods dry up. Economic growth will decline. High inflation in Britain will also discourage firms from investing, because of the uncertainty that inflation brings with it. Firms will also expect to see governments intervene to reduce inflation and this will also discourage them from investing. Less investment leads to lower growth and fewer new jobs in the future.

Low inflation, on the other hand, will result in Britain being competitive. Orders for British goods will rise. Firms will want to invest and take on new workers. All this will bring about falling unemployment, higher growth, and an improved balance of payments situation. To some extent, this was the position from 1982 to 1985, as can be seen from Figure 68.2. Falling inflation is matched by higher growth. But unemployment continued to rise. So perhaps the Chancellor was wrong when he argued that there is no 'conflict' between inflation and unemployment.

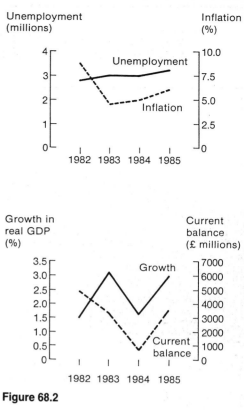

Figure 68.2

Describe and analyse the present government's economic objectives. Consider the extent to which those economic objectives are in conflict. Research material for this can be obtained from past copies of the *Economic Progress Report* (published by the Treasury) and from newspaper articles.

Fiscal Policy

1 Read the article carefully and then study the statistics. You have to prepare a report for the Opposition on the likely effects of the Chancellor's measures. In particular, you need to consider the effects on:

(a) unemployment;
(b) inflation;
(c) the balance of payments;
(d) the rate of economic growth.

Once you have prepared your report, you may want to discuss what actually happened after March 1972.

Figure 69.1 Unemployment (excluding school leavers)

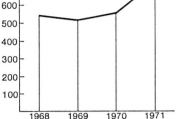

Figure 69.2 Inflation

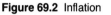

Figure 69.3 Growth (in GDP at constant prices)

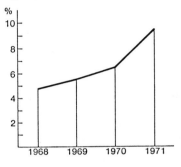

Figure 69.4 Current balance on the balance of payments

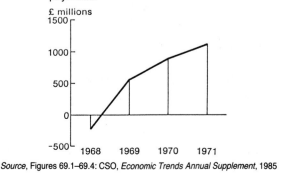

Source, Figures 69.1–69.4: CSO, *Economic Trends Annual Supplement*, 1985

£1,211m tax cuts in 72–73

The main features of the Chancellor's budget are:

● total tax cuts of £1,211m. By far the single most important item in this is a cut in income tax which should mean that every taxpayer pays £1 a week less in tax.

● increased help to companies which invest. Companies will be able to pay less tax if they undertake investment. Total cost to the Government is estimated at £200m a year.

● increased help for Britain's high unemployment regions (the "Development Areas"). Companies investing in these areas will be able to get back 20% of the cost of any investment made.

● overall, the Chancellor's measures will lead to tax cuts and extra government spending of an estimated £1,391 million a year.

The Chancellor, Mr Anthony Barber, said that the purpose of his Budget was "To revitalise British industry so that it can open up the new frontiers of Europe. To achieve a rate of growth twice as fast as in the past decade. To secure a growing prosperity which can be sustained into the foreseeable future and which will benefit all our people."

He claimed that the UK now had "the most powerful combination of national and regional investment incentives since the war".

The estimated effect of the budget will be to add another 2% to national output (taking into account direct and multiplier effects), 1½% of which is attributed to income tax cuts.

The Chancellor said that his budget was not "inimical" to the fight against inflation. He pointed out that business had repeatedly claimed that a faster growth of output was, via the effect on productivity and profitability, one of the most effective means of restraining price increases.

Adapted from the *Financial Times*, 22 March 1972.

Controlling the Economy

By adopting various policy measures, governments can affect the economy. This unit and the next two, will consider these various measures.

A main weapon is FISCAL POLICY. Fiscal policy is government policy with regard to government spending, taxation and borrowing. Fiscal policy can affect the economy in a number of ways. First, it may affect the *level of demand* in the economy. If a government spends more and/or raises less money in taxation, then there will have to be an increase in the amount that the government borrows – the PUBLIC-SECTOR BORROWING REQUIREMENT or PSBR will go up. An increase in the PSBR will mean that the private sector will have more money to spend. This situation will have come about either because the private sector is paying less in taxes than before, or it will have money as a result of extra government spending. For instance, if the government has spent more on roads, then the private sector will end up with that extra money in the form of wages, orders for raw materials, etc. Economists disagree, however, about the exact link between PSBR and aggregate demand.

Keynesian economists argue that an extra £1 of government borrowing will increase national income by more than £1. This is known as the MULTIPLIER EFFECT. The argument is that if the government increases, say, spending in hospitals by £1, then that will lead to a £1 increase in income. But whoever receives that £1 (workers, firms, etc.) will spend it, creating further income in the economy. The money will keep travelling round the economy (or round the circular flow described in Unit 48), each time creating extra income as it changes hands.

Monetarists, however, argue that there is no multiplier effect. In fact £1 of extra borrowing by the government will mean that the private sector will not be able to borrow that £1. Extra public spending CROWDS OUT private spending, so that an increase in the PSBR has no overall effect on aggregate demand in the economy.

Second, fiscal policy can affect the distribution of income and wealth in the economy. By making the rich pay more in taxes than the poor, and by increasing spending on programmes that benefit the poor rather than the rich, the government can make the distribution of income and wealth more equitable. Making the poor pay more in taxes and reducing spending on programmes designed to help the poor will increase income and wealth inequalities in the economy.

Third, fiscal policy can affect the decisions of industrial consumers, workers and firms.

- If a government gives cash grants or reduces taxes to firms making investment, then total investment in the economy should rise.

- Workers may work harder, if incentives to work are increased. This can be done by reducing the marginal rate of income tax (i.e. the rate of tax on the last pound earned by the worker). Or it can be done by reducing unemployment benefits, so that the difference between income in work and out of work is increased.

- Entrepreneurs can be encouraged to start up in business and expand through a whole variety of measures – e.g. reduced marginal tax rates on income and profits, investment grants, and tax privileges on borrowed funds.

- Firms can be encouraged to take on more workers through reducing taxes on the employment of workers – the main tax in the UK being employers' national insurance contributions.

K E Y   T E R M S

FISCAL POLICY – government policy with regard to public expenditure, taxation and borrowing.

PUBLIC-SECTOR BORROWING REQUIREMENT (PSBR) – the difference between total government revenue and total government expenditure.

MULTIPLIER EFFECT – the theory that extra spending will lead to further increases in spending in the rest of the economy.

CROWDING OUT – the belief that extra government spending leads to less spending by the private sector.

Monetary Policy

Government keeps interest rates high as money supply keeps growing at too fast a rate

Banks eager to lend money to personal customers. Interest rate cut expected

Money supply growth sparks off renewed fears of inflation

Companies call for lower interest rates to help reduce costs and increase price competitiveness

Building company gone into liquidation. The company blames "too high mortgage rates" which have caused a slump in demand for new houses

Credit card companies report less spending since interest rates were increased

Increased money supply explains the recent reduction in interest rates

Company defers investment plan due to "too high interest rates"

Pound falls on foreign exchange markets. Government steps in to stop the fall by increasing interest rates

Mortgage rates up again as Government increases interest rates

STUDY POINTS

1 Write a report explaining why the money supply and the rate of interest is important in an economy. In your report, make use of each of the examples above. Structure your report round the following:

(a) What is the relationship between the rate of interest (which is the *price* which has to be paid if money is borrowed) and the supply of money? If you have any difficulty in answering this, go back to units 12 and 13 which discuss supply and price.

(b) Explain the possible link between the money supply and inflation.

(c) Explain the link between the value of the pound and the exchange rate.

(d) Explain the link between the rate of interest and the level of spending in the economy.

'Hopes for a cut in British interest rates received a sharp setback yesterday with the announcement that the money supply rose far beyond its target range last month.' (*Source: Financial Times*, 8 May 1985)

Since 1976 UK governments have attempted to fix a limit to the rate of growth of the money supply – this is the 'target range' mentioned in the extract. In doing this, they have automatically had to fix interest rates (the interest rate is the price of money).

As was shown in Unit 53:

- a reduction in the money supply will lead to a rise in interest rates;

- lower interest rates (assuming that the demand for money does not change) are caused by a rise in the money supply.

So in the extract, the writer says that interest rates are unlikely to fall, because the government has failed to keep the growth of the money supply within its limits. The government is now going to have to tighten its control and this reduction in the rate of growth of the money supply will mean higher interest rates.

Reasons For Controlling the Money Supply

There are three main reasons why a government might want to control the money supply and interest rates.

- First, as was discussed in Unit 63, monetarists believe that inflation is caused by excessive increases in the money supply. Controlling the money supply is therefore the key to controlling inflation.

- Second, many economists believe that lower interest rates will increase aggregate demand in the economy. If interest rates come down, consumers will be more tempted to borrow money for cars, houses, etc., and firms will be more tempted to borrow money for investment. Increased demand will help boost growth and reduce unemployment.

- Third, interest rates may be raised to help increase the value of the pound. Higher interest rates will help attract foreign investors to buy pounds to invest in Britain. More demand for pounds will lead to a higher value of the pound.

Techniques of Monetary Control

In the UK, the Bank of England is responsible for implementing MONETARY POLICY. It is important to remember that most of the money supply is made up, not of notes and coins, but of money in bank accounts. So controlling the money supply means, in practice, controlling the amount of money in the banking system.

A technique that has been used for a long time is called OPEN MARKET OPERATIONS. Here the Bank of England either borrows more money than it needs to finance the PSBR or it repays money owed by government to the rest of the economy. Borrowing more money than is needed is called OVERFUNDING. It has the effect of reducing the amount of money in the hands of the consumers, firms, banks, etc. – i.e. it reduces the money supply. It also pushes up the rate of interest, because the money supply is reduced.

Another technique is for the Bank of England to issue MONETARY DIRECTIVES. Directives were used extensively in the 1950s, 1960s and 1970s. The Bank of England would order the banks not to lend out more than a certain figure, or not to allow their deposits to grow by more than a certain percentage. Restricting lending by the banks should help restrict the money supply. In practice, banks tended to find ways round these restrictions.

SPECIAL DEPOSITS are another form of control that is now disused. The Bank of England would order the banks to lend it a certain amount of money. The banks would therefore be left with less money to lend to customers, and the money supply would go down.

FUNDING is the name given to the process of changing short-term government borrowing to long-term government borrowing. The effects of funding depend upon the particular rules of the banking system. One effect is likely to be a rise in long-term interest rates and a fall in short-term interest rates, as the demand from the government for short and long-term funds changes.

The Bank of England also has the power to change interest rates, if it wants. But unless this is backed up by other measures, such as the ones already described, it will not be able to keep interest rates at this new level, because market forces will restore the old level of interest rates.

In general, governments have found it very difficult to control the money supply, a point highlighted by the extract from the *Financial Times* at the beginning of this unit.

1 Why might a government wish to control the money supply?

2 Explain how the Bank of England can reduce the money supply through open market operations.

3 Distinguish between special deposits and directives.

4 Explain, using a demand and supply diagram, why a fall in the money supply will raise interest rates.

5 The Bank of England funds its debts by selling more long-term stock and using the money to buy up short-term stock. Use demand and supply diagrams to explain what will happen to interest rates for (a) short-term funds and (b) long-term funds.

COURSEWORK SUGGESTION

Take any three-month period. Describe what has happened to interest rates and the money supply over that period. Analyse why changes have occurred, particularly looking at the effect of the control of monetary variables exerted by the Bank of England. Consider the extent to which monetary policy has been effective over the period. This project will require a thorough reading of the financial press (particularly the *Financial Times*) over the period.

KEY TERMS

MONETARY POLICY – government policy with regard to the money supply and interest rates.

OPEN MARKET OPERATIONS – the buying and selling of government securities by the Bank of England in order to influence the stock of money in the economy.

OVERFUNDING – a form of open market operations where the Bank of England sells more government stock than is needed to finance the PSBR.

MONETARY DIRECTIVES – instructions from the Bank of England to the banks to restrict the growth of borrowing and lending.

SPECIAL DEPOSITS – loans that banks are forced to make to the Bank of England. This results in less money in the banking system and hence a lower money supply.

FUNDING – the substitution of long-term government debt for short-term government debt.

Data Response Questions
Units 67–70

Unit 67 Regional Inequalities

Who will act to stop the rot?

THE West Midlands Forum of County Councils warns that the region is developing into two societies, and unless the Government devises urgent and positive policies to rectify the stagnation, deep trouble lies ahead.

The forum sees an inner-city wasteland of poverty, decay and social unrest for the unemployed, while those in work escape to the shire counties.

The government is urged to seek more development aid from the EEC, to step up training in new technology, to modernise existing industry, and generally make the area more attractive to entrepreneurs.

The Government must take positive action, because the West Midlands is not the only area of the country that is decaying in a dangerous manner.

The CBI may give bright reports on booming trade, but the good news is only for those already in work. The job prospects are gloomy, and will remain so until some direct action is taken.

Source: Express and Star, 5 June 1985

1 What is meant when it is said that the West Midlands is developing into 'two societies'? (*2 marks*)

2 What can cause a region to 'decay'? (*3 marks*)

3 What measures might a Government take to prevent this decay from occurring? (*2 marks*)

4 What are the costs of regional decay to society? (*3 marks*)

Unit 68 Government Economic Policy

PYM TELLS THATCHER
YOU'VE FAILED

By **JULIA LANGDON**
Political Editor

SACKED Foreign Secretary Francis Pym had a stark message for Mrs Thatcher last night: Your policies have failed.

Mr Pym said that the Government's economic policies had not worked, were not working – and must be changed.

In the most devastating attack by one of Mrs Thatcher's ex-ministers, Mr Pym pointed out:

● Unemployment has nearly tripled and is still rising.

● Growth in the economy is only about half of one per cent a year.

● Industry in Britain is less competitive than in other countries.

Mr Pym, speaking at Oxford University, said: "I do not see how we can possibly be satisfied with the success of our policies – and nor do most people in the country."

Source: Daily Mirror, 15 May 1985

1 Explain what is meant in the article by:
(a) 'economic growth';
(b) 'less competitive' industry. (*4 marks*)

2 What major goals of government policy does Mr Pym argue the government has failed to achieve? (*1 mark*)

3 What major goals of government policy does Mr Pym not mention in his attack on the government? (*1 mark*)

4 To what extent should the control of unemployment be the most important goal of government policy? (*4 marks*)

Unit 69 Fiscal Policy

Car firms seek Thatcher boost

An urgent call for action to help the Midlands motor industry survive and challenge its rivals went to the Government today.

The plea comes in a campaign drawn up by the Society of Motor Manufacturers and Traders which asks Whitehall to remove obstacles to the industry's growth.

The society is asking the Government to cut car tax levels, improve roads, bring down interest rates and to achieve a realistic exchange rate with the pound to increase exports.

Suzanne Hinton, the society's head of external affairs, said: "The Government must give us the same level of support that governments in other car manufacturing nations such as France, and Italy give their motor industries."

The campaign brochure underlines the vital part the production of vehicles and components plays in the Midlands, a region where twice as many people as anywhere else depend on the motor industry.

The society says the industry has fought back from the recession and the terrible job losses and is striving to hold its own with the best of the world's vehicle producers.

The campaign document going to the Government – The Motor Industry in the Midlands – says there are 40,000 Midlands jobs in vehicle production, a figure multiplied many times by workers in component factories.

Source: Express and Star, 11 July 1985

1 Explain what measures the Society of Motor Manufacturers and Traders is asking the Government to take. *(3 marks)*

2 Explain how *two* of these measures would (a) help the car industry and (b) help other industries. *(4 marks)*

3 Why might Government spending on the car industry have a multiplier effect on the rest of the economy? *(4 marks)*

4 What is the opportunity cost of *two* of the measures suggested by the Society? *(4 marks)*

Unit 70 Monetary Policy

No easy task

THE behaviour of sterling M3, which is still one of the government's two targetted money measures, is not all that the Chancellor might desire.

Pinpointing the reasons why it is growing so quickly, though, is not an easy task. The September increase in sterling lending to the private sector of £1 billion was below recent figures.

The most convincing explanation so far is that corporate borrowing is up because of the spate of take-overs and mergers. And that, of course, is not likely to prove inflationary.

The Government is nevertheless left with a credibility problem.

One option is to go back to the old policy of over-funding the borrowing requirement, so that private sector liquidity is mopped up by excess debt sales and sterling M3 slows down.

Source: The Guardian, 9 October, 1985

1 Which measure of the money supply is mentioned in the article? *(1 mark)*

2 Increased lending by banks to private sector consumers and firms will increase the money supply. Explain why this is so. *(2 marks)*

3 Explain carefully in your own words a possible reason why the money supply is 'growing so quickly'. *(2 marks)*

4 (a) What is 'overfunding'?
   (b) Why might overfunding help reduce the rate of growth of the money supply? *(5 marks)*

Essay Questions
Units 67–70

1 'The Government in its budget increased income tax.'
   (a) Suggest *three* reasons why the government might have decided to increase taxes in its budget. *(9 marks)*
   (b) Explain why this increase in income tax could lead to unemployment in the economy. *(6 marks)*
   (c) To what extent would a rise in unemployment help reduce inflation? *(5 marks)*

2 (a) Describe *three* types of money in the UK. Explain why they are money. *(9 marks)*
   (b) How might a government attempt to control the growth of the money supply in the UK? *(6 marks)*
   (c) Why might the government want to control the rate of growth of the money supply? *(5 marks)*

Incomes Policy and Competition Policy

A history of incomes policy

Before 1966, governments had urged workers and employers not to push wages up too much. The first full prices and incomes policy was launched in August 1966 by the Labour government. The policy was *statutory* i.e. it was a law, and workers or firms who broke the policy could be prosecuted. A Prices and Incomes Board was set up and all pay rises had to be approved by them.

The terms of the policy were:

- August 1966 to December 1966 – a wages freeze i.e. no workers were allowed pay rises.
- January 1967 to June 1967 – a period of 'severe' restraint, when only 'special cases' were entitled to a pay rise.
- July 1967 to March 1969 – a period of low pay rises with a government target of keeping pay rises to 3½% per annum.
- March 1969 onwards – the government tried to keep overall wage rises to 3½% but controls were much looser than before.

In 1970, the Labour party lost the general election and a Conservative government was formed. It abolished all pay restraint, but rising prices forced it to reintroduce another statutory policy in 1972. The terms of this were:

- November 1972 to April 1973 – a prices and wages freeze.
- April 1973 to September 1973 – workers were allowed increases of £1 per week plus 4% of their wages.

- November 1973 onwards – workers were allowed either an extra £2.25 a week or a 7% pay rise, whichever was the greater. Workers could also obtain pay rises to compensate for inflation (i.e. index-linking).

The miners went on strike in November 1973, demanding much larger pay increases than the incomes policy allowed. The Conservative government called a general election on this issue. It lost the election in February 1974. The new Labour government then put in place its own incomes policy. This was *voluntary* – it was not backed by law, but was an agreement between the TUC and the government. The terms of the incomes policy were as follows:

- Autumn 1974 to July 1975 – 'voluntary restraint' but no figure for maximum pay rises was stated.

- August 1975 to July 1976 – a flat rate pay rise of £6 a week for all workers.
- August 1976 to July 1977 – a minimum pay rise of £2.50 a week up to a maximum of £4.50 a week *or* a rise of 5% whichever was the greater.
- August 1977 to July 1978 – a maximum pay rise of 10% with an allowance for any productivity gain.
- August 1978 onwards – a maximum pay rise of 5%, plus an allowance for productivity.

The voluntary pay policy broke down from the autumn of 1978, as groups of workers refused to accept the suggested maximum of 5%. In May 1979, the Labour party lost the general election and the Conservative government of Mrs Thatcher refused to have anything to do with incomes policies.

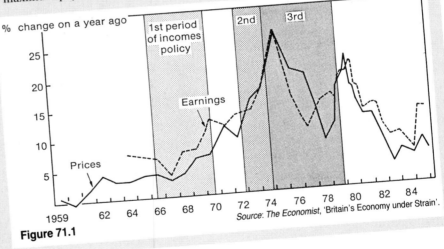

Figure 71.1

Source: The Economist, 'Britain's Economy under Strain'.

STUDY POINTS

1 Explain the meaning of the following terms associated with incomes policies:
  (a) statutory policy
  (b) wages freeze;
  (c) wage restraint;
  (d) index-linking;
  (e) flat-rate pay rise;
  (f) productivity pay rise.

2 What is the purpose of an incomes policy?

3 Look at the graph. What was happening to inflation before each of the three incomes policies of the 1960s and 1970s was imposed? Why do you think governments adopted prices and incomes policies?

4 Did any of the three incomes policies succeed in reducing inflation?

Prices and Incomes Policy

Units 69 and 70 considered two major policies at a government's disposal – fiscal policy and monetary policy. Units 84 and 85 consider trade and exchange rate policy. In this unit, we look at two other important policy weapons available to government, namely incomes policy and competition policy.

A PRICES AND INCOMES POLICY is a measure designed to control inflation. As we saw in Unit 64, many economists believe that inflation is caused by increases in costs – the cost–push view of inflation. One way to keep costs and therefore prices down is to limit the amount by which prices and wages can increase in the economy. In 1966 and 1972, for instance, the governments of the day introduced price and incomes policies that 'froze' prices and incomes in the UK economy – i.e. they were not allowed to increase. By fixing the level of prices and wage increases in the economy, a government should be able to control inflation. There have been three periods of major prices and incomes policy in the UK: 1966–70, 1972–4 and 1975–9, as illustrated in Figure 71.1. They had three major points in common:

- they were all imposed as a crisis measure, because inflation was climbing rapidly;
- they were all successful to start with in bringing down inflation;
- they all collapsed and were followed by a period of very high inflation.

The prices and incomes policies collapsed mainly because of hostility from workers and firms. Workers did not like incomes polices, because they felt that their wages could be higher without the policy. Firms did not like controls on the prices they wanted to charge. Nor were they very keen on the income restraint. Although wage costs were kept under control, firms often found it difficult to recruit workers in shortage areas. Normally, they would have reacted to a shortage of a particular type of worker by offering higher wages. A lack of key workers could seriously hamper production.

Competition Policy

Traditionally, COMPETITION POLICY has attempted to control the powers of monopoly firms to prevent them exploiting the consumer, as discussed in Unit 37. Since 1979, however, competition policy has come to have a much wider meaning and a much more important role. Monetarists tend to believe that free markets work more efficiently than controlled markets. Many markets in the UK are not 'free' in this sense.

- Labour markets are often not free, because workers join together in trade unions to protect their interests. This, monetarists argue, pushes up wages in the industry and therefore reduces employment. So a government that wishes to bring down unemployment must reduce trade union power and increase free-market forces in the labour market.
- Product markets are often not free, because the state has a monopoly on production. What needs to be done here is to privatise state-owned industries or to introduce competition to the market – e.g. by replacing local authority refuse services by refuse services run by private firms who have tendered for the contract.
- Service-sector markets are often not free, because of restrictive trade practices. These are agreements between workers or firms in an industry to limit competition. An example of this was the Stock Exchange rules, which meant that only a small number of firms could trade directly in shares. The ending of restrictive trade practices should drive down prices for consumers and increase employment in the industry.

So competition policies, it is argued, can reduce prices to consumers (i.e. they can lower inflation) and, because consumers will now buy more products at the cheaper price, they will reduce unemployment. What is more, quite apart from the advantages of lower inflation and lower unemployment, consumers are offered more *choice* of products, as a result of increased competition. This, however, is a view held by only some economists. Others believe that the effects of competition policy are likely to be so small that there will be no noticeable effect on prices or employment. Indeed, as will be seen in Unit 85, one group of economists believes that less competition could well be the answer to Britain's employment problems.

CHECKPOINTS

1 What is meant by 'freezing' prices?
2 Explain how an incomes policy could control cost–push inflation.
3 Why do workers resist an incomes policy?
4 Explain how competition policy can, in theory, help reduce prices and increase employment.

COURSEWORK SUGGESTION

Research the incomes policy of 1975–9. Describe and analyse why the incomes policy was felt to be necessary, the form that it took, its effect on inflation, and the reasons for its breakdown. Try to assess the extent to which the incomes policy was successful in its objectives.

KEY TERMS

PRICES AND INCOMES POLICY – a policy that controls the increase in prices and wages in the economy.

COMPETITION POLICY – a policy designed to increase the power of free-market forces in the economy.

The Management of the Economy

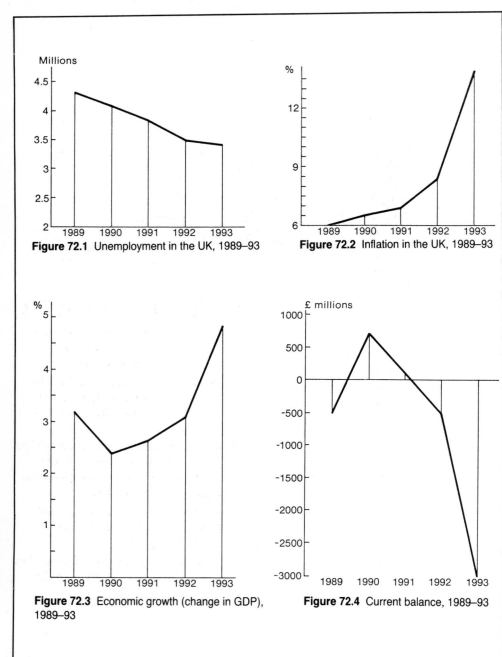

Figure 72.1 Unemployment in the UK, 1989–93

Figure 72.2 Inflation in the UK, 1989–93

Figure 72.3 Economic growth (change in GDP), 1989–93

Figure 72.4 Current balance, 1989–93

S T U D Y   P O I N T S

Figures 72.1, 72.2, 72.3 and 72.4 give statistics for the British economy over the period 1989 to 1993. You are the Chancellor of the Exchequer preparing your budget in March 1994. Your task is to decide what policy measures to take. Currently there is no prices and incomes policy in force. Prepare your budget statement.
(a) Comment upon the trends shown in

(i) unemployment (ii) inflation (iii) growth and (iv) the current balance.
(b) State which of these trends represent problems for the UK economy.
(c) What economic policy measures could the Government take to help solve these problems?
(d) What effect would these measures have on the other two variables shown in the data?

'**Bold blueprint to cut the dole queues**' according to the headline in the *Daily Express*. Those same policies were called 'the economics of the madhouse' by an MP. As these two quotes illustrate, there are very deep differences of opinion between economists (and politicians) about how to run the economy. In this unit, we will consider two approaches, the monetarist one and the Keynesian one.

The Monetarist View

Since 1979, the UK has been governed by a prime minister, Mrs Thatcher, whose views can be described as monetarist. The four main economic policy objectives of government are low inflation, low unemployment, high growth and a current account balance or surplus. Monetarists argue that:

- *Inflation* is caused by excessive growth in the money supply. Monetary policy must therefore act to restrict the growth of the money supply. Fiscal policy must work to produce a low PSBR so that the government does not have to print the money it needs to cover its spending.

- *Unemployment* is caused by a lack of competitiveness in the economy as a whole, and by failures in the market for labour in particular. Monetarists argue, therefore, that tax rates should be reduced in order to increase incentives to work. Workers should accept lower wage rates to prevent themselves from being 'priced out of jobs'. Generous welfare payments to the unemployed should be cut to encourage people to take jobs. Trade unions should lose their power to fix wages which are too high.

- *Growth* will be increased, if the UK becomes more competitive. Cutting tax rates, privatisation, reducing union power, cutting welfare benefits, helping small businesses – all these measures will help growth.

- The *current account* will look after itself as long as the government does not attempt to fix an artificial rate of the pound.

Monetarists argue that a government does not have the power to spend its way out of a recession. Extra public spending will reduce private spending, so there will be no extra demand in the economy. But the government can attempt to influence the SUPPLY SIDE of the economy. Encouraging new firms to set up, existing firms to expand, unemployed workers to take on work, firms to invest, etc. will increase the supply of goods and services to the economy.

Keynesian Views

Keynesians argue that there is no point in encouraging extra supply in the economy, if the goods that are produced cannot be sold. What is more, governments can change the level of *demand* in the economy through the size of the budget deficit, the PSBR. In more detail, Keynesians argue that:

- *Inflation*, if caused by cost–push factors, can be controlled by prices and incomes policies. If inflation is demand–pull in nature, then the government will have to accept higher unemployment if it wishes to lower inflation by reducing public spending and/or increasing taxes.

- *Unemployment* is caused mainly by a lack of demand in the economy. Governments need to increase demand by increasing the budget deficit, the PSBR. However, many Kenyesians believe that much of the unemployment in Britain today is structural. Here they would agree with monetarists that supply-side measures such as extra investment are essential.

- *Growth* can be stimulated by keeping a high level of demand in the economy. This will encourage firms to invest, because firms know they will be able to sell their products.

- The *current account* can be kept in balance either through the use of import controls or by devaluing the pound. Keynesians disagree amongst themselves as to how effective each policy could be, or whether the policies would be effective at all. This debate will be considered in Units 84 and 85.

Overall, monetarists believe that the government's role is to control the money supply and to help free-market forces work. The government has only a limited role and cannot directly control either unemployment or the growth rate. Keynesians argue that the government can have a powerful effect on the economy and believe that free-market forces can reduce the economy to ruins, if left to themselves. According to them, governments have to correct free-market forces to ensure that the economy is running at full employment.

CHECKPOINTS

1 Explain why monetarists believe that monetary policy is very important for a government.

2 What policies would monetarists use to reduce unemployment? How does this compare with a Keynesian approach?

3 What do monetarists believe will be the effect on the economy, if the government increases its spending without increasing taxes?

4 What are 'supply-side' policies? How might these policies help reduce unemployment?

5 How would Keynesians suggest that inflation can be controlled in the economy?

COURSEWORK SUGGESTION

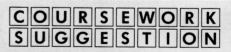

Examine the economic policy of a particular government in recent history (e.g. the Thatcher administration from 1979). Describe its policies, and the problems that it faced. Analyse and assess the extent to which the policy of that government succeeded in its objectives.

KEY TERM

SUPPLY-SIDE ECONOMICS – the study of the total supply of goods, services and factors of production to the economy.

Regional Policy

THE METROPOLITAN DISTRICT OF DONCASTER

Population: *290 000*

Main town: *Doncaster*

Geography: *In the south and east, mainly rural with isolated villages. In the west are many of the mining villages. In the north, the district reaches the farming and mining area of West Yorkshire.*

Communications: *Within 2 hours by rail of London, Birmingham and Manchester. Excellent motorway link-up to Humberside ports and, via the A1 and M1, to the South. The South Yorkshire Canal, running through the district, can handle sizeable barges and cargo vessels.*

LOCAL INDUSTRY

This is dominated by a few large manufacturing companies. These include British Rail Engineering (production and repair of trains and track), International Harvesters (tractors), Bridon (wire, wire rope and fibre rope), Pegler-Hattersley (valves, taps and compression fittings), ICI Fibres (nylon yarns) and Rockware (glass containers). The largest employer is British Coal. There are a very few firms employing between 300–800 workers. Remaining employment is found in a reasonably well-developed patchwork of small companies.

UNEMPLOYMENT

The unemployment rate stands at 19%, rising to nearly 25% in some parts of the district. In an 18 month period between 1980 and 1981, Doncaster lost 8000 manufacturing jobs. Over the past ten years, plant closures have included General Electric Company, British Mohair Spinners, Fairbrother Textile Company, Burton's, two sweet manufacturers — Nuttall's and Parkinson's — and lawnmower manufacturers Ransome, Simms and Jefferies. Job losses over the next twelve months include 3500 at British Coal and 350 at British Rail Engineering.

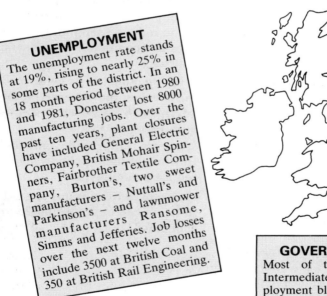

DONCASTER

GOVERNMENT HELP

Most of the district is an Intermediate Area. The unemployment black spots have Development Area status.

STUDY POINTS

You have been appointed by the District Council to evaluate Doncaster's economic problems and to put forward proposals which will deal with them. In your report, you must:

1 State the economic problems that Doncaster faces.

2 Evaluate what help is already given to help combat these problems.

3 Suggest what the local council could do to alleviate the situation.

4 Point out the opportunity costs of your proposals.

'In the 12 years since the UK's Industry Act was introduced in 1972, the Government has paid out £5.5 bn in regional assistance.' (*Source: Financial Times, 25 January 1985*)

In Unit 67, it was shown that there are very large economic differences between the various regions of the UK. The South of England is relatively more affluent than the rest of the UK. In Unit 49, it was argued that a major cause of this was the growth of industry in the South at the expense of the rest of the UK. Governments since the 1930s have attempted to narrow this gap between the regions through **REGIONAL POLICY**. As the above quote states, £5.5 bn was spent in the 1970s and early 1980s alone. What can governments do about this problem and how effective have actual policies been?

Demand-side Policies

One way of tackling high unemployment and low incomes in a region would be to increase demand for goods and services in that region. More spending would result in more jobs and higher wages, as more labour is demanded. This policy, however, has not been attempted in the UK, simply because an increase in spending in a region is likely to benefit other regions far more, as consumers buy goods produced elsewhere in Britain or abroad. So traditional Keynesian policies of increasing demand in the economy are unlikely to help the problem regions.

Supply-side Policies

What governments, both Keynesian and monetarist, have attempted to do instead, is to implement supply-side policies. This means creating new work places (jobs) through additional investment. Firms need to be attracted to the problem regions to invest there, rather than not investing at all or investing in the more prosperous regions of the UK. This will increase the supply of goods and services produced in the problem regions, helping to reduce unemployment and raise incomes.

Since the 1930s, governments have offered a variety of incentives to businesses. In 1986, these included:

- Grants of 15% on new buildings, machinery and equipment, with a minimum of £3000 per work place (i.e. job) created to a maximum of £10 000 per work place. For instance, if a businessman invested £5 million and created 120 jobs, then the firm would get 15% of £5 million (i.e. £750 000 of that) back from the government in grants. The maximum grant the firm would get for creating 120 jobs would be 120 × £10 000 (i.e. £1 200 000), and the minimum grant would be 120 × £3000 (i.e. £360 000). The grants can only be obtained if a company invests in the worst unemployment areas in Britain, which the government has called DEVELOPMENT AREAS. These Development Areas are shown on Figure 73.1.

- Additional grants of money, if the government feels that these are needed to create jobs. They are available in both Development Areas and Intermediate Areas. INTERMEDIATE AREAS are areas where unemployment is high, but not as high as in Development Areas.

- Cheap rents on government-built factories in Development and Intermediate areas.

- Training grants for workers, again in both Development and Intermediate Areas.

Success Or Failure?

Far less is spent today in real terms by the government on regional policy

Figure 73.1 UK Development Areas

than in the 1960s. Governments have cut back on public spending and regional policy has suffered. What is more, governments are less hopeful of curing unemployment today in, say, Glasgow, when the whole of the economy is suffering high unemployment, than 20 years ago when the economy was mostly at full employment.

It was stated at the start that £5.5 bn was spent on regional policy between 1972 and 1984, over a period when unemployment increased nearly sixfold in the economy. Was regional policy useless? The answer is probably no. If there had been no regional policy, unemployment in areas such as Wales and Scotland would probably have been even higher. Government grants do help create jobs. But those

grants have an opportunity cost. The government has to decide whether creating jobs in Glasgow is more important than building hospitals in Kent or spending more on defence.

1 Why is regional policy necessary in the UK?

2 How would a cut in taxes for all people living in Liverpool:
(a) affect jobs for those in Liverpool;
(b) affect the rest of the UK?

3 Explain what incentives are offered to businesses to create jobs in the problem regions of the UK.

4 Calculate the amount of grant that a company setting up in a Development Area would automatically be entitled to receive in the following cases:

Value of investment in new factories and equipment (£)	Number of jobs created	Grant (£)
100 000	4	
5 000 000	20	
200 000	10	

5 Why does regional policy have an opportunity cost?

COURSEWORK SUGGESTION

Arrange to interview several firms that have recently established themselves in a Development Area of the UK. Prepare a detailed questionnaire which assesses why the firms set up in those areas and the influence that regional incentives had upon their decisions. Write a report describing your findings. Compare and contrast the reasons for the firms' decisions. Try to evaluate the extent to which the complete abolition of regional incentives would lead to less investment in Development Areas.

KEY TERMS

REGIONAL POLICY – government policy that attempts to readjust regional economic imbalances.

DEVELOPMENT AREAS – areas of the UK designated by the government as eligible for regional assistance because of their high unemployment.

INTERMEDIATE AREAS – areas of less high unemployment, but still eligible for some regional assistance.

The Redistribution of Income

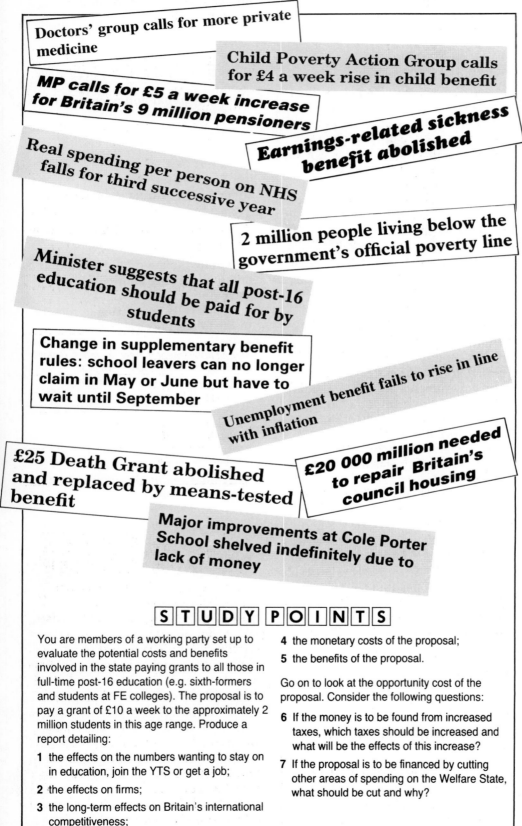

Doctors' group calls for more private medicine

Child Poverty Action Group calls for £4 a week rise in child benefit

MP calls for £5 a week increase for Britain's 9 million pensioners

Earnings-related sickness benefit abolished

Real spending per person on NHS falls for third successive year

2 million people living below the government's official poverty line

Minister suggests that all post-16 education should be paid for by students

Change in supplementary benefit rules: school leavers can no longer claim in May or June but have to wait until September

Unemployment benefit fails to rise in line with inflation

£25 Death Grant abolished and replaced by means-tested benefit

£20 000 million needed to repair Britain's council housing

Major improvements at Cole Porter School shelved indefinitely due to lack of money

S T U D Y   P O I N T S

You are members of a working party set up to evaluate the potential costs and benefits involved in the state paying grants to all those in full-time post-16 education (e.g. sixth-formers and students at FE colleges). The proposal is to pay a grant of £10 a week to the approximately 2 million students in this age range. Produce a report detailing:

1 the effects on the numbers wanting to stay on in education, join the YTS or get a job;

2 the effects on firms;

3 the long-term effects on Britain's international competitiveness;

4 the monetary costs of the proposal;

5 the benefits of the proposal.

Go on to look at the opportunity cost of the proposal. Consider the following questions:

6 If the money is to be found from increased taxes, which taxes should be increased and what will be the effects of this increase?

7 If the proposal is to be financed by cutting other areas of spending on the Welfare State, what should be cut and why?

The Welfare State

It was shown in Unit 17 that large differences in income and wealth exist between individuals in the UK. If the government did not intervene, some individuals would die of malnutrition or poor health, simply because they did not have the income to buy essential goods and services. The young, the old, the sick, the handicapped and the unemployed would be most vulnerable.

To prevent this from happening, all Western European democracies have established some form of welfare provision. In the UK, this has come to be called the WELFARE STATE. The welfare state was established after the Second World War and it was based upon the recommendations of the Beveridge Report, which was published in 1942. Lord Beveridge argued that five main problems faced the country:

- *want*, which could be overcome by the existing national insurance scheme and by a social security system;
- *disease*, which could be overcome by the setting up of a free National Health Service;
- *ignorance*, which could be attacked by more and better schooling;
- *squalor*, which could be avoided by more and better housing;
- *idleness* (i.e. unemployment), which could be tackled by greater government control of industry.

Forty years after the setting up of the welfare state, we know that poverty, disease, squalor and unemployment are still with us. But it is almost certainly true that, without the welfare state, differences between the rich and the poor would be much greater, and the poor would be much poorer.

The welfare state was created by the Labour government of 1945–51. This photograph shows Aneurin Bevan, Minister for Health, marking the site of one of the first National Health Clinics in the UK.

Public Spending and Taxation

Income and wealth are redistributed by the government through its spending and through taxes. Spending on welfare programmes tends to benefit the poor more than the rich. Spending on social security benefits is for the most part used to raise the income levels of the poorer sections of society. Supplementary benefit, for instance, can only be claimed by people on low incomes. Spending on health, education and housing helps the poor, because they are supplied with services that they would not otherwise be able to afford.

This spending is paid for through taxes. The government redistributes income by making higher-income earners pay more in tax than they receive from government spending and

by using that surplus to pay for benefits to poorer people in society. Some taxes are PROGRESSIVE – the higher the income, the higher the proportion or percentage that is paid in tax. Income tax is progressive. A worker earning £6000 a year might pay 10% of total income in income tax. A worker earning £30 000 might pay 30%. (Note, however, that a tax where the higher the income the more that is paid in tax is not necessarily a progressive tax. A worker earning £6000 a year might pay £600 in tax. A worker earning £30 000 might pay £601. This is *not* a progressive tax, because the percentage paid in tax has declined dramatically as income increases.) UK taxes that are generally considered to be progressive are income tax, capital gains tax and capital transfer tax.

Not all taxes are progressive. Some are PROPORTIONAL, where the percentage paid in tax stays the same as income changes. Others are REGRESSIVE – the percentage paid in tax actually falls as income rises. Examples of taxes that are generally considered to be proportional or regressive are excise duties, VAT and local authority rates.

By spending on programmes to help the poor and paying for them by raising taxes on the better off, the government is able to ensure a more equal distribution of income and wealth. 'More equal' does not of course mean that it is more desirable or fairer. Some people argue that the present system is unfair because it takes from individuals who have earned money to give to others who have done nothing to deserve these benefits. Others argue that the system does not go far enough in helping the disadvantaged in society and that present inequalities

are unacceptable. This, of course, is a debate about how scarce resources are allocated in an economy. Society has to choose between different degrees of inequality, and such choices are always difficult to make.

CHECKPOINTS

1 What was the Beveridge Report and what did it recommend?
2 What are the main parts of the welfare state in the UK today?
3 How does government spending help the poor in the UK today?
4 What is the difference between a progressive and a regressive tax?
5 State whether each of the following is a progressive, proportional or regressive tax:

Income (£)	Tax paid (£)	Percentage of income paid in tax (£)	Type of tax
(a) 5 000	1000		
10 000	3000		
(b) 6 000	600		
10 000	700		
(c) 800	20		
8 000	200		
(d) 4 000	1000		
15 000	3000		

COURSEWORK SUGGESTION

Compare the position of your own household with that of other households with regard to the welfare state. From Chapter 5 of *Social Trends* (published by HMSO), find statistics relating to the redistribution of income through taxes and benefits (Table 5.19 in the 1985 edition). Use the breakdown of income, benefits and taxes to estimate the income, benefits and taxes of your own household. Compare your household with other typical households described in the statistics. Try to assess the extent to which the different households benefit or lose from the welfare state.

KEY TERMS

The WELFARE STATE – the system that ensures that every member of the population receives adequate food, shelter, health care and education.

PROGRESSIVE TAX – a tax where the higher the income of the taxpayer, the larger the percentage of total income paid in tax.

PROPORTIONAL TAX – a tax where the percentage of total income paid in tax remains the same at different income levels.

REGRESSIVE TAX – a tax where higher-income earners pay a lower proportion of their income in tax compared to lower-income earners.

Data Response Questions
Units 71–74

Unit 71 Incomes Policy and Competition Policy

Professions must compete too

A key question for the 1980s is how much of economic activity should be subject to the discipline of market forces. Before talking of getting rid of the Welfare State, free marketeers should consider competition amongst the professions.

Take, for instance, accountants. In order to enter the profession, the would-be accountant has to pass an examination set by the Institute of Chartered Accountants, the body which represents accountants. But these examinations have become much tougher over the past ten years. It isn't clear that the work that accountants do has become any harder. But the high failure rate of candidates does mean that the supply of new accountants is restricted and that must be good for accountants' earnings.

Adapted from the Financial Times, 11 March 1985

Newly-qualified accountants 'in short supply'

BRITAIN is experiencing a serious shortage of young and partly-qualified accountants, according to a survey on the profession published today.

The shortage has boosted salaries for newly-qualified accountants aged 23 to 26 by almost 15 per cent in the London area, says the spring survey on salaries published by Accountancy Personnel, the recruitment agency.

Source: Financial Times, 22 April 1985

1 What is meant by 'market forces'? (2 marks)
2 Explain how competition in accounting is restricted. (2 marks)
3 What are the effects of these restrictions? (3 marks)
4 What are the costs of these restrictions to (a) consumers (b) workers? (4 marks)
5 Why might an abolition of restrictions lead to (a) lower unemployment and (b) lower prices? (4 marks)

Unit 72 The Management of the Economy

Directors urge £2.5bn tax cuts

MR NIGEL LAWSON, Chancellor of the Exchequer, was urged by directors yesterday to concentrate his Budget on tax cuts, with renewed efforts to curb public spending.

The Institute of Directors, in its Budget submission, also suggested that Mr Lawson should raise his borrowing target for 1985-86 from the £7bn assumed in his autumn statement, to £8bn.

By increasing this target, the institute believes the Chancellor would have room for £2.6bn in tax cuts – on conservative estimates – rather than the £1.5bn he suggested in November.

It also argues that cutting taxes would be one of the quickest ways of reducing unemployment.

Source: Financial Times, 16 January 1985

1 Describe the Budget suggestions made by the Institute of Directors. (4 marks)
2 Explain in detail the arguments that:
   (a) 'cutting taxes would be one of the quickest ways of reducing unemployment';
   (b) the government can't 'spend its way out of trouble'. (6 marks)

Unit 73 Regional Policy

Cumbria evaluates status changes

THE GOVERNMENT has announced that Cumbria is to lose its Development Area status. What this means is that industry setting up or expanding in Cumbria will no longer be entitled to receive government grants and other forms of assistance.

The County Council says that Cumbria received £22.5 million of regional assistance last year. However, much of that went to one company, British Nuclear Fuels at Sel-

lafield, and created very few jobs.

The County believes that government grants have not attracted much new industry to the area. But it has been a crucial feature in persuading existing companies to stay and expand. Two companies that have grown recently in this way include Ashley Accessories which makes electrical fittings and the chemicals and detergents company, Albright and Wilson.

Adapted from the *Financial Times*, 25 January 1985

1 What is meant by 'Development Area status'? (*2 marks*)

2 Why should having Development Area status help attract industry to an area? (*2 marks*)

3 What impact did Development Area status have on Cumbria? (*2 marks*)

4 How and to what extent may the loss of Development Area status hit Cumbria? (*3 marks*)

Unit 74 The Redistribution of Income

WELFARE STATE BIG CUTS

THE Government is planning a savage attack on the welfare state.

Benefits will be slashed and, in future, linked to the performance of the economy.

The cutbacks were promised yesterday by Chancellor Nigel Lawson.

He told cheering Tories that the days of "open ended commitment" to social

spending were over, and warned that there must be no "special pleading".

Mr Lawson said: "Can we afford a system which encourages idleness and irresponsibility and discourages initiative and enterprise?

Can we do justice to the really needy if we extend benefit to those well able to look after themselves?"

Source: *The Mirror*, 11 May 1985

1 What is the 'welfare state' and what is its purpose? (*4 marks*)

2 What does the Chancellor of the Exchequer propose to do, according to the article? (*2 marks*)

3 What are (a) the costs and (b) the benefits to society of relatively generous levels of welfare benefits? (*4 marks*)

Essay Questions
Units 71–74

1 'The UK is suffering from rising unemployment but falling inflation.'
(a) Describe *two* different measures which the Government could take to help reduce unemployment. (*4 marks*)
(b) Describe *two* different measures which the Government could take to help reduce inflation even further. (*4 marks*)
(c) To what extent would these measures also help increase the economic growth of the UK? (*6 marks*)
(d) How effective will these measures be in reducing unemployment and inflation? (*6 marks*)

2 'Britain is divided into two regions – the South rich and prosperous, the rest of the country poor and disadvantaged.'
(a) Describe *four* ways in which differences in living standards between regions could be measured. (*8 marks*)
(b) Give *two* reasons why the South is more prosperous than the rest of the UK. (*6 marks*)
(c) What policies could a government pursue to reduce regional inequalities? (*6 marks*)

The Theory of Comparative Advantage

In Japan, it costs 1000 yen to produce a bottle of whisky: in Britain it costs £2. In Japan it costs 8000 yen to produce a simple camera: in Britain, it costs £20. This can be summarised like this:

Cost of Production

JAPAN	1000yen	8000yen
U.K.	£2	£20

STUDY POINTS

1 What is the opportunity cost of producing 1 camera in Japan i.e. how many bottles of whisky could have been produced for the same cost as one camera?

2 What is the opportunity cost of producing 1 camera in the UK?

3 Which country can produce whisky more cheaply (relative to cameras)?

4 Which country can produce cameras more cheaply (relative to whisky)?

5 Each year, the Japanese buy 8 million bottles of whisky and 1 million cameras. How much in total would it cost the Japanese if all cameras and all whisky were produced in Japan?

6 Each year, the British buy 20 million bottles of whisky and 1 million cameras. How much in total would it cost the British if all cameras and all whisky were produced in the UK? Japan and the UK decide to trade whisky for cameras at an exchange rate of 1 camera for 9 bottles of whisky.

7 How many cameras can Japan make instead of the 8 million bottles of whisky she produces?

8 How many cameras will she now produce if she also carries on producing the 1 million cameras as before?

9 How many bottles of whisky can the UK now produce (including the 20 million bottles produced before) if she switches resources from the production of cameras to whisky?

10 Japan offers to trade 1 million cameras for whisky with the UK. How much whisky can she obtain in exchange?

1 How many cameras and how much whisky is now available for sale in Japan? Is Japan better or worse off than before trade took place?

2 How many cameras and how much whisky is now available for sale in the UK? Is the UK better or worse off than before trade took place?

'Italy sold 28 million pairs of leather shoes to Britain in 1983 at an average price per pair of £6. So it might come as a surprise to learn that Britain managed to sell 321 000 pairs to the Italians at an average price of £12 per pair, and it's quality which appears to be the characteristic which captures the Italians to buy British.' (*Source: The Guardian*, 4 June 1985)

Why should Italians buy British shoes when Italy is one of the world's leading producers of shoes? Why is Italy a more important producer of shoes than Britain anyway?

Specialisation

To answer these questions, we need to develop the theory of *specialisation*. Specialisation, discussed in Unit 7, means that producers specialise in producing products or performing tasks. One example of specialisation is the division of labour. If specialisation is to make economic sense, producers must specialise in what they are best at producing.

Figure 75.1 gives some sample figures for the production of shoes in the UK and in Italy. For the sake of argument, assume that Italy and the UK only produce shoes and that the only cost of production is labour. It can be seen from the table that Italy is better at producing ordinary shoes than the UK because it costs only 10 man-hours to produce a pair of ordinary shoes in Italy, but 20 man-hours in the UK. Italy is said to have an ABSOLUTE ADVANTAGE in the production of ordinary shoes. On the other hand, the UK has an absolute advantage in the production of quality shoes – i.e. the UK is better at producing quality shoes than Italy. So it would make sense for Italy to make ordinary shoes and exchange them for quality shoes made in the UK.

But what would happen if Italy

were better at producing both ordinary shoes and quality shoes than the UK? i.e. Italy has an absolute advantage in the production of both ordinary shoes and quality shoes. It still pays for each country to specialise. Which country will produce what depends upon which country is relatively better at producing each product. Look at Figure 75.2. Italy can produce both quality shoes and ordinary shoes at less man-hour cost than the UK. In Italy, it costs just 10 man-hours to produce a pair of ordinary shoes, whereas in the UK it costs 20 man-hours. Quality shoes cost 30 man-hours in Italy, but 40 in the UK. Italy therefore has an absolute advantage in both the production of ordinary shoes and quality shoes.

Figure 75.1

Cost of production (man hours)	Italy	UK
1 pair of ordinary shoes	10	20
1 pair of quality shoes	25	16

Figure 75.2

Cost of production (man-hours)	Italy	UK
1 pair of ordinary shoes	10	20
1 pair of quality shoes	30	40

Comparative Advantage

However, we can show that it will be to the advantage of both countries, if each specialises and then they trade. In Italy, it takes three times as long to produce a pair of quality shoes as it does a pair of ordinary shoes (30 man-hours compared to 10 man-hours). So the opportunity cost of producing a pair of quality shoes is

three times that of producing a pair of ordinary shoes. In the UK, a pair of quality shoes costs only twice as much as a pair of ordinary shoes (40 man-hours compared to 20 man-hours). So the UK is relatively better at producing quality shoes than Italy. The UK is said to have a COMPARATIVE ADVANTAGE in the production of quality shoes. Italy, on the other hand, can produce ordinary shoes relatively more cheaply than the UK. It costs Italy ⅓ a pair of quality shoes to produce one pair of ordinary shoes (10 man-hours compared to 30 man-hours), whereas it costs the UK ½ a pair of quality shoes to produce one pair of ordinary shoes (20 man-hours compared to 40 man-hours). So Italy has a comparative advantage in the production of ordinary shoes.

By concentrating on the production of ordinary shoes, in which it has a comparative advantage, a country like Italy can export these and import other products such as quality shoes, which would be relatively more expensive to produce in Italy. The UK should concentrate on producing and exporting what it is relatively best at doing – in our example, that was the manufacture of quality shoes. The theory of comparative advantage helps us to understand why one of the world leaders in the manufacture of shoes should be importing shoes from the UK.

CHECKPOINTS

1 What is meant by 'specialisation'? Name *four* examples of specialisation in the world economy.

2 (a) It costs the UK £3 to produce a record and £1 to produce a blank cassette. What is the cost

of a record in terms of cassettes?

(b) Japan can produce either 100 000 records or 200 000 cassettes for the same cost. What is the cost of a record in terms of cassettes?

(c) Which country has the comparative advantage (i.e. has the lowest relative cost) of producing (a) records; and (b) cassettes?

(d) If the UK and Japan were to trade cassettes for records, what would the UK export and what would it import?

3 The USA and France face costs shown in Figure 75.3

(a) What is the cost of 1 unit of chemicals in terms of barley (i) in the USA; (ii) in France?

(b) Which country has a comparative advantage (i) in chemicals; (ii) in barley?

(c) If the USA and France were to trade chemicals for barley, what would the USA export and import?

Figure 75.3

Costs of production (man-hours)	USA	France
1 unit of barley	2	5
1 unit of chemicals	1	2

COURSEWORK SUGGESTION

Take a traditional UK manufacturing industry which has declined since 1945, such as steel, the motor-cycle industry, textiles or shipbuilding. Describe the decline and analyse the effects it has had on the UK economy. Which countries in the world are now producing these goods? Why has the comparative advantage in the production of these goods shifted to other countries? Consider the extent to which the UK could ever regain its comparative advantage in this industry.

KEY TERMS

ABSOLUTE ADVANTAGE – where one producer is better at producing a product than another producer.

COMPARATIVE ADVANTAGE – where one producer can produce a good at a relatively cheaper cost in terms of other goods than another producer.

Exports and Imports

STUDY POINTS

Consider Figure 76.1.

1 What has happened to exports as a share of total spending in the UK economy since 1948?

2 Why are exports now more important for British industry and British workers than in 1948?

Consider Figure 76.2.

3 Explain how the UK's visible trade changed over the period 1973 to 1984.

4 Calculate the difference in value of (a) imports and (b) exports of mineral fuels and lubricants in 1973 and 1984. Why has there been this large change?

5 Why is the shrinking share of manufactured goods in total UK exports of importance to the British economy?

Consider Figure 76.3.

6 Which are now the most important and the least important areas of the world with which Britain trades? How has this changed since 1973?

7 Suggest reasons why this change in the direction of visible trade might have taken place.

Figure 76.1 Share of exports in total UK spending (exports of goods and services at market prices, final expenditure on goods and services at 1980 market prices)

£ thousand millions at constant (1980) prices

Export of goods and services at market prices

Total expenditure at market prices.

Percentage share of exports in total expenditure

12.8% (1948) 14.8% (1958) 16.0% (1968) 21.6% (1978) 22.0% (1984)

Figure 76.3 Visible trade by area

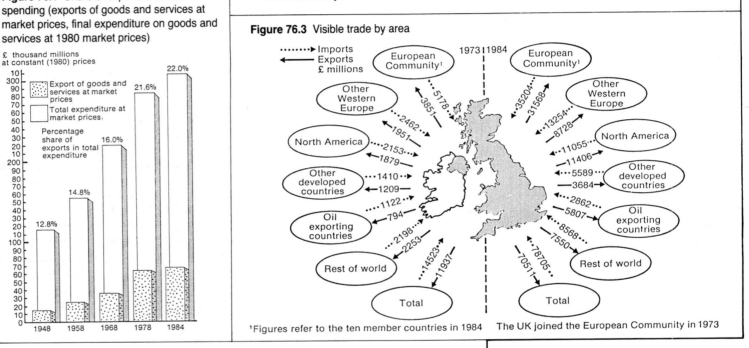

······► Imports
◄—— Exports
£ millions

1973 | 1984

European Community[1]

Other Western Europe

North America

Other developed countries

Oil exporting countries

Rest of world

Total

[1]Figures refer to the ten member countries in 1984

The UK joined the European Community in 1973

Figure 76.2 Visible trade by commodity (figures in brackets are % of total)

£millions

	Exports		Imports	
	1973	1984	1973	1984
Food, beverages and tobacco	849 (7)	4693 (7)	2832 (20)	8936 (11)
Basic materials	420 (4)	1989 (3)	1692 (12)	5420 (7)
Mineral fuels and lubricants	374 (3)	15367 (22)	1320 (9)	10193 (13)
Semi-manufactured goods	4013 (34)	16332 (23)	3731 (26)	17923 (23)
Finished manufactured goods	5910 (50)	25804 (37)	4704 (32)	31780 (40)
Other	371 (3)	6326 (9)	244 (2)	4453 (6)
Total	11937	70511	14523	78705

Sources: CSO, *Monthly Digest of Statistics*, No. 471 and CSO, *United Kingdom Balance of Payments*, 1984.

Britain has a long history as a trading nation. When Britain was the most advanced industrial country in the world in the nineteenth century, it **IMPORTED** (i.e. brought into the country) raw materials from all over the world. It **EXPORTED** (i.e. sold abroad) goods manufactured from these raw materials. Since the Second World War, Britain has become even more dependent on foreign trade. As Figure 76.1 shows, the share of exports in total expenditure in the UK has risen from 12.8% in 1948 to 22.0% in 1984. If exports and imports were to cease suddenly, the British economy would collapse overnight – which shows just how *interdependent* Britain is with the rest of the world.

Visible Trade

Approximately two-third of Britain's exports and imports consist of trade in goods – or VISIBLES, as they are called in foreign trade jargon. Figure 76.2 shows UK exports and imports by commodity, and how this has changed over the period 1973–84. As mentioned, the UK has traditionally imported raw materials – basic materials such as iron and mineral fuels and lubricants such as oil – and semi-manufactured goods such as steel bars, and then turned these into manufactured goods, some of which have then been exported. This traditional pattern, which to some extent still held true in 1973, has fundamentally changed. Two very important changes can be seen in the statistics:

- Britain has become a major exporter of oil. From virtually nothing in 1973, oil came to account for over one-fifth of total visible exports by 1984.

- Britain's trade in manufactured goods has suffered a major reversal. Traditionally, the UK has exported far more manufactured goods than it has imported – as was the case in 1973. By 1984, the situation had been reversed. Britain now imports far more manufactured goods than it exports. Deindustrialisation cost more than 2½ million lost jobs between 1973 and 1984.

Figure 76.3 shows Britain's main trading partners and the changes that have occurred since the UK joined the European Economic Community (the EEC) in 1973. The statistics show that trade with the EEC has grown rapidly, so that today nearly 50% of all visible trade is conducted with Britain's Common Market partners. Equally, trade with the 'rest of the world' has declined in relative importance. No longer is British trade dominated by the pattern of buying raw materials from developing countries and selling them back manufactured goods.

Invisibles

Approximately one-third of the total value of the UK's trade is made up of INVISIBLES – trade in services. These include services such as:

- banking and insurance;
- tourism;
- interests, profits and dividends on money lent and borrowed from abroad;
- defence – maintaining British forces overseas, while US forces are stationed in Britain.

Britain's export of services has shown strong growth since the Second World War.

The significance of these trends in trade is further discussed in Unit 79.

Money Flows

When the UK exports, goods and services flow *out* of the country. Foreigners, in return, pay for those goods and services, so money flows *into* the country. When the UK imports, goods and services flow *into* the country, but money flows *out* to pay for them. So if the UK buys wine from France, an import for the UK, money goes out of the UK. Similarly, if a Briton takes a holiday in France, money leaves the UK and so this, too, is classified as an import. On the other hand, a French firm buying British shirts would be an export, because money would flow into the UK. Equally, a German firm buying insurance from a UK company would be an export for the UK, as money would flow into the UK to pay for the premium.

CHECKPOINTS

1 Distinguish between:
   (a) an import and an export;
   (b) a visible and an invisible.

2 State whether the following are (i) an export or an import for the UK; and (ii) visible trade or invisible trade:
   (a) a British car sold to the USA;
   (b) French cheese sold in Britain;
   (c) a British tourist holidaying in Spain;
   (d) British Airways buying a plane from Boeing (USA);
   (e) the American Air Force maintaining an air base in East Anglia;
   (f) the British government maintaining an embassy in Iran;
   (g) the British government buying American nuclear missiles;
   (h) an Italian oil company sending its profits from its North Sea oilfield from the UK to Italy.

3 How has the size and composition of UK trade changed over the past twenty years? Outline two factors that have caused these changes.

COURSEWORK SUGGESTION

Take one particular category of exports and imports (e.g. chemicals or textiles). Describe how exports and imports of this product have changed over time, geographically, in volume and by value. Analyse why these changes have occurred. Consider the effects on the UK economy. Sources of statistics include *Abstract of British Historical Statistics* (by B. R. Mitchell and P. Deane, published by Cambridge University Press, 1962); and *Annual Abstract of Statistics, United Kingdom Balance of Payments* and *Overseas Trade Statistics of the United Kingdom* (all published by HMSO).

KEY TERMS

EXPORTS – products sold to foreigners. Products leave the country in return for money coming in.

IMPORTS – products bought from foreigners. Products enter the country in return for an outflow of money.

VISIBLE TRADE – trade in goods.

INVISIBLE TRADE — trade in services.

The Balance of Payments

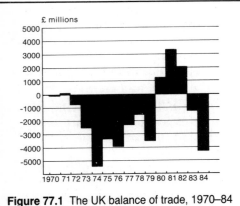

Figure 77.1 The UK balance of trade, 1970–84

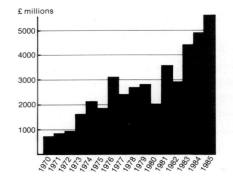

Figure 77.2 UK invisible balance, 1970–84

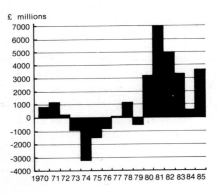

Figure 77.3 The current balance, 1970–84

Figure 77.4 Investment and other capital transactions, 1970–84

Source: (for all figures) CSO, Economic Trends

STUDY POINTS

1 The balance of trade is the difference between the value of the exports of *goods* and the imports of *goods*. Describe how the balance of trade changed over the period 1970–84.

2 Invisible trade is trade in *services*. The balance on invisible trade is invisible exports minus invisible imports i.e. exports of services minus the import of services. Why has invisible trade been very important to the British economy since 1970?

3 The current balance is the difference between total exports (both of goods and services) and total imports. Describe how the current account has changed since 1970.

4 Suggest reasons why it might be undesirable for the current account to be negative (i.e. for imports to be greater than exports).

5 How do you think North Sea oil affects the current account (i.e. how does it affect exports and imports)?

6 The investment and other capital transactions account records the international borrowing, saving and investing by the UK abroad and by foreigners in Britain. If a British company, for instance, lends money abroad, then money will flow out of the country and this is shown by a minus figure on the account. If a foreign company were to buy shares in Britain, then money would come into the country and this would be shown by a plus sign on the account. The balance on the investment and other capital transactions account is the difference between money coming into the country to be saved and invested and money leaving the country to be saved and invested. What does it mean if the account shows a minus sign?

7 In which years was the investment and other capital transactions accounts (a) positive and (b) negative? Which is the better position to be in? Explain your answer.

8 Why do you think a country cannot go on borrowing money for ever?

The Balance of Payments Account

Unit 76 considered the UK's pattern of trade and distinguished between exports and imports, and visibles and invisibles. This unit will consider other transactions made abroad, and how all these are brought together in the balance of payments account.

The BALANCE OF PAYMENTS ACCOUNT shows all the UK's financial transactions with foreigners. There are two main parts to the account. The CURRENT ACCOUNT shows the income and expenditure of the UK over a period of time. Its income is the money received from exports of visibles (goods) and invisibles (services). Its expenditure is the money paid to foreigners for imports to the UK. The CAPITAL ACCOUNT shows the investments, savings and borrowings of the UK, over a period of time.

The balance of payments must always balance – i.e. the money leaving the country must exactly equal the money coming in. This is no different from your own accounts. The money you spend and save must be exactly the same as the money you receive and borrow. Over any particular period of time, the different parts of the account need not balance. The UK can export more than it imports and use the surplus created to invest abroad, just as you can save money by not spending all the money you earn. Or the UK can import more than it exports and pay for this by borrowing from abroad or running down savings.

The Current Balance

Since 1945, exports and imports have tended to grow in value each year, even after inflation has been taken into account. This shows that the UK is becoming more and more economically interdependent with the rest of the world.

Of particular interest, though, is the balance between exports and imports.

Figures 77.1–77.3 show three balances:

- the **BALANCE OF TRADE** which is the difference between visible exports and visible imports;
- the **INVISIBLE BALANCE** – invisible exports minus invisible imports;
- the **CURRENT BALANCE** – total exports minus total imports (or the balance of trade plus the invisible balance).

An example of how these three balances are calculated is shown in Figure 77.5.

It can be seen that the UK tends to run a balance of trade deficit – that is, the nation tends to import more goods than it exports. On the other hand, the invisible balance is always in surplus – that is, the UK exports more services than are imported. The current balance – the sum of the balance of trade and the invisible trade – swings from surplus to deficit. Oil has been a major factor in changes in the current balance in the 1970s and 1980s. The fourfold increase in the price of oil in 1974 helped push the current balance into massive deficits in 1974 and 1975. On the other hand, production of North Sea oil, which started slowly in 1976 and made the UK self-sufficient in oil by the early 1980s, allowed the current account to go into surplus from 1980 onwards.

The Capital Account

The capital account shows transactions made for the purpose of investment, saving and borrowing. For instance, a Japanese company buying pounds to set up a factory in the UK would be an inflow of money to the UK. So too would a British company borrowing dollars to finance expansion in Britain. On the other hand, a British bank buying shares in New York, or a British company buying a French company would represent an outflow of money from the UK. These would all be recorded on the **INVESTMENT AND OTHER CAPITAL TRANSACTIONS** section of the balance of payments. The balance on this part of the accounts is shown in Figure 77.4.

The government, too, buys and sells foreign currency. Its transactions are called the **TOTAL FOR OFFICIAL FINANCING**.

1 In which part of the balance of payments account would the following transactions be recorded:
   (a) a US company buying shares on the London Stock Exchange;
   (b) a British tourist holidaying in Spain;
   (c) a British company selling cars to France;
   (d) a French company buying a British firm;
   (e) the government buying up £100 million of sterling with its foreign currency reserves.
   Which of the above transactions are inflows of money to the UK (and therefore given a 'plus' sign on the balance of payments account) and which are outflows (and given a minus sign)?

2 The figures in Figure 77.6 refer to the UK balance of payments, 1984. Calculate (a) the balance of trade, (b) the invisible balance and (c) the current balance.
   Figure 77.6

	Exports	Imports
Visible	60 600	61 300
Invisible	35 000	31 300

3 Explain why a foreign loan taken out by a British firm would be given a *plus* sign on the *capital* account, whereas the interest payable on that loan would be given a *minus* sign on the *current* account.

Figure 77.5 An example of the current balance (£ million)

Visible exports	700	Invisible exports	300	Total exports	1000
Visible imports	800	Invisible imports	100	Total imports	900
Balance of trade	−100	Balance on invisible trade	200	Current balance	100

BALANCE OF PAYMENTS ACCOUNT – the record of all financial transactions with foreigners.

CURRENT ACCOUNT – the part of the balance of payments account where the value of exports and imports is recorded.

CAPITAL ACCOUNT – the part of the balance of payments account where the value of investment, saving and borrowing is recorded.

BALANCE OF TRADE – visible exports minus visible imports.

INVISIBLE BALANCE – invisible exports minus invisible imports.

CURRENT BALANCE – exports minus imports.

INVESTMENT AND OTHER CAPITAL TRANSACTIONS – the record of investment, saving and borrowing made by foreigners in the UK and by the UK abroad.

TOTAL FOR OFFICIAL FINANCING – government transactions (buying and selling foreign currency).

Describe how the balance of trade has changed over the past twenty years. Analyse why these changes have taken place. What effect, for instance, have changing exchange rates or North Sea oil had on the balance of trade? Consider the effects of these changes on the British economy. Sources of statistics include the *Annual Abstract of Statistics*, *United Kingdom Balance of Payments*, and *Overseas Trade Statistics* (all published by HMSO).

Exchange Rates

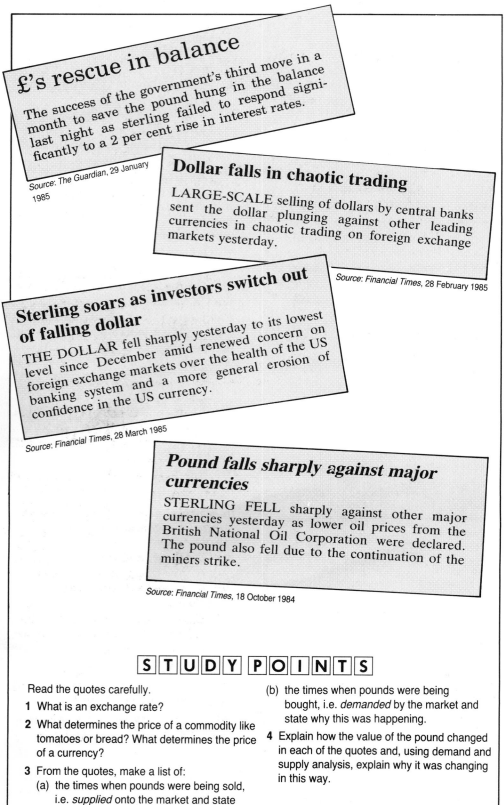

£'s rescue in balance

The success of the government's third move in a month to save the pound hung in the balance last night as sterling failed to respond significantly to a 2 per cent rise in interest rates.

Source: The Guardian, 29 January 1985

Dollar falls in chaotic trading

LARGE-SCALE selling of dollars by central banks sent the dollar plunging against other leading currencies in chaotic trading on foreign exchange markets yesterday.

Source: Financial Times, 28 February 1985

Sterling soars as investors switch out of falling dollar

THE DOLLAR fell sharply yesterday to its lowest level since December amid renewed concern on foreign exchange markets over the health of the US banking system and a more general erosion of confidence in the US currency.

Source: Financial Times, 28 March 1985

Pound falls sharply against major currencies

STERLING FELL sharply against other major currencies yesterday as lower oil prices from the British National Oil Corporation were declared. The pound also fell due to the continuation of the miners strike.

Source: Financial Times, 18 October 1984

- 'The pound staged a dramatic recovery in the world's currency markets yesterday.'
- 'Dollar up as pound falls to record low.'
- 'The trade-weighted index stood at 76.2, unchanged from yesterday.'

Headlines such as these occur frequently. They all refer to the value of the pound sterling. What is this value and how is it determined?

The Value of the Pound

The pound can be seen as a commodity, like tomatoes or LPs or bars of chocolate. Pounds are bought and sold all over the world. They are bought and sold in exchange for other types of money – French francs, Spanish pesetas, US dollars, German deutschmarks, etc. You may have sold pounds to a bank or a bureau de change to get foreign currency for a holiday. When anything is bought and sold, it is bought and sold at a price. This price represents the value of the pound, and is known as the FOREIGN EXCHANGE RATE. So the price of the pound is quoted as so many US dollars per pound, so many French francs per pound and so on.

Price

Like anything that is bought and sold, the price of the pound is fixed by the forces of demand and supply. Pounds are:

- *demanded* (i.e. bought) to pay for British exports, and to invest and save in the UK;
- *supplied* (i.e. sold) to pay for imports from abroad, and to invest and save outside the UK.

When demand for the pound goes up – more exports perhaps are sold, or foreign money comes into London attracted by high interest rates – then the price of the pound will go up too. When the supply of pounds increases – caused perhaps by increased imports or money leaving the country to be

S T U D Y   P O I N T S

Read the quotes carefully.

1 What is an exchange rate?

2 What determines the price of a commodity like tomatoes or bread? What determines the price of a currency?

3 From the quotes, make a list of:
   (a) the times when pounds were being sold, i.e. *supplied* onto the market and state why this was happening.

   (b) the times when pounds were being bought, i.e. *demanded* by the market and state why this was happening.

4 Explain how the value of the pound changed in each of the quotes and, using demand and supply analysis, explain why it was changing in this way.

invested abroad – then the value of the pound will go down.

There are a number of reasons why the value of any currency fluctuates from year to year. The main ones are:

- *Changes in the current balance* (the current balance is exports minus imports). If, say, the balance goes from being positive (or 'in the black') to being negative (or 'in the red'), then more pounds will be supplied than before to pay for those imports, relative to the number of pounds demanded by foreigners to pay for exports. So the value of the pound will go down. The value of the pound will tend to go up, however, if the current account is in surplus. Inflation is one major factor causing imports to increase faster than exports, pushing the current account into the red. If Britain's inflation rate is higher than that of other countries, British goods will become less price-competitive, encouraging imports and making it more difficult for British firms to export.

- *Changes in interest rates.* A rise in interest rates in the UK encourages other countries to invest in the UK. The demand for pounds rises, increasing the value of the pound. When domestic interest rates fall, the value of the pound tends to decline.

- *Speculation.* If the buyers and sellers of currency feel that the value of the pound is going to go down in the future, they will not buy or demand pounds now. So the value of the pound will fall. If, on the other hand, they believe that the value of the pound is going to rise, they will buy pounds now and try to make a profit out of a rising

pound. FOREIGN CURRENCY SPECULATORS – people, firms, banks, whose aim is to make money by simply buying and selling currencies – are a major influence on the value of any single currency, like the pound, today.

Expressing the Value of the Pound

The value of the pound can be given in terms of any single currency: £1 = $1.20, £1 = 11 francs, £1 = 2 deutschmarks, etc. But it is difficult to judge quickly whether the value of the pound has gone up or down, if, for instance, it has gone up against the dollar, but down against the French franc. To get over this problem, the UK government calculates an average value of the pound against the currencies of our major trading partners. This average is called the 'trade weighted index' or the 'STERLING EXCHANGE RATE INDEX'.

A Diagrammatic Analysis

Changes in the value of the pound can be explained using a demand and

supply curve. Consider Figure 78.1. The shift in the demand curve from D to D' (i.e. at any given price, more pounds are demanded in the market) could be caused by a rise in UK exports, a rise in interest rates in London, or speculation that the pound will rise in future. This shift in the demand curve would cause the value of the pound to rise from OB to OC. A shift to the right in the supply curve (i.e. at any given price more pounds are supplied onto the market) would cause the value of the pound to fall from OB to OA. This increase in supply could have been caused by a rise in imports, a fall in interest rates in London, or speculation that the value of the pound will fall in future.

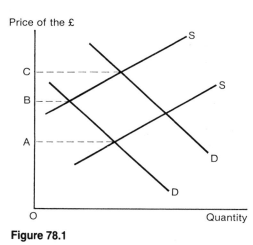

Price of the £

Figure 78.1

1 The value of the pound is £1 = $1.5, £1 = 12 French francs and £1 = 2 deutschmarks. How many:
   (a) French francs can you buy for £5;
   (b) US dollars can you buy for £100;
   (c) German deutschmarks can you buy for £50 000?
   What is the value of 1 deutschmark in French francs?

2 Explain how the value of the pound is determined.

3 Explain whether owners of pounds sterling will buy pounds or sell pounds:
   (a) if there is a rise in UK imports;
   (b) if there is a rise in UK exports;
   (c) if interest rates rise in New York;
   (d) if there is speculation that the value of the pound will fall over the next six months.

4 Using a demand and supply diagram, illustrate the effects of (a) to (d) in question 3 above.

5 What is the 'sterling exchange rate index' and why is it calculated?

K E Y   T E R M S

FOREIGN EXCHANGE RATE – the price at which one currency is bought and sold for another currency.

FOREIGN CURRENCY SPECULATOR – a person or organisation that makes money by buying and selling foreign currencies in anticipation of changes in their value.

STERLING EXCHANGE RATE INDEX – an average value of the pound against the currencies of the UK's major trading partners.

The Significance of the Balance of Payments and Exchange Rates

Figure 79.1 Current balance, 1989–94

	£ millions
1989	− 653
1990	+3235
1991	+6993
1992	+4923
1993	+3246
1994	+ 624

Figure 79.2 Investment and other capital transactions, 1989–94

	£ millions
1989	+2157
1990	−1887
1991	−7399
1992	−3392
1993	−5111
1994	−3287

Figure 79.3 Exchange rate against major trading partners, 1990 = 100

1989	103
1990	100
1991	102
1992	105
1993	108
1994	110

Figure 79.4 Unemployment in the UK, 1989–94

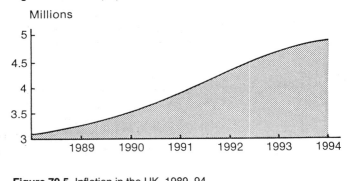

Figure 79.5 Inflation in the UK, 1989–94

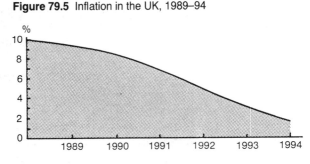

DEMOCRATIC PARTY MANIFESTO

Economic Policy

Unemployment is the main economic problem that faces Britain today. It not only directly affects the lives of millions of unemployed workers and their families but also represents a huge cost to the rest of society. The Democratic Party is committed to reducing unemployment by:

- extra public spending of £10 billion on roads, schools, hospitals, sewers and grants to private firms for investment;
- cutting the exchange rate by 20% to make Britain more competitive;
- stopping British investment overseas and, if necessary, borrowing money from abroad to pay for new investment in private industry.

STUDY POINTS

You are the newly elected Democratic government of the UK in 1995. Your manifesto commits you to certain economic policies.

1 What effect will the rise in public spending have on:
(a) total spending in the economy and, therefore, on
(b) imports, and, therefore on
(c) the current balance?

2 How will the fall in the exchange rate affect:
(a) the ability of British exporters to compete abroad;
(b) total exports;
(c) the ability of British companies to compete against foreign imports in the UK;
(d) total imports;
(e) the current balance?

3 What effect might reducing foreign investment by Britons have on:
(a) investment at home in British industry;
(b) the supply of pounds for sale on the foreign exchange markets and, therefore, on the exchange rate of the pound;
(c) the competitiveness of British industry?

4 What are likely to be the effects of your policies on:
(a) unemployment;
(b) the incomes of workers;
(c) investment by British industry;
(d) inflation?

- 'Current account record deficit.'
- 'Pound slides again.'
- 'Record investment abroad.'

Units 77 and 78 considered the balance of payments and exchange rates. But why are they important? Does it matter if the pound is high or low, or if the current account is in surplus or deficit?

The Current Account

Between 1973 and 1975, the UK experienced record deficits on its current account. In 1973, imports exceeded exports by £981 million; in 1974, by £3273 million; in 1975, by £1521 million; and in 1976 by £875 million. Did it matter? The simple answer is yes, because the UK could not have continued to have large deficits. It is easy to see why.

To run a deficit on current account, the economy has to run a surplus on the capital account – i.e. it has to borrow money. This is no different from the finances of an individual – if a person wants to spend more than he or she has earned, he or she has to borrow. Eventually, the foreign debt of a country can get so large that other countries refuse to lend any more. This actually happened to a number of countries in the late 1970s and early 1980s. These countries included Poland, Mexico, Brazil and Argentina. By 1976, the British government was borrowing from the International Monetary Fund (the IMF), the international bank that lends money to countries in financial difficulties. If the UK deficit had continued, eventually no country would have lent to the UK

and it would have gone bankrupt. Thus a country cannot run a deficit on the current account for ever.

The Capital Account

Since 1979, Britain has been investing much of the proceeds of North Sea oil abroad. In 1981, for instance, the UK invested over £7000 million abroad. Economists differ about whether or not this is a good thing.

- By investing abroad, the UK is building up a 'nest egg' for the future. Interest, profits and dividends on the money (which are recorded on the current account) can be brought home to the UK and be spent.
- By investing that money in the UK, British industry could have been built up to make it more competitive on world markets, creating jobs and income in the process.

Exchange Rates

Is a high pound or a low pound good for Britain? Consider this extract:

> 'The Yanks are coming – to buy British clothes. They like the cut – and they love the price now their dollar will buy 91p worth of our goods against only 69p a year ago. America's vast JC Penny chain of 1700 department stores will soon announce big orders for British made clothes.' (*Source: Daily Mirror*, 19 February 1985)

The fall in the value of the pound against the dollar has meant that British goods have become cheaper in dollar terms. Americans are buying more UK exports. Similarly, US goods

are now much more expensive in the UK, so the UK will buy fewer US goods. This illustrates the two sides of a low value of the pound:

- It is good for exports and for jobs in Britain.
- It is bad for prices, because the price of imported goods will now be higher. The consumer therefore cannot afford to buy as many of the goods as before.

So there is no simple answer as to whether a high pound or a low pound is 'good' for Britain.

Control of the Foreign Exchanges

It is very important to realise that in all of this, the government plays only a very small part. It is *not* the government, on the whole, which imports and exports, invests and borrows abroad, or buys and sells foreign currency. This is done by millions of individuals and organisations. It is therefore very difficult for the government to control exchange rates or the balance of payments. This is something that will be discussed in more detail in Unit 84.

C H E C K P O I N T S

1 What is meant by a current account deficit?

2 Explain why a country cannot run a current account deficit on a long-term basis.

3 Is it better to run a surplus or a deficit in the capital account?

4 Explain the economic effects of a rise in the value of the pound.

C O U R S E W O R K S U G G E S T I O N

Examine the value of the pound over the past twelve months. Explain why the value of the pound has changed. Analyse the likely effects of this change in value on the British economy as a whole and your local area in particular. Try to decide whether the changes are likely to prove beneficial or not.

The lower the value of the pound the more American tourists will come to the UK and buy British goods.

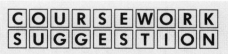

raphs; SW1, 2	The pound	Bank Buys	Bank Sells		12	+7	+2
					13	+7	+3
arwick; War-					14	+5	+5
					15	+7	+1
	Australia $	2.18	2.14		16	+7	+4
	Austria Sch	24.50	23.30		17	+5	+5
Solano d paint-	Belgium Fr	71.80	68.00				
	Canada $	2.195	2.095		18	+6	+8
Sicilia;	Denmark Kr	12.98	12.28		19	+5	+7
nsington	Finland Mkk	8.02	7.52				
	France Fr	11.07	10.52		20	+8	+3
	Germany Dm	3.49	3.31		21	+6	+2
	Greece Dr	214.00	199.00				
	Hong Kong $	12.30	11.80		22	+6	+
on Rep-	Ireland Pt	1.155	1.095		23	+7	+
Guildhall	Italy Lira	2385.00	2265.00				
Drama,	Japan Yen	261.00	247.00		24	+5	+
	Netherlands Gld	3.91	3.72		25	+8	+
ol String	Norway Kr	11.07	10.52				
Holland	Portugal Esc	232.00	220.00		26	+5	+
	Spain Pta	4.05	3.35		27	+6	+
y Anne	South Africa Rd	221.00	209.00				
St Giles	Sweden Kr	11.24	10.69		28	+8	+
EC2, 4.	Switzerland Fr	2.91	2.76		29	+7	+
ry Bicket;	USA $	1.60	1.53				
	Yugoslavia Dnr	530.00	490.00				

Retail Price Index: 381.6
New York: The Dow Jones industrial average closed up 3.22 at 1,789.43.

Data Response Questions
Units 75–79

Unit 75 The Theory of Comparative Advantage

Switching on again to British radios

LOW-COST PORTABLE radios are to be manufactured in Britain again for the first time in years.

A radio which will cost about £25 was unveiled in London yesterday by Ross Electronics, a small British company with a successful record in other audio products.

Far Eastern suppliers have dominated the mass market for radios for 20 years. While imports accounted only for 1 per cent of the British Market in 1959, they rose to more than 50 per cent in five years. British manufacture has been in decline since, says a trade report.

Ross Electronics, claims to have more than 50 per cent of the British market for headphones. Until last year Ross had its headphones made in Taiwan but has started manufacturing them in the UK.

In addition to saving on freight and duty, the company believes, it can make them more cheaply in the UK. The headphones and the new radio have been designed for capital-intensive production.

The labour content accounts for less than 10 per cent of the manufacturing cost, states Mr Marks.

Source: Financial Times, 20 May 1985

1 Describe how the production of radios in Britain has changed over the period since 1950. *(2 marks)*

2 Which countries developed a comparative advantage in the production of radios over that period? *(1 mark)*

3 Explain how and why Ross Electronics may be able to shift comparative advantage for low-cost portable radios back to Britain. *(7 marks)*

Unit 76 Exports and Imports

Sharp rise in non-oil exports

BY MAX WILKINSON, ECONOMICS CORRESPONDENT

BRITAIN'S exports rose to a record £6.9bn in February, although imports were also running at a high level of £7.2bn.

The latest figures from the Department of Trade and Industry yesterday showed that non-oil exports rose steeply to £5.1bn.

Imports of manufactured goods have risen. Their volume in the three months to February was 4 per cent higher than the average for last year. This was more than matched, however, by the rise in exports of manufactured goods, 6 per cent higher in the latest three months compared with last year's average.

Source: Financial Times, 27 March 1985

1 What was the value of Britain's exports in February 1985? *(1 mark)*

2 What was the value of oil exports in February 1985? *(1 mark)*

3 Give four examples of non-oil exports from the UK. *(2 marks)*

4 Describe how trade in manufactured goods changed in early 1985. *(2 marks)*

5 Why does the UK need to export goods? *(4 marks)*

Unit 77 The Balance of Payments

GKN lifts its stake in Spain's car firms

Engineering group GKN is to boost its stake in the Spanish motor industry, which now produces more cars than Britain.

GKN is taking over two leading companies in the motor components market in deals reputedly costing around £15 million.

It is taking control of Ayra Durex, which produces constant velocity joints and propeller shafts, with annual sales of £23 million. GKN's stake in the business goes up from 35 to 66 per cent.

GKN is also buying Indugasa, which produces £40 million worth of constant velocity joints annually. It is jointly owned by Spanish vehicle maker SEAT and the French car firm Citroen.

GKN has not disclosed the cost of the two deals but brokers estimate that the Ayra share purchase was probably worth around £4 million while Indugasa cost at least £10 million.

GKN is seeking to widen its influence as a multinational company to make it less dependent on the declining UK engineering industry.

Spain has emerged as a leading car making country in the past five years, with major investments by Ford, General Motors and Fiat.

Last year it produced about 1.25 million cars against Britain's 900,000.

Source: Express and Star, 1 October 1985

1 What has GKN purchased in Spain? *(1 mark)*

2 Where will this purchase be recorded on the UK Balance of Payments Accounts and why? *(4 marks)*

3 Why might the purchase lead, in future years, to an increase in:
   (a) visible exports and
   (b) invisible exports for the UK? *(4 marks)*

4 What are:
   (a) the costs and
   (b) the benefits of the purchase for the UK economy? *(6 marks)*

Unit 78 Exchange Rates

Behind the fall in sterling

THERE ARE three reasons why sterling is in crisis again. First, and most important, the sterling exchange rate is linked to the price of oil. Just as sterling was very strong during the second oil price explosion of 1979–80, so it has been tending to fall as the price of oil has fallen over the past couple of years.

Secondly, the markets may believe that domestic monetary policy is too loose – too much money in the economy will help create inflation and a loss of competitiveness as well as allowing extra spending on imports. This factor is often over-emphasised in the City of London.

The third factor is the government's failure to intervene at the right time in defence of sterling. The government's failure to increase interest rates at the right time meant that, when the pound did start to fall rapidly, the rise in interest rates had to be even greater than if prompt action had been taken.

Source: adapted from the Financial Times, 15 January 1985

1 What is meant by a sterling 'crisis'? *(4 marks)*

2 What two forces determine the price of a currency? *(2 marks)*

3 Explain, in terms of these two forces, why, according to the article, the pound was falling. *(9 marks)*

The Data Response Question for **Unit 79** can be found on page 221.

Essay Questions
Units 75–79

1 (a) Explain the difference between an export and an import. *(4 marks)*
   (b) Give *two* examples of *visible* exports for Britain. *(4 marks)*
   (c) What is meant by a 'deficit' on the current account. *(4 marks)*
   (d) What are the implications for a country if it has a current account deficit? *(8 marks)*

2 'Pound falls in hectic trading.'
   (a) What is meant by a 'falling pound'? *(6 marks)*
   (b) How is the value of the pound determined? *(8 marks)*
   (c) What are the consequences for exports and imports of a falling pound? *(6 marks)*

The European Economic Community (1)

STUDY POINTS

1 The statistics compare the countries of the EEC with the USA, Japan and the USSR. Prepare a report detailing the major differences.

2 How would you expect the various figures shown in the data to change by the year 2000, given the changes shown over the period 1960–83? Say why you would expect these changes to occur.

Note: The statistics only relate to the ten countries belonging to the EEC in 1985. They do *not* include Spain and Portugal who joined in 1986.

Figure 80.1 Composition of the EEC in 1986

Figure 80.2 Motor vehicles and television sets per 1000 inhabitants

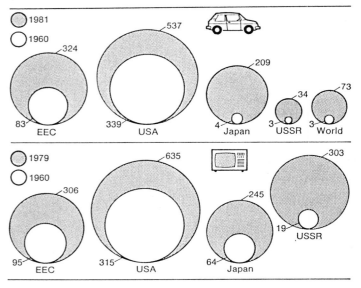

Figure 80.3 Land area and population growth

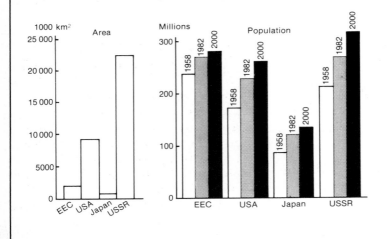

Figure 80.4 Gross domestic product at market prices per head

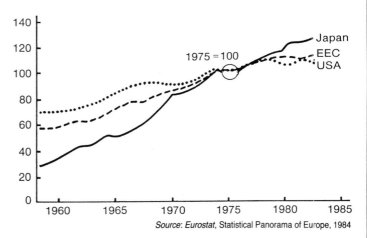

Source: Eurostat, Statistical Panorama of Europe, 1984

The EEC

The European Community (the EC, also known as the 'EEC' or 'European Economic Community' or the 'Common Market') was established in 1957, when six countries – France, West Germany, Italy, Belgium, the Netherlands and Luxemburg – signed an agreement called the Treaty of Rome. The politicians who helped found the EC wanted to set up a Europe that would no longer go to war against itself. Only by having a united Europe could there be no repetition of the two world wars experienced since 1914.

The first step in this dream was the setting up of a united economic Europe – and so, for most of its history, the EC has been known as the European Economic Community. The UK, Eire and Denmark joined the Community in 1973. Greece followed in 1981, and Spain and Portugal in 1986.

Free Trade

A united economic Europe implies that there will be no more restrictions on economic activity between, say, London and Paris than there are say, between London and Birmingham. This means that there must be *free trade* between all the member countries of the EEC. An essential part of achieving this was the formation of a CUSTOMS UNION. In a customs union:

- There is free trade between member countries.
- All goods and services imported from outside have the same trade restrictions placed upon them. An important part of this is the COMMON EXTERNAL TARIFF. A shirt imported from the USA will have the same tariff placed upon it if it is imported into the UK, as it would if imported into France or Greece.

Free trade means more than just the setting up of a customs union. There are many barriers to free trade between countries, such as:

- different safety standards on products;
- laws limiting the movement of workers between countries;
- laws limiting the power of firms to set up business in other countries;
- agreements between companies to limit competition in particular countries.

In order to try and combat these restrictions, the Common Market has established a number of *common policies*. The most important of these is the Common Agricultural Policy, which will be discussed in the next unit. Other common policies include:

- *Regional policy*. As in the UK, each member country has differences in economic standards between regions. The richest part of the EEC is known as the 'Golden Triangle', whose limits can be drawn from Milan in Italy, to London in the UK, to Hamburg in West Germany. The EEC regional policy is supposed to help reduce inequalities by giving aid to the less prosperous regions of the community.
- *Social policy*. The aim of the EEC is to bring all the welfare systems of member countries into line with each other. Very little progress has been made towards achieving this difficult objective. At the moment, the Social Fund pays out grants mainly for resettling and retraining workers.
- *Competition policy*. Free trade can only be achieved if firms are free to compete in all countries of the EEC. The competition policy of the Community is designed to prevent restrictions on this from occurring.

For instance, companies are not allowed to prevent other companies from competing in their markets; nor are groups of companies allowed to fix prices between themselves.

The commemorative 50 pence piece, minted to mark the UK's entry into the Common Market in 1973 – the nine interlocking hands represented each member country.

C H E C K P O I N T S

1 Which countries originally formed the Common Market? Which countries have joined since 1957?

2 Explain how a customs union works.

3 In 1986, Spain and Portugal joined the EEC. Both countries had imposed very high tariffs on imported cars.
   (a) What will happen now to these tariffs?
   (b) What will be the effect on Spanish car workers?

4 Name two common policies of the EEC and describe how they operate.

C O U R S E W O R K   S U G G E S T I O N

Describe one major policy of the European Economic Community. Analyse its effects upon trade within the Community and on trade between the Community and non-member countries. Who has benefited from this policy, who has lost out and why? To what extent has this policy contributed to greater efficiency within the Community?

K E Y   T E R M S

CUSTOMS UNION – a group of countries between which there is free trade and which all impose identical tariffs and quotas on goods coming in from countries outside the union.

COMMON EXTERNAL TARIFF – the tariff or tax that is imposed by all EEC countries on goods coming into their country from outside the EEC.

The European Economic Community (2)

Why cheap isn't cheerful

SPECIAL SALES of cheap, EEC butter have made a nonsense of the UK butter market, according to the marketing director of Butterdane, John Howard. Butterdane is the marketing arm of the Danish butter industry. Mr Howard's views are echoed by his colleagues responsible for most of the other established butter brands.

At prices from 33 pence a half pound pack upwards, cheap butter has destroyed consumers' brand loyalties, halted the bulk of conventional butter sales, and done nothing to halt the underlying decline in butter consumption, which fell 11 per cent last year.

Overall consumption of butter in the first four weeks of this year was up by more than a quarter compared with a drop of almost 12 per cent in the last quarter of 1984, but no-one in the industry is fooled that this is other than a brief hiccup in butter's slide towards an ever smaller market share. "These gains will quickly dissipate," Mr Howard notes gloomily.

The end of the cheap sales is expected to be followed by a lull in buying, as consumers eat the stockpiles of cheap supplies now resting in their freezers.

The Government decided last week not to argue in Brussels for any continuation of the other, regular, EEC butter subsidy, which in Britain has held the retail price at two pence a pack below the level it would otherwise be. This decision was taken on health grounds, as part of the official recognition that animal fats contribute towards heart disease, which in the UK is more rife than elsewhere in Europe.

Meanwhile, stockpiles of frozen butter continue to rise, in spite of EEC efforts to curb milk production and in spite of the cheap butter sale. Butter that would have gone into the shops this year but for cheap butter, have gone into Intervention cold stores instead.

A spokesman for the Intervention Board says that UK butter stocks for which there is no ready buyer amount at the moment to 136,000 tonnes, which is 25,000 tonnes, more than this time last year. There is even some concern that the existing cold store capacity may be inadequate to cope, particularly in Northern Ireland where the other day they had only room left for another 8,000 tonnes of surplus butter.

Source: The Guardian, 19 March 1985

STUDY POINTS

Your task is to prepare a report explaining *why* there is a butter mountain, *how* this butter mountain could be eliminated and what would be the *costs* and *benefits* of doing so. Structure your report round the following points.

1 Explain why consumers are buying (or *demanding*) less butter than farmers are producing (or *supplying*). If possible, draw a demand and supply diagram to show this.

2 Explain that if producers can't sell their butter at an EEC-agreed minimum price (the intervention price), then the EEC will buy it from the producers at that price and put it into store. If possible, show on your demand and supply diagram how much butter the EEC will need to buy in order to keep minimum prices for butter above the price where demand equals supply.

3 Explain the costs and benefits to butter consumers, butter producers and EEC taxpayers of each of the following methods of eliminating the butter mountain:
   (a) reducing the intervention price to the point where what consumers demand and what farms supply is equal;
   (b) keeping the intervention price at its present level but selling butter from the Intervention Stores at a much reduced price.
   (c) restricting by licence the amount of butter that can be produced in the EEC so that demand and supply of butter are equal;
   (d) selling EEC butter at a knock-down price to countries outside the EEC;

4 Explain why the EEC demand for butter is likely to fall in the future and how this will affect the problems of over-production of butter in the EEC.

The Common Agricultural Policy (CAP)

Should the UK be a member of the EEC? This question is one which has been asked ever since the European Economic Community was first thought of in the early 1950s. Many Britons today still believe that the UK would be better off outside the EEC than in it. This unit considers the economic arguments for and against membership.

One of the main costs of membership for the UK is the Common Agricultural Policy. When the EEC was first set up in 1957, agriculture was the single most important industry in the Community. If free trade were to become a reality in the EEC, then agriculture seemed an obvious starting point.

The main aims of CAP were:

- to increase agricultural productivity – i.e. raise the amount produced per worker in the industry;
- to ensure a fair standard of living for workers in the industry;
- to stabilise markets, e.g. preventing large changes in price;
- to ensure that no food shortages ever developed in Europe;
- to ensure that consumers could buy food at reasonable prices.

These aims were to be achieved mainly by fixing minimum prices for products. This minimum price is known as the *intervention price*. If a farmer cannot sell his produce at this price on the open market, then the EEC will buy it from him at the intervention price. The idea was that when free-market prices rose again, the EEC would sell off the produce it had bought. The cost to European taxpayers would be small and the aims of CAP would be achieved.

What has actually happened has

been rather different. Consider this extract:

'Housewives swooped on stores yesterday in a rush for free butter. Nearly 500 000 half-pound packets were given away free in West Berlin. The stampede started after housewives were told they would be given a half-pound of butter free for every packet they bought. The giveaway was launched by the Common Market in an experiment to find a way to reduce its huge 900 000 ton butter mountain.' (*Source: Daily Mirror*, 16 May 1985)

CAP today is a very expensive policy, which has resulted in high prices, together with mountains and lakes of unsold produce. The extract above relates to one agricultural product, butter. Since the start of CAP, farmers have been able to put strong political pressure on the EEC to fix high intervention prices. This results in higher farm incomes. But it has also resulted in intervention prices being above the market price. Consumers have not been willing to buy all the butter, for instance, that farmers have produced. The EEC has had to keep on buying up food, and this has resulted in, among other things, the 900 000 ton butter mountain.

This is shown in Figure 81.1. The only price at which consumers will demand exactly what farmers supply is OA. This is the '*market price*'. If the EEC sets an intervention price of OB, then farmers will supply OG, but consumers will only want to buy OE. The result is that the Common Market has to buy EG and put the produce into store.

Part of the EEC 'butter mountain' in cold storage in The Netherlands.

With too high a price set, the Community does not find an opportunity to sell off produce in store at the market price. So it has to dispose of the produce by other means. The extract referred to surplus butter being given away to Berlin housewives. Other ways of disposing of mountains (e.g. butter) or lakes (e.g. wine) have been to sell it cheaply to the Russians or developing countries, feed it to animals, or simply destroy it.

CAP has been costly to the UK because:

- CAP prices are higher than world prices for food. If Britain could buy food from the cheapest source, it could save at least £1000 million a year.

- Spending on CAP forms 60–70% of the EEC budget. If spending on CAP were reduced, the UK might be able to reduce its budget contribution, possibly saving a few hundred million pounds a year.

Other Costs and Benefits

Higher food prices are just one cost of Community membership. Another cost is the budget contribution that the UK has to make. The UK pays more into EEC funds than it receives. Britain has also seen many of its jobs disappear, as European firms have proved more competitive than British ones. On the other hand, entry to the EEC has created jobs in Britain as British firms have gained markets in Europe. It is very difficult, if not impossible, to say whether more jobs, and therefore income, have been gained in the UK than have been lost following entry. What is true, though, is that if the UK were to leave the Community, many jobs would be lost in British industry, as the EEC would put up tariff and quota barriers against UK goods without there being any guarantee that new jobs would be created to replace those lost.

C H E C K P O I N T S

1 **Explain how the Common Agricultural Policy fixes prices for agricultural products in the Community.**

2 **What are the aims of CAP? To what extent are they fulfilled in practice?**

3 **How do 'mountains' and 'lakes' appear?**

4 **Outline the arguments for and against British membership of the EEC.**

C O U R S E W O R K   S U G G E S T I O N

Find out how the EEC supports beef and dairy producers in the Community. Analyse the problems that are caused by this support. What measures have been taken to overcome these problems? Try to assess the extent to which EEC policies produce an efficient allocation of scarce resources in this sector of the agricultural industry.

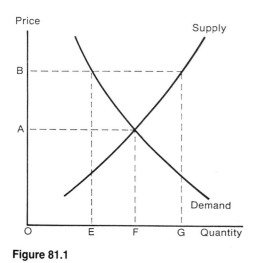

Price

B

A

O   E   F   G   Quantity

Supply

Demand

Figure 81.1

The Developing World (1)

Figure 82.1 GNP per capita, 1982 (US $)

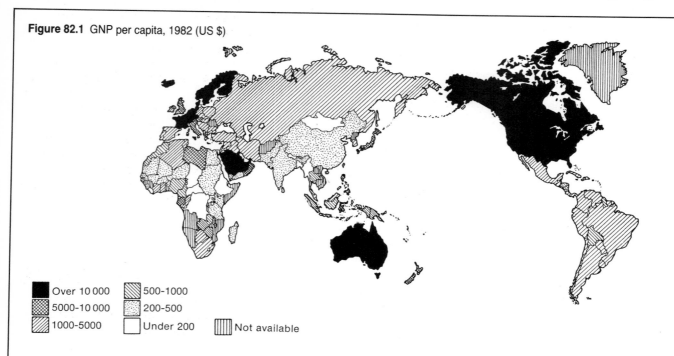

- ■ Over 10 000
- ▨ 5000-10 000
- ▨ 1000-5000
- ▩ 500-1000
- ⠿ 200-500
- ☐ Under 200
- ▤ Not available

S T U D Y P O I N T S

Prepare a report on the world economy. In your report:

1 Describe how the population of the world is distributed geographically. It might be helpful to mark on an outline map of the world the continents named in Figure 82.2. (Either trace the world outline from Figure 82.1 above or obtain a map from your teacher.)

2 Describe how the world's income is distributed. To do this, use Figure 82.1 which shows GNP per capita (i.e. income per person) in US dollars. In 1982, £1 was roughly equal to $1.5. So an income of $400 a year would be worth approximately £270 a year. Show that high income countries (often called 'developed' countries) tend to be situated in the North of the world while low income countries (often called 'developing' countries) tend to be situated in the South.

3 Use Figure 82.3 to show the link between how long people live, on average (their 'life expectancy'), and their income (GNP per capita). Suggest *five* reasons why this link might exist.

Figure 82.2 Distribution of the world's population

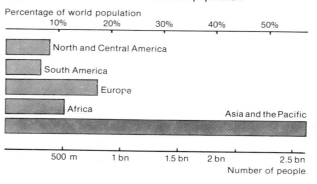

Percentage of world population

- North and Central America
- South America
- Europe
- Africa
- Asia and the Pacific

Number of people

Figure 82.3 Life expectancy and GNP per capita

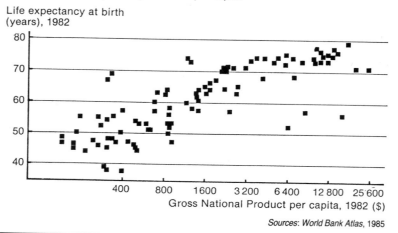

Life expectancy at birth (years), 1982

Gross National Product per capita, 1982 ($)

Sources: World Bank Atlas, 1985

Characteristics of the Developing World

The world's population stands at around 4 billion. Three-quarters of these people live in the DEVELOPING or THIRD WORLD, and only a quarter live in the DEVELOPED first and second worlds. The *first world* is made up of rich, industrialised, developed, Western, for the most part democratic countries, such as the USA, the UK and Japan. The *second world* is made up of less well off, but still relatively rich, Eastern-bloc Communist countries, such as the USSR and Poland. The developing world, where most people live, is made up of very much poorer countries in South America, Africa and Asia. Figure 82.2 shows how the world's population was distributed in 1982.

Developing countries represent the largest group of countries in the world, both by area and by population. But in terms of income and wealth, they lag behind the first two worlds.

No two developing countries are the same, and therefore it is dangerous to try and generalise. However, developing countries usually show a number of the following characteristics:

- *Low incomes per person.* Figure 82.1 shows the GNP per capita (gross national product or income per person) for countries in the world today. Note that India, China, Pakistan and Bangladesh, with a quarter of the world's population, have average incomes of less than $400 a year. Note, too, that the developed countries are found mainly in the North. Hence the gap between rich and poor countries is often referred to as the 'North–South divide'.
- *Low life expectancies for their population.* Figure 82.3 shows that you are far more likely to live longer, if you live in a high-income country than if you live in a low-income country.
- *High rates of population growth.* Many children still die in developing countries, but such deaths were even more common 100 years ago. In order to maintain family size, parents had to have lots of children. Today, more children survive, but it takes time for social attitudes to change. People still have large numbers of children. There is strong evidence to suggest that as incomes rise and parents see that more children are surviving, family size will come down.
- *A less well-educated population.* By no means everybody, for instance, is able to read and write.
- *Relatively little capital.* Everything, from factories and machines to roads and schools, is far less abundant than in developed countries.
- *Low labour productivity.* A less well-educated workforce, with less capital, produces less per worker than in the industrialised countries of the developed world.
- *Poor housing.*
- *Poor sanitation.* For instance, many people in developing countries do not have access to clean piped water for drinking and washing.
- *Poor health standards.* Common diseases, no longer seen in the rich developed countries, kill millions in developing countries. Malnutrition, too, is still a big killer.

The Poverty Cycle

All aspects of poverty in developing countries are interlinked. For instance, low productivity of developing world workers means that they can only earn low wages. This, in turn, means that they cannot afford to eat sufficiently well, which leads to poor health. With low wages, they cannot afford to live in good-quality houses with adequate levels of sanitation, which again leads to health problems. High mortality (death) rates encourage parents to have large families, but this leads to too many workers chasing too few jobs and consequently to low wages. Each individual problem is part of the much larger problem facing developing countries – namely, such a lack of economic resources that many of their inhabitants cannot even satisfy their basic human needs. The basic economic problem is much more acute in India than it is in the USA.

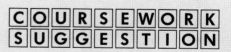

The Developing World (2)

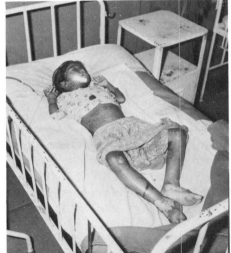

S T U D Y   P O I N T S

You are a committee of experts studying how best to distribute foreign aid.

1 Identify, from the photographs, problems facing a typical third world country.

2 Describe specific projects which could be paid for by aid which would help solve some of these problems in a village or town in the developing world.

3 Assess the costs and benefits of this aid.

Interdependence

The links between the rich, industrialised nations of the world and the poorer developing countries are numerous. Economically, all the nations of the world are interdependent, if only because of trade. The developed world is vitally dependent upon the developing world for raw materials – everything from oil to copper to coffee. If the developing countries were to cut off their supplies to the developed world, the economies of the developed world would be plunged into chaos. This can be shown by the traumatic effects of restrictions on the supply of oil to the developed world in 1973/4 and 1978/9.

The third world has also been developing its own industries, producing mainly low-technology products such as textiles and steel, or assembling high-technology goods manufactured in the developed world. This has presented developed countries with costs and benefits. Consumers in the first world have been able to take advantage of low prices for these goods. On the other hand, the equivalent industries in developed countries have found it difficult to compete, and millions of jobs have been lost.

One very worrying trend for developing countries is that the prices of goods they export to the developed world have not tended to keep up with the prices of goods developed countries sell to them (i.e. the developing world has suffered a long-term decline in its terms of trade). Poorer countries need to export more raw materials and manufactured goods to the rich countries to pay for the same amount of developed world products. What this means is that the rich countries have been able, on average, to secure a larger percentage of the increase in income and wealth worldwide than they would otherwise have done at previous prices. It is one

Are the developing countries exploited by the developed world?

of the reasons why the gap between the rich countries of the world and the poorer countries has widened over the past thirty years.

Aid

Developed countries do give FOREIGN AID to the developing world. This ranges from emergency aid to fight famines, to money which helps the long-term development of a country. Much foreign aid is used to buy goods from developed countries, including armaments, which may do little to increase standards of living for the inhabitants of the country. Some aid is given in the form of 'SOFT' LOANS – loans that carry little or no interest. There are also vast flows of money which are lent to developing countries by ordinary commercial banks in the West at market rates of interest. This, however, can hardly be said to be 'aid'.

There is much controversy over whether aid has been beneficial to developing countries. On the one hand, there is no doubt that aid, if correctly administered, can have a very powerful impact on living standards. Provision of food for the starving, or clean water for those without it, or simple technology capital to make goods in demand in the local economy will certainly help the inhabitants of a developing country. On the other hand, it is far less clear that a new steel mill, or a new dam, will improve living standards for a large number of people, especially if the money to buy these items has come from a loan on which interest has to be paid, rather than as a gift.

CHECKPOINTS

1 What is meant by 'economic interdependence'?

2 What food products does Britain import from the developing world?

3 How would a rise in the price of coffee beans affect: (a) a coffee-producing country such as Brazil; and (b) the UK?

4 What would be the effect on the developed world, if the developing world stopped all exports of oil? What would be the effect on the developing world?

5 The British government provides foreign aid for a developing country to build a steel plant. What will the effects of this be on: (a) the developing country; and (b) the UK?

6 How might the development of a poor country such as Bangladesh, which exports textiles, help or harm the interests of (a) British workers and (b) British consumers?

COURSEWORK SUGGESTION

Use *British Aid Statistics* (published by HMSO, and available from your local large reference library), to describe the pattern of UK overseas aid in recent years. Describe who receives foreign aid and what sort of projects are supported. Analyse how foreign aid patterns have changed. Try to decide whether the UK ought to give more foreign aid, and whether current aid is effective in helping poor people in developing countries.

KEY TERMS

FOREIGN AID – gifts or loans of money from the rich developed countries to poorer developing countries.

SOFT LOANS – loans at low rates of interest.

Data Response Questions
Units 80–83

Unit 80 The European Community (1)

COSTA PACKET

AFTER years of debate, the terms on which Spain and Portugal should be allowed to join the Common Market have been finally agreed. In nine months, the ten will become twelve.

"The cost to the existing 10 members will be heavy at the beginning," said a spokesman. "But in the long run, hopefully, we will all benefit." *Hopefully?*

Taxpayers will not even have the compensation of knowing that they will be able to buy cheap produce from Spain and Portugal.

If there was a genuine free Common Market these two countries could flood Europe with cheap wine, fruit, vegetables, fish – and workers.

But under the deal agreed on Saturday, they will not be allowed unrestricted access because of the disastrous effect this would have on the 10's home industries. Instead, there will be a transition period of up to 10 years.

For instance:

● **WINE:** imports of cheap Spanish and Portuguese plonk will be regulated for seven years.

● **FRUIT AND VEGETABLES:** In order to keep up High Street prices, Spanish and Portuguese imports (oranges, lemons, apples, lettuces and mushrooms, for example) will have to pay the present import levies – varying between seven and 25 per cent – for the next four years.

"But that isn't good enough," says a spokesman for Britain's National Farmers' Union. "The transition period should be seven years if we are to stave off their unfair competition."

Source: *Daily Express*, 1 April 1985

1 Which countries form 'the ten' of the Common Market mentioned in the article? *(2 marks)*

2 What are the possible costs of Spanish and Portuguese membership of the EEC for the UK farmer? *(3 marks)*

3 What might be the advantages of membership for:
   (a) the British consumer;
   (b) British industry? *(5 marks)*

Unit 81 The European Community (2)

Now Europe faces a sugar mountain

Common Market taxpayers will have to find hundreds of millions of pounds to store surplus sugar, because of a collapse in world prices.

The Common Market Commission in Brussels has decided to suspend exports outside the community and to put surplus sugar into public store.

Until now exporters have received a subsidy of £253 a tonne, which has meant sugar has been sold outside the community for as little as 25p a kilo bag, half the British price.

Surplus sugar in the EEC will now be stockpiled and taxpayers will have to pay the cost of buying it off the market and of the storage.

The cost of tackling the sugar mountain in Britain alone is likely to top £100 million this year.

Source: *Express and Star*, 28 June 1985

1 What is a Common Market 'mountain'? *(1 mark)*

2 Explain how 'mountains' are created. *(2 marks)*

3 Why is the EEC set to create a sugar mountain? *(2 marks)*

4 What would happen to sugar beet farmers in the UK if this mountain were not created? *(2 marks)*

5 What are the costs of mountains to:
   (a) EEC taxpayers;
   (b) EEC consumers? *(3 marks)*

The retail price of sugar is being held at an artificially high level through the intervention of the EEC. But measures such as stockpiling – while benefiting sugar producers and dealers – are costly to taxpayers and consumers and generally unpopular.

Unit 82 The Developing World (1)

A paper mill's tale

ONE HUNDRED bumpy kilometres north-west of Hanoi is a Swedish-financed pulp and paper mill. It is the biggest Western aid project in Vietnam.

The project is designed to develop Vietnam's forestry industry. It involves felling trees in an area near the Chinese border, transporting them south to the mill by river and road, pulping the timber, and manufacturing writing and printing paper to help meet the needs of Vietnam's 60 million people.

But the project has encountered many difficulties. One problem has been that, whilst there was an overabundance of trees to fell in the area, not enough initially reached the mill. This was because access roads were not built in time. This problem now appears to be solved but others remain.

The sophisticated Swedish equipment is posing problems of repair for local Vietnamese technicians. Wood-cutters upstream have been neglecting to cut correct timber lengths, resulting in extra cutting work at the mill site. The Swedes have also accused Vietnam of forcibly recruiting forest workers and making them work under miserable conditions.

Some people now believe that it was a mistake to build the mill – such large, complicated projects are near impossible to implement successfully in a poor developing economy like Vietnam's.

This may well be right. On the other hand, not only are the Vietnamese now producing paper, they are also learning how to use more sophisticated technology and developing management skills.

Adapted from the *Financial Times*, 3 April, 1985

1 What is the Swedish mill producing? *(1 mark)*

2 What economic resources were needed to produce paper? *(2 marks)*

3 Which of these resources had to be specially provided for the project? *(1 mark)*

4 What have been:
(a) the costs and
(b) the benefits of the mill to Vietnam? *(6 marks)*

Unit 83 The Developing World (2)

Tea exports falling

THE INDIAN Government is worried that the value per unit of tea exports is falling. In 1984, the country earned its highest ever unit value of Rs 34.69 (£2.30) a kilogram and the export earnings from tea rose to a record Rs 7.45bn. That record is unlikely to be repeated.

The government thinks that if the industry concentrates more on value-added items – such as instant tea, tea bags and packet teas – part of the expected fall can be made up. But the industry says there is a limit to what can be done about raising value-added tea exports.

Source: Financial Times, 3 June 1985

1 Explain what is meant by 'value per unit of tea exports.' *(3 marks)*

2 Who will (a) suffer and (b) benefit due to this fall in value. Why? *(4 marks)*

3 Why will production of more 'value-added items' benefit (a) Indian tea companies and (b) Indian workers? *(4 marks)*

4 Explain *two* costs to the Indian economy of concentrating on more value-added items. *(4 marks)*

Essay Questions
Units 80–83

1 (a) What is the 'European Community'? *(8 marks)*
(b) Describe briefly how the Common Agricultural Policy works. *(8 marks)*
(c) Explain one benefit to the UK of its membership of the EC. *(4 marks)*

2 (a) Describe *four* features of poor developing countries of the world such as those found in Africa or Asia. *(8 marks)*
(b) Analyse ways in which the developed countries of the world, such as the UK, could help the economic development of the developing countries. *(12 marks)*

Exchange Rate Policy

Government prepared to take action on fall in sterling

BY PHILIP STEPHENS AND PETER RIDDELL

THE GOVERNMENT is extremely concerned about the recent slide in sterling on foreign exchange markets.

The Treasury yesterday acted quickly to deny weekend press reports that ministers were indifferent to the sharp fall in the pound.

The Prime Minister and the Chancellor of the Exchequer discussed the position on the telephone and were said to be "dismayed" by such suggestions.

The Whitehall line was that the present broadly non-interventionist strategy in relation to the long-term level of sterling would continue but that this did not mean a completely hands-off approach in face of sudden large movements.

Labour leaders will this morning consider whether to press for an emergency Commons statement this afternoon on sterling or to wait for the Chancellor's speech in tomorrow's debate on unemployment.

Source: Financial Times, 14 January 1985

Industry delighted at fall of pound

By Our Industrial Staff

THE FALL of sterling has been an almost unmitigated boon for British industry.

Leading industrialists, who three years ago were complaining bitterly about the high value of sterling are delighted with the current exchange rate.

Mr George Russell, managing director of British Alcan Aluminium, said: 'Compared to what I was facing three years ago this is a joy-ride.'

Source: Financial Times, 14 January 1985

MEMORANDUM   TO THE CHANCELLOR

What are our options? I should like an immediate report on:

a) What we could do to stop the slide in sterling (if that's indeed what we want to do).

b) Why we should want to stop the pound falling. I need hardly remind you that our top priority must be the fight against inflation. I believe our balance of payments position is still strong.

c) How we should react to comments from British industry that a falling pound is actually good for them.

You must brief directly whoever is going to speak for the government in tomorrow's debate on unemployment. We can head off the demand for an emergency Commons statement today.

The Prime Minister

S T U D Y P O I N T

1 Pretend you are the Chancellor and prepare a report for the Prime Minister as requested.

Altering the Value of a Currency

The value of the pound is fixed by the forces of demand and supply. Governments have the power to alter the value of a currency by altering its demand and supply. Consider this extract:

> 'Central banks sold between $1.5 bn and $1.75 bn today. The intervention drove the dollar from a high of 3.45 deutschmarks to 3.27 deutschmarks in two hours. The pound sterling rose 3.6 cents on the day.' (Adapted from the *Financial Times*, 28 February 1985)

Governments in Western Europe felt that the value of the US dollar was too high and therefore that the value of their currencies was too low. They sold US dollars, which they owned in their gold and foreign currency reserves. These reserves are held by central banks, like the Bank of England. Selling US dollars meant that the supply of dollars increased. With increased supply, the price of the US dollar fell, and hence the value of other currencies such as the German deutschmark or the British pound rose.

The power of a central bank to alter the value of a currency is severely limited. It cost $1.75 bn to alter the value of the dollar by just 3.6 cents against the pound on 27 February 1985. Central banks hold only a relatively small stock of gold and foreign currency. In 1985, for instance, the Bank of England held about $8 bn worth of reserves – only enough to repeat the operation of the 27 February four and a half times.

Today, the main way in which a central bank alters the value of its currency is through changing interest rates. Consider this newspaper extract:

> 'The Government moved decisively yesterday to push up the cost of borrowing in an attempt to break sterling's slide on foreign exchange markets.' (*Source: Financial Times*, 15 January 1985)

The 'cost of borrowing' is the rate of interest. If interest rates rise in the UK, it becomes more attractive than before to invest in the UK rather than, say, in New York or Paris. The result is that some savers are now tempted to move their savings into London: this increases the demand for pounds. What is more, some UK savers will be tempted to leave their money in London rather than move it abroad: thus the supply of pounds to be exchanged for foreign currency will decline. Higher demand and lower supply of pounds will increase the value of the pound.

Despite its frequent use, changing interest rates is not a very powerful way of influencing exchange rates. The 2% rise in interest rates on 14 January 1985, in the extract above, did not even manage to stop the fall of the pound – the selling pressure on the pound from private sources was too great. In practice, governments find it difficult, if not impossible, to fix an exchange rate.

Devaluation

Changing the exchange rate can have an effect on the current account of the balance of payments. A DEVALUATION of the currency (i.e. a fall in its value) is likely to improve the current account position, reducing a deficit or increasing a surplus. A fall in the value of the pound will mean that the price of British exports to foreigners will fall. A £6000 car, for instance, sold at $2 = £1 would cost an American $12 000. At $1 = £1, it would only cost $6000. Foreigners are therefore likely to buy more British exports. Imports into the UK, on the other hand, will be more expensive to British consumers. So the volume of imports should decline. The exact implications of this on the current balance depend upon the elasticities of imports and exports (see Unit 14).

If one assumes, as may well be the case for the UK economy, that the demand for imports is inelastic, while the demand for exports is elastic, then, following devaluation, the total value of imports will rise. This is because, although fewer imports are bought by volume, each import costs more. For instance, if a 10% rise in price led to only a 5% fall in quantity demanded, the total value of spending on imports would rise by approximately 5%. Equally, the total value of exports will rise. The price of exports remains the same to the exporter (but becomes cheaper to the buyer of course), while sales increase. If sales increased by 10%, the total value of exports would rise by 10% too. So long as the increase in the value of exports is greater than the increase in the value of imports, then the current account on the balance of payments will improve.

☐C☐H☐E☐C☐K☐P☐O☐I☐N☐T☐S☐

1 What determines the value of the pound?

2 Suppose the Bank of England sells dollars and buys pounds. What will be the effect on the value of the pound and why?

3 Why should raising UK interest rates help increase the value of the pound?

4 What is meant by a 'devaluation' of the pound?

5 Explain how a revaluation of the pound is likely to lead to a worsening in the current account position.

☐C☐O☐U☐R☐S☐E☐W☐O☐R☐K☐ ☐S☐U☐G☐G☐E☐S☐T☐I☐O☐N☐

Describe how the value of the pound has changed over the past twelve months, and how the Bank of England has intervened to alter its value. To find out the necessary information, look through copies of a daily newspaper, preferably the *Financial Times*, for the past twelve months. These should be available from your nearest large local library. Analyse why the value of the pound has changed. Consider the likely effects of these changes on the current account in the future.

☐K☐E☐Y☐ ☐T☐E☐R☐M☐

DEVALUATION – a fall in the value of the currency.

Protectionism

WAR THE JAPS HAVE WON

DIRTY TRICKS HAVE MADE THEM £2.8bn

DIRTY TRICKS HAVE MADE THEM £2.8bn

THE Japanese have a big yen for exporting their products all over the world.

But when the tables are turned and foreign firms try to export to Japan the answer is nearly always — *Ah, NO!*

For they have set up a great wall of Japan to keep out as many foreign goods as possible.

All they are willing to import are top-quality goods like Scotch whisky and designer clothes which they cannot make as well themselves.

In the last ten years, our trade deficit with Japan has shot up **TEN TIMES** to a staggering £2,843 million. And that was in spite of repeated promises from the Japanese that they would curb their exports and allow in more imports.

Many British firms are frustrated and furious about their inability to penetrate the Japanese markets.

The Sun has compiled a list of tricks used by the Japanese to keep imports out:

● **AH, NO**: The Japanese often use their complex language to their own advantage.

Many Japanese businessmen can speak and write English.

UK-JAPANESE TRADING GAP		
1964	1974	1984
-£15m	-£251 m	-£2,843 m

£4,000 m — £3,768 m

£3,000 m

£2,000 m

£1,000 m — £925 m — £572 m — £321 m

JAPANESE SALES TO UK
UK SALES TO JAPAN

Goods

But when it suits their business they choose not to understand.

● **AH, NO**: A highly-complex system of testing imported foreign goods has been set up.

The process can take up to a year and is expensive for Western firms.

● **AH, NO**: Over-rigorous standards are laid down by the Japanese for many engineering goods.

● **AH, NO**: A complicated distribution network exists in Japan which is very difficult to penetrate.

Examples of how the Japanese have used their inscrutability and red tape include:

CHOCOLATE giant Cadbury's uses a special emulsifying agent which is not approved by Japan.

Every other nation in the world has no objection to the substance.

PLANEMAKERS British Aerospace cannot sell their highly-successful B.Ae 146 commuter airbus to Japan.

The plane is designed for two-man operations. Outdated rules in Japanese aviation industry say an aircraft weighing more than 35 tons must have a *three-strong crew*.

FARMERS in Britain cannot sell pork to Japan – even though the meat is the most popular in the Japanese diet.

The Japanese complain that Britain imports some meat from Latin America where there is foot-and-mouth disease.

DRUGS companies cannot break into Japan because of miles of red-tape.

Questionnaires running up to 20,000 pages for new drugs have to be filled in first.

When the Japanese go hunting for orders overseas, they are ruthless.

Their biggest trick is to offer huge loans to potential customers at vastly-reduced interest rates.

The Japanese Government also holds the yen down at the artificially low level.

Source: The Sun, 23 May 1985

STUDY POINTS

Read the article carefully. You are a civil servant who has been asked by the Prime Minister to prepare a report on the problem posed by the Japanese. You have been asked to recommend what action, if any, the British Government should take. In your report, you should consider:

1 The nature of the problem and its effects, good as well as bad, on British jobs, incomes and goods available to the consumer.

2 What action the British Government could take.

3 The benefits and costs of each course of action for the British economy.

Reasons For Protectionism

There has been an increase in protectionism in the world economy since the mid-1970s. PROTECTIONISM is the restriction of imports into a country through government regulations. There are a variety of protectionist measures including:

- TARIFFS or *customs duties*. These are taxes imposed on imported goods. They raise the price of imports to consumers and so make them less attractive.

- QUOTAS. These are limits on the quantity of a product that can be imported into a country (e.g. no more than 100 000 cars a year can be imported).

- *Regulations*. A country may, for instance, have unique safety regulations, which means that potential imports are 'unsafe' and so cannot be sold in that country. Or the country may make it very difficult for importers to get import licences for goods.

Protectionism can give rise to major benefits for an economy. Fewer imports can mean that domestic industries will produce what would otherwise have been imported. This creates not only jobs, but extra income for the domestic economy. Domestic production may also lead to exports, as firms gain expertise in the production of goods.

Another argument in favour of protectionism is the *infant industry* argument. An economy may wish to start up a particular industry, such as steel making or car manufacturing. In the early stages, the industry is bound to be uncompetitive with foreign competition. It will have high start-up costs and not produce large enough quantities to reap sufficient economies of scale. Protecting an industry like this from imports will allow it to grow and prosper. When it is eventually strong enough, import controls can be removed.

Reasons in favour of Free Trade

The opposite of protectionism is FREE TRADE. The great advantage of free trade is that consumers can buy the products that are most competitive, whether they are produced at home or abroad.

But it is not only consumers who may benefit. Many economists argue that free trade rather than protectionism is the way to create jobs and prosperity. Their argument is that protectionism encourages protected industries to be inefficient. They have no incentive to become efficient and produce goods that consumers want to buy at the keenest prices. Such industries are unlikely ever to develop into strong industries capable of conquering export markets. Free trade, on the other hand, forces firms to become efficient or else they go bankrupt. If a firm can beat off imports at home, then it stands a good chance of being a successful exporter. Competition brought about by free trade produces efficient industries and thus leads to jobs and prosperity. What is more, if all countries follow free trade policies, each country will specialise in those products in which it has a comparative advantage and this, as Unit 75 showed, produces gains to consumers in all countries.

Increased protectionism can be self-defeating if other countries retaliate. If the UK were to ban all imports of Japanese cars, there would be little benefit for the UK if Japan were to retaliate by banning an equivalent value of UK imports.

Despite all these arguments in favour of free trade, it is true to say that some of the most successful economies in the world today – such as Japan and West Germany – have pursued or currently pursue protectionist policies. The country most associated with free trade – the UK – has not proved particularly successful at increasing its income. With high unemployment worldwide, it is perhaps not surprising that many countries see protectionism as an easy way of protecting jobs in their country.

Would protectionist measures benefit British industry?

CHECKPOINTS

1 What is the difference between a tariff and a quota?

2 Why do countries adopt protectionist policies?

3 What are the arguments in favour of free trade?

4 Why might other countries retaliate if the UK imposed protectionist measures?

COURSEWORK SUGGESTION

Describe the main forms of protectionist policies used in the world today. Explain why there has been a growth of protectionism in the world since the 1970s. Consider the extent to which protectionism could solve the problems of countries tempted to use such policies.

KEY TERMS

PROTECTIONISM – the restriction of imports into a country by government measures.

TARIFFS – taxes on imported goods. Also often called *customs duties*.

QUOTAS – limits on the quantity of a commodity that can be imported.

FREE TRADE – trade without protectionist barriers between countries.

Economic Systems (1)

China comes to market

ONCE, THE best selling fashion was watches, says Wang Tsuan. He is manager of the Xidan department store in one of Beijing's main shopping centres. This year, it is hair tonics, lipsticks and face preparations. Next year who know what will be the best selling fashion?

It is now Wang's job to find out. 'I have to please customers – or I fail', he says. Not so long ago, this didn't matter. Central planners decided what the store would sell and which factories would make the goods. They determined, too, the price of the goods and the pay of the staff. So what if goods were poor quality, the staff unfriendly, the management slow, the store shabby and uninviting and the customers dissatisfied?

Today these things matter very much to Wang. He is responsible for selecting and buying the 32 000 items sold in

his store. He is responsible for meeting, as best he can, the demands of his 150 000 customers a day. And he will largely determine the pay and conditions of his 2900 staff. Much of his time is now spent visiting suppliers – not just to buy, but to criticise and to sack if the goods are not up to scratch.

'If the quality is not right I stop buying', he explains. He is required to make a profit – to pay for shop improvements and to pay the bonuses earned by staff who perform well.

Wang admits that it is increasingly difficult to keep up with the demands of his customers. Incomes at about £200 a year are still well below Western standards, but are growing fast. Most Chinese now have black and white television sets and would like to have the colour television imported form Japan, now selling

in Wang's shop for about £470. Many will now have fridges, electric fans and perhaps even automatic washing machines.

Wang and his customers are part of an economic revolution that is changing the way the world's biggest nation lives. Where economic life was once vertically organised – decisions about every aspect of economic life being made at the top by government – it is now being changed by exposure to market forces and competition. Where being rich was once condemned as anti-social and 'bourgeois', private enterprise and profit is now actively encouraged. Where workers could expect a job for life whatever their effort, now a new 'responsibility system' is being introduced. Few corners of Chinese life have remained unaffected by these changes.

Source: Sunday Times, 17 March 1985

STUDY POINTS

Read the extract carefully and then consider carefully the following:

1 Who is Wang Tsuan?

2 China is a 'planned economy'. What this means is that what is produced and what can be bought in the shops is decided by government (the central planners), and not by individual firms and customers. According to the extract, what was the effect of this system on a department store such as Wang's and on its customers?

3 China is now experimenting with a private or free enterprise system in some industries. What this means is that firms and their customers, and not the government, decide what is to be produced. Describe *five* ways in which this has affected Wang's department store, its workers and its customers.

4 The last paragraph describes changes in the Chinese government's attitude towards production and workers. Discuss the advantages and disadvantages to the owners of firms, to workers (including the

unemployed) and to consumers of:
(a) allowing some individuals to become rich instead of distributing the income and wealth produced by the economy more evenly among all people;
(b) rewarding good workers by bonuses or higher pay while paying workers who are not so productive less or even sacking them;
(c) encouraging competition among firms, instead of government deciding which firm is to produce which goods.

5 In Britain, some goods, such as television sets, are provided by private firms through the free market mechanism, while others, like health care, are provided by government and are centrally planned. Would it be better for Britons if the National Health Service were privatised so that consumers had to pay for health care (visits to doctors, hospital treatment, etc.) and doctors and hospitals competed with each other for patients? Explain your answer carefully.

No two economies are organised in exactly the same way, but they all have to solve three fundamental problems:

- *What* should be produced in the economy? For instance, what quantities of food or televisions or banking services should be produced?

- *How* should production be organised? For instance, should machinery be used; how many workers should be employed; should production take place in London or Glasgow?

- *For whom* should production take place? Should everybody be entitled to an identical share of production, or should some receive more than others?

Economists distinguish between four different economic systems which resolve these problems in different ways. These will now be looked at in turn.

Traditional Or Subsistence Economies

A SUBSISTENCE ECONOMY is one where there is little specialisation and little trade. People tend to live in family groups, and these families grow most of their own food, make their own houses, gather their own fuel and provide their own leisure activities – i.e. to a great extent they are self-sufficient. It is called a 'subsistence' economy because it is very difficult, without a great deal of specialisation and trade, to do more than subsist (i.e. provide the basic necessities for living). It is a 'traditional' economy because it is the type of economy that has existed all over the world since man began being economically active. It is only in relatively recent history that more 'advanced' types of economy have developed.

What, how and for whom to produce are decisions that are answered by looking to the past. If a society has managed to survive for

An example of China's 'modernisation' – a supermarket in Beijing.

some time, then what was done in the past must have been successful. So in traditional economies there is often resistance to change and to new ideas. No two traditional economies are the same, so it is impossible to describe typical economic mechanisms by which resources are allocated.

Free-market Economies

A FREE-MARKET ECONOMY is one where decisions are made through the market mechanism. The forces of demand and supply, without any government interference, determine how resources are allocated.

What to produce is decided upon by the level of profitability for a particular product. Buyers cast their spending 'votes' in the market place. For instance, consumers may buy 200 000 British cars a year. That may not be enough to make the car company in Britain profitable. Car sellers would need either to sell more cars, or to sell the same number of cars at a higher price, in order to earn a reasonable or 'normal' rate of profit. Investors are then discouraged from investing in that industry. They will put their money into higher-profit industries. As a result, fewer British cars will be produced. What is produced is therefore fixed by what it is most profitable to produce in an economy.

How production should be organised is equally determined by what is most profitable. Firms are encouraged through the market mechanism to adopt the most efficient methods of production.

As to for whom production should take place, production is *allocated* to those who can afford to pay. Consumers with no money cannot afford to buy anything. Millionaires can purchase large quantities of goods and services.

Command Economies

A COMMAND ECONOMY is one where all economic decisions are made by the government. The government decides what to produce, how it is to be produced and how it is to be allocated to consumers. This involves a great deal of planning. Hence such economies are often called PLANNED ECONOMIES. Planned economies tend to be run by governments who, in theory at least, want to see greater economic equality between consumers. By state planning, goods and services can be produced to satisfy the needs of all the citizens of a country, not just those who have the money to pay for goods.

Mixed Economies

A MIXED ECONOMY is one where some goods and services are produced in the free-market sector of the economy, but others are produced by the state – i.e. it is a mixture of a pure free-enterprise market economy and a pure command economy.

CHECKPOINTS

1 Imagine that you live in a traditional economy and you are a farmer. Make a list of all that you would have to produce to keep yourself alive.

2 A farming community in the developing world has been farming in the same way for hundreds of years. The people are so poor that, if the next crop fails, they will starve. A government worker comes to the village to persuade the farmers to change their farming methods completely. Why do you think that the farmers might be very reluctant to change?

3 Owners of fish and chip shops are finding it difficult to cover their costs, whereas health food shops are making large profits. What effect will this have on the number of fish and chip shops and health food shops operating in the UK? How do profits allocate resources in an economy?

4 Which of the following goods or services are produced mainly in the market sector of the UK economy, and which are produced mainly in the state sector and allocated through a planning mechanism: (a) education; (b) television sets; (c) gas cookers; (d) health care; (e) defence; (f) roads; (g) cars; (h) petrol?

5 Imagine that you are Prime Minister and that Britain is a command economy. What goods would you choose to produce? How would you allocate those goods?

KEY TERMS

TRADITIONAL or SUBSISTENCE ECONOMY – an economy where specialisation and trade are limited, and where there is a great degree of self-sufficiency.

FREE MARKET or FREE ENTERPRISE ECONOMY – an economy where resources are allocated through the market mechanism.

COMMAND or PLANNED ECONOMY – an economy where resources are allocated by the state through a system of planning.

MIXED ECONOMY – an economy where some resources are allocated via the market mechanism and some via the state.

COURSEWORK SUGGESTION

Describe the National Health Service and private medical care in the UK. Explain how each system allocates resources, how each is funded and on what basis consumers are able to use the services. Try to decide which system provides the most efficient health care in the UK.

Economic Systems (2)

Cost to the community

Lambeth Council disagrees strongly with the policy of selling council houses. Why is this ?

The main reason is that we believe the overriding duty of the local authority is to providing housing for the people who need it most rather than just for those who can afford to buy.

We are not against home ownership as such. Indeed, before the Tory government cut off the funds we had helped many hundreds of families to purchase and improve their own property. In 1979 we gave more mortgages than any other borough in London.

But home ownership must not be at the expense of the many people who can never hope to buy and for whom renting on the private market is practically impossible. An indication of the huge demand for council housing in this borough is the 16,000 households on the waiting list.

The Council owns 49,310 flats and houses. Every year about 2,000 households move out allowing other households to move in.

If the total number of Council homes is reduced by selling them off, those in need of decent homes will have to go on waiting.

It is only too obvious that the best property - houses with gardens for example - will prove the most attractive to purchasers. Less desirable property will be left and the 7,000 tenants seeking transfers to better or more suitable accomodation will find their choice severely limited.

The Council is also likely to lose money by selling its homes. To build them, Lambeth has to borrow the money and repay it with interest over 60 years. Even if a property is sold the loan still has to be repaid.

Building in an inner city area like Lambeth is very expensive and the cost of replacing homes that are sold will be far more than the Council can hope to receive from selling them. This will mean greater pressure for increased rates and higher rents for remaining tenants.

December 1985

R.452   Lambeth Council

Your right to buy your home

A guide for council, new town and housing association tenants

The Department of the Environment & the Welsh Office 1985

STUDY POINTS

1 The British government has decided to end all government intervention in the housing market in order to make it a totally free market. To this end, it has decided to force local authorities to sell off all council houses and other dwellings to the highest bidders. All controls relating to rents and tenancies are to be abolished too. Your task is to prepare a report detailing the likely effects of these measures. In particular, you need to consider the effects on:

(a) rents of rented property and the prices of owner-occupied property;
(b) the freedom of choice of consumers in the housing market;
(c) the quality of housing services offered to consumers;
(d) the future supply of houses by builders and landlords;
(e) the poor and the homeless;
(f) landlords and existing house owners;
(g) the distribution of resources in the UK.

Free-market versus Command economies

There are no pure free-market economies nor pure command economies in the world today. The USA, however, is the most important 'free-market' economy. About 75% of total output is produced by the private sector. The other 25% is produced by the government. As was shown in Unit 55, *public* goods, such as defence, would not be provided by the free-market mechanism. Other *merit* goods, such as education, would not be provided in sufficient quantity. So any modern state has to allocate resources for these goods via a taxation and government-spending programme.

In a command economy, it is impossible to regulate all markets. Even in the most planned economies of the world, such as the USSR or Poland, some goods and services are provided through a free-market mechanism. An economy where 75% of the goods are provided by the state would be called a command economy. In a mixed economy, such as the UK or France or Norway, the balance between state provision and free-market provision is more or less equal.

Efficiency

Would it be better for the UK to have more production or to be less organised by the free-market mechanism or by the state? The Conservative Party argues that more free-market production would increase efficiency. The Labour Party argues the contrary. To decide who is right is not easy because a variety of aspects of efficiency need to be considered.

Take, as an example, the provision of medical care. In the USA, it is provided mainly by the free-market mechanism. Consumers have to pay for any medical services they use. In the UK, medical care is provided by the state through the National Health Service. Almost all services are free to consumers (although they are not free to society of course – they are paid for through taxes). Aspects of efficiency that need to be considered include:

- *Distribution of resources.* In a free-market system, resources are allocated to consumers only if consumers are able to pay for them. In the USA, if you are ill, but have no money, you cannot get treatment. In the UK, treatment is given on the basis of need. If the health services do not have the resources to treat patients, then the patients either go untreated or are placed on waiting lists.

- *Choice.* In the USA, consumers have the freedom to choose which doctor to go to, or which hospital to use. Under the UK National Health Service, there is far less choice.

- *Cost.* The UK spends a lower proportion of its total income on health care than almost any other advanced country. It could be argued that British health care is less good than that of other economies. On the other hand, it could be that Britain's state health system is much cheaper, but still provides the same level of service. A state system allows economies of scale to be achieved. Doctors are encouraged to think about what is best value for money, rather than how they can profit from charging for treatment which is of dubious value.

- *Quality.* State-provided services are often accused of being poor quality. Workers know that they do not have to sell products in a competitive market, so they do not strive to provide good-quality products. On the basis of this argument, the National Health Service would provide a better service to customers if it were privatised.

The quality and quantity of goods available for consumption and how they are distributed are very important aspects of the efficiency of an economy. Other aspects include:

- The degree to which an economy is stable. An economy racked by high inflation, or continuing bouts of high unemployment, is less efficient than a more stable economy.

- The rate at which the economy grows. A fast-growing economy that provides increases in the standards of living of its citizens is more efficient than one that grows only slowly or not at all.

- The degree to which the long-term interests of the economy are taken into consideration. An economy that destroys the environment, or its historical heritage, may be able to achieve high rates of growth today, but it is impoverishing future generations who will have to pick up the bill for such growth.

Because there are so many ways of comparing the efficiency of different types of economy, it is impossible to say whether or not the free-market system or a command economy is the better. What has to be considered, for each country in the world, is whether or not a move towards more state planning or more private provision would improve efficiency in the economy, and so go further towards solving the basic economic problem of the allocation of scarce resources.

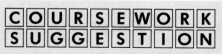

CHECKPOINTS

1 Why is it not possible to have a pure free-market economy?

2 Give *four* examples of (a) command economies, (b) free-market economies and (c) mixed economies in the world today.

3 Why is there likely to be greater choice of goods and services in a free-market economy than in a command economy?

4 What are the advantages of a free-market economy compared to a command economy? What are the disadvantages?

COURSEWORK SUGGESTION

Find out about the workings of a command economy, such as the USSR or Poland. Describe how resources are allocated in the economy. Analyse the successes and problems of the economy. Consider the impact on efficiency in the economy, if more markets were freed.

Data Response Questions

Units 84–87

Unit 84 Exchange Rate Policy

See-sawing pound hits Midlands exporters

Fears over flagging exports continue to worry business leaders in the West Midlands. But prospects for home orders look rosier.

The quarterly trade survey by the region's chambers of commerce says export order books have become even thinner over the past three months.

Group chairman Roy Fellows, of Wolverhampton, said: "Companies have real worries on the export front caused by a mixture of the high value of the pound and the sheer uncertainty of what exchange rates will be from one day to the next."

But the survey still showed a level of optimism, with almost half the companies predicting a rise in overall sales compared with only 11 per cent expecting a fall.

Nearly three-quarters of firms singled out lower interest rates as the factor most likely to improve their prospects.

Source: Express and Star, 10 October 1985

1 What is meant by 'flagging exports'? (1 mark)

2 Explain carefully why Midland export orders might have been hit by trends in exchange rates. (5 marks)

3 Explain how Midland companies could be helped to export more. (4 marks)

Unit 85 Protectionism

Fair play on free trade

LABOUR'S plan to set a 45 per cent limit on foreign car imports into Britain and to heavily subsidise British Leyland is half right.

Dedicated to the religion of free trade, the flood of foreign cars into Britain over the years has been a source of embarrassment to the Conservative Party.

The motor industry has not been the only area to suffer from the disparity between the weight of foreign goods that have poured into Britain and the amount that our trading partners take in British goods.

The shoes and textile industries have been devastated as a result of cheap exports from developing countries that have taken virtually nothing from Britain in return.

In recent years the Japanese have not only crucified the British motor industry but also used Britain as a base to exploit the European markets.

Though in purist terms the introduction of import limits is contrary to the philosophy of free trade, the aspect of fair play makes it relevant.

However, there is the great danger that heavy state subsidy of BL would merely be an open invitation to return to the days of massive wage claims, daily strikes, shoddy work and an uncompetitive product that nobody wants to buy.

Limiting imports would help our motor industry, but unless we are producing cars that we ourselves desire, at prices that match or better competitors, the exercise would be futile.

The export factor is still vital, and if we would not buy the cars ourselves, it is madness to assume that foreigners would.

Source: Express and Star, 1 June 1985

1 What does Labour plan to do? (1 mark)

2 What would be (a) the benefits and (b) the costs of such a policy to the UK? (6 marks)

3 Explain whether or not you believe that Britain should trade with countries that 'have taken virtually nothing from Britain'. (3 marks)

Unit 86 Economic Systems (1)

Cheap labour sparks business boom in Ciskei

THE CISKEI is South Africa's newest 'independent republic'. It advertises itself as Africa's most beautiful business climate. The Ciskei does indeed have a beautiful landscape, but it is also full of the shacks of hungry and unemployed blacks.

The Ciskei National Development Corporation (CNDC) is responsible for the economic development of the country. In its first five years, only 4500 jobs were created in the industrial sector. 1981–2 brought that total to 7700 and it is understood that this higher rate of job creation is being maintained. Industrial investment in 1981–2 almost doubled from R32m to R63m (£16.4m to £32.3m).

CNDC says that this increase is due to the free enterprise policies of the government and to the generous incentives available to businesses. The incentives include a cash allowance of 95% of total wages bills for 7 years, an effective rate of interest of 3.3% on loan capital, rail transport rebates, cheap power, and so on.

The explanation for the boom, however, must also be connected to the fact that the Ciskei has no labour laws, no minimum wage and no trade unions – what might be described as an extreme example of a free labour market. The result is very low wages. Dimbaza Foundries, for example, which is half British owned, reckons that wage levels are about one-half of what they would have to pay elsewhere. They say their present average wage is R120 a month (about £61). But these wage rates are quite high compared to most companies. There are cases, especially for female labour, where the hourly rate is 30–40 cents an hour (about 15–20 pence).

There is no shortage of labour at whatever rates. At independence last December there were 666 000 'Ciskeians' living in the territory. So 7700 jobs created over six years is a drop in the ocean – and the CNDC would not disagree.

Adapted from the *Financial Times*, 1983

1 Where is 'the Ciskei'? *(1 mark)*

2 What is the role of the Ciskei National Development Corporation (CNDC)? *(2 marks)*

3 What inducements are offered to attract businesses to the area? *(2 marks)*

4 A company sets up in the Ciskei.
   (a) It has a weekly wage bill of £1000. How much of that will be paid by the Ciskei Government?
   (b) It borrows £20 000 for new buildings. How much interest per year (in £s) will it have to pay? *(4 marks)*

5 What level of wages is paid to local black workers? *(1 mark)*

6 Why are wages so low? *(4 marks)*

7 What type of economy is the Ciskei? *(1 mark)*

8 To what extent do free labour markets in the Ciskei benefit (a) local black citizens (b) the owners of companies setting up in the Ciskei? *(5 marks)*

Unit 87 Economic Systems (2)

Russia's press catches up with enemies of the people

The Supreme Soviet is meeting tomorrow to approve next year's budget and the next five-year plan. The main thrust of economic policy is to provide the man in the street with more take-home pay and to improve the range and quality of the goods he can spend it on.

The money is coming from the productivity surge which the economy has enjoyed since Soviet leaders recently began a crackdown on absenteeism and corruption, and perhaps more importantly launched the widespread use of incentive payments.

Mr Chernenko, the Socialist leader, said in his budget speech: "Can there be any other explanation than the most phenomenal blundering for the simple lack of any decent shoes in our shops? And what about children's shoes? There just aren't any. It can't be right that here we are in winter and the shoe shops are stuffed with summer sandals. You can never buy the right shoes for the time of year."

Adapted from *The Guardian*, 26 November 1984

1 What is the main aim of Soviet economic policy in the late 1980's? *(1 mark)*

2 What type of economy is the USSR? *(1 mark)*

3 What problems does the Soviet economy face? *(4 marks)*

4 Why does planning in the USSR create the inefficiencies described in the article? *(4 marks)*

5 (a) What is an 'incentive payment'?
   (b) Explain why the use of incentive payments is a step towards a more market-orientated economy. *(5 marks)*

Essay Questions
Units 84–87

1 'The USA is considering imposing import restrictions on Japanese computers.'
   (a) What are 'import restrictions'? Give examples of *two* different types of import restrictions. *(8 marks)*
   (b) Why might a country like the USA want to impose import restrictions? *(6 marks)*
   (c) What are the costs to a country of import restrictions? *(6 marks)*

2 (a) In the UK, part of our output is produced by private firms and part by government. Explain how private firms and government decide what to produce and who should receive what they have produced. *(8 marks)*
   (b) What type of economy is the USSR? Who decides what to produce and who should receive that production in the USSR? *(6 marks)*
   (c) What is the role of profits in a free market economy? *(6 marks)*

Data Response Questions
Units 41, 42, 63, 64 and 79

Unit 41 Sole Proprietorships and Partnerships

Jobs boom on cards – 'despite the Tories'

Britain's self-employed workers aim to create at least 750,000 new jobs over the next two years, says a survey. But many of them say it is no thanks to the Government.

Fifty nine per cent said the Government had done little to help them to succeed.

The survey was carried out by Gallup for the Legal and General Assurance company.

Legal and General says that if each firm took on only one extra employee it would mean 750,000 new jobs.

The report found that on average the self-employed work a 55-hour week, have little time for taking holidays and miss out on family life because they are working so hard.

But they enjoy the independence and see it as a chance to make more money.

Three out of four said they would not go back to working for someone else, even if the job and money matched their current earnings.

More than a third started their own business because they wanted to be their own boss, and 17 per cent because they were out of work.

Running a business is often a family affair.

Nearly a quarter of the people surveyed had joined the family business and 57 per cent had their spouses helping them.

Source: Express and Star, 16 October 1985

1 How many firms were surveyed by Gallup? (*1 mark*)

2 What did the survey find were
   (a) the costs
   (b) the benefits to workers of being self-employed? (*6 marks*)

3 Why is running a small sole proprietorship more risky to the owner than being a shareholder in a limited company? (*3 marks*)

Unit 42 Joint-Stock Companies

Tony Jackson reports on the share sale prospects of an unusual drug company

Weighing up Wellcome's worth in the market place

THE Wellcome Foundation, which this week announced its intention to go public early next year, has one of the least public profiles of all the world's big drug companies. This is largely because of its unusual structure — an essentially charitable organisation, owned by a trust which distributes all the profits derived from its ownership to medical research.

However, the Wellcome Trust has announced its intention to sell an initial 20 per cent of the foundation in a Stock Exchange flotation. This has no effect on the way the company is run. The trust has decided that to carry on its charitable programme it would like to spread its sources of income, using the proceeds of the flotation to make investments elsewhere.

The decision, however, pushes the company into the limelight not least because the stock market is curious to know what it is to be offered. Wellcome is not easy to value in market terms. Pharmaceutical companies which tread a line between jackpot success and failure, seldom are. Early guesses of £1.5bn for the whole company seem exaggerated, but a figure of nearly £1bn, looks feasible.

1 What does the Wellcome Foundation produce? (*1 mark*)

2 What is it intending to do according to the article? (*2 marks*)

3 Who will be the owners of the company after the flotation? (*2 marks*)

4 Who will have control of the company after the flotation? (*2 marks*)

5 What will be the total value of the new shares sold in the Foundation? (*3 marks*)

6 Why is the Wellcome Foundation making this flotation? (*5 marks*)

Unit 63 The Causes of Inflation (1)

Government reasserts link

The Chancellor Mr. Lawson, speaking at a Tory Party conference in Wales, emphasised again the link between inflation and the rate of growth of the money supply. He warned that too much government spending would lead to inflation because the money supply would have to grow too fast to pay for the increased spending. Lower inflation, he stressed, was essential if Britain's economic recovery were to continue and this could only be achieved through strict control of public expenditure.

1 What does Mr Lawson believe is the cause of inflation?
(2 marks)

2 Explain why Mr Lawson believes that increased government spending would lead to an increase in the money supply.
(3 marks)

3 What, according to Mr Lawson's argument, would be the economic results of an increase in public expenditure?
(5 marks)

Unit 64 The Causes of Inflation (2)

Home loans cut helps inflation down to 5.9pc

Inflation fell to 5.9 per cent in September – its lowest rate since February, according to the Retail Price Index published today.

The drop, from 6.2 per cent in August, was due mainly to the recent cut in mortgage rates.

Other prices also fell during September, including petrol and some fresh fruit and vegetables.

Overall, prices in the month came down by 0.1 per cent, according to the figures from the Department of Employment.

The news was welcomed by Employment Secretary Lord Young, who said "With further petrol price cuts to come and good news on factory gate prices, we could look forward to an even lower rate of inflation next month."

The main item in September's figures was the reduction in mortgage rates, which were cut by 1.25 per cent. This alone reduced the Retail Price Index by nearly 0.4 per cent.

Source: Express and Star, 11 October 1985

1 What is the 'Retail Price Index'? *(2 marks)*

2 Explain why inflation fell in September 1985. *(2 marks)*

3 (a) What is the 'cost–push' theory of inflation?
  (b) How does the article suggest that inflation has been cost–push in nature? *(6 marks)*

Unit 79 The Significance of the Balance of Payment and the Exchange Rate

Boom ahead for holidays in Britain as £ falls

BY DAVID THURLOW

THE British have rediscovered the delights of Britain – and it points to a first class year for the tourist trade.

Early returns from tour operators all over the country are 15 per cent up on this time last year. The English Tourist Board says cautiously: "It's very encouraging but too early to go further than that."

However, there are two clear signs that Britain is going to be booming in 1985. The **weak pound** is bringing in foreigners and making the British think twice about expensive holidays abroad. And **bad publicity** about violence in Spain is putting them off going there.

In the traditional holiday town of Bournemouth, bookings are already up on last year.

In 1984 more than 2,200,000 holidaymakers packed the Dorset town.

Promotion officer Judith Pratt said: "It looks good again. There is a rekindling of interest and rediscovery of England.

"It's not so smart to go abroad as it used to be. It's losing some of its grandeur and it's not as up-market because most people can afford it."

Source: Daily Express, 25 March 1985

1 What is meant by a 'weak pound'? *(2 marks)*

2 What does the article argue will happen to the demand for UK holidays in 1985? *(1 mark)*

3 Explain the link between a weak pound and an improved current account balance on trade in holidays. *(4 marks)*

4 To what extent is the demand for foreign holidays price elastic? *(3 marks)*

Index